Praise for *Yoga and the Luminous*

"A valuable group of Chapple's essays (old and new) about Yoga ... Chapple is both a scholar and practitioner of Yoga, and one can see elements of both trainings in this book.."

— *Religious Studies Review*

"In *Yoga and the Luminous*, we get an historical summary about yoga schools of the three classic religions of India, with *Yoga Sūtra* of Patañjali as the theme of the monograph. This marvelous monograph also weighs in years of personal practice, understanding and diligence of the author ... Students and teachers ... alike would find *Yoga and the Luminous* a good reading."

— *Jinamañjari*

"...Chapple's insights—the result of 30 years of reflection and writing on yoga—are potent, and he is a gifted writer. The book is a pleasure to read, surveying important themes in the theory and practice of yoga."

— *CHOICE*

"Anyone with an interest in Yoga must consider *Yoga and the Luminous* as a starter guide."

— *Midwest Book Review*

YOGA

AND THE LUMINOUS

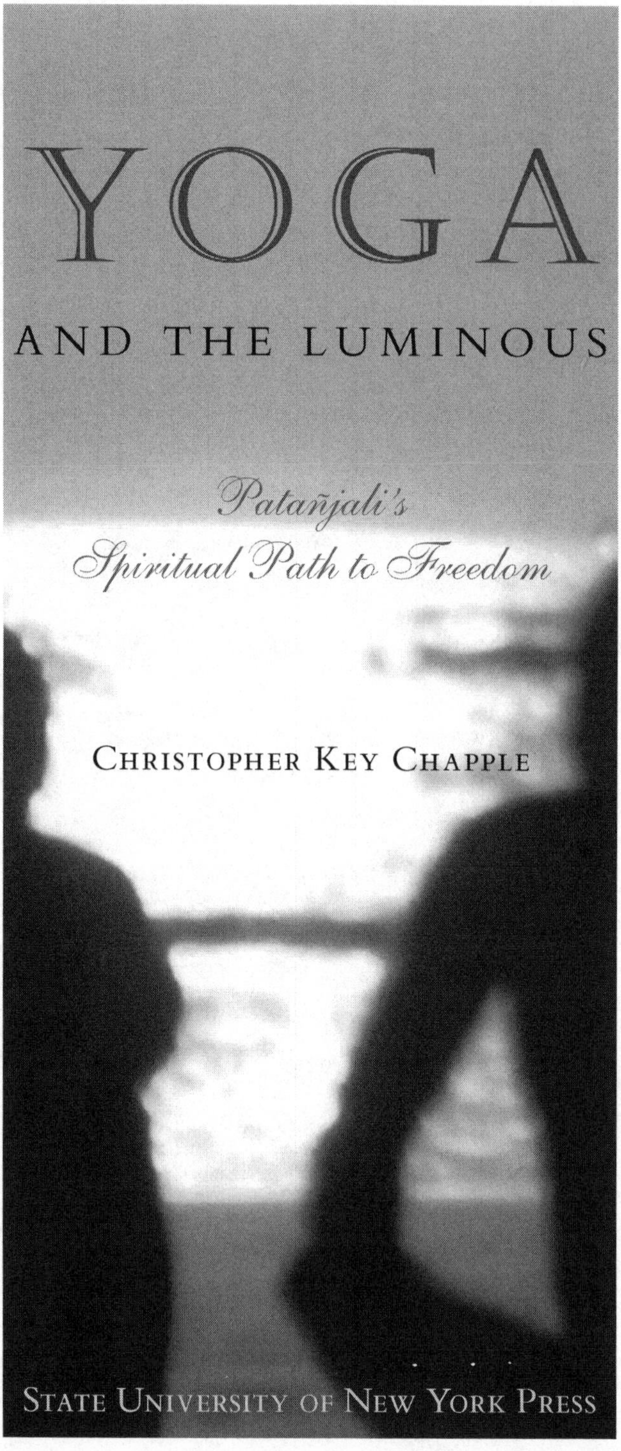

YOGA

AND THE LUMINOUS

Patañjali's Spiritual Path to Freedom

CHRISTOPHER KEY CHAPPLE

STATE UNIVERSITY OF NEW YORK PRESS

Published by
STATE UNIVERSITY OF NEW YORK PRESS, ALBANY

Printed in the United States of America

For information, contact State University of New York Press, www.sunypress.edu

Production and book design, Laurie D. Searl
Marketing, Susan M. Petrie

Photographs courtesy of Nicole DePicciotto
Yoga models: Trampas Thompson (cover), Nicole DePicciotto, and Jeff Horne

Library of Congress Cataloging-in-Publication Data

Chapple, Christopher Key.
Yoga and the luminous : Patañjali's spiritual path to freedom / Chistopher Key Chapple.
p. cm.
English and Sanskrit (also romanized).
Includes bibliographical references and index.
ISBN 978-0-7914-7475-4 (hardcover : alk. paper)
ISBN 978-0-7914-7476-1 (pbk. : alk. paper)
1. Yoga. 2. Patañjali. Yogasūtra. I. Patañjali. Yogasūtra. English & Sanskrit. II. Title.

B132.Y6C555 2008
181'.45—dc22 2007036976

10 9 8 7 6 5 4 3 2 1

to

Dylan Edward Chapple

and

Emma Catherine Chapple

Contents

	Preface	ix
	Acknowledgments	xiii
	Abbreviations	xv
1	The Yoga Tradition	1
I	The Practice of Yoga	
2	Sāṃkhya Philosophy and Yoga Practice	19
3	Precepts and Vows in Yoga and Jainism	31
4	Imitation of Animals in Yoga Tradition: Taming the Sacred Wild through Āsana Practice	49
5	Patañjali on Meditation: Undoing the Thinking Self	61
II	Yoga and Liberation	
6	Luminosity and Yoga	71
7	Living Liberation in Sāṃkhya and Yoga	83

III Patañjali's *Yoga Sūtra*

8 Approaching the *Yoga Sūtra* 103

9 The *Yoga Sūtra* of Patañjali: Continuous Text and Translation 115

10 Translation Methodology and Grammatical Analysis 139

11 "Samādhi pāda" 143

12 "Sādhana pāda" 163

13 "Vibhūti pāda" 183

14 "Kaivalya pāda" 203

IV Interpreting Yoga

15 Reading Patañjali without Vyāsa: A Critique of Four *Yoga Sūtra* Passages 219

16 The Use of the Feminine Gender in Patañjali's Description of Yogic Practices 237

17 Contemporary Expressions of Yoga 249

Notes 261

References 279

Index of Sanskrit Terms 287

Index 295

PREFACE

Why another book on Yoga? Beginning over a century ago, several fine books have been published on the Yoga tradition, including *Raja Yoga* by Swami Vivekananda, *Yoga as Philosophy and Religion* by Surendranath Dasgupta, *Yoga: Archaic Techniques of Ecstasy* by Mircea Eliade, *The Yoga Tradition* by Georg Feuerstein, and *The Integrity of the Yoga Darśana* by Ian Whicher, among many others. This particular book takes a fresh look at some aspects of Patañjali's Yoga system that have been previously overlooked and reexamines some well-worn themes. It begins with a historical overview of Yoga practice and its place within the context of the religions of India. The book discusses the sequence of practices outlined in Patañjali's eightfold system, taking a close look at its relationship with Sāṃkhya philosophy. It includes a word-by-word translation of Patañjali's *Yoga Sūtra* followed by an exploration of how some sequences of *sūtras* might be interpreted in light of text-critical and feminist methodology. The book concludes with a sociological assessment of Yoga's growing popularity and its prospects for the future.

Yoga has deep roots within the Śrāmanical side of religiosity in India, meaning that Yoga emphasizes interior experience, meditation, renunciation, and ethical alacrity, in contrast with the Brahmanical traditions, which speak more emphatically of ritual, the nondual nature of ultimate reality, and full participation in the mores and taboos of Hindu society. Yoga holds closer affinity with Jainism and Buddhism than with its Vedānta and Bhakti cousins. It profoundly influenced the articulation of the Sikh religious faith and captured the imagination of the Muslim world as well. Yoga is now widely practiced by Jews and Christians.

Yoga practice takes an individual on an inward journey. It begins with taming one's impulses through the cultivation of ethical precepts and molding a positive outlook through the application of virtues. It requires the harnessing of the energy generated within one's body and breath. It culminates in a threefold interiority of concentration, meditation, and becoming whelmed or enraptured. Through Yoga, one enters a rarefied state of consciousness, a transparency and luminosity described by Patañjali as being "like a clear jewel."

By looking word by word at Patañjali's text, one detects a rhythm and flow that returns like a spiral to the Yoga's central theme: overcoming negative karma and obtaining freedom from affliction. Patañjali celebrates numerous styles of Yoga and holds tightly to a metaphor that first appears in the *Ṛg Veda*: "Two birds sit on the same tree. One eats sweet berries, while the other merely observes." For the Yoga tradition, this signifies the two states of life, referred to in Buddhism as the relative (*samvṛtti*) and the absolute (*paramārtha*). In Sāṃkhya, the realm of *prakṛti*, associated with the feminine, constantly changes, while the witness consciousness or *puruṣa* merely gazes, remaining inactive. Vedānta attempts to conflate the two into a united state, claiming the former to in some way be deceptive or unreal. Yoga proclaims that both really exist in all their complexity and that only through experiencing the pain associated with change can we feel our freedom. Consequently, Patañjali celebrates the feminine gender, both grammatically and practically, acknowledging that through the power of awareness one comes to see and gain mastery over this complex relationship and engage the manifest world, deemed as feminine, through a process of purification.

This book emerges from more than thirty years of practice, study, and reflection. Meditation and Yoga first entered my life during my teen years, when I interviewed Philip Kapleau, author of *The Three Pillars of Zen*, began to sit, and initiated an *āsana* practice. In 1972, I joined Yoga Anand Ashram, where under the tutelage of Gurāṇi Añjali (1935–2001), I embarked on a systematic process of Yoga training. Simultaneously, I began undergraduate and graduate studies in Indian philosophy, Sanskrit and Tibetan languages, the history of religions, and theology. Some passages in this book were written more than twenty years ago. The translation emerged from a seven-year joint study project at Yoga Anand Ashram that extended from 1981 to 1989. Numerous people contributed to the translation, including Eugene Kelly (for a while known as Yogi Anand Viraj), Yogi Anand Satyam (formerly known as Sal Familia), Roy Mitchell, Glenn James, Bill Bilodeau, Tom Affatigato, and Kathe Jeremiah. The late Loretta Quintano devoted long hours to typing the first manuscript. The translation was first published in India by Sri Sat Guru Publications in 1990. It served as the basis for a study group of scholars, Yoga teachers, and practicioners that met in my home from 1996 to 2001 and is used on an ongoing basis at the Hill Street Center for Yoga and Meditation in Santa Monica. We are pleased to make this work more widely available.

Though certainly not definitive or exhaustive, this book seeks to explore Yoga through the prism of practice, while keeping sight of its historical context and its philosophical contribution.

Acknowledgments

Numerous people contributed directly and indirectly to this book, including:

Gurāṇi Añjali
Maureen Shannon-Chapple
Yogi Anand Satyam
Padmani Higgins
Eugene Kelly
Roy Mitchell
Kathe and Don Jeremiah
Joanne and Bill Bilodeau
John and Karen Doukas
Glenn and Theresa James
Dylan and Emma Chapple
Carol Turner
Virginia Huynh
Nicole DePicciotto
Carol Rossi
Lisa Walford
Denise Kaufman
John Hick
Thomas Berry
James Fredericks
Ian Whicher
David Carpenter
Veda Bharati
Gerald Larson
Antonio T. DeNicolas
Georg Feuerstein
T. K. V. Desikachar
Vivian Richman
Wynanda Jacobi
Linda Schultz
Saradeshaprana
Allison Andersen
Barbara Michels
Beth Sternlieb
Cris Antunes
Ron Stark
Stephanie Petersen
Douglas Renfrew Brooks
John Friend
Edwin Bryant
Stuart Sarbacker
Peggy Dobreer
Jasmine Lieb
Aaron Reed
Todd Vander Heyden
John and Denise Hughes
Viresh Hughes
Laura Cornell
John Talbert
George van den Barselaar
Donovan Duket
Jim and Barbara Mathieu
John Casey
Matt Dillon
Laura Dern
Amy Davis
Jodi Shaw
David Gordon White
Daniel Michon
Navin and Pratima Doshi
Purusottama Bilimoria
Yajneshwar and Sunanda Shastri
and many others

ABBREVIATIONS

BG	*Bhagavad Gītā*
CU	*Chāndogya Upaniṣad*
SK	*Sāṃkhya Kārikā*
SKGB	*Sāṃkhya Kārikā of Īśvarakṛṣṇa with the Commentary of Gauḍapāda*
SU	*Śvetāśvatara Upaniṣad*
YS	*Yoga Sūtra*
YSVB	*Yoga Sūtra of Patañjali with the Commentary of Vyāsa*

1 The Yoga Tradition

Yoga has spread far from its home in India, yet its message has remained the same: one can experience freedom and spontaneity through the adoption of a specific way of life, defined by ethics, movement, and meditation. This philosophy has a long history in North America, beginning with the discussion of Yoga and the Upaniṣads by the transcendentalists. In 1893 an authentic Indian teacher, Swami Vivekananda, introduced Indian philosophy to the American public at Chicago's Parliament of World Religions. Yoga proved very popular in the early twentieth century particularly due to the efforts of the Ramakrishna-Vivekananda Mission and the Self-Realization Fellowship of Yogananda. Both these organizations continue their work at centers throughout the country.

During the past thirty years, there has been a resurgence of interest in Yoga, but with a difference. No longer are Americans at the mercy of third-hand accounts of Yoga, relying on translations given through the medium of translators who rewrite texts extensively to make them comprehensible to the Judeo-Christian mind. Nor is the spectrum of teachings available limited to the Neo-Vedantic syncretism that captured the imagination of the masses from the 1920s to the 1960s. Philosophers, Sanskritists, and a new wave of Yoga teachers have enriched our interpretations and brought a new understanding of this ancient discipline. Yoga teachers are exacting radical transformations in their students, requiring extended periods of serious *sādhana* study. Studios established by followers of the primary disciples of Krishnamacharya, such as B. K. S. Iyengar and Pattabhi Jois have found a niche within the fabric of American life.[1] In some cases, new followers of Yoga undergo a phase of "Hinduization," wherein the Indian mindset is rehearsed, recited, and embodied. This approach can be found in the practice of devotional (*bhakti*) Yoga in the Hare Krishna movement. In other cases, some Indian gurus in the

West have "modernized" their teachings and tolerate behavior that would not be found in India. The Kripalu movement in Massachusetts has pioneered a style of Yoga management that emphasizes democratic principles rather than reliance on a central figure.

Whether Hinduized or not, the contemporary followers of Yoga have, for the most part, questioned their fundamental approach to life. The superiority of Western advances in science are no longer taken for granted; the horrors of chemical pollution, increased cancer rates, and rampant stress have soured the comforts brought by technology. Due to a number of cultural changes enacted in the late sixties and early seventies, the notions of progress and development are no longer seen as ultimately healthy or even worthwhile. Many modern-day practitioners find in Yoga an integrated spiritual practice that serves as an antidote to the cynical, sedentary, and often opulent lifestyle that has developed in the postmodern world.

The Yoga tradition perhaps can be traced to the earliest identifiable phase of religion and culture in India, the Indus Valley civilization (ca. 3500 BCE). In seals and small statues, artists of these early cities depicted figures in meditative poses, somewhat recognizable in later tradition as named Yoga postures.[2] Although Yoga does not appear as a discrete practice in the literature of the four Vedas, the Upaniṣads (ca. 600 BCE ff.) refer to Yoga and list several of its practices. Buddhist and Jaina texts explicitly list practices of Yoga beginning approximately 350 BCE, and by the year 200 CE various styles and modes of Yoga became codified by Patañjali in his *Yoga Sūtra*. Because Yoga emphasizes practices for mystical religious experience without specifying a fixed theological perspective, it has been appropriated in one form or another by nearly all the religions found in India, including Christianity. [3]

Patañjali defined Yoga as a state of consciousness bereft of pain or discomfort during which the preoccupations of the mind cease. He stated that Yoga can be applied to alleviate human suffering (*duḥkhaṃ*), leading to a state of purified witnessing. The Buddha taught various forms of yogic meditation to help one achieve *nirvāṇa*. The Jina advocated the scrupulous observance of the yogic practice of vows with special emphasis on nonviolence (*ahiṃsā*) to advance one toward *kevala*. The *Bhagavad Gītā* described three styles of Yoga: Action or Karma Yoga, Knowledge or Jñāna Yoga, and Devotion or Bhakti Yoga. The Sufi mystics of India taught the goal of *tauḥīd* or complete union, a state not unfamiliar to yogic thinkers. The Sikhs of India included many yogic practices in their religious life. In these various traditions, Yoga established a common discourse of interpretation for religious experience that can be understood across cultures and traditions.

The *Yoga Sūtra* of Patañjali is now studied by Yoga practitioners worldwide. It helps to orient Yoga students into ethical behavior, movement, breathing, and meditation practices that characterize a serious undertaking of Yoga. Yoga deals explicitly with liberative states of consciousness (*samādhi*), listing several varieties and diverse means to achieve them. For cross-cultural purposes, its emphasis on practice is extremely useful, as it discusses process, not doctrine or belief. Fundamentally, Yoga explains how and why we hold beliefs and feelings and prescribes methods for transcending them. Yoga does not dogmatically dictate *what* to believe, feel, or do, but seeks to cultivate understanding leading to self-mastery.

LOWER SELF AND HIGHER SELF, SEEN AND SEER

Yoga regards life as a continuing relationship between two fundamental experiences, *prakṛti* or the manifest realm and *puruṣa/ātman*, one's higher self. The *ātman* or "true nature" is amply described in the Śvetāśvatara Upaniṣad:

> Than whom there is naught else higher,
> Than whom there is naught smaller, naught greater,
> The One stands like a tree established in heaven.
> By that, *puruṣa*, this whole world is filled.
> That which is beyond this world
> Is without form and without ill.
> They who know That, become immortal;
> But others go only to sorrow.[4]

In reading this or any other text describing a person's highest nature, it is important not to regard the self as a static state. When reified or objectified, the concept of higher self loses its dynamism. The self is an experience, a body-feel, a state of silent absorption. Though not described through conventional language, it nonetheless is not an unattainable ideal.

The state of absorption, wherein the separation between subjective and objective breaks down, is referred to in the *Bhagavad Gītā* as the "higher self." Although this contrasts with the "lower self," both are necessary for human life; their relationship is reciprocal, not mutually abnegating.[5] The elements, senses, mind, and emotions comprise the lower self. Difficulties in life arise because one identifies wholly with the lower forms of embodiment, residing only in the ego, ignoring the higher self. The seer (*puruṣa-ātman*) is always a witness, always neutral and inactive, and hence easy to ignore or overlook.[6] Due to lack of alertness, the Seer or higher self (*puruṣa*) becomes buried and one identifies with the Seen (*prakṛti*): *draṣṭṛ-dṛśyayoḥ saṃyogo heya-hetuḥ*.[7] This attribution of consciousness to an aspect of the non-conscious *prakṛti* results in ego identification and suffering. The ego or *ahaṃkāra* erroneously claims experience to be its own and fixes the world as seen from its own limited perspective. The lower ego self elevates itself to the status of highest priority: all that matters is what relates to the "me." With this attitude in control, a damaging rigidity arises, and the pain of *saṃsāra* continues. With each selfish action, a seed for further action is planted; as these seeds mature and flourish, strengthening selfish motives, the primal, pure *puruṣa* mode of detached witnessing becomes concealed. The breath of life is constricted, and the suffering (*duḥkha*) continues.

In such states, the Seer (*puruṣa*) and Seen (*prakṛti*) no longer interact in reciprocity; only the ego is apparent. The antidote for this "disease" is found through meditation, during which the nonselfish, *puruṣa* state may be engaged and embodied. To achieve this goal, the *Yoga Sūtra* prescribes many different paths, all aiming to effect *citta-vṛtti-nirodha*, the suppression of mental modifications.[8] The mental modifications, which define the nature of the Seen, are five in number: cognition, error, imagination, sleep, and memory.[9] When these are held in abeyance, the highest self gains ascendancy, and the freedom of detachment is made present.

YOGA AS PATH

Essentially, Yoga is technique. Its elaborations on the causes of suffering (*kleśa*) provide a conceptual framework for understanding the operations of the ego, ultimately to be transcended through meditation. Yoga provides a phenomenological investigation of suffering and its transcendence, its sole presupposition being that each person has the ability to reach a state of liberation. The closest "definition" of liberation in the *Yoga Sūtra* is *dharma-megha*, a beautifully metaphoric and appropriately vague term that lends itself to a variety of interpretations, including "cloud of virtue."

How can Yoga, a tradition steeped in Indian culture and atmosphere, be translated for application by Westerners? Have the attempts made by various Indian teachers been successful? Can Yoga be applied universally to enrich non-Asian religious practices? In order to answer these questions, the basic presupposition of Yoga must be examined, to see if the needs that gave rise to Yoga are also relevant in the postmodern, technological era. Along with virtually all systems of Indian philosophy, Yoga is predicated on the supposition that humankind is plagued with discomfort and suffering (*duḥkha*) and that this suffering can be alleviated. The *Yoga Sūtra* states that "the pain of the future is to be avoided" (*heyaṃ duḥkham anāgatam*).[10] To the extent that this analysis holds true, Yoga can be applied by any individual seeking self-fulfillment of a spiritual kind. If someone has perceived a degree of suffering in life, Yoga practice offers a means to transcend that suffering. Unless one shares the basic intent of alleviating pain, the suitability of Yoga would be questionable.

All over the world, Yoga and systems related to Yoga are being practiced; discontented people are searching for viable paths of transformation. Part of the appeal of Yoga lies in the many diverse means it prescribes. Patañjali offers the practitioner an abundance of practices. The student of Yoga is told that the liberating suppression of the mind's unruliness is achieved through well-cultivated practice and detachment. One who applies faith, energy, mindfulness, nondual awareness, and insight (*śraddhā, vīrya, smṛti, samādhi, prajñā*), is said to gain success.[11] Another way is to devote one's meditation to the primal teacher, *Īśvara*, who remains untainted by the ravages of change inflicted by association with *prakṛti*.[12] This teacher defies objectification as an external deity, being also identified with the recitation of the syllable *oṃ*, a self-generated vibration within the body of the practitioner. Appropriate behavior in interpersonal relationships is seen to be another tool for self-evolution: "One should cultivate friendship with the joyful, compassion for the sorrowful, gladness toward those who are virtuous, and equanimity in regard to the non-virtuous; through this, the mind is pacified."[13] The emphasis here is on flexibility, being able to recognize a situation and act as called for. Goodness does not suffice in all circumstances; at times, the best lesson is provided by restraint, as in the cultivation of equanimity among those who are nonvirtuous (*apuṇya*).

Breathing is seen as a means to achieve the peace of *nirodha*.[14] By recognizing the most fundamental of life's processes, a closeness to self is achieved. The word *ātman* is in fact derived from the verbal root *āt*, breathe. The *Chāndogya Upaniṣad* tells the story of a contest among the bodily functions of speaking, seeing, hearing, thinking, and breathing. Each respective faculty takes a turn at leaving the body and remaining away for a year. When speaking leaves, the body becomes dumb; when the eye leaves, blindness results; upon the departure of the ear, deafness follows; and when the mind leaves, a state of mindlessness sets in. But when the breath begins to go off, "as a horse might tear out the pegs of his foot-tethers all together, thus did it tear out the other Breaths [speaking, etc.] as well. They all came to the breath and said 'Sir! Remain! You are the most superior of us. Do not go off!'"[15] Of all bodily functions, the breath is the most fundamental, without which life is not possible. In gaining control over the breath, the yogin masters the other senses, including the thinking process.[16]

Other practices prescribed in the *Yoga Sūtra* include directing one's consciousness to one who has conquered attachment (*vīta-rāga*) or meditating on an auspicious dream experience or centering the mind in activity or cultivating thoughts that are sorrowless and illuminating or by any other means, as desired.[17]

The purpose of these various practices is to diminish the influence of past actions that have been performed for selfish or impure motives (*kleśa*). These motives are five in number and catalogue pitfalls in the path. The first, nonwisdom (*avidyā*) is seen to be the cause of the other four. Patañjali describes this *kleśa* as "seeing the self, which is eternal, pure, and joyful, in that which is non-self, non-eternal, impure, and painful."[18] The "I" mistakes its limited experience for the ultimate reality, and life is pursued through combinations of the other four *kleśas*: from the attitude based solely on self-orientation and self-gratification (*asmitā*) or clinging (*rāga*), despising (*dveṣa*), or because of an insatiable desire to hold on to life (*abhiniveśa*).[19] These influences, which define the ego, must be lessened through Yoga in order for the experience of freedom to take place.

The Yogic process of transformation begins at the ethical level through the practices of disciplines (*yama*) and constructive action (*niyama*). Through the adherence to particular behavioral practices, the yogin begins to erode the past impressions that have bound one to a life of rigidity. For the yogin, freedom is found through disciplined action. By restraint from violence, stealing, hoarding, and wantonness, and through the application of truthfulness, the influences of the self-centered past are lessened. Cultivation of purity, contentment, forbearance, study, and devotion to a chosen symbol (*īśvara-praṇidhāna*) establishes a new way of life, deconstructing the old, pain-ridden order and constructing a new body of free and responsible action. *Yama* and *niyama*, although listed first among Patañjali's eight limbs, are not to be seen as preliminary practices. As Feuerstein points out, "it would be quite wrong to interpret these 'members' as stages, as has often been done. Rather they should be compared with functional units, which overlap both chronologically and their activity."[20]

The world is intended and constructed through personal behavior, and the world created by the practitioner will continue to operate, even when the state of liberation or *kaivalyam* is reached. The *Sāṃkhya Kārikā* states that even when the highest wisdom has been attained, and *prakṛti* has displayed herself and retreated, the force of past impressions causes the body to continue to operate, just as a potter's wheel spins on even after the kick of the potter ceases.[21] Similarly, the state of *dharma megha*, so tersely mentioned in the *Yoga Sūtra*, does not seem to imply that life evaporates. Rather, this may be seen as a cloud wherein the totality of the nondual experience is made apparent, and all distinctions of "grasper, grasping, and grasped" dissolve.[22] In conventional consciousness, the world stands against and apart from the experiencer. Through Yoga, self unites with circumstance, and the ground of all possibilities is laid open. Life does not cease but is freed from the constraints of a limited perspective.

The system of Yoga presents various avenues by which the pettiness of self-centered orientation may be overcome and the fullness of human potential may be realized. Yoga emphasizes ethical behavior, movement, and meditation. This meditation may be guided or shaped by the notion of deity. Yoga suggests that one chooses his or her own deity ideal (*iṣṭa devatā*).[23] This open approach is Hinduism at its best and even defies the label "Hindu." In fact, the practice of choosing one's deity form spread throughout Asia with Buddhism, which developed an entire pantheon of Buddhas and bodhisattvas. In both Hinduism and Buddhism, the human condition is regarded in much the same manner. Two pathways are open to humankind, one associated with affliction (*kliṣṭa*) and one oriented toward enlightenment (*akliṣṭa*). By continually generating afflicting behavior or "words," one is bound to misery. By cultivating the opposite, the practitioner of meditation builds a life of responsible freedom. Both systems set forth ideal religious figures to emulate. These gods, goddesses, or Buddhas inspire one to persist on the spiritual path.

Because of its existential and practical thrust, the concepts of the *Yoga Sūtra* hold a nearly universal appeal. Like the Buddha, Patañjali emphasizes suffering as the prime catalyst to spark the spiritual quest. Like the *Ṛg Veda* and the Sāṃkhya school, the *Yoga Sūtra* divides its characterization of experience into the seer and the seen and suggests that Yoga requires the pacification of the seen to allow the seer or pure consciousness to emerge. Like Jainism, it requires strict adherence to five ethical practices: nonviolence, truthfulness, not stealing, sexual restraint, and nonpossession. Presaging later devotional or *bhakti* schools, it suggests that one should model oneself after an idealized deity (*īśvara*), defined as the perfect soul "untouched by afflictions, actions, fruitions, or their residue."[24]

The brilliance of Patañjali lies in his ability to weave together key theological themes that in a different context would be seen as incompatible or contradictory. By restricting his discussion to techniques for alleviating distress, by delicately avoiding a commitment to a specific deity manifestation, by appealing for adherence to a foundational set of ethical precepts, and by personalizing the process of spiritual self-discovery, Patañjali evades many conflicts that normally would arise regarding the existence of God and the existence or nonexistence of a soul. He does not overtly deny the possibility of

God as do many Buddhist and Jaina thinkers, nor does he downplay the validity of human experience as do many later thinkers of the Advaita Vedanta schools. He evokes a minimalist though thorough approach to overcoming the negative influences of past karma, advocating the application of reflective analysis, ethical precepts, and physical as well as mental disciplines.

A VEDĀNTA APPROACH TO YOGA

The emphasis on the transcendent nature of consciousness in Indian philosophy led some theorists to postulate an underlying universality within the world's religious traditions. Although this idea might seem quite modern, the *Ṛg Veda* itself, arguably as old as if not older than the Hebrew Bible, proclaims, "To what is one, sages give many a title"[25] and "the One has developed into All."[26] The theme of oneness can also be found in the great sentences of the Upaniṣads (*mahāvākya*) and the nondualist philosophy of Śankara (ca. 700 CE).

The Neo-Vedānta taught by Swami Vivekananda a century ago advanced this theory of oneness as both a way to harmonize the world's religious traditions and to alleviate human alienation. He wrote, "As manifested beings we appear to be separate, but our reality is one, and the less we think of ourselves as separate from that one, the better for us. The more we think of ourselves as separate from the Whole, the more miserable we become."[27] Though the Vedānta emphasis on oneness and unity might tend to deemphasize or even trivialize individual and/or cultural differences, it nonetheless provides a compelling appeal for religious harmony and provides a rationale for respecting the religions of others.

American and British literature has long held a great fascination with the Vedānta concept of Brahma or the absolute. Ralph Waldo Emerson wrote several poems inspired by his reading of Indian texts in translation, including the aptly titled "Brahma," which was inspired by the *Bhagavad Gītā*. This poem revels in the inner nature of religious experience and pokes fun at the gods who seek but can not attain *samādhi*:

> If the red slayer think he slays,
> Or if the slain think he is slain,
> They know not well the subtle ways
> I keep, and pass, and turn again.
>
> Far or forgot to me is near;
> Shadow and sunlight are the same;
> The vanished gods to me appear;
> And one to me are shame and fame.

They reckon ill who leave me out;
When me they fly, I am the wings;
I am the doubter and the doubt,
And I the hymn the Brahmin sings.

The strong gods pine for my abode,
And pine in vain the sacred Seven;
But thou, meek lover of the good!
Find me, and turn thy back on heaven.[28]

Similarly, W. Somerset Maugham (1874–1968) waxed eloquent in *The Razor's Edge* about Vedānta, creating a rhapsodic summary of Indian philosophy, "According to the Vedantists, the self, which they call the atman and we call the soul, is distinct from the body and its senses, distinct from the mind and its intelligence."[29] Maugham attributes to Larry, the lead character in this novel, a life-transforming blissful experience, which he describes tentatively as "oneness with reality."[30]

Despite the glowing narratives about the nondual nature of religious experience found in the Upaniṣads and later literature influenced by Vedānta, the Yoga tradition does not espouse a monism. It grounds itself in the recognition of multiple points of view and, in fact, argues for individual exploration and discovery as the only means to liberation. Yoga texts examine different paths while acknowledging the need for common guidelines for spiritual practice. We have already introduced a plurality of practices as found in the *Yoga Sūtra* of Patañjali. Several other texts of Yoga also exist, including a series of Upaniṣads on Yoga, extensive Yoga passages in the great epic *Mahābhārata*[31] (including the *Bhagavad Gītā*), and in various texts of Buddhism. The *Yogavāsiṣṭha*, an eleventh-century text, combines strands of Indian thought including Vedānta, Buddhism, and Yoga in an expressive epic style. Haribhadra's *Yogadṛṣṭisamuccaya*, an eighth-century Jaina text, juxtaposes numerous Yoga systems, takes a firm stand on issues of ritual purity, and serves as Haribhadra's biographical statement on the issues of conversion and religious conviction, an enduring theme in the broader religious traditions of India. Yoga also found prominence in the intellectual discourse of Sikhism and Islam, underscoring the plurality of theological schools that adopted some form of Yoga practice.

THE *YOGAVĀSIṢṬHA*

The desire to reconcile different meditative traditions finds expression in the *Yogavāsiṣṭha*, a text developed over several centuries, reaching its present form by the eleventh century. The *Yogavāsiṣṭha* emphasizes a Vedānta-style universal consciousness but also delineates practices of Yoga.

Demonstrating the author's familiarity with Sāṃkhya, Mahāyāna Buddhism, Vedānta, and Yoga, the *Yogavāsiṣṭha* states,

> This is seen as the Puruṣa of the Sāṃkhya philosophers,
> the Brahman of the Vedāntins,
> The Vijñāptimātra of the Yogācāra Buddhists,
> And the Śūnya of the Śūnyavādins.[32]

This sweeping statement seems to equate various religions or theological perspectives. More significantly, it indicates a style of doing theology or studying religions that seems thoroughly modern in its ecumenism.

To understand this interest in developing a broad theological perspective, it is helpful to explore the context for the discourses contained in the *Yogavāsiṣṭha*. Rāma, despairing over the burdens of kingship and in quest of transcendent knowledge, has approached his teacher Vasiṣṭha for answers. Vasiṣṭha outlines the central metaphysics of Indian thought, teaching Rāma about the unseen, eternal, changeless aspect in contrast to the apparent, finite, changing reality of human life and responsibility. In the style of the *Bhagavad Gītā*, he urges Rāma to integrate these two aspects through the performance of Dharma, to take up his kingly duties. As he prospers, so also his kingdom will prosper. Included in this survey summation of Indian thought are Vedāntic monism, the Yogācāra "mind-only" and Mādhyamika emptiness schools of Buddhism, and the Sāṃkhya spiritual psychology of the silent witness.

Each of these schools was represented in India during the time of the composition of the *Yogavāsiṣṭha*, around 1100 CE. The king or kings symbolized by Rāma for whom these discourses were intended would need to be familiar with each of these traditions to be effective in his rule. In a pluralistic polity, sensitivity to diverse perspectives is essential to maintain peace. The rhetoric put forth by the *Yogavāsiṣṭha* allows the king to regard each religion with respect. By appealing to the universals, the government becomes the protector of virtue in its specific and various forms.

The *Yogavāsiṣṭha* integrates aspects of diverse schools into a coherent theological view. However, Vasiṣṭha states that the world relies on the workings and habits of the mind; it changes frequently. Moreover, he urges Rāma to transcend the realm of desire and change through performing his required tasks with zeal, working for the benefit of all his subjects. By acting selflessly, both goals are achieved: rising above the cares of the world while yet performing what needs to be done to maintain the world order. This approach integrates the teachings of Karma Yoga as found in the *Bhagavad Gītā*: by performance of action without attachment one attains an equanimity that sanctifies the nature and content of one's actions, setting an example for others. It also provides a working model for the adoption of a tolerant point of view, essential for the maintenance of harmony in a social setting characterized by diversity.

THE *YOGADṚṢṬISAMUCCAYA*: JAINISM AND YOGA

The Jaina tradition, similar to Sāṃkhya and Yoga, does not espouse a universal common soul or consciousness but asserts a multiplicity of souls, each on an individual, heroic quest, with the ultimate goal found in the elimination of all karma. Jainism emphasizes the scrupulous practice of nonviolence (*ahiṃsā*) as the path to liberation.

The *Yogadṛṣṭisamuccaya*, written in the eighth century of the common era, presents Haribhadra's comparative analysis of several Yoga schools from a Jaina perspective. Born into the Brahmin caste, Haribhadra, according to hagiographical tradition, converted to Jainism after hearing a Jaina nun outline the basic precepts of nonviolence, karma, and liberation (*kevala*). Drawing upon his extensive training in the Vedas and Vedānta, and building on his studies of Buddhism, he pioneered the tradition of doxological texts, which summarize rival schools of thought quite fairly. His *Saddarśanasamuccaya* provides a thoughtful, accurate summary of the prevailing theological and philosophical schools of medieval India.

In the *Yogadṛṣṭisamuccaya*, Haribhadra applies this methodology not only to theories of Yoga but also to various groups of its practitioners. He recasts Patañjali's eightfold limbs in terms of a goddesslike tradition. The Disciplines (*yama*) take on the name Mitrā; Observances (*niyama*) become Tārā; Postures (*āsana*) become Balā; Breath Control (*prāṇāyāma*) becomes Dīprā; Inwardness (*pratyāhāra*) becomes Sthirā; Concentration (*dhāraṇā*) becomes Kāntā; Meditation (*dhyāna*) is called Prabhā; while Absorption (*samādhi*) takes on the name Parā. Each of these titles evokes a goddess, whose qualities may be translated into English as Friendly, Protector, Power, Shining, Firm, Pleasing, Radiant, and Highest, respectively. Haribhadra also describes four Yoga schools and arranges them in a hierarchy that privileges nonviolence and purity as essential for proper Yoga practice.[33]

Haribhadra criticizes some Yoga practitioners as deluded, chiding them for fanning the flames of desire while thinking they are free. He praises others for their adherence to proper ethical behavior. However, while he clearly states his negative opinions regarding animal sacrifice and trying to quell desire by attempting to satisfy it, Haribhadra also advances a viewpoint that emphasizes a need to look beyond differences toward the commonalities of Yoga practice. He states that all yogis seek to overcome suffering and that this can be accomplished by diligent practice, keeping good company, and studying the scriptures. In keeping with the Jaina tradition of avoiding extreme views, he criticizes the Buddhist emphasis on impermanence and the Vedāntin teaching of illusion. Nonetheless, he presents a tableau of spirituality that sees a common ground and purpose to the pursuit of Yoga, regardless of the theological tradition to which it is attached.

BUDDHISM AND YOGA

The Buddhist tradition is closely linked with Yoga. Both Buddhism and Yoga place emphasis on the centrality of human suffering, the need to meditate in order to gain clarity, and gradual processes of purification required to attain the shared goal of *nirodha*, or the cessation of the causes that lead to suffering. The Brahma Vihāras in the *Yoga Sūtra* (the cultivation of friendliness, compassion, sympathetic joy, and equanimity [I :33]) derive directly from the teachings of the Buddha, as will be examined in chapter 15. The emphasis on suffering or *duḥkha*, found in *Yoga Sūtra pāda* II, correlates directly to the first truth of the Buddha. The release from suffering for Buddhism is found in right view, right resolve, right speech, right action, right livelihood, right effort, right mindfulness, and right concentration (*samādhi*). Patañjali offers a similar eightfold practice of precepts, observances, movement, breath, inwardness, concentration, meditation, and *samādhi*. Winston King has suggested a correlation between states of yogic *samādhi* and stages of Theravada Buddhist meditation (Pāli: *jhāna*, Sanskrit: *dhyāna*).[34]

In the later Mahāyāna Buddhist tradition, we find that *dharma megha samādhi* is considered to be the tenth and highest level attained by the bodhisattva.[35] Similarly, *dharma megha samādhi* plays a central role in Patañjali's system. Mahayana Buddhism also refers extensively to a concept known as 'emptiness' or *śūnyatā*, which it equates with an elevated state of insight. Similarly, Patañjali refers to a state of being "empty of own form" (*svarūpa-śūnya*, I:43, III:3, IV:34) that he regards to indicate entry into the state of *samādhi*. However, not all the references to Buddhism are direct borrowings or affirmations of the system. Seemingly in response to the Yogācāra notion that all things proceed from the mind, he states that the reality of the external world cannot be disputed (IV:16) but that the mind itself can be purified of tinge or coloration (IV:17). The tradition of Vajrayāna Buddhism or Tantra holds many common themes with classical and Haṭha Yoga, including veneration of the guru and meditation on the *cakras*.

SIKH YOGA

Another tradition that acknowledged and incorporated various aspects of classical Yoga is Sikhism, founded by Guru Nanak (1469–1538) in northern India. According to Trilochan Singh, Bhai Gurdas (1551–1636) referred to Patañjali as an "enlightened sage."[36] The sacred writings of Sikhism, the *Guru Granth Sahib*, discuss Haṭha Yoga. Guru Nanak uses the word *Yoga* to refer to his own religious system, which he calls "Gurmukh Yoga," "Gurmat Yoga," or "Sahaja Yoga." The Sikh scriptures make frequent reference to the Sāṃkhya and Yoga theories of *puruṣa* and *prakṛti*. Concepts and practices from the later Haṭha Yoga traditions are also recognized, such as *prāṇa*, *kuṇḍalinī*, and the *ṇadīs*. Guru Nanak, who lived at a time when Gorakhnath school of Yoga was widely practiced,[37] was highly critical of their "selfish individualism." According to Trilochan Singh, Guru Nanak visited their centers throughout India up into Afghanistan in an attempt to convince them of the preeminence of God or the Akal, the timeless *puruṣa*.[38]

In America, the Sikh Yoga developed by Yogi Bhajan starting in Los Angeles' East-West Center in 1969 utilizes the very techniques criticized as excessive by Guru Nanak. In particular, Yogi Bhajan's practices include breathing exercises and Yoga postures designed to elevate the *kuṇḍalinī* through various *cakras*. Other aspects of American Sikh Yoga follow traditional Sikhism, including belief in one God, rising before sunrise, not cutting one's hair, following a vegetarian diet, serving the community, living as a householder, and being available for military service.[39] Though Daniel Michon, who has studied Sikhism extensively in India, claims that physical aspects of Yoga are not readily apparent in the Punjab, the mention of the concepts of *puruṣa* and *prakṛti* and the practices of what Guru Nanak calls a "Gurmukh Yoga" in the *Guru Granth Sahib* indicate a close connection between the two forms of Yoga.

ISLAM AND YOGA

The Muslim world has long held a deep interest in the religions and spiritualities of India. Intellectuals from within the Muslim community sought out and translated two primary philosophical texts on the Yoga tradition, the *Yoga Sūtra* and the *Yogavāsiṣṭha*. Additionally, a third text, the *Amṛtakuṇḍa*, was translated into Arabic, which explains yogic physiology and practices, for which the original Sanskrit or Hindi has been lost. Patañjali's *Yoga Sūtra* was translated into Arabic by al-Biruni (d. 1010). The *Laghu Yogavāsiṣṭha* was translated into Persian by Nizam al-Din Panipati for the Mughal emperor

Jahangir in the late 1500s and, according to Fathullah Mojtaba'i, "is the earliest exposition of Vedānta philosophy written in a language that could be read outside India."[40] It includes descriptions of various Yoga practices.

Perhaps the most pervasive awareness of Yoga within the Muslim world came through a text known as the *Amṛtakuṇḍa*, rendered as the *Hawd mā al-hayāt* in Arabic and as *The Pool of the Water of Life* in English. This text, which has been translated into English by Carl Ernst (forthcoming, State University of New York Press), describes various styles of breath control, different Yoga postures, inner visualizations, and meditation exercises. It provides something of a manual for the practice of Sufi Yoga and was widely disseminated in Arabic, Persian, Turkish, and Urdu translations. Ernst surmises that this text first appeared in the fifteenth century and combines aspects of the Gospel of Thomas with the Koran, Hellenistic philosophy, and Sufism, all within the context of Haṭha Yoga practice. Though Ernst is careful to point out that Sufism did not originate from India, as R. C. Zaehner[41] and other scholars have hypothesized, this text amply demonstrates that Sufis in India were aware of indigenous forms of meditation and Yoga.

PLURALISM, TOLERANCE, AND YOGA

Pluralism has been the core of what can be called the "Hindu faith," from the seals of the Indus Valley culture and the Vedic pantheon of gods and goddesses to the contemporary coexistence of Vaiṣṇavas and Śaivas. Likewise, Hindus have always lived in a pluralistic society, side by side with Greeks,[42] Jainas, Buddhists, Zoroastrians, Muslims, Sikhs, Jews, and Christians.

Conceptually, Hinduism has dealt with this multiplicity through a creative application of a theory of universalism. The Jainas state that all beings want to live; the Buddha proclaimed that all beings suffer; the *Dharmaśāstras* state that all people seek wealth, pleasure, and societal harmony. The Neo-Vedānta of Vivekananda specifically emphasizes the need to study multiple traditions, citing Ramakrishna's immersion into mystical Islam, goddess worship, and the teachings of Jesus.

In many ways, the modern academic discipline of religious studies follows the Vedic adage, Truth is one, though the paths are many. Many academic departments, though within the context of a largely Christian worldview, seek full representation of all major faiths on their faculties. The Roman Catholic Church proclaimed during the Second Vatical Council that

> religions to be found everywhere strive variously to answer the restless searchings of the human heart by proposing "ways," which consist of

> teachings, rules of life, and ceremonies. The Catholic Church rejects nothing which is true and holy in these religions. She looks with sincere respect upon those ways of conduct and of life, those rules and teachings which, though differing in many particulars from what she holds and sets forth, nevertheless often reflect a ray of that Truth which enlightens all.[43]

Both the academic disciplines of religious studies and the Roman Catholic advocacy of interreligious dialogue exhibit a pragmatism that resembles India's age-old attempt to deal with multiplicity.

Tolerance, dialogue, and syncretism are important qualities of the Hindu tradition that bear contemporary relevance. Patañjali's universalization of spirituality outlines an implicit argument for tolerating the existential reality and choices of others. Haribhadra provides a model for conducting a thoughtful, probing study of the religious thought of one's neighbors. The author of the *Yogavāsiṣṭha* shows that syncretism can be an effective tool for promoting societal peace.

The religious traditions of India extend from Indus remnants and Vedic chants to classical formulations, epic embellishments, medieval devotionalism, and the rationalistic apologetics of Aurobindo and Vivekananda. This rich legacy demonstrates the subtlety of theological reflection and nuance in response to changing needs within Indian society. It also underscores the difficulty of defining religion within India or confining it within a fixed set of doctrines, practices, or beliefs. Yoga traditions and their practices offer an important response to plurality that might be helpful as India continues to grapple with this ongoing issue and as scholars of religions continue their search for paradigms through which to conduct interreligious dialogue. By emphasizing spiritual practice and remaining mute on disputations of theological issues, Yoga has emerged through the centuries not only with effective methods for spiritual practice but also with an adaptability that accords well in multicultural contexts.

Given the basic thrust of Yoga as practice, not belief, it has served as a bridge between cultures and diverse religious forms for millennia. At the beginning of this chapter, Vivekananda was mentioned as a great bringer of Eastern truths to the West. He was certainly far from the first Indian to transmit Indian philosophy to foreign places. Bodhidharma took Zen to China.[44] Padmasambhava introduced Buddhist meditation techniques in Tibet. Closer to the Western world, major texts on Yoga such as the *Yogavāsiṣṭha* were translated into Persian during the thirteenth century. At even earlier times, Indian influence on Greek and Roman thinking through various trade routes is well documented.[45]

This dialogue between India and the world has not been a one-way street. Mughal rule greatly influenced large sectors of the population; India now contains the world's second largest Muslim population. British rule in India led to a new cultural and philosophical exchange. A sizeable group of respected English scholars held the native philosophies of India in high regard. Concurrently, Indians began imbibing in European traditions. Ram Mohan Roy (1772–1833), partly due to his exposure and exchange with Christian missionaries in Bengal, contributed greatly to the revitalization of Hinduism, incorporating some aspects of church services into the meetings of Brahmo Samaj. This in turn influenced later Hindu movements and undoubtedly made Vivekananda's message more easily understood during his lecture tours of the late ninteenth century and early twentieth century.

Meditation does not strive to create a new cultural identity but provides the occasion for insight into the very presuppositions that determine the need for personality. Yoga does not require an identity crisis wherein a better self-image is sought; rather, Yoga stems from a desire to examine and overturn *all* notions that perpetuate clinging to one's self-identity. Yoga, in itself, is cross-cultural. It can be used by Hindus, Buddhists, Christians, Sufis, and Sikhs, but the practice cannot be bound by the symbols chosen or the language used to convey its teachings.

Americans and Europeans are intellectually and spiritually prepared to benefit from Asian meditation techniques. However, unless the needs spoken to by the traditions are the needs motivating practice, the would-be practitioner runs the risk of self-deception and perhaps a few wasted years. Education about Yoga must accompany education in Yogic techniques to ensure that the remedy suits the illness. Yoga is a cross-cultural tool for cultivating religious insights and has demonstrated a universal applicability. Its effectiveness rests on a desire to transcend suffering; for one who shares this desire, Yoga offers a way of release.

I *The Practice of Yoga*

2 *Sāṃkhya Philosophy and Yoga Practice*

In this section of the book, we will approach the actual practice of Yoga, beginning with a philosophical overview of the system. We will then address the topics of Patañjali's eight limbs through three thematic chapters, dealing with ethics, movement, and meditation, respectively.

Yoga and Sāṃkhya combine religion and psychology. They hold the essential presupposition that at the core of human experience and transactional behavior resides an unseen seer, a silent witness to all activity who remains forever untouched. This principle is called "*puruṣa*."

SĀṂKHYA

To complement the unrevealed consciousness, which can never be objectified or discussed without resorting to inadequate metaphors, the *Sāṃkhya Kārikā* of Īśvarakṛṣṇa (ca. AD 300) posits a realm of activity, *prakṛti*, which provides experience for *puruṣa* to witness, and, through its quiescence, allows for the higher states of spiritual insight (*jñāna*). *Puruṣa* was never created, nor does it create (SK III). *Prakṛti* serves as the feminine matrix of creation. She divides into twenty-three functions (*tattva*) expressed through three modalities or *guṇas*. The *guṇas* manifest themselves into a state of heaviness or lethargy (*tamas*), passionate activity (*rajas*), or buoyant luminosity (*sattva*). Though itself uncreated, *prakṛti* gives rise to all creation, in the following sequence. First, *buddhi* appears, the "great one" (*mahat*). Then *ahaṃkāra*, the sense of I, follows, further dividing into *sattvika* and *tamasika* dimensions. On the *sattvika* side, *ahaṃkāra* generates the mind, the five senses, and the five motor organs. On the *tamasika* side, it generates the five subtle elements (*tanmātra*): sound, touch, form, taste, smell. Further *tamas* causes the gross elements to emerge from the subtle, hence space, wind, fire, water, earth. These twenty-

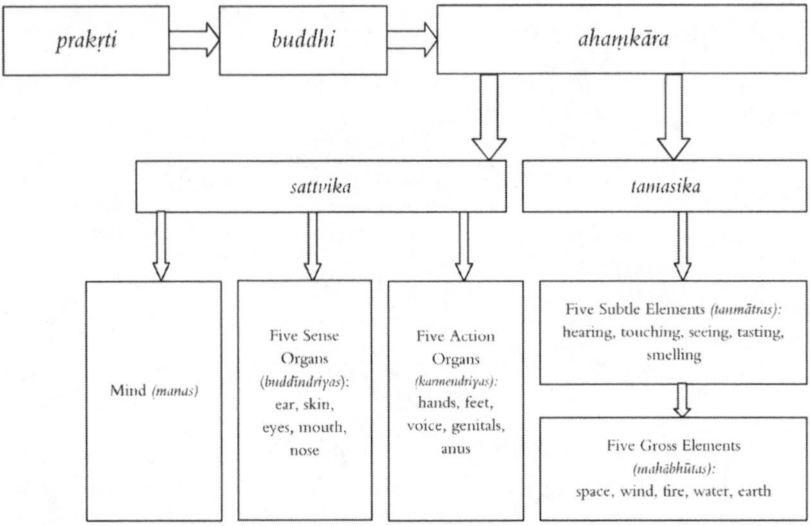

Figure 1. The 24 Functions of *Prakṛti*

five functions, as noted in figure 1 above, account for both the subjective, human realm and the external world.

The *buddhi*, the first of *prakṛti's* creations, is critical in the Sāṃkhya explanation of reality. The word *buddhi* derives from the verb root *budh*, which means to awaken. The word Buddha, the awakened one, derives from the same root. In the context of Sāṃkhya, *buddhi* shapes the reality to which, in a sense, one awakens. *Buddhi* serves the special function of relaying and interpreting experience to *puruṣa*. As seen in figure 2, the *buddhi* consists of four diametrically opposed pairs of qualities (*dharma*, *adharma*; *jñāna*, *ajñāna*; *virāga*, *rāga*; *aiśvaryam*, *anaiśvaryam*) with virtue contrasting with vice, knowledge with ignorance, dispassion with attachment, and strength with weakness. The *buddhi* determines not only the particulars of experience but also its mood or mode (*bhāva*) as well. If the *buddhi* resides in the negative domain of nonvirtue, ignorance, attachment, and weakness, pain (*duḥkha*) pervades experience. If it carries the opposite tendency, pleasure (*sukha*) follows. One critical *bhāva* holds the key to spiritual unfoldment: the knowledge mode (*jñāna bhāva*) fulfills the ultimate purpose of Sāṃkhya, liberation.

Note that *buddhi* operates within the domain of *prakṛti*; *puruṣa* has no need for liberation, as it remains always untouched, despite the dramatic play of *prakṛti's* creation. Rather, *prakṛti* needs liberation. Through a tragic case of

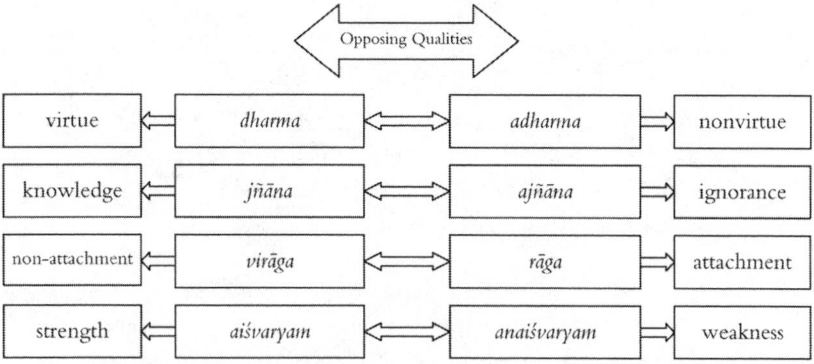

Figure 2. The Eight *Bhāvas* of *Buddhi*

mistaken identity, she erroneously attributes agency to the ego or *ahaṃkāra*, who claims all experience. Through the cultivation of knowledge, the difference between *puruṣa* and *prakṛti* is discerned, effecting liberation:

> From analysis of the *tattvas*, [one says]:
> "I am not: I own nothing; the 'I' does not exist."
> Thus, knowledge (*jñāna*) arises which is
> complete, free from error, pure, and absolute.
>
> *evaṃ tattvābhyāsān nā'smi na me nā'ham ity*
> *apariśeṣam, aviparyayād viśuddham*
> *kevalam utpadyate jñānam.*[1]

Identification with *prakṛti's* creation ceases, though experience in fact continues. From the forces of past impressions, the body lives on, "like a potter's wheel."

Two aspects of Sāṃkhya distinguish this system from Vedānta and other forms of monism and theistic philosophy. First, Sāṃkhya's dualism is relentless: *puruṣa* and *prakṛti* must in no way be equated or related; the mistaken notion that they are somehow related is the root of all pain. The key to knowledge lies in seeing the difference. Second, Sāṃkhya refuses to attach any appellations to the absolute. *Puruṣa* remains ever unnamed, never substantialized or objectified. The *puruṣa* cannot be named or seen nor become the object of speculation. No metaphor for the absolute suffices. Liberation is attained only when *prakṛti* musters up within herself sufficient discriminative knowledge (*jñāna*) to realize her mistaken identity. By surrendering all claims of self-identity, she frees herself.

YOGA

In the second of Patañjali's *sūtras*, we find the definition of Yoga: *Yogaś citta-vṛtti-nirodhaḥ*, Yoga is the restraint of fluctuations in the mind. These four key philosophical concepts of the mind and its fluctuations, restraint, Yoga, and the witness will be discussed below, with reference to the implications Yoga holds for defining reality and the significance of life.

CITTA-VṚTTI

The term *citta*, variously translated as "mind," "mindstuff," "internal organ," "mind-complex," "consciousness," "thinking principle," or "psychic nature," is central to the Yoga system.[2] *Citta* may be described as a network of functions (*tattvas*) that allows for the relay of information to the inactive experiencer (*puruṣa*). These functions include the inner organ (*antaḥkaraṇa*), composed of *buddhi*, *ahaṃkāra*, and *manas*, in conjunction with sense and motor organs (*buddhīndriyas* and *karmendriyas*), and their objects. The *citta* is regarded as the vehicle for perception, wherein the contents of experience take form for presentation to the *puruṣa*. It is also the receptacle for the effects of *karma*, the residue left by activity (*saṃskāra* or *vāsanā*), which conditions future actions. The *citta* in its pure state is like an unprogrammed computer. It takes coloration with the arising of each *vṛtti*, a fluctuation or wave that pervades the *citta* in the form of various perceptions, thoughts, memories, and emotions.

Five fluctuations or *vṛttis* are listed and described in the first section of the *Yoga Sūtra*.[3] In valid cognition (*pramāṇa*), objects are perceived: *pramāṇa* is any experience wherein *prakṛti* finds full manifestation in one of the gross elements. Such experience is verified via three avenues: perception, inference, or a credible verbal account (*pratyakṣa, anumāna, āgama*). Any perception of plants, animals, automobiles, buildings, clothing, oceans or inference or testimony about any such object, belongs to the first class of *vṛtti*. Such "things" are, metaphorically speaking, no more than a ripple (*vṛtti*) in the field of objectivity (*citta*). The second class of fluctuation, error (*viparyaya*), is considered to be a misguided ripple, that is, one that does not correspond to reality. The next category of fluctuation, imagination (*vikalpa*), involves a notion, not necessarily an error, which does not correspond to an object but may in fact serve a useful function. Examples of *vikalpa* would be metaphor and simile in poetry. In states of meditation, the engagement of *vikalpa* is considered important in the strengthening of the mind. In the sleep fluctuation (*nidrā*), one thought predominates to the exclusion of others, perhaps analogous to a brain scan wherein sleep is registered as a distinct, uniform wave pattern. Memory (*smṛti*), the last fluctuation or *vṛtti* listed, operates exclusively on the level of the inner organ (*antaḥkaraṇa*), wherein the contents of a previous experience are returned to consciousness via thought, although there is no longer any corresponding structure on the gross level. These five *vṛttis*—valid cognition, error, imagination, sleep, and memory—represent five discrete movements, five gauges of, or access points to, reality that account for all—or nearly all—human experience. Each, as listed in the system, is explicitly mechanical; this analysis, which explains the contents and scope of awareness, is not unlike the account of the states of consciousness that might be given by a contemporary neuropsychologist.

The five fluctuations of the mind summarize the normal range of human functioning, encompassing three modes of conventional transactions: things (as registered in *pramāṇa*), thoughts (in *viparyaya*, *vikalpa*, and *smṛti*), and sleep (*nidrā*). Each of these states is linked directly to a subjective appropriator, an "I" that claims the experience. In *Yoga Sūtra* IV:4, we find that "states of awareness (in particularized form), arise from the sense-of-I (*asmitā*) exclusively." That is, the perceptions of discrete objects or thoughts as described in the *citta-vṛtti* complex arise from the sense of self (*ahaṃkāra*). In such a state, the "higher" self, the noncreative witness (*puruṣa*), the actual registrar of data, is forgotten; the ego or *ahaṃkāra* "grabs" the experience, thinking it to be its own. As described in *Yoga Sūtra* II:6, the unseen seer (*puruṣa*) is blended into the seen in the process of *saṃyoga*, the mistaken linking of *puruṣa* with *prakṛti*. The result is evolution (*pariṇāma*), the emergence of the *that*, the reification and solidification of the world in the form of fluctuations or *vṛttis*. This movement, the perception of things, thoughts, or sleep as appropriated by the self and therefore separate from it, constitutes conventional experience.[4]

The reality of *prakṛti* and hence of *citta-vṛtti* is not denied. However, what in common usage are referred to as "things" (*vastu*) are in the yogic system seen as fluctuations stemming from the sense-of-I. These "things" are reinforced by education. The learning process, that is, the acquisition of appropriate names for certain mental fluctuations, dictates how the "world" is to be experienced and engaged. A table, once learned to be a table, is almost always intended and used as a table. Conventional reality, once sedimented, becomes unmoveable; perspective is restricted to limited languages of things and how the sense-of-I relates to those things. In such conventional consciousness (*citta-vṛtti*), life is spent in the unending generation of essentially the same patterns, like the bar in a ripple tank, continually emanating a surface of interfering waves, with still water, the bearing of other possibilities, forgotten.

NIRODHA

Mental fluctuations or *citta-vṛtti* are, by nature, fraught with the causes of affliction (*kleśa*), rooted in ignorance (*avidyā*), and characterized as impermanent, impure, and painful (*anitya, aśuci, duḥkha*).[5] As stated in *Yoga Sūtra* II:15, "to the one who possesses discrimination, all is pain" (*duḥkham eva sarvam vivekinaḥ*). However, Yoga does not stop with existential despair; we are not condemned to eternally generate the same painful wave patterns. As with Sāṃkhya and Buddhism, the purpose of Yoga is the cessation of pain, effected by states of restraint (*nirodha*) through which the wave-generating pattern is brought under control. This restraint, which is defined *as* Yoga, takes many forms. Here the *Yoga Sūtra* sketches myriad paths of practice, appropriately suited to the intensity of the practitioner. In regard to the restraint process, this wide range of methods indicates an emphasis on the ongoing application of Yogic techniques, not a deadening of the mental faculties wherein the operations of consciousness are switched off. The artistry of various forms of restraint indicates the subtle and complex nature of Yoga practice.

The *Yoga Sūtra* offers three main Yogas by which this practice is effected. The first of these, the application of practice (*abhyāsa*) and dispassion (*vairāgya*), transforms randomly produced fluctuations or *vṛttis* into responsible intentions (*pratyaya*), thus inducing a "working state" of restraint or *nirodha*. Practice, as "the effort of being established (*sthitau*),"[6] includes a wide range of nineteen techniques to stabilize the mind, while the cultivation of dispassion prevents the practitioner from appropriating the results of such practice in a selfish manner. The second Yoga, Kriyā Yoga, involves the threefold cultivation of austerity (*tapas*), self-study (*svadhyāya*), and devotion to *īśvara* (*īśvara-praṇidhāna*).[7] The third Yoga, the one most commonly identified with Patañjali, is eightfold Yoga, which includes the familiar "stages" of ethics (*yama*, and *niyama*), movement (*āsana*), breath control (*prāṇāyāma*), inwardness (*pratyāhāra*), and interior Yoga (*dhāraṇā, dhyāna*, and *samādhi*). All Yogas share a common technique and purpose: control over the mind's fluctuations.

The means used to still the mind is summarized in *Yoga Sūtra* II:33: "In the case of inhibiting thoughts, there should be the cultivation of opposites (*pratipakṣa bhāvanam*)." This applies not only to the ethical *yama/niyama* practices in the eightfold scheme, but to various techniques mentioned in the first section that prescribe purifactory practices. For instance, it is recommended to cultivate faith, energy, mindfulness, concentration, and wisdom;[8] to develop friendliness, compassion, gladness, and equanimity in the presence of those who present the opposite;[9] to generate thoughts that are sorrowless and illuminating,[10] and so forth. Each of these techniques requires a restructuring of the thought processed, a transformation from mundane thinking (*citta-vṛtti*) to responsible intention (*pratyaya*).

Three practices, the last of the eightfold scheme, are described as "inner Yoga." Concentration (*dhāraṇā*) is holding the *citta* in one spot;[11] meditation (*dhyāna*), the singularity of intention (*pratyaya*);[12] absorption (*samādhi*), the shining forth of the intended object devoid of inherent form (*svarūpa śūnya*).[13]

No discussion of Yoga would be complete without some mention of the various levels of *samādhi*, the most well known of various practices (*abhyāsa*) described in Patañjali's first chapter. Several states and stages are listed, most particularly in *sūtras* I:17, I:18, and I:41–51. Vijñānabhikṣu defines *samprajñāta* as "the suppression of all functions save the one related to the object of meditation . . . [It] leads to the perception of the Reality or Essence and thus puts an end to all the troubles of life." The second, *asamprajñāta*, is said to be the "suppression of all functions . . . [which] destroys the impressions (*saṃskāra*) of all antecedent (mental functions)."[14] In the later descriptions, one concentrates first with speculation (*savitarka*). In the later stage of *nirvitarka*, there is no longer any patina or interpretation applied to the object intended; it shines (*nirbhāsa*) as if it were "devoid of inherent form."[15] At an even higher level, in *savicāra* one reflects on the root causes of emotion, while in *nirvicāra samādhi*, the distinction between knowing and knower blurs: the analogy of radiance or clarity extends to oneself (*adhyātma*). Eventually, all distinctions of "grasper, grasping, and grasped" dissolve.[16] In this state, a total transformation has taken place.

When there is no longer even the slightest tendency to separate a self from things or vice versa, there arises a vision of discernment (*viveka khyāti*), identified as *dharma megha samādhi*. Vijñānabhikṣu isolates *sūtra* I:41 as descriptive of the pinnacle of Yogic attainment: "To the one of suppressed faculties belong a concentration and consubstantiation in (matters relating to) the perceiver, the means of perception, and the object perceived, as in a transparent gem."[17] Neither subject nor object, perceiver or world, emerges as substantial or separate; the world is, so to speak, carried in the body of the "experiencer," who is now designated, according to Vijñānabhikṣu, as a Jivan Mukta.[18]

Yoga requires the restraint of the fluctuations of mind (*citta-vṛtti-nirodha*). However, this should not be misconstrued as negation of life: both Yoga and Sāṃkhya affirm the existence of the "objective world" (*prakṛti*), using various proofs.[19] *Prakṛti* is real; the external world is not denied. However, the purpose of Yoga is not to describe the world "out there" but is, rather, to show a means by which the practitioner may have direct access to the intended world without the interference of impure residues: the point is how to sever projects, present from a time without a beginning, that obscure the direct perception of this reality. The technique is almost shamanistic: the yogin excises a part of his corpus or being—*citta-vṛtti*—so that the totality of life may emerge, as represented by the unseen witness (*puruṣa*). The predominance of mental fluctuations (*citta-vṛtti*) obscures this experience. The cultivation of restraint (*nirodha*) serves to replace the compulsive tendency to reify the world with a concentration that reveals, if only for a moment, that everpresent, everinactive witness (*puruṣa*).

YOGA

The *Sāṃkhya Kārikā* and the *Yoga Sūtra* have often been regarded as calling for the severance of *puruṣa* from *prakṛti*; concepts such as 'liberation' and 'self-realization' have been interpreted in an explicitly world-rejecting manner, as have been concepts of Buddhist '*nirvāṇa*.' Max Muller prefers to retitle Yoga as "viyoga" (separation), citing Bhojarāja's commentary.[20] Almost one hundred years later, Feuerstein echoes the same refrain, stating, "The essence of Patañjali's Yoga can be said to consist in the separation (*viyoga*) of these two realities (*puruṣa* and *prakṛti*)."[21] Feuerstein finds this emphasis on separation "philosophically unattractive."[22] It is the case that Yoga does require a distancing of oneself from worldly attachments, including, for some, retreat into a more spiritual environment. Yoga does entail renunciation. Taken to its logical limit, the absolute separation of *prakṛti* and *puruṣa* can even be interpreted as death. Yet, the *Sāṃkhya Kārikā* acknowledges that the potter's wheel continues to turn.[23] The *Yoga Sūtra* states that "even the wise possess the will-to-live."[24] Although the practice of Yoga is certainly a fine preparation for death, Yoga is a way of life, as indicated by the references to *nirbīja samādhi* and *citi-śakti* (I:51, IV:34). By applying the disciplines of Yoga, one cultivates a life oriented toward purity, setting a context for experiences of liberation.

In states of *citta-vṛtti*, the "I" (*ahaṃkāra*) thinks it is the seer. When it is revealed that "I am not the seer" (cf. *SK* 64: I do not exist, nothing is mine, I am not), a perception of the distinction of seer from seen arises (*viveka khyāti*). This serves to break down the theoretical self (*ahaṃkāra*) that stood apart from the object. In *dharma megha samādhi*, when the "I" no longer appropriates experience, there arises the "consubstantiation of seer, seeing, and seen," a state of unitive attention. In the thirteenth chapter of the *Bhagavad Gītā*, the one who sees the field (*prakṛti*; *citta-vṛtti*; *ahaṃkāra*) as distinct from the knower of the field (*puruṣa*) is called wise. Krishna advises Arjuna, "He who sees his self not to be the doer, he sees indeed."[25] *Puruṣa* and *prakṛti* are seen as fulfilling separate and discrete functions, but both are necessary and present, even in the act of "truly seeing." When the seer is perceived as distinct from the "I" that claims, the yogin then loses interest in the generation of compulsive *citta-vṛttis*; in a sense, there is no longer anyone home to collect the interest.[26] Nothing is claimed by the "I." With this movement, the sediment of prior conditioning (*saṃskāra*) is cleared away; objects shine forth devoid of inherent form (*svarūpa śūnya*); the consciousness-of or "I-vs.-that" consciousness has retreated; and the consciousness-I-count-on is revealed, if only for a moment. This process is an ongoing one, involving continued sacrifice of perspectives. In moments where sacrifice finds its culmination (and any yogic practice would be considered sacrifice), there is a state of *nirodha*: the *manas/ahaṃkāra-citta-vṛtti* complex is stilled, and absorptive vision (*samādhi*) emerges. In this state, attention cannot be separated from the intended; awareness is both subject-free (*anahaṃvādi*) and object-free (*nirvastuka*). Yoga may thus be defined not as a union of an appropriating self with objects of appropriation nor as a Cartesian separation of the thinker from the thought, but rather as a moment in which there is the nonseparation of knower, knowing, and known.

PURUṢA

Yoga is concerned with reality as presented by and arising from the intention and attention of the particularized consciousness; it is not fundamentally concerned with the origination or control of the fixed external reality established by *citta-vṛtti*. The process of Yoga, rather than taking the experiencer for granted, takes the experienced for granted (there is nothing new anyway, just new combinations of the same old elements) and seeks to unveil the experiencer, the unseen seer referred to in the Upaniṣads. The only constant factor binding experiences is the sense of the unseen seer; both subjectivity and objectivity, though real, are continually in the flux of the three *guṇas*. The purpose of Yoga is to reveal reality as it relates to the seer and, through certain practices, break through to the point of consciousness where there is no distinction between seer and seen. Many names are given to this process: the various *samādhis*, *kaivalyam*, *dharma megha*, *viveka khyāti*, *nirodha*. All are equated with this unseen seer, *puruṣa* or *ātman*, a presence that can be expressed only metaphorically.

The reading of Yoga as entry into states of existential unity may be seen as parallel to the philosophy of Ortega y Gasset, which calls for the saving of both self (cf. *puruṣa*) and circumstance (cf. *prakṛti*).[27] Yoga can also be read as a means of revelation: through the suppression of *citta-vṛtti*, the truth of things at hand is revealed. This concept of revelation would not be foreign to the Quakers or to the theologian George Tyrrell or even perhaps to Thomas J. J. Altizer, who writes of a state wherein "we discover and embody a pure immediacy in response to a totally anonymous presence."[28]

In a work entitled *I and That*, Alex Comfort articulates this search for the unseen seer in a biological language, referring to this quest for the "inner person" as a search for "homuncular identity." The following passage explains this neurological approach:

> In crude terms, "homuncular identity" means the conviction or experience that there is "someone inside," distinct from the outer world, the body and the brain, in whom the processes of experiencing, willing and so on are focused, and this "someone" objectivized both these processes and itself. If we look closer, however, this experience does not refer to any soul, true self, inner reality, divine spark, or, indeed, anything so complex as these: such experiences and hypotheses refer to other matters. The inner "someone" who is objectivized in human thinking is a reference point or *point of observation* on which inner and outer experience are felt to converge, and from which initiatives are felt to issue is not a ghost, but a kind of bottleneck in the circuitry. Rather than representing some transcendental core or hot-spot of being, this self is a *point of view*, an intrapolated locus round which experience is structured, and like other reference points is dimensionless and virtual.[29]

This explanation of awareness corresponds in some respects to the descriptions of consciousness-function in Yoga and Sāṃkhya. *Puruṣa* is said to be "witness, seer, inactive,"[30] comparable to a "point of observation" or the "locus round which experience is structured." Both systems are purely functional; both demythologize experience, dispensing with the need for some inner spirit or outer god. With new interpretations of how the brain works, Yoga and Sāṃkhya may gain new recognition as a sophisticated neurophysiology with soteriological implications.

One of the great feats of Indian philosophy is its penchant for pointing at the unspeakable without naming it. Mādhyamika Buddhism is perhaps the most vivid example. Similarly, Sāṃkhya and Yoga recognize that any appellation of consciousness is betrayal; yet they do not negate its presence. *Puruṣa*, in isolation, that is, without data to receive, is devoid of attributes, reflects nothing upon the *buddhi*, is free from any limiting constraints and thus unknowing, unknowable, and unknown. Analogously, *vikalpa* or imagination is our only recourse to discussion of the *puruṣa* as pointed out by Vyāsa and reiterated by Vijñānabhikṣu. *Puruṣa* is the silence prior to all sound. *Īśvara*, referred to as the "*prāṇava* (*oṃ*)," is the closest of all approximations to *puruṣa* and hence an appropriate object of meditation. *Oṃ* is a "saying" that is simultaneously no-saying and all-saying, the closest sound to silence.

CONCLUSION

Three languages are present in the *Yoga Sūtra*. One speaks of conventional reality, of things and thoughts, of all the variations of life and the wide range of possible experiences. Another language points to a totality of consciousness that is prior to the particularities of perception. The third language, the predominant language of the *Yoga Sūtra*, speaks of a method by which that totality may be attained: it is the language of responsible engagement, of practice, of meditation, of creative imagination. In a radical sense, it is this third language that makes human life possible, the language through which culture may be saved.

The first language, that of *citta-vṛtti*, describes *saṃsāra*, *samvṛtti*, the "play of the *guṇas*," regarded to be painful. The second language, that of the *puruṣa/ātman*, is a language of metaphor and paradox, the essence of salt mixed in water, that which is eternally uninvolved, the ever-present witness. The third language, the language of Yoga, unites the two, providing the path by which neither is forgotten or taken for granted. On the one hand, it requires the cultivation of constructive thoughts (*abhyāsa*); on the other hand, it requires a distance from any thoughts cultivated (*vairāgya*). It is both ambivalent and imperative, pain-discerning and pleasure-discerning. The world thus revealed is as large as the viewer, and for the one with skill, that view or world or body experience is defined (metaphorically) as an ever-expanding cloud or *dharma-megha*.

The language of Yoga incorporates death—the separation of seer from seen—into life. And this language includes a "mastery," the development of *siddhis* through which the world, when seen as proceeding from *citta*, may be manipulated. This third language engages the first two in such a way as to reveal the precognitive, mobile consciousness for the sake of enriching, verifying, and vivifying the consciousness-of: the two languages are engaged in tandem. The language of Yoga allows for a responsible union of both conventional and absolute modes without the presence of defiled interpretation.

Yoga systematically lays out the means to what Freud called "oceanic experience"—the merging of "I" and "that." *Dharma megha*, the culmination of this process, may thus be interpreted as a contextual sphere wherein the process of evolution—the engagement of the world—takes place not through *saṃyoga*, the confusion of *puruṣa* for an aspect of *prakṛti* which promulgates finite existence, but through Yoga, a movement wherein the world is both sacrificed and embodied: objects are no longer separated from the perception of them, and perception is not restricted to the perspective of a limited point of view.

3 *Precepts and Vows in Yoga and Jainism*

The beginning two stages of Patañjali's eightfold Yoga require the adaptation of one's daily life to conform to higher ethical standards. The first group, the precepts or disciplines (*yama*), includes five vows: non-violence (*ahiṃsā*), truthfulness (*satya*), not stealing (*asteya*), impulse control (*brahmacarya*), and nonpossession (*aparigraha*). The second group, the observances (*niyama*), include the cultivation of purity (*śauca*), contentment (*santoṣa*), austerity (*tapas*), study (*svadhyāya*), and dedication to one's chosen ideal deity (*īśvara praṇidhāna*). The precepts seek to engender patterns of restraint from deleterious behavior. The observances take a more positive approach, seeking to plant the seeds of wholeness and enduring well-being.

What prompts an individual to adopt these precepts and observances, which in many instances require a radical altering of one's lifestyle? Generally, one would need to undergo a process of conversion, a change of heart arising from a landmark event in one's process of self-discovery. This chapter begins with a psychological exploration of how a transformative religious experience as articulated by William James might prompt one to adopt the code of precepts and observances outlined by Patañjali. The practice of the precepts will then be explored in light of Yoga, Jainism, and my own *sādhana* training.

WILLIAM JAMES AND WALT WHITMAN

William James writes extensively about the process of conversion and its relationship to making an ongoing ethical commitment. He describes it in the context of several different religious traditions and defines conversion as follows: "To be converted, to be regenerated, to receive grace, to experience religion, to gain an assurance, are so many phrases which denote the process, gradual or sudden by which a self hitherto divided, and consciously wrong, inferior and unhappy, becomes unified and consciously right superior and happy, in consequence of its firmer hold upon religious realities."[1] James states that this experience, regardless of the particular religious tradition, changes a person. For James, religious ideas move the core of one's being: "To say that a man is 'converted' means, in these terms, that religious ideas, previously peripheral in his consciousness, now take a central place, and that religious aims form the habitual centre of his energy."[2] In conjunction with this transformation, James states that a purity arises that alters one's actions within the world: "The shifting of the emotional centre brings with it, first, increase of purity . . . [T]he cleansing of existence from brutal and sensual elements becomes imperative."[3] In other words, an individual who has undergone the process of conversion feels a compulsion and responsibility to move away from one's base impulses and develop a more elevated, more ethical lifestyle.

James cites the life and work of Walt Whitman as an example of a modern American saint, an individual he considers to have been touched and transformed by conversion. He quotes William Bucke's classic book, *Cosmic Consciousness*, in regard to Whitman:

> His favorite occupation seemed to be strolling or sauntering outdoors by himself, looking at the grass, the trees, the flowers, the vistas of light, the varying aspects of the sky, and listening to the birds, the crickets, the tree frogs, and all the hundreds of natural sounds. It was evident that these things gave him a pleasure far beyond what they give to ordinary people . . . All natural objects seemed to have a charm for him. All sights and sounds seemed to please him . . . He never spoke deprecatingly of any nationality or class of men, or time in the world's history, or against any trades or occupations . . . not even against any animals, insects, or inanimate things, not any of the laws of nature, nor any of the results of those laws, such as illness, deformity, and death. He never complained or grumbled either at the weather, pain, illness, or anything else.[4]

Bucke writes about a link between immersion into cosmic consciousness and the moral life:

> The prime characteristic of cosmic consciousness is a consciousness of the cosmos, that is, of the life and order of the universe. Along with consciousness of the cosmos there occurs an intellectual enlightenment which alone would place the individual on a new plane of existence—would make him almost a member of a new species. To this is added a state of moral exultation, an indescribable feeling of elevation, elation,

> and joyousness, and a quickening of the moral sense, which is fully as striking, and more important than is the enhanced intellectual power.[5]

After citing Bucke's descriptions of this relationship between conversion and ethics, William James then makes a direct connection between Bucke's articulation of cosmic consciousness and the Yoga tradition. He writes, "In India, training in mystical insight has been known from time immemorial under the name of yoga."[6] Quoting Swami Vivekananda, he writes that in the highest states of Yoga, "There is no feeling of I, and yet the mind works, desireless, free from restlessness, objectless, bodiless. Then the Truth shines in its full effulgence, and we know ourselves—for Samādhi lies potential in us all—for what we truly are, free, immortal, omnipotent, loosed from the finite."[7] James notes that a profound religious experience can lead to the control of sexual impulses and sobriety, affirming similar statements in the *Yoga Sūtra*. This brings us to a discussion of the first of the two Indian philosophical and religious traditions that we will explore in the course of this chapter: Yoga.

YOGA PHILOSOPHY AND ETHICS

In the Yoga tradition, *samādhi* comprises the core conversion moment. In Patañjali's *Yoga Sūtra* (ca. 200 CE), this is defined as a state where "one's thoughts diminish and one becomes like a clear jewel, assuming the color of any near object, with unity among grasper, grasping, and grasped."[8] In other words, one becomes transparent to one's surroundings, blending in with and taking on the qualities of others. Rather than applying one's own standard to reality, one can fully experience things as they present themselves. Such a person becomes liberated from the influences of past karma and can dwell moment by moment, adapting to circumstance and situation. From this experience, one feels a connectedness between oneself and other beings, which can bring a heightened sense of responsibility and accountability. As a result, a desire to cultivate and abide by a higher moral standard, as suggested by Bucke, may ensue.

Ethics plays a central, foundational role in the eightfold path outlined by Patañjali. By the second century of the common era, Patañjali had compiled an array of practices under the philosophical umbrella of the Sāṃkhya metaphysical school and promulgated a system of Yoga that borrows from Vedic, Jaina, and Buddhist schools of thought and practice. Unlike Sāṃkhya, and like Jainism, Buddhism, and the Dharmaśāstra materials of the Brahmanical Hindu tradition, Patañjali emphasizes the importance of ethical practices in the practice of Yoga, both in preparation for states of *samādhi* and, in a sense, in affective response to the experience of *samādhi*. He suggests that one may cultivate "friendliness, compassion, happiness, and equanimity" as a means of achieving *samādhi*.[9] He later lists the five precepts that delineate the ethical practices of Yoga: nonviolence (*ahiṃsā*), truthfulness (*satya*), not stealing (*asteya*), impulse control in the form of sexual restraint (*brahmacarya*) and nonpossession (*aparigraha*).[10] Interestingly, this list predates Patañjali by at least five centuries and forms the core ethical system for the Jaina religious tradition, particularly as found in the *Ācārāṅga Sūtra* (ca. 400 to 300 BCE). In this chapter, I will intertwine a discussion of the ethics of both Yoga and Jainism as found in these two texts. Additionally, I will explore the psychological and theological impetus for the practice of these ethical precepts, as summarized in karma theory.

The theory of karma in Hindu thought can be found in the Upaniṣads and the Yoga tradition. The *Yoga Sūtra* specifies that karma comes in three colors (black, white, mixed,[11] perhaps corresponding to the three *guṇas* of *tamas*, *rajas*, and *sattva*) and that all karma presents itself as vitiated with a combination of five impurities or *kleśas*.[12] Patañjali lists these impurities as ignorance, egoism, attraction, repulsion, and clinging to life.[13] These five bind an individual within rebirth (*saṃsāra*) and a blind repetition of prior action based on conditioning seeds (*bija* or *saṃskāra*) deposited through routine, indiscriminate pursuit of desire. Patañjali defines ignorance as: *anitya-aśuci-duḥkha-anātmasu nitya-śuci-sukha-ātma-khyātir avidyā*

> Ignorance is seeing
> the transient as intransigent,
> a sullied thing as pure,
> a painful experience as pleasure,
> and the ego as one's true self.[14]

Knowledge here refers not to knowing the size and shape of things but entails wisdom resulting from a process of introspectively regarding the ultimate purpose of things. By seeing the evanescent quality of apparent reality, one develops the ability to stand aloof from the drama of catching and holding without pause or reflection.

This analysis extends to the ego itself. By noticing that the attributes through which an individual holds to a fixed sense of self generally are subject to constant change, rigidity and fixity can be loosened. In the process, one comes to understand the twin dynamic of attraction and repulsion, the realm of opposites, of likes and dislikes, that often drives an individual to seek out preferences and avoid discomforts without a depth of understanding. This interplay of ignorance and ego, allurement and repulsion, repeats itself again and again, accustoming a person to a repetitive rhythm that lulls one into a sense of thinking the world could not be different or more important than a constant repeat of what has been played before.

However, this ignorant worldview leads ultimately to discomfort. Our bodies age, our friends and relatives may predecease us, our expectations in life can lead to disappointment. As an antidote, Yoga karma theory suggests that we seek out an understanding of the origins of things and their ultimate purpose. Patañjali states: "*heyaṃ duḥkham anāgataṃ*" (The pain of the future is to be avoided [through contemplation]).[15] By examining the seed causes of repetitive behavior, one can anticipate and restructure one's comportment within the world and restructure one's behavior in a manner enhanced by dignity. In the first section of the *Yoga Sūtra*, Patañjali states that the practice of concentration can wear away the seeds of past action (*saṃskāra*).[16] In the second section of the *Yoga Sūtra*, Patañjali prescribes cultivating the opposite (*prati-pakṣa-bhāvanam*), literally, using the other wing.[17] The prime tool to achieve this goal can be found in the ethical practices of the five great vows.

Patañjali's *Yoga Sūtra* describes these vows in a series of six aphorisms. He begins with an assessment of the need to control one's thoughts and actions, pointing out that if one does not abide by these precepts, suffering and endless ignorance will result: "Discursive thoughts like violence, etc., whether done, caused or approved, consisting in lust, anger, or delusion, and whether mild, medium, or intense, have as their endless fruits dissatisfaction and ignorance. Thus, cultivation of opposites is prescribed" (II:34). He then states each of the five required practices, and indicates a benefit to each one:

> When in the presence of one established in nonviolence, there is the abandonment of hostility. (II:35)
> When established in truthfulness, there is correspondence between action and fruit. (II:36)
> When established in nonstealing, whatever is present is all jewels. (II:37)
> When established in sexual restraint, vigor is obtained. (II:38)
> When steadfast in nonpossession, there is knowledge of "the how" of existence. (II:39)

Swami Jyotir Mayananda, a twentieth-century Yoga teacher who resided in Puerto Rico and Florida for many years, wrote,

> An aspirant must be able to understand that every negative thought process must be controlled the moment it emerges from the unconsciousness in the form of a tiny ripple. Just as a spark of fire can be

> easily crushed between one's fingers, but, when it is allowed to grow, even the most advanced fire-extinguishing methods become ineffective. Forests are consumed in blazing fire. In the same way, an evil thought-wave must be nipped in the very bud. It is easy to control it with the art of *Pratipaksha Bhavana*. But, when it is allowed to stay and grow in the mind, it assumes various perverse forms so that it is very, very difficult to recognize it, and it is further difficult to eradicate it. Thus, an aspirant must control and sublimate every thought wave that promotes violence, falsehood, impurity, greed, discontent, and lack of devotion to God.[18]

Through the control of thoughts by the practice of these five vows, a control of one's thinking process emerges that enhances an ethical way of life. Jyotir Mayananda has given multiple reflections on how to practice each of these five disciplines and quoted various others, including Mahatma Gandhi and Ramana Maharshi, regarding this topic. A few of his reflections are as follows:

> When you keep your mind free from developing thoughts of hatred and anger even under provocative conditions, you are practicing mental non-violence.[19]

> There is no strength greater than Truth. There is no wealth greater than Truth. By the pursuit of Truth, one acquires boundless willpower.[20]

> Stealing in the broad sense has many subtler implications. In its grossest expressions this vice manifests in thieves, robbers, swindlers and similar criminals. But it continues to exist in different forms in all people, until the Yogic insight eliminates it.[21]

> On the human level, lack of control in seeking sex-pleasures, and lack of the recognition of social and moral restraint in sex-relationships, is an expression of degeneration and deterioration of personality.[22]

> [W]hen a Yogi develops the quality of non-covetousness, he becomes a true master of his possessions. He is no longer possessed by the objects that he possesses . . . The virtue of non-covetousness holds manifold blessings for the individual as well as the world outside. To the individual it opens the ever-increasing expansions of the Self; and to the world it promotes harmony, economic balance, love and understanding.[23]

Swami Jyotir Mayananda has reflected on the broader ramifications of ethical practice and suggests an array of practical applications for nonviolence, truthfulness, not stealing, sexual restraint, and nonpossession.

From 1973 until 1985, my wife and I lived within a small spiritual community that practiced classical Yoga under the guidance of Gurāṇi Añjali, a woman from Calcutta.[24] At Yoga Anand Ashram in Amityville, New York, students in the applied method (*sādhana*) classes are given a discipline and/or observance to practice for the week. The first time I heard about this approach to spiritual practice was in conversation with Carole Zeiler in the Student Union at the State University of New York at Buffalo in 1972. A member of the Ashram, she said that she had received her *sādhana* in the mail, and she was to practice nonviolence or *ahiṃsā*, which meant, among other things, that she needed to find cookies made without eggs! I became intrigued with the detail of this practice, which was my first introduction to dietary orthopraxy. Several months later, after moving to Long Island, I entered a *sādhana* class, and each week brought a new challenge. How could I make my life more austere? We routinely observed a weekly fast and weekly day of silence as a practice of austerity (*tapas*). But what more could be done? We worked at not walking off with little things such as pencils or hording intangible things such as time while practicing not stealing (*asteya*), another of the five ethical disciplines in the first stage of Patañjali 's eightfold path.

Truthfulness (*satya*) was always a great challenge. How could I resist the temptation to exaggerate? Was my being in the world fully authentic? Though my wife and I shared these practices with one another, the bulk of our days were spent on a university campus where such topics were not appropriate to bring up in conversation. So we cultivated a life of ethical introspection rooted in Patañjali's Yoga while engaged in our studies and campus jobs, enjoying the company of our fellow Yoga students while in class at night and on the weekends. In little and big ways, we forged a different path than that dictated by the culture that was promoting disco dancing and the hustle. Perhaps the biggest culture gap came with the practice of nonpossession (*aparigraha*). For our teacher, this meant avoidance of debt. In India, lending policies have historically been draconian. Until recently, even houses were paid for with cash. We came to value and stretch our meager resources and live a truly simple lifestyle that has carried over to a certain extent in our adult years.

In order to give a sense of the day-to-day nature of the practice of ethics in the Yoga tradition, I have included some entries from my journals, written in the 1970s and 1980s.

> *Asteya* [is] physically not stealing, not taking, respecting others' possessions. [It is] mentally not stealing, not harboring belittling thoughts which diminish another's self respect; not stealing space

from another person's mood. Spiritually, there is nothing outside of one's self to steal (1976).

Ahiṃsā, protecting bugs, seeing people.

Satya, being firm with myself in the world; being honest with others and yet trying not to hurt them.

Asteya, not taking time from others; not imposing myself.

Brahmacarya: putting myself in situations of confrontation with thoughts. The purpose of *brahmacarya* on the physical level and the mental level is to conserve energy; on the spiritual level it is to see all beings of both sexes as the same as oneself, to see the light within and not the gross alone.

Aparigraha: appreciating and not grasping (1976).

Aparigraha means not holding on, not possessing, not hording, not appropriating, not collecting or amassing. It is a negative term with an implicit positive meaning. By negating the obvious, the subtle becomes explicit. By eliminating attachment, a freedom arises, a knowledge that life is beyond or more than the accumulation of material goods. By stripping away the "fluff" of life, the cloud of possessions that generally surrounds the common person, the essence of life is revealed. By eliminating or reducing the physical commodities needed to maintain the body, the body itself takes on a new importance and commands a new respect. In the process of giving up, an understanding arises as to why the previous possession is not needed and an appreciation and understanding arises for what remains.

I remember back in Buffalo in 1972 when Carole would receive *sādhana* in the mail and we would practice it. She would briefly explain it and then give some examples of how other people in the Ashram had practiced it. The first time I practiced *aparigraha* I decided that I would not buy anything. I had enough food for the week, my dormitory room was paid in full for the semester, and, as a student, I had few needs or responsibilities. It was a wonderful experience. I felt a purity, a control, an appreciation for my simple Spartan life. But when I was home with my parents and had to go to the store for them and buy some food, it was an agonizing time, as I did not wish to break the vow I had made to myself. I bought the food that my father had asked me to pick up but it became such a big thing to me. The whole process of purchase on that particular day was as big in my consciousness (and conscience) as the Empire State Building. Later, when I told Carole about what had happened, she got a laugh out of it.

Throughout that first year of Yoga before I came to the Ashram, I kept my possessions to the absolute minimum. I don't recall buying any clothes. I only bought books if absolutely necessary. At that time I did not yet have a car, which was truly a liberating experience. But then, when I decided to move to Long Island, I had to get a car. I put all my possessions (some books and notebooks and letters) in an old cardboard banana box and all my clothes in a parachute bag and, at age 18, drove off with everything I owned to the Ashram in Amityville. Then, for several weeks, *aparigraha* continued. I moved from house to house of various Ashram members and pillars before finding a room to rent for $18 per week. And so my simple, single lifestyle continued for the next year with an old used car, a rented room (tiny in size), some books, and a few clothes.

Then I became a householder. Fortunately, because we had nothing, friends and relatives gave us only functional items as wedding presents. As time moved on and as we went from two rooms to three and a half rooms to five rooms, extra objects began to pile up: old magazines, worn out clothes, and so forth. And we received gifts which went beyond the "utensils of an ascetic" as suggested in scripture. These provided the occasion for the continued practice of *aparigraha*, cleaning up and throwing out things periodically.

One phase of *aparigraha* practice stands out in my mind. My duties as *pūjāri* brought me to the Ashram at dawn each day to change the flowers and recite the Gayatri Mantra in the four directions. The timing of the sunrise was such that my hair would not be dry by the time I had to go out to go to the Ashram. Because my hair needed to be washed every day, this presented a problem. So, I began to use one of the gifts we had been given, a hand held hairdryer. Then, one morning during a week we were practicing *aparigraha*, it occurred to me that this behavior was silly. It wasted electricity, my mornings began with an orange plastic gun shooting hot air at my head, and it was a waste of time as well. Admittedly, I might have caught cold, going out in freezing temperatures with wet hair. But enough was enough . . . I got my hair cut short, and dried it as well as I could with a towel: I literally had fewer possessions, setting the hair dryer (and much of my hair) aside. My newly clipped haircut felt lighter both physically and emotionally, and we simultaneously reduced our consumption of electricity. *Aparigraha* came very close to me that week, touching, as it were, my very body.

In keeping possessions to a bare minimum, there is a lightness and a power. There is a power in conservatism: being aware of lights left on, keeping the thermostat low, and so forth. This results not in drudgery or fear but produces a sense of freedom in the recognition that bodily maintenance can be achieved with relative comfort on little money.

There is an openness and emptiness in the practice of *aparigraha*. In the realm of experience there are three facets to perception: the grasped (*grāhya*), the grasping (*grahaṇa*) and the grasper (*grahītṛ*). The term *aparigraha* implies the negation of all these: the objects that can be grasped, whether in the form of thoughts, tendencies, cars, books, and the rest; the act of grasping, of compulsively intending outward to said objects; and the grasper, the notion that there is a self who can appropriate objects. This negation brings with it a freedom, a detachment from ascribing inherent, lasting reality to the things that comprise experience.

On the one hand there is the absolute, untainted, pure consciousness, free of focus on sense of self, free of process, objectless, unmanifest, undivided, and the rest. On the other hand there is the world of possessions, of relationship, of activity, of change, of cause and effect. The challenge of spiritual life is to reconcile the two through the conscious transformation (*nirmāṇa*) of the relative into a reflection of the absolute. In this paradigm, objects, senses, and self take on a new light; they potentially serve as reminders of the absolute, catalysts for meditative experience. Every positive implies its opposite; no battery works with only one charge. Thus, each experience provides the occasion for the realization of its opposite. The very act of taking at the same time is not taking. The very possession of wealth serves as a meditation on poverty; likewise, poverty serves as a reminder of wealth. Once the truth is recognized that every occurrence reflects dialectically its opposite and hence has no meaning in itself, a type of compassion arises, generated from the vision that all these objects are like children, without a parent, a child who needs guidance and support. The floor becomes an object to be cherished, upheld, appreciated, and washed because it is in the radical sense of the word, a lost soul. It has no meaning other than what I decide to give to it. Things have no meaning unless they are taken up, held, made real, and appreciated. In *aparigraha* the fixity of the world dissolves, but this dissolution in return provides for the maintenance of life from a fresh perspective.

The play between taking and not-taking becomes a rhythm, a breath, a wave, an inhale and exhale, one implying and giving way to the other. By not taking, I am taking; by taking, I am not taking. As I put down a book I am taking up an empty hand. As I reach for a pen, I give up the hand once more. As I take up one step, I leave the other step behind.

It is very difficult to discuss the taker, because by reifying the taker with the word, the taker is subject to all the problems inherent in subject and object. However, the anonymous taker, the taker that is not nominalized, serves as a vehicle for all experience. All things move through the taker, yet in an absolute sense the taker moves no thing. It is only in the taker that the discussion of relative and absolute can take place; the taker, as intermediary, is like a fulcrum on which the see-saw of experience rests. When the taker sees clearly, then the absolute is seen in the relative and vice versa, but the two are not confused. The relative is seen as absolute only because it is subject to constant change; the absolute is seen as relative because for the purified taker this experience as presented in life becomes an analogy for the absolute, points to ultimate meaning or consciousness. Thus, it is the taker who decides not to take, which ultimately leads to the taking up of all things. Without the taker, there can be no realization and no life.

Aparigraha, as a discipline to be performed, serves as the means to purify the taker and provide a rubric in which the difference between taking and not-taking is seen, leading to a compassion for all objects as children.

There is an austere aspect to *aparigraha*; it is only by giving up, doing without, suffering even a little, that appreciation can be developed for what is held. Once objects are appreciated, then, like children they will run to the parent, offering their services and support, presented innocently and freely. *Yoga Sutra* II:39 states that the nature of all objects becomes known through nonpossession. With this knowledge arises a gentle type of power, a power that comes from, paradoxically, indifference *and* appreciation simultaneously. April 6, 1980.

In doing *satya* there is a recognition that a thing arises due to the attention given it, whether an object or mood. The being or truth of an experience takes place due to the experiencer; there is no object separate from the experience and experiencer of it. Thus, at the "core" of any *satya* experience is the recognition of subject and object, the two being mutually dependent and hence, in reality or *satya*, inseparable. There is a unity in *satya*, a connection wherein the substantial borders of experience are blurred.

In the quietness, in the moments when I just am with breath, there is a great peace, a tranquil life (soon to be charged with action) but with a recognition of the great power of *sat* or existence. This happens on the frontier regions of *sat*, in the dialectical space between no action and action, in between not doing and doing.

A less theoretical example of the power of *satya* occurred when I almost got hit by a car. I had the fortunate experience of later confronting the driver. I pointed out to her that she was irresponsible in her driving. For her, this was a jarring experience. As I spoke, I felt the presence and power of speech; my words shaped her reality, readjusted her truth. It shook her; she resisted and then apologized. The lesson I learned was that truth is created by responsibility. I could have gone on my way and ignored the accident and she would have gone on her merry way, unaffected. At least through the confrontation she was presented the possibility of improving her driving habits and general awareness of pedestrians.

For Nietzsche, the only truth came in the realization of the falsity of all things. To ascribe truth or verity to any object implies that it is lasting or eternal. Life shows us otherwise. Even our bodies, which are closest to us, are a deception, governed by our thoughts and fears and aging. My body is not the same as it was; in it there is no lasting truth. Yet it cannot be dismissed or denied. Because phenomena such as bodies are dependent, they must be nurtured, upheld, supported. The world takes on a sense of urgency, a newness, a sacredness, when seen through the prism of *satya* as temporary or ephemera. Like a child, the world does not know how to live by itself. It requires constant attention and careful, patient understanding. Truth necessitates care. Without care there can be no world, no *satya*, no life. Intentionality shapes the world; object proceeds from project.

Satya is identified with language, but a language that includes not only the written and/or spoken word but the unspoken as well. *Satya* is structure; it holds things together. From that structure, from language, all things proceed.

One small task that has absorbed me is the "training" of some morning glory creepers on our fence. Usually every other day I spend several minutes undoing the vines from the tomatoes and whatever else they've swirled into and re-guide them along the picket fence. This is a simple sort of task, but a relationship, a *sat*, has grown between the plants and myself; in becoming their "friend" or even parent, there is an affirmation of their existence, a caring, a quiet joy. It is a silent act of truth, producing a mood that sustains and nurtures both myself and the plant. August, 1980.

Reading this scant sampling from hundreds of pages of journal reflections, I am reminded of how the ethical mind becomes cultivated in the Yoga. Each week we would be assigned an ethical precept upon which to reflect. We were encouraged to post the word on the refrigerator, to repeat the word again and again, and to reflect and write about the experience. Sometimes we would be assigned a single practice for weeks on end. Other times we would be asked to write down the names of the five disciplines and pick a new one from a bowl each morning.

The practice of these disciplines engages the memory. I struggled at times to remember which discipline I was practicing. I had to stretch to apply the vow on some occasions. On other occasions, it stood by me like a cherished friend. By creating a groove through repeated returns to the word and its meaning, a new way of engaging in the world emerged. The "cultivation of opposites" gave me permission to confront my fears, to understand my pettiness, and in some instances transcend what I had always assumed to be myself.

In the Buddhist tradition, moral sensibilities arise via two avenues. The first, referred to as "*apatrapā*," is practiced when others tell one to perform specific correct behaviors. The second, known as *hrī*, arises from the heart. One has learned and interiorized the path of making the correct choice. Rather than being imposed externally, this higher form of moral life spontaneously arises from within oneself.

The cultivation of spiritual practice or *sādhana* begins with instruction from someone whom one respects and trusts. This person has dedicated herself or himself to giving advice to others based on personal experience. However, the actual experience of that person, that teacher, is far less important than the willingness of the *sādhaka* or spiritual practitioner to enter her or his own path. By taking the tools offered by a teacher, one takes the opportunity to reform, to remold, to refashion oneself. The daily or weekly practice of the five vows offers fertile ground for the planting of new seeds. The thoughts engendered by the remembrance of nonviolence, for instance, automatically begin a process of deconditioning and reconditioning. In the training received by my wife and myself, our circumstances themselves provided the context for our makeover. Our marriage, our work, and eventually our children to whom this book is dedicated all became the ground through which we were able to apply these principles and practices.

As I trained to become a theologian, I drew from this early training, particularly within the area of ethics. For instance, in a book titled *Nonviolence to Animals, Earth, and Self in Asian Traditions*, I attempt to apply the practice of the five great vows to environmental ethics:

> The first vow, *ahiṃsā*, requires respect for and protection of all life forms, stemming from the premise that even a blade of grass is not different from oneself in its essential vitality. Advocates of vegetarianism claim that abstention from eating meat not only spares the lives of animals, but also helps contribute to a healthy ecosystem. The third vow, not stealing, means that one abstains from taking what does not belong to oneself. This can be particularly instructive for people of the "developed world" who continue to consume the majority of the world's resources, spewing forth pollution as a primary byproduct. The fourth vow, that of nonpossession, is tacitly environmental. The less one owns, the less harm has been committed to one's ecosphere. On a practical level, the fifth vow, sexual restraint, can be seen as one way to hold down population growth. Psychologically, it can be used as an exercise in post-patriarchal interpersonal relations, in which regarding other bodies as potential objects for sexual gratification or the seeing of others as manipulable is transformed into seeing other people and other people's bodies as not different from oneself.[25]

I have also employed reflection on the five great vows to other contexts in my professional life, writings about the protection of animals, responses to war, human rights, and other topics. The application of these disciplines, rather than appealing strictly to the rational faculty, calls up an affective response, a response built on memories of past practice and experiences. Numerous memory points become activated in the process of making ethical decisions. By engaging the ideas and methods of the ancient system as taught by traditional teachers for hundreds of years, some new solutions to contemporary issues might be found.

JAINISM AND THE PRACTICE OF NONVIOLENCE

The Jaina tradition refers to the conversion moment described by William James as "*saṃyak dṛṣṭi*," described as seeing things as equal or same. Both this term and the Hindu term *samādhi* contain a variation of the word *sama* or sameness as well as a variant that relates to vision (*dhi*, *dṛṣṭi*). In both traditions, this experience can result in a profound change in a person. In the Yoga tradition, it is said that *samādhi* can lead one to overcome past habits, eventually leading to a state of purity or seedlessness. In the Jaina tradition, it can enable one to progress up the ladder of spirituality (*śreṇi*) toward the world of perfection (*siddha loka*). In both Hinduism and Jainism, we find extensive discussion of conversion, in the sense intended by William James. Having had a glimpse into the state variously known as cosmic consciousness, *samādhi*, or *saṃyak dṛṣṭi*, one then assiduously pursues an internally inspired ethical course that transforms action from mundane repetition of personal preferences or cultural conformity into a concerted effort to recapture the inspiration felt in the state of cosmic connectedness.

In the Jaina tradition, the starting point for authentic spirituality begins with this moment of conversion. Dr. Padmanabh S. Jaini has described the state of *saṃyak dṛṣṭi*, which is documented to last from a single instant up to forty-eight minutes, as a temporary experience of feeling liberated from all fettering karmas: "So great is the purity generated by this flash of insight that enormous numbers of bound karmas are driven out of the soul altogether, while future karmic influx is severely limited in both quantity and intensity."[26] This moment entails a leaving behind of preoccupation with the body, with psychological states, and with possessions. The gross forms of anger, pride, deceit, and greed are "rendered inoperative." One "no longer perceives things as 'attractive' or desirable' but one penetrates to the fact that every aspect of life is transitory and mortal."[27] At this point a resolve sets in to change one's lifestyle and to adopt the purposeful observance of the vows (*vrata*) of Jainism.

One anthropological account of this conversion experience has been documented by James Laidlaw. He records a moment in the life of a woman who subsequently decided to become a Jaina nun: "The decision came one morning when she walked into the kitchen. There was a cockroach in the middle of the floor, 'and I just looked at it and suddenly I thought, "Why should I stay in this world where there is just suffering and death and rebirth?"'"[28] This woman embarked on a changed life, renouncing her family, her name, any claims to wealth, all in order to begin a life of austerity designed to minimize harm to all living beings.

The earliest full account of the five precepts that govern and define the life of both practitioners of Yoga and of the Jaina faith can be found in the *Ācārāṅga Sūtra*, the earliest surviving Jaina text, which was composed three hundred years before the common era. Though the vows are identical to those listed above in the context of the *Yoga Sūtra*, this particular listing is more expansive with its language than Patañjali. The *Ācārāṅga Sūtra* articulates the five great vows as follows:

> I renounce all killing of living beings, whether subtle or gross, whether movable or immovable. Nor shall I myself kill living beings, nor cause others to do it, nor consent to it.[29]

> I renounce all vices of lying speech arising from anger or greed or fear or mirth. I shall neither myself speak lies, nor cause others to speak lies, nor consent to the speaking of lies by others.[30]

> I renounce all taking of anything not given, either in a village or a town or a wood, either of little or much, of small or great, of living or lifeless things. I shall neither take myself what is not given, nor cause others to take it, nor consent to their taking it.[31]

> I renounce all sexual pleasures, either with gods or men or animals. This vow also includes the following: not to "continually discuss topics relating to women," not to "regard and contemplate the lovely forms of women," not to "recall to his mind the pleasures and amusements he formerly had with women."[32] It also states that "a Nirgrantha does not eat and drink too much, or drink liquors or eat highly seasoned dishes" and that a "Nirgrantha does not occupy a bed or couch affected by women, animals, or eunuchs."[33]

> I renounce all attachments, whether little or much, small or great, living or lifeless; neither shall I myself form such attachments, nor cause others to do so, nor consent to their doing so.[34]

Each of these five vows helps to encourage the monk, nun, or layperson to work diligently for self-perfection.

By recognizing the interrelated nature of life, one develops a respect for other life forms. Mahavira himself, who 2,500 years ago standardized Jainism as it is practiced today, was considered a keen observer of nature: "Thoroughly knowing the earth-bodies and water-bodies and fire-bodies and wind-bodies, the lichens, seeds, and sprouts, he comprehended that they are, if narrowly inspected, imbued with life."[35] This perception of the beauty and complexity of nature formed the foundation for the great teaching of nonviolence (*ahiṃsā*) that so aptly characterizes the Jaina faith.

Mahatma Gandhi gave voice to an ethical path within the world that transformed the history of the twentieth century. Gandhi not only enacted the liberation of India from colonial British rule but also inspired the civil rights movement in the United States during the 1960s. Gandhi had a conversion experience while being ejected from a train in South Africa and from this jolt changed the political climate within the world for the latter half of the twentieth century.

Mahatma Gandhi built his campaign to free India of colonial rule in part with inspiration from his Jaina friends, most notably Rajchandra Bhai. Equipped with a resolve to be respectful to all beings, Gandhi explored all five vows in his work, most notably nonviolence (*ahiṃsā*), holding to truth (*satyagraha*), sexual restraint (*brahmacarya*), and owning as little as possible (*aparigraha*). His selfless toil resulted in a free India, and his core ideology shaped India's self-identity and economic reforms until the liberalization of trade laws in the early 1990s under Rajiv Gandhi.

A core precept of Gandhian ethics is to examine oneself first. At a 2002 meeting of the American Academy of Religion in Toronto, Arun Gandhi,[36] one of Gandhi's grandchildren, told the story of the young mother who implores Gandhi to tell her son, under doctor's orders, to eat fewer sweets. Gandhi tells her to come back in a week, at which time he lectures the young man to good effect. When the mother asks why Gandhi needed to wait so long to deliver this important message, Gandhi replied, "Why Madame, one week ago, I myself ate sweets daily. Before I could hope to alter your son's habits, I needed a week to correct my own excesses." In other words, the moral life begins with one's own patterns and practices. The self-correction afforded by the disciplines and observances of the Yoga tradition provide the necessary structure for the cultivation of personal ethics and practices.

4 *Imitation of Animals in Yoga Tradition*

Taming the Sacred Wild through Āsana Practice

The role of animal-human relations has become a newly emerging field of study. In years past, particularly in the Western philosophical tradition as found in Aristotle and Descartes, animals were deemed utterly other than and subservient to the human order.[1] Studies in the contemporary field of ethology have shown that animals possess a highly developed emotional life and a capacity for thinking.[2] In Indian philosophy, animals hold a different ontological status due to the doctrine of reincarnation. Each animal can be viewed as having once been a human being or as a potential future human being. This perceived continuity between the animal and human realms has been well documented in Buddhist and Jaina literature,[3] leading to a twofold ethical regard for animals. First, from various stories, primarily the Jātaka narratives about past lives of the Buddha, animals hold the power to make ethical choices. Second, humans have an ethical responsibility to minimize harm to animals, as violations of this precept would lead to eventual harm to oneself. The strong karmic stance espoused in the tradition of India creates a worldview conducive to animal protection, as seen in the many animal shelters of India[4] and the advocacy of vegetarianism, particularly in the Jaina and Vaiṣṇava traditions.[5]

The Yoga precept of nonviolence (*ahiṃsā*), the first and foundational vow practiced by Jainas and yogis, stems from a larger context of a deep respect for animals within the ancient Śrāmanical tradition. Animals are to be respected and treated carefully. Animals are also regarded as holding special power which can be harnessed through imitation. Early cultures throughout the world, from the Palaeolithic art of France to the more highly developed early civilizations of Egypt and Mesopotamia, China and the Aztecs all venerate animals in some way; most also include therioanthropic images. The concept of the 'totem animal' is very significant among the aboriginal peoples of

Australia, who imitate animals in movement and in sound. Shamans, specialists in healing who cultivate special power through their relationships with animals, are found in nearly all traditions. This chapter will explore how people, like shamans, take on the power of animals in the Indian subcontinent, particularly through the ritual and physical practices of Yoga.

India has had a long relationship with animals. The earliest archaeology in the Indian subcontinent has unearthed artifacts from 3000 BCE that indicate various ways in which the early people of India interacted with animals. These artifacts from the cities of Mohenjodaro and Harappa in the Indus Valley (modern Pakistan) include representations of animals in statues, in small seals, and in masks. As noted by the archaeologist Jonathan Mark Kenoyer,[6] these objects had both instructional and cultic purpose. The masks were used to conceal one's identity and replace it with an identity at least partly animal. Some statues portray human figures imitating feline animals in the manner of the Lion Pose or Siṃhāsana, as it is called in later Yoga texts.[7] Of particular interest is the seal that depicts a meditating figure surrounded by animals. This motif recurs throughout later Indian art and literature. Eventually this figure takes the name of Paśupati, meaning Lord of the Beasts, an epithet for the god Śiva.[8] These images of animals and of humans imitating or masquerading as animals indicate a shamanic relationship between the two realms. The Indus Valley people were particularly adept at portraying the power and particular abilities associated with specific animals.

In order to understand the significance of animals in later Yoga traditions, we need to discuss briefly the nature of shamanism, first in general and then in the context of India. Mircea Eliade describes the importance of shamanic rituals that display intimacy with specific animals as follows:

> Imitating the gait of an animal or putting on its skin was acquiring a superhuman mode of being . . . by becoming this mythic animal, man becomes something far greater and stronger than himself . . . He who, forgetting the limitations and false measurements of humanity, could rightly imitate the behavior of animals—their gait, breathing, cries, and so on—found a new dimension in life: spontaneity, freedom, "sympathy" with all the cosmic rhythms and hence bliss and immortality.[9]

These remarks by Eliade underscore the important relationship cultivated between humans and animals from prehistoric times.

Studies of the tribal cultures of India indicate that even today animals play an important role in the training and acquisition of power by healers. The Santal tribe of northern India requires its potential *ojhas* or healers to take the shape of calves, tigers, spiders, chameleons, and other animals and insects.[10]

The tribal cultures of India continue to flourish alongside Sanskritized Hindu culture, Arab-influenced Muslim culture, and modern English-speaking culture in India, influenced by Britain and America. Tribal or autochonous cultures in such regions as Orissa have influenced and shaped local expressions of religiosity. Mainstream Hinduism includes veneration of animal gods such as Hanuman, the loyal monkey, and Ganesh, the elephant-headed deity.

Two great meditators who developed specialized techniques of Yoga were closely associated with animals. The Buddha used extensive animal parables in his teachings that related to his past lives and the past lives of his students.[11] Mahavira Vardhamana, also known as the Jina, was a great teacher of Jainism. Before his renunciation of worldly life he rode in a palanquin adorned with animals. After his enlightenment (*kevala*), he advocated protection of all animal life and himself was described in terms of representing the best qualities of various animals.

The *Ācārāṅga Sūtra*, an important Jain text from approximately 300 BCE, states that Mahavira Vardhamana, later known as the Jina or Spiritual Victor, decided to embark on the path of meditation and renunciation, descended from a palanquin "adorned with pictures of wolves, bulls, horses, men, dolphins, birds, monkeys, elephants, antelopes, *sarabhas* (fantastic animals with eight legs), yaks, tigers, and lions."[12] When he successfully attained liberation (*kevala*) through his yogic austerities, he was described in terms of the animal realm:

> His senses were well protected like those of a tortoise;
> He was single and alone like the horn of a rhinoceros;
> He was free like a bird;
> He was always waking like the fabulous bird Bharunda;
> Valorous like an elephant, strong like a bull;
> Difficult to attack like a lion . . .
> Like the earth he patiently bore everything;
> Like a well-kindled fire he shone in his splendor[13]

Animals were noted for their particular abilities and accomplishments. To imitate these fine qualities was considered a sign of spiritual attainment, not unlike the process found in the shamanic tradition, as described by Mircea Eliade above.

Buddhism, Jainism, and the broader Hindu tradition all developed techniques through which to enhance meditative concentration. Each of these traditions referred to these disciplines as "Yoga." The *Yoga Sūtra* of Patañjali, which dates from the second century of the common era, refers to animals twice. It states that one can develop the power of an elephant.[14] It also refers

Rooster (Kukkuṭa-āsana)

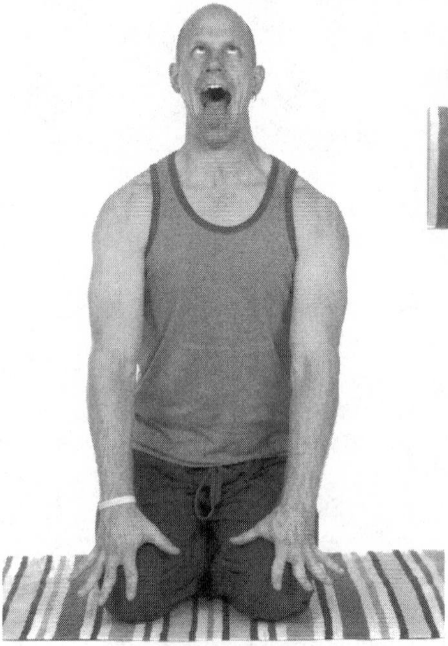

Lion (Siṃha-āsana)

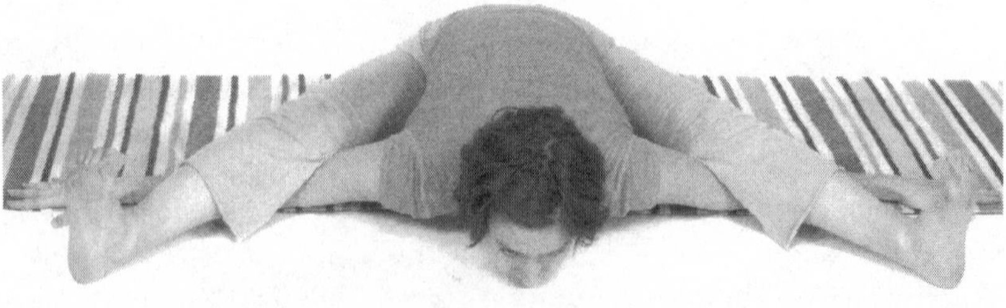

Tortoise (Kūrma-āsana)

Cow's Head
(Gomukha-āsana)

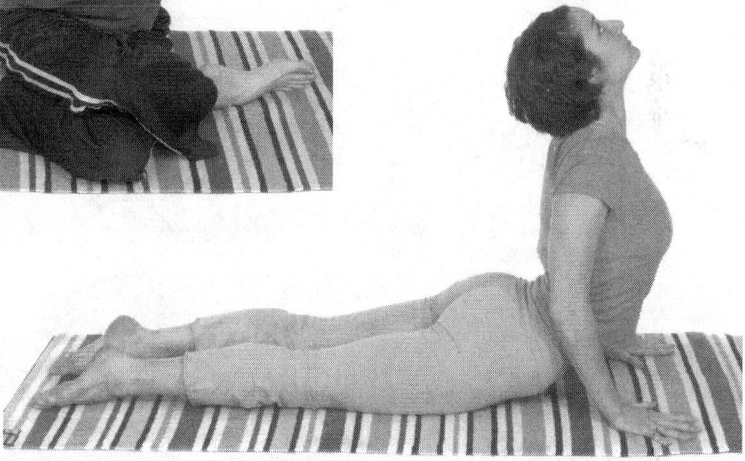

Cobra (Nāga-āsana)

Peacock (Mayūr-āsana)

Eagle
(Garuḍa-āsana)

Scorpion
(Vriścika-āsana)

Rabbit
(Śaśa-āsana)

Crow
(Kāka-āsana)

Locust
(Śalabha-āsana)

to the Kūrma or tortoise *nādi*, an energy pathway located in the upper region of the body through which one attains stability. It also extols Yoga postures or *āsanas* as the means to attain steadiness and ease.[15]

In later times these postures (*āsanas*) come to carry the names of animals. The *Haṭha Yoga Pradīpikā*, written by Svatmarama in the fifteenth century, lists several poses named for animals. Some examples are the Cow's Head pose (Gomukha-āsana),[16] the Tortoise pose (Kūrma-āsana),[17] the Rooster pose (Kukkuṭa-āsana),[18] the Peacock pose (Mayūr-āsana),[19] and the Lion's pose (Simha-āsana).[20]

Additionally, later Yoga manuals such as the *Gheraṇḍa Saṃhitā* include several additional poses named for animals, including the Serpent pose (Nāga-āsana), the Rabbit pose (Śaśa), the Cobra pose (Bhujaṅga-āsana), the Locust pose (Śalabha-āsana), the Crow pose (Kāka-āsana), the Eagle pose (Gauruḍa-āsana), the Frog pose (Māṇḍūka-āsana), and the Scorpion pose (Vṛiścika-āsana), to name a few.

Some Yoga postures are named after nonanimal objects such as the bow (Dhanur-āsana) or take their name from human physiology such as the Head-Knee (Janu-Sira-āsana) or from geometry such as the triangle poses (Trikona-āsana). However, a session of performing Yoga unavoidably includes poses that place the practitioner in a state of imitating an animal.

As a not very skilled but consistent practitioner of Yoga postures, I would like to suggest that Yoga practice does have an emotional effect that goes beyond mere strength or flexibility of the body. By imitating an animal, one takes on a new demeanor, influenced by the qualities of the animal whose shape and form and stance one emulates. In the performance of the Peacock pose, one feels a sense of balance, pride, an affirmation of one's ability to move competently in the world. In the Eagle pose, one feels a sense of entwinedness and focus, a honing of one's vision and purpose. In the Cobra pose, one feels both a tremendous gravity and a rising up, a sense of being weighted and glued to the earth, yet yearning and stretching to rise above. In the Lion pose one feels positively regal, refreshed, and energized. At the close of a Yoga session one feels renewed and in a sense redefined, prepared to encounter the world with greater agility and balance.

The relationship between animals and Yoga postures leads to various questions. Did these postures arise because people imitated animals, as we find in shamanistic religious practices? Or did the posture originate first, with the developers of Haṭha Yoga naming the pose after the fact for whatever came to mind?

In the context of India, animals are part of one's everyday reality, even in the cities. One encounters cows, goats, cats, dogs, and numerous other animals on a daily, sometimes continuous basis. People often feed birds before taking their own meal. Birds fly into the home at dinnertime, expecting acknowledgment. Gurāṇi Añjali, my own teacher of Yoga, urged her students to observe animals, to learn from them. One has a sense that the attention required to move into and sustain a Yoga pose carries a connection with the ancient shamanic tradition of animal imitation.

However, it could also be argued that a danger lies in overromanticizing the mysterious or shamanic aspects of animal mimesis. For instance, Denise Kaufman, a prominent Yoga teacher in Los Angeles, suggests that one adopt a largely empirical attitude toward doing Yoga and relating with animals. In an interview she commented:

> Animals move; people can learn about movement from animals. House pets stretch all day long, creating space in their joints. Animals sit in different kinds of positions. Monkeys and apes do things with their hands. Perhaps as humans we need to reclaim our four-leggedness. Getting down on all fours stimulates the pranic flow. Sitting in chairs tightens the hamstrings and the lower back. Animals don't sit on furniture; they have not built things contrary to their nature.[21]

From her perspective, Yoga involves recapturing our animal physicality and reconditions the body to establish itself within a nontechnologically enhanced environment.

I would suggest that the naming of Yoga postures is more than merely a convenient, descriptive artifice and that the relationship between sacred power and the human cannot be divorced from the harnessing of the deep images evoked by intimacy with the animal world. We have seen how the early peoples of India revered animals, depicting them in tableaux of adornment and surrounding their early sacred meditating yogi with animals. Animals find prominence in classical literature. The later medieval Yoga texts explicitly prescribe animal poses as integral to mystical attainment.

Perhaps most significantly, we learn to be empathetic and connected with nature from our experience of and relationship with animals. As Thomas Berry has noted, our consciousness as humans, our development and affectivity, radically depend upon our openness and sensitivity to the natural order:

> We know a mockingbird by the variety of its songs, by its size, by the slate gray color of its feathers and by the white patch on its wings and the white feathers in its tail . . . In every phase of our imaginative, aesthetic, and emotional lives we are profoundly dependent on the larger context of the surrounding world. There is no inner life without

> outer experience. The tragedy in the elimination of the primordial forests is not the economic but the soul-loss that is involved. For we are depriving our imagination, our emotions, and even our intellect of that overwhelming experience communicated by the wilderness. For children to live only in contact with concrete and steel and wires and wheels and machines and computers and plastics, to seldom experience any primordial reality or even to see the stars at night, is a soul deprivation that diminishes the deepest of their human experiences.[22]

To the extent that Yoga heightens our senses and brings us into visceral relationship with the nonhuman realm, our own sense of worth, well-being, and connectedness becomes enhanced.

Beyond the outward imitation of animals through the practice of postures, Yoga also works to cultivate a growing awareness of the power of breath (*prāṇa*). Through regulation of the breath clarification of the mind (*citta-prasāda*) can arise.[23] By performing control of breath, one can stabilize the body and overcome a myriad of distractions, such as dullness, carelessness, laziness, and sense addiction.[24] Cultivation of the breath eventually leads to a state described by Patañjali as "dissolving that which covers [one's] inner light" (*prakāśa*).[25] Through this process of intentional radiance, described more fully in chapter 6, one gains a sense of inwardness and interiority, of gatheredness in the Quaker sense of the world. By no longer seeking external stimuli or agreement or affirmation, one takes an internal stance that resonates with rather than resists the powers of the innately beautiful world that surrounds and enfolds us.

In daily Yoga practice as taught at Yoga Anand Ashram, morning begins with a recognition of the sunrise, a cleansing ritual, and a sequence of movements (*āsanas*) and breath regulation (*prāṇāyāma*). About midway through my twelve-year training in Yoga, in the summer of 1980, we engaged in an intense and protracted class of *prāṇāyāma*. It included multiple rounds of *mūla bandha* (anal contractions), *jālandhara bandha* (chin to chest lock), and *uḍḍiyana bandha* (stomach contractions), as well as alternate nostril and other forms of breathing, conducted after at least thirty minutes of Yoga postures. Simultaneously, during this period, we were asked to practice truthfulness (*satya*). During this time, we also kept journals, and two entries in particular captured the *élan* of this experience:

1) Words have no absolute and lasting meaning; emotions and even experiences cannot be adequately expressed with words.
2) The nature of the universe is dualistic. For example, there is the good and the bad, the positive and the negative, the left and the

> right side, male and female, subject and object, the unmanifested and the manifested, night and day, etc. Each of these experiences is an experience of my body. Skill in action comes when I stand in the center, the central pillar of my being: 100 percent attached and 100 percent detached. The dualities are necessary, however, in order for me to live my life; I have to see the two in order to see the one.
>
> 3) My desire creates the universe in which I live.
> 4) Anything which depends on another thing is perishable. Any time I depend on or look for another person's approval I lose my own integrity.
> 5) The breath moves all living things. The breath is life. Through feeling the breath in my life I feel the breath in the universe.

This sequence of reflections suggests that groundedness in one's interiority through the breath can generate feelings of intimacy and connection.

The combination of calm breath and rootedness in silence also yielded an interesting passage that reveals a direct perception of the power of intention:

> Another experience of *satya* occurred while sitting, as I usually do, at the close of the day, in our back lawn, facing the woods and the sun setting through the trees. I have worked with an exercise, a twist of consciousness, wherein the light between the trees takes on the cloak of reality, while the trees themselves are "intended" into the void . . . one framework of reality is replaced by another, thus disclosing the intentional nature of all reality. The world is focus and focus is subject to change and tuning. With the view of *satya*, there is a lightness, flexibility.

Working with the body, working with the breath, pushing ethical reflections to their limits and deeply inside, a powerful change of perspective takes hold of the Yoga practitioner. This inward grounding, known in Sanskrit as *pratyāhāra*, prepares one for the next phase of Yoga's journey, the process of concentration, meditation, and *samādhi*.

5 *Patañjali on Meditation*

Undoing the Thinking Self

heyaṃ duḥkhaṃ anāgataṃ
The pain of the future is to be avoided.
—*Yoga Sūtra* II:16

The ordinary person is primarily a thinking being. Our thoughts define who we are, what we like, and what we dislike. We constantly remind ourselves of who we are by thinking the thoughts that we think. One of the greatest philosophers of Europe, Rene Descartes, expressed this unabashedly when he wrote "*Cogito ergo sum*: I think therefore I am." Thought has become the primary locus for personal identity in the modern world. We cherish our thoughts, and we hold them to be our own. We are trained since infancy to "think for ourselves," to "develop our own opinions" and "respect the opinions of others."

However, the great yogic philosopher Patañjali held another perspective on thought. Rather than lauding thought as the baseline for identity, rather than holding thought to be something sacrosanct and definitional, he maintained that thought must be used judiciously and cautiously, always directed toward a higher goal. Otherwise, thoughts become the very source and core of our profanity, moving us further from our true identity, our true self, our true existence. For Patañjali, the greatest insight into the nature of things, the highest skill that a human can attain lies in the conquest of thought through the careful application of yogic techniques. Yoga, as defined by Patañjali, involves the "suppression of thought, the restraint of mental fluctuations."[1]

Patañjali regarded thoughts to come in five varieties: true cognition, error, imagination, sleep, and memory.[2] Furthermore, he suggested that in most circumstances these thoughts are impure, afflicted with the burdens of ignorance, egoism, pleasure, disdain, and clinging to life,[3] burdens that infect and prolong our karmic constitution.[4] An identity linked to such thoughts stands as firm as the vacillating impulses of thought itself: that is to say, the grounding for such identity, when subjected to close scrutiny, is, at best, flimsy. It can be assaulted easily by the attitudes that other people put forth and can be easily molded by changing circumstances. If I place great value upon the written work I compose, new data may render it untrue; someone else's criticism might assail its style. If my identity is bound up in the craft of writing, then my emotional states and the very thoughts I hold to be my own are open to assault from all sides: my own self-doubt and the opinions of others. As long as I think that the thoughts I think and express are my own, my self is subject to fluctuation and hence unstable.[5] As long as I remain attached to thoughts about me in which I find solace, I remain distanced from any hope of groundedness.

For Patañjali, stability and true identity are found in a realm that is other than thought. By quelling the persistent, nagging, thinking voice that claims selfhood for its own, Patañjali asserts that true identity, the power of pure witnessing or *citi śakti*, can be attained.[6] By undoing that which one thinks one is, the true self can be found. If this insight experience shines even for a moment, it can help establish a path toward a reconditioned sense of being, a yogic identity rooted not in the evanescent but in that which sees change but does not itself change.

In developing the *Yoga Sūtra*, Patañjali compiled a host of techniques to facilitate this process. The very first of these that he mentions involves the joint application of practice and release from desire, a diligent distancing that reminds aspiring yogis not to forget the goal of quelling thought and advises a holding back from throwing oneself into passionate activity. This practice and release, when applied over a long period of time, stabilizes and quiets one's sense of identity.[7] In concert with this twofold practice, Patañjali also advocates the observance and application of two primary ethical systems to rein in and gain control over one's realm of activities. Both of these are found also in earlier renouncer systems: Jainism and Buddhism.

Like Jainism, Patañjali advocates adhering to the five *mahāvrata* or great vows of nonviolence (*ahiṃsā*), truthfulness (*satya*), not stealing (*asteya*), nonlustfulness (*brahmacarya*), and nonpossession (*aparigraha*).[8] Patañjali, referring to these collectively as *yamas* or disciplines, places them at the very beginning of his eightfold Yoga path (*aṣṭāṅgayoga*). Each of these restrains a person from excessive involvement with worldly affairs, reminding one that true identity cannot be found in the control or manipulation of things, events, or persons to serve one's own selfish desires. To kill a spider because one finds it repulsive is an act of amazing arrogance. To lie and deceive in order to save one's face is none other than hypocrisy. To take something that one has not earned, whether it be money or recognition, violates propriety. To use someone sexually for reasons of ego or mere physical gratification dehumanizes that person and oneself. To collect trinkets and accomplishments to adorn one's self-concept merely cements the thoughts that inevitably bind us. It has been said that we don't own things; things own us. The ethics of Yoga requires the undoing of each of these activities in an effort to loosen the thoughts and consequent actions stemming from selfish desires that ensnare us ever more deeply in firmly held notions about ourselves, notions that become brittle and easily broken. Using this fivefold renouncer ethic, one can undo the knots created by attachment. The nonviolent, abstemious, quieted self can gradually approximate the pure consciousness that Yoga upholds as the supreme human state.

As in Buddhism, Patañjali advocates the observance of the Brahmavihāra, the cultivation of thoughts that minimize our separation from others.[9] If we encounter a person with no redeeming qualities, we are encouraged to bring forth feelings of equanimity, not disgust. If we encounter the successful, Patañjali suggests joy, not jealousy. He advises developing compassion for those in the midst of unhappy circumstances and cultivating friendliness toward those who are doing well. This ethic, while acknowledging the undeniable differences between individuals, provides methods for minimizing the otherness of persons. For Sartre, hell was other people; Patañjali encourages using the other as a vehicle for modulating our own emotionalities, an important step in gaining control over the mind.

As an aid to get ourselves out of petty self-concerns, Patañjali suggests that we cultivate positive observances within our day-to-day life. These constitute the second phase of his eightfold scheme, the *niyamas*. Like the *yamas* mentioned above, the *niyamas* include five components: purity (*śauca*), contentment (*santoṣa*), austerity (*tapas*), spiritual study (*svādhyāya*), and devotion to a higher ideal (*īśvara praṇidhāna*). This last phase urges us to devote ourselves to the service and pursuit and emulation of the perfect yogi or Īśvara, often translated as "Lord or God."[10] Acknowledging that each individual imagines her or his ideal independently, Patañjali defines this chosen deity (*iṣṭa devatā*) in the most general of terms, saying that it is untouched by the afflictions of ignorance (*avidyā*), egoism (*asmitā*), pleasure (*rāga*), disdain (*dveṣa*), and clinging to life (*abhiniveśa*).[11] By repeating the name of this ideal, and by conforming one's thoughts and actions to what one imagines such an exulted presence would model, stability and inwardness arise.

The body, the living temple, the abode of thought, also becomes a vehicle for stabilization in Patañjali's system. When positions of ease and strength are gained through the practice of *āsana* (the third of Patanjali's eight steps) the mind can be fixed.[12] The breath when properly regulated through *prāṇāyāma* (Patañjali's fourth phase) stills the mind.[13] Mastery of these preliminary phases leads one into the fifth state, *pratyāhāra*, a withdrawal from attachment to the things of the world. When the energy centers of the heart, throat, and forehead can be felt, power is gained that is no longer theory, notion, or opinion, but a direct experience that can inspire the reconstruction of self-identity.[14] Other body felt experiences such as dreams and feelings of exultation and release can also be used as a foundation for stabilizing the mind.[15]

And finally, the mind itself can be used to undo the mind. By focusing on the thoughts and sensory experiences offered by a single object, the mind can discover its own power.[16] When one can hold the mind on a thing, the mind that normally dissipates one's power can make one stronger. This strength then leads to the disappearance of the physical object, to its absorption into one's self or the absorption of self into it. An intimacy is gained with what once was considered utterly other than oneself. This process takes place through the inner limbs of Yoga, the final three phases known as *dhāraṇā*, *dhyāna*, and *samādhi*.

The first phase of this inward path is concentration or *dhāraṇā*. This term can be best understood by looking at its root verb *dhṛ*, "to hold." By holding the mind on a particular object for a fixed period of time, one develops a relationship, a thoughtfulness, and a deep memory of that object. Soon one not only becomes established with that object during discrete times of fixed sitting but also encounters the power of that object throughout the day, quietly and unexpectedly. For instance, if one spends ten minutes in the morning devoting one's attention to the song of a mourning dove or the fragrance and beauty of a rose, one then enters the day with a mind and body poised and receptive to hear more clearly, smell more acutely, and see more elegantly. The power to hold and focus ones's mind opens one to the immediacy of the intended object and the many other myriad possibilities of which the particular object is just one manifestation. As a possible example of the practice of *dhyāna*, let us consider establishing concentration on a tree. At first, one searches out an appropriate candidate. In New York State, it might be a stately maple. As a California resident, I turn my focus each morning to the bottlebrush tree in my backyard. With regularity, I observe the tree, taking note of its shape, the curvature of its limbs, the nature of its leaves, and, in the spring and summer, its spectacular puffy red flowers laden with bright yellow pollen. I have grown to discover that this tree holds many secrets. Small sparrows nest deep in its protected darkness. Favorite visitors such as hummingbirds and bumblebees come to the tree for its nectar. On some days, the winds toss its drooping limbs from side to side. On other days, they hang with poignant silence. I see this tree. I let it speak to me, and I speak to it, allowing my thoughts to rest there and return there each morning.

When the existential mood or *bhāva* generated by the concentration of the mind takes on power without requiring support; when one can maintain focus on one's state of centeredness, then one enters the state of true meditation or *dhyāna*. The mind in this state becomes whelmed with an unspeakable sense of focus. Without flitting from one external support to another, whether in the form of objects or ideas, the mind holds to one place without straying.[17] When arising from such meditation, there remains no residue, no clutter of afflicted thoughts to plague or haunt the meditator.[18] Through skillful meditation, the distractions of unbridled thought can be avoided.[19]

When one truly knows a tree, it becomes one's friend. Its stability and special form of fragility provide quiet comfort. When sitting with the tree, moments of repose relieve one from the need to think, deliver one from the need to generate thoughts and reflections pertaining even to the tree itself. The tree, rooted and reaching, earthbound and arching heavenward, becomes more than a tree, more than a metaphor, and opens one into true contemplation and meditation.

The final state of Patañjali's eightfold Yoga scheme, the culmination of his system, is referred to as "*samādhi*." This critical term is derived from two prefixes and a root word that literally translate as "together-here-putting" or putting things together. It has been rendered as "absorption," "concentration," "unitive attention," but is best defined by Patañjali as a state that emerges from the "diminishment of mental fluctuations, like a precious or clear jewel assuming the color of any near object."[20] It can be with support or seed (*sabīja*), characterized in fourfold fashion as with gross object (*savitarkā*), free of gross object (*nirvitarkā*), with subtle object (*savicārā*), and free of subtle object (*nirvicārā*). In such a state, one would enter into a state of oneness with either an object or notion, such that one's consciousness becomes indistinguishable from it. When the power of absorption transcends the particular external object or thought and reaches into the depth of one's psychic structures (*buddhi*), then one attains the state of *nirbīja samādhi*, through which the underlying structures of the mind become purified.

Facility in *samādhi*, when undergirded with concentration and meditation, is referred to as "*saṃyama*." It allows one to accomplish a host of special powers such as knowledge of the past and future, an understanding of one's prior condition in an earlier birth, an ability to "read" the thoughts and intentions of others, a skill that allows one to go unnoticed, a sense of one's own mortality, the development of great strength, the acquisition of knowledge about the movement of heavenly bodies, and insight into the operation of the *cakras* and the workings of the mind.[21] However, Patañjali regards the acquisition of such powers or *siddhis* to be merely a·distraction from the true task of overcoming the compulsive activities of the mind and discerning clearly the difference between the changing seen and the unchanging seer.[22]

Patañjali describes this highest state in various ways. He speaks of clarity of authentic self that leads into true righteousness (*ṛta*)[23]; he speaks of being free from involvement with the realm of manifested reality or *prakṛti*,[24] of cultivating a purity of consciousness free from passion.[25] He speaks also of entering into *dharma-megha samādhi* or the "cloud of virtue *samādhi*" through discriminative discernment, a state from which no afflicted action proceeds. In his concluding verse, Patañjali claims that Yoga culminates in the emergence of pure consciousness (*puruṣa*) and the power of higher awareness (*citi śakti*).[26] Meditation empowers one to discern the difference between the realm of unending and ultimately fruitless production and repetition of mind-driven activity fraught with ego and desire, and the realm of pure witnessing, a state of nonattachment. Always bearing in mind the distinction between the unspeaking seer and that which is seen and thought about, one becomes liberated from the trap of ascribing fixed reality to the world, a world in which one constantly sets oneself up as a candidate for pain. Through perseverance and purification, the meditator can leave behind identification with the myriad changes endemic to the human condition and establish and stabilize the ongoing cultivation of purified consciousness, supported with the ongoing application of ethical precepts.

In a state of *samādhi*, the tree upon which one gazes can be felt as the trunk of one's own body, the roots as one's own legs and feet, the leaves as one's myriad thoughts, rustling in the breeze. This experience of uniting the external with the internal through the application of *saṃyama* slowly erodes the notion that the self is different from the world and that the world is different from the self.[27] Through remembrance of such insight and by its repeated application, the seeds of desire that manifest in selfishness and defensiveness begin slowly to dry up.[28] By practice through the mind, the mind itself surrenders and turns from defense to service, turns from resistance into wakefulness. By not forgetting the lessons of meditation, a yogic life rooted in stability and compassion rather than endless thought and futility can be built.

For Patañjali, this life of Yoga through meditation and meditative action requires an honest examination of one's own self-definition in yogic categories. The root and source of one's anxiety and pain (*duḥkha*) is thought; thoughts are perpetuated because of past actions (*saṃskāras*), which are generally fraught with impurity and affliction (*kleśa*).[29] By applying various techniques of Yoga practice, the influence of past actions slowly wears away, lessening the anxiety and pain normally associated with the human condition. To devote one's thoughts and attention to a guru, to place one's body in service of a higher ideal through *sevā*, to work diligently at being ethical in one's dealings with others, to sit quietly and observe the breath, to chant the names of gods or goddesses are all methods that recondition our being away from impurity toward the state of Yoga. For Patañjali, this reversal of the mind from outward obsession to inward stability is the highest of all possible human achievements.

II *Yoga and Liberation*

6 *Luminosity and Yoga*

The universe revealed through a meeting with the Light contrasts with the profane Universe—or transcends it—by the fact that it is spiritual in essence. The experience of Light radically changes the ontological condition of the subject by opening him to the world of the Spirit . . . [A] meeting with the Light produces a break in the subject's existence, revealing—or making clearer than before—the world of the Spirit, of holiness, and of freedom.

—Mircea Eliade, *History of Religions*

Light, most especially the camphor flame, is thus an extraordinarily potent condensed symbol of the quintessentially Hindu idea . . . that divinity and humanity can mutually become one another.

—C. J. Fuller, *The Camphor Flame*

Mircea Eliade wrote extensively about the centrality of light as the constant religious image appearing throughout the many traditions he studied from around the world over a period of decades. In reading the *Yoga Sūtra*, the core text of the tradition that defined Eliade as a leading scholar of the history of religions, themes of light and luminosity pervade the text, peering out in each of the book's four sections. This chapter will follow Patañjali's treatment of light, lightness, and clarity as a constant root metaphor for the process of yogic attainment. In the process, I will address a fundamental persistent question that arises in regard to Yoga's approach to the lived world. Can Yoga as a philosophical system be seen as providing an avenue for active engagement with the world without abrogating its teleology? Can *nirodha* (restraint) and *kaivalyam* (aloneness or isolation) be seen as compatible with an ongoing relationship with the fluctuations of the mind?

One generally approaches the Yoga tradition by looking at its self-definition: *yogaś-citta-vṛtti-nirodha*.[1] This can be translated as "Yoga is the restraint of the mind's fluctuations," leading to an overall philosophy and practice that emphasizes control and perhaps even suppression. Following this experience, one is said to reside in one's own nature,[2] an allusion to *puruṣa*, the eternally free, ever-present witness consciousness. Though this remains the definitive explanation of Yoga, I would like to suggest that the living application of this experience can be understood by examining the places in Patañjali where he discusses the "shining forth" or discernment of *puruṣa* or witness consciousness, referred to in each of the four sections (*pādas*) of the text. For most scholars, this event underscores the so-called dualistic world abnegating nature of the Yoga system. It is generally supposed that the world of active engagement ceases in order for the *puruṣa* to be discerned. In this chapter, building on themes introduced in chapter 2, we will explore how the *Yoga Sūtra* presents a much fuller and alluring account of the process of lightening one's karma than is generally acknowledged, a path that inherently affirms the world while seeking a state of transparency and luminosity.

PĀDA ONE: BECOMING THE CLEAR JEWEL

The *Yoga Sūtra*, as with most Indian philosophical texts, announces its purposes,[3] defines its telos[4] [as given above], and then outlines its theory of knowledge and reality.[5] The description of actual Yoga practice does not begin until sūtra I:12, where Patañjali emphasizes ongoing practice (*abhyāsa*) and the cultivation of dispassion (*vairāgya*). In the Sāṃkya system of Īśvarakṛṣna, only knowledge (*jñāna*) leads to liberation. Patañjali puts forth repeated practice of Yoga techniques combined with dispassion as the first of many effective tools for attaining the state of Yoga. Dispassion (*vairāgya*) is said to lead to (or proceed from, as will be discussed) the discernment of *puruṣa*: "That highest [release]—thirstlessness for the *guṇas*—proceeds from the discernment (*khyāti*) of *puruṣa*."[6] Here we see a theme that occurs throughout the text: first seeing things as no more than combinations of *guṇas*, then ascending from heaviness (*tamas*), through passion (*rajas*) to lightness (*sattva*) and then finally dissociating oneself even from this lightest state of purity. At that moment, the goal of luminosity has been attained: *prakṛti* is held in abeyance and, the witness consciousness alone stands.

Patañjali describes four other instances in the first *pāda* of this clarified witness consciousness being revealed without insisting that the world itself dissolve. The first involves the Brahma Vihāra, the famous ethical observances of friendliness, compassion, sympathetic joy, and equanimity borrowed into Yoga from the Buddhist tradition.[7] It could be argued that this "clarification of the mind" (*citta-prasāda*) refers only to an intermediary state, that this is merely a preparatory place to higher states of consciousness. However, if we look at this state in the context of the Pāli Canon, we can see that this is not the case. During his lifetime, the Buddha proclaimed that five hundred of his disciples achieved liberation or nirvana and declared them to be *arhats*. Identical with the formula given in the *Sāṃkhya Kārikā*, each *arhat* declared, "I am not this, there is no self, I have nothing." Subsequent to this attainment, the Buddha described each as dwelling in the "Brahma Vihāra," the abode or sanctuary of the religiously accomplished. Richard Gombrich writes that this was an assertion of the comportment of the enlightened ones, not merely a method of meditation.[8] I would suggest that this shows a process of active engagement whereby "clarification of mind" becomes an epithet for the applied and active insight undertaken on the part of the accomplished yogin in daily affairs.

The next reference to luminosity can be found in *Yoga Sūtra* I:36: "Or having sorrowless illumination." Though brief, this attainment indicates that a flooding of light (*jyotis*) has occurred, through which sorrow has been expelled. Again, the Buddhist allusions in this passage are clear, as well as an indication of a state of being or awareness that does not nihilistically deny the redeemability of that which can be perceived.

This brings me what is perhaps my favorite *sūtra*, one that to my estimation has been both overlooked and misinterpreted:[9] "[The accomplished mind] of diminished fluctuations, like a clear jewel assuming the color of any near object, has unity among grasper, grasping, and grasped."[10] This *sūtra* juxtaposes two key images: the state of mind as having diminished fluctuations and the quality of a clear jewel. First, the linkage between diminished fluctuations and *citta vṛtti nirodha* must be acknowledged. This *sūtra* defines the several processes for controlling the mind and achieving various forms of *samāpatti* (unity) and *samādhi* (absorption). This can be seen as not different from the process of *nirodha*, due to the direct reference to the diminishment of fluctuations. Yet this does not lead to the elimination of the mind or objects or the processes of perception. Instead, a specialized form of awareness—dare we say *puruṣa*—is revealed in which the separation between grasper, grasping, and grasped dissolves. Though Vyāsa suggests that this refers to three different foci of awareness, I would prefer to place the emphasis on the term *samāpatti*. In this state of unity (*samāpatti*), ego, senses, and objects lose their separation from one another revealing a state akin to kinaesthesia, a state of being whelmed or absorbed—in short, moving into the depths of mystical at-one-ment. The world itself does not cease; merely the barriers that fence the self from world and world from self disappear. This verse, embedded innocuously at the three-quarter point, defines and, in my thinking, gives high profile and importance to the processes of *samādhi* (*savitarkā*, *nirvitarkā*, *savicārā*, *nirvicārā*) that follow.

The image of clarity recurs at the end of this sequence:

In skill with *nirvicārā*
Clarity of authentic self occurs.
There the wisdom is *ṛtam* bearing[11]

Ṛtam refers to the peak Vedic experience wherein the purposes and intent of sacrifice (*yajña*) are fulfilled, resulting in a moment of perfect equipoise.[12] Earlier I mentioned the ascent from *tamas* through *rajas* to *sattva*. One has ascended from unity with gross objects, first with thought and then without thought, to unity with subtle objects, presumably the *vāsanās* or residues or *saṃskāras* of past action that condition our personality and behavior. As one gains facility in this state of unity, "clarity," earlier associated with the Brahma Vihāra and the notion of an authentic or somehow purified or elevated self arises. Again, this does not state that the world has been discarded or disengaged. In fact, the reference to *ṛta* proclaims that this accomplishment leads to a wisdom through which the flow of life (the goal of the Vedic philosophy) may reach its fullness.

PĀDA TWO: THE SEER AND THE SHEDDING OF LIGHT

Patañjali summarizes the Sāṃkya system in verses 15–28 of the second section or *sādhana pāda*. In the process, he emphasizes the purpose and function of the manifest world, the realm of the seen. In a nearly direct quote from the *Sāṃkhya Kārikā*, Patañjali writes, "The seer only sees; though pure, it appears intentional. The nature of the seen is only for the purpose of that (seer). When its purpose is done, it disappears; otherwise it does not disappear due to being common to others."[13] First, I want to establish the relationships among the process of seeing, the seer, and luminosity. According to the Sāṃkhya scheme, a correspondence exists between the subtle elements, contained within the body, the sense organs manifested through the body, and the gross elements (*mahā bhūta*-s). The nose and smelling correspond to the earth, the mouth and tasting correspond to water, and the eyes and seeing correspond to light or *tejas*, the element that illumines and extends warmth. In the *Puruṣa Sūkta*, the two eyes correlate to the sun and the moon. Hence, in the Sāṃkhya system, the function of the seer is to literally cast light upon the things of the world. Although this may seem to be a childlike inversion of how we have come to understand physical principles, this perspective nonetheless reveals certain wisdom: there can be no world that has meaning apart from one's perception of it. This does not deny the reality of the external world but underscores the importance of perspective and relationality in any endeavor or circumstance.

According to the psychology of Sāṃkhya and Yoga, the predispositions of karma exist in the seen, not in the seer.[14] Hence, though the limited ego claims to be the owner of personality, in fact personality and action can only emerge due to the presence of what the *Chāndogya Upaniṣad* refers to as the "unseen seer." Everything that can be perceived is perceived for the sake of that seer, but, mistakably, the limited self assumes that the world exists for the sake of its own limited gratification, hence ensnaring the individual within its limitations. When the seen sees that "she" is not the seer, that is, when the purpose of the realm of activity is seen as providing experience to the unseen seer, then the "seen" and all the attachment it connotes disappears. One stands alone in silence, liberated. This takes place through a process of "unfaltering discriminatory discernment," a term that receives further mention in the third and fourth sections,[15] as will be discussed later.

Images of light appear in the two places in the second *pāda*: the accomplishment of purity (*śauca*) and the performance of breath control (*prāṇāyāma*). Purity, of all the disciplines (*yama*) and observances (*niyama*), holds the distinction of bringing one to the point of perfect *sattva*. It is considered to be an apt preparation for "the vision of the self" and generates a more philosophically laden description than any of the other nine disciplines or observances: "From purity arises disassociation from one's own body, noncontact with others, purity of *sattva*, cheerfulness, onepointedness, mastery of the senses, and fitness for the vision of the self."[16] This discussion of purity begins with a description of the process of turning away from physical attraction, the most obvious aspect of *tamas*. With increased purity, one gains a host of benefits: increased *sattva*, a cheerful disposition, enhanced focus, mastery of the senses (which receives fuller treatment in the third section), and finally "fitness for the vision of the self." This last attainment places one again in the realm that links vision, the luminous sense, with the self.

A double entendre can be found in each of these references. On the one hand, vision of the self can refer to looking at and seeing the self, which, as we will see in IV:19, cannot happen because the self can never become an object. That leaves us with the alternate reading, the other part of the double meaning: construing the compound here as a genitive *tat puruṣa* compound, translated as "the self's vision." The practice of purity holds the allure of the physical realm in abeyance, allowing for the seer to simply see. This accomplishment is the "vision of the self," referring to a clarified process of perception rather than the notion that the self is seen as a fixed substance.

The next of the eight limbs to include reference to light and luminosity occurs in the discussion of *prāṇāyāma*. The fourth state of *prāṇāyāma*, somewhat similar to the description of purity above, entails "withdrawal from external and internal conditions."[17] With this inwardness comes an intensification of *sattva*. Elliptically referring perhaps to visionary experiences articulated in the later Haṭha Yoga texts, Patañjali writes, "Thus, the covering of light is dissolved." This "enlightening" experience then allows for enhanced power and concentration: "And there is fitness of the mind organ for concentrations."[18] In the prior two chapters we discussed experiences that arise from the joint application of breath control and the cultivation of inwardness. In those *sūtras*, breathing exercises set the stage for an illuminative experience.

PĀDA THREE: THE SHINING

Splendor and radiance can be found in the description of Patañjali's eighth limb, *samādhi*, in the third or *Vibhūti pāda*. Echoing the earlier reference to the clear gem and to the point or moment where the purpose of the seen has been completed, Patañjali writes, "When the purpose alone shines forth as if empty of own form, that indeed is *samādhi*." When the purpose—that is, all things exist for the sake of providing experience to the seer—is known, then a crystalline luminosity, a seeing-things-as-they-really-are takes place. And from the mastery of this, again recalling the description of wisdom in I:48, arises the "splendor of wisdom."[19] This level of *samādhi* clearly allows for a world engaged through the aegis of wisdom.

Nine additional *sūtra*s in the third section include references to light and illumination. Applying *saṃyama* on the sun brings "knowledge of the world."[20] By gazing upon that which the sun illuminates, one gains an understanding of the world. Moving into interior reflection on the *cakra*s, concentrating on the highest *cakra*, "the light in the head" brings about "vision of the perfected ones," the *siddha*-s or invisible helpmates to those who practice Yoga. The next reference, in the midst of a description of various fabulous attainments and powers, brings us back to the philosophical purpose of the text: "When there is no distinction of intention between the pure *puruṣa* and the perfect *sattva*, there is experience for the purpose of the other (*puruṣa*); from *saṃyama* on purpose being from the self, there is knowledge of *puruṣa*."[21] Again "knowledge of *puruṣa*" begs to be interpreted as "*puruṣa*'s knowledge." Strictly speaking, *puruṣa* cannot possess anything, even knowledge, but this allows a process of alluding to an elevated state of consciousness without allowing anyone to claim it.

In the descriptions of light as associated with *saṃyama*, Patañjali employs three images in quick succession. The first states that the power of breath, specifically "mastery of the middle breath" yields radiance (*jvalanam*).[22] This might refer to the physical result of being well oxygenated, when, for instance, one's cheeks become rosy after a brisk walk or some form of physical exertion. The second image talks about concentrating on the lightness of cotton (*laghu-tūla*), which allows one to move through space (*ākāśa-gamanam*).[23] By identifying with something as flimsy as cotton, one takes on its qualities of free movement. The third image talks of moving beyond even the body toward the "great discarnate" (*mahāvideha*).[24] This reference links to the earlier discussion on rising above the manifest aspects of *prakṛti*.[25] In the first mention of the discarnate (*videha*), a desire to become again involved with *prakṛti* lingers.[26] In contrast, in the third section, this concentration on the discarnate results in the destruction of the covering of light (*prakāśa-āvaraṇa-kṣayaḥ*),[27] a much more positive assessment of this yogic accomplishment. This also refers back to the prior *pāda*, where the practice of breath control also removes the covering of light.[28]

The remainder of the third section discusses how one's *sattva* increases successively. First one masters the elements (*bhūta-jaya*).[29] Then one attains perfection of the body (*kāya-saṃpad*).[30] Next one rises above the body to gain mastery over the sense organs (*indriya-jaya*).[31] This results in mastery over that which causes the world to become manifest, the latent aspect of *prakṛti* (*pradhāna-jaya*).[32] At this level, as in the stage of *nirvicāra samādhi* mentioned in the first section, one is able to control the impulses (*saṃskāras*) that normally condition human craving and the pursuit of desire. Hence, as in the Upaniṣads, where one rises from the food-made body to the mind-made body to the emotion-body and finally attains the self, one first masters the relationship with the external elements, then one's body, then one's senses, including the mind, and gains control over the emotions. However, the final attainment requires an even higher level, defined as the "discernment of the difference between *sattva* and *puruṣa*." The final verses of the third section nicely underscore the need for increasing levels of lightness, until one reaches *kaivalyam*:

> Only from the discernment of the difference
> between *sattva* and *puruṣa* can there be
> Sovereignty over all states of being
> and knowledge of all.[33]
> Due to release from even this,
> in the destruction of the seed of this impediment,
> arises perfect aloneness (*kaivalyam*).[34]
> There is no cause for attachment and pride
> upon the invitation of those well established,

> because of repeated association with the undesirable.[35]
> From *saṃyama* on the moment and its succession,
> there is knowledge born of discrimination.[36]
> Hence, there is the ascertainment of two things that are similar,
> due to their not being limited (made separate) by differences
> of birth, designation, and place.[37]
> The knowledge born of discrimination is said to be liberating,
> (inclusive of) all conditions and all times, and nonsuccessive.[38]
> In the sameness of purity between the *sattva* and the *puruṣa*,
> there is perfect aloneness (*kaivalyam*).[39]

Though I will discuss this portion of the text at length in chapter 15, let me paraphrase the trajectory of this important description of the liberative process. Liberation hinges on discerning the difference between one's best purity and the modality of pure witnessing. One cannot hang a shingle on one's purity; this leads to passion, attachment, and pride; one becomes susceptible to flattery. As one sloughs off all identification from moment to moment, one develops the critical skill of dwelling in a state of constant discrimination (*khyāti*). Hence, one keeps a constant vigil and can discern the difference between the purity attained in the state of *videha-prakṛti-laya*, the most rarefied form of *sattva* that occurs within the realm of *prakṛti*, and the witness. The two are so close. *Prakṛti* has resisted all attempts to act on prior compulsions (*saṃskāras*) and move again in the realm of attachment and passion. In dwelling in that perfect state of abeyance one becomes outwardly indistinguishable from the witnessing consciousness, but the voice that remains within *prakṛti* would continue to deny any such connection. Later commentators (Vācaspatimiśra, Vijñānabhikṣu) referred to this relationship in terms of reflection (*pratibhā*), indicating that the world reflects itself to the witness in its pure state, without any interfering patina of sullied interpretation.[40]

THE FOURTH *PĀDA*: LUMINOSITY

The process of inverse evolution (*prati-prasava*) leading to increasing levels of luminosity is described yet again in the fourth section of the *Yoga Sūtra*. The first concept that indicates a special relationship between the purified *sattva* of *prakṛti* and the *puruṣa* is the concept of "*prayojakam*," the initiator. Patañjali describes this function of *prakṛti* as "the one mind among many that is distinct from activity."[41] This would probably be the intellect or *buddhi* in its most subtle form of *sattva*, which we saw above as associated with *kaivalyam*.[42] All mind is in some sense active but this "one mind" is like *puruṣa* and hence pure. In the next verse, Patañjali, again elliptically, refers to an unspecified something that arises from mind that, despite its being "born" and hence in the realm of *prakṛti*, he nonetheless refers to as pure (*anāśayam*): "There, what is born of meditation is without residue."[43] This reflects the theme in I:50: "The *saṃskāra* born of it obstructs other *saṃskāra*s." This state of purity does not obliterate the world but in some way perhaps transforms it.

The next verse pertains to notions of color, which can only be perceived through the sense of sight, and hence require some form of illumination:

> The karma of a yogin is neither white nor black;
> that of others is threefold.[44]

This verse discusses what the Jains refer to as the "*leśyas*" or combinations of karmic impulses that obscure the luminosity (the energy, consciousness, and bliss) of the soul, referred to in Jainism as "*jīva*." In Jainism, these colors vary from black to blue to red to yellow to white; the perfected Jaina (*siddha*) rises above all colors in the state referred to as "*kevala*." Patañjali refers to the varieties of color as mixed and, like Jainism, suggests that the perfected one goes beyond all coloration.

Continuing the theme of colors, Patañjali later suggests that the attitude one takes toward objects depends upon the "anticipation" or projection of the mind that perceives any given object. Appealing to one of the classic proofs given in the *Sāṃkhya Kārikā* for the existence of *puruṣa*, he states that all these changes are due to the "changelessness of their master, *puruṣa*."[45] To complete this argument about the relationship between that which is objectively seen and the seer, he states that the object does not possess revelatory powers but becomes illumined only through the presence of the seer. Only through the seer can the world be known, although the seen, particularly in its mistaken assumption of ego identity, seeks to claim all experience. Patañjali advances this argument as follows:

> An object of the mind is known or not known,
> due to the anticipation (of the mind) that colors it.[46]
> The fluctuations of the mind are always known
> due to the changelessness of their master, *puruṣa*.[47]
> There is no self-luminosity of that (*citta-vṛtti*)
> because of the nature of the seen.[48]

The seen can never see itself. Light ultimately comes from the highest source of illumination, which stands separate, even aloof, illuminating the things of the world through its gaze. When one sees that one does not really see, then the compulsion to grasp and cling to the ego identity ceases. Patañjali writes that "the one who sees the distinction discontinues the cultivation of self-becoming."[49] Having observed and understood that the world appears to be as one assumes it to be because of the structures of one's mental conditioning, one gains the liberating perspective that allows a retreat from the self-generating status quo.

The conclusion of the *Yoga Sūtra* describes this process of heightened awareness as a gradual letting go of being invested in the continuation of the world as self-construed. This results in the cryptic description of a liberated state, defined as the "cloud of *dharma samādhi*." This has been interpreted, appropriately, in many ways. On the one hand, the term *dharma* can be seen in light of its Buddhist counterpart, as a constituent of existence. This usage can also be found in the only other passages where Patañjali uses the term. In III:13 and 14, Patañjali discusses *dharma* as the nature or essential quality of a thing and says that things take on their particular character due to the nature of the *dharma*. In the level of *dharma-megha samādhi*, this essence or nature has been purified and lightened to the point where rather than manifesting in the shape of a concrete reality, it remains as evanescent as the water vapor in a cloud, indicating that it perhaps has been resolved to its most subtle or *sattvika* form. In terms of the technical Jaina usage of '*dharma*,' it has attained its most refined state of movement. And in the traditional, nontechnical Hindu sense of '*dharma*,' this state might indicate that all unvirtuous activities have been overcome and that one dwells only in a *dharma* characterized by the *sattva-guṇa*. The following verse seems to support this final interpretation: "From that, there is cessation of afflicted action,"[50] which causes Vyāsa to state that one has attained living liberation, the only reference to this cherished state in his entire commentary.

In either case, the progression from gross to subtle culminates to completion in this last verse of the *Yoga Sūtra*. The process of outward manifestation (*pariṇāma*) has been reversed, called back to its origin. The inertia that leads to *tamas* has been reversed through the practices of Yoga. The *guṇas*, even *sattva* itself, have performed their function of providing experience and liberation for the seer, the *puruṣa*, the original source of illumination, although, paradoxically, *puruṣa* never actively illumines. This returns the Yoga practice to the state referred to in the third *sūtra* of the first pāda, the state of standing in *sva-rūpa*. This is not, however, a static state. The conclusion of the *Yoga Sūtra* does not require the cessation of all luminosity but instead avers to the notion of an ongoing presence of consciousness, referred to as "*citi śakti*," the power of higher awareness. The *Yoga Sūtra* does not conclude with a negation of materiality but with a celebration of the ongoing process of dispassionate yet celebratory consciousness.

> Indeed, in [that state of] reflection,
> for the one who has discriminative discernment
> and always takes no interest,
> there is the cloud of *dharma samādhi*.[51]
> From that, there is cessation of afflicted action.[52]
> Then, little is to be known
> due to the eternality of knowledge
> which is free from all impure covering.[53]
> From that, the purpose of the *guṇas* is done
> and the succession of *pariṇāma* concluded.[54]
> Succession and its correlate, the moment,
> are terminated by the end of *pariṇāma*.[55]
> The return to the origin of the *guṇas*,
> emptied of their purpose for *puruṣa*,
> is *kaivalyam*, the steadfastness in own form,
> and the power of higher awareness.[56]

Just as in the description of *prāṇāyāma* removing the covering of light,[57] so also this concluding phase of Yoga philosophy brings an end to all impurity (*tadā sarva-āvaraṇa-mala-apetasya*).[58] It does not, however, mean that the world itself ceases.

In studies of Hindu thought, it is difficult to escape the notion, promulgated by the language of the tradition itself as well as Christian critiques of the tradition, that Hinduism denies the world. The language of the Buddha and Rāmakṛṣṇa alike call for a leaving behind of the world in search of higher values. However, does this really mean the rejection of the world? Does it mean that the world should only be condemned and shunned? Or does it mean that only the impure aspects of the world must be transcended? The concluding verses of the *Yoga Sūtra* certainly seem to allow for the engagement of a purified sense of one's place in the world, through which one is established and living in a purified consciousness, having understood and reversed the lure of the lower *guṇas*.

In recent studies of attitudes toward nature, several authors, including Callicott and Nelson, have suggested that Hindu philosophy negates the world and has helped cultivate an attitude of indifference or even contempt for nature. In a long-term study of the life and work of Sunderlal Bahuguna, a leading environmental activist in India, George James reaches quite a different conclusion about what some consider to be an ambiguous attitude toward the natural world. Referring to the Chipko movement for forest preservation, James writes:

> Chipko is unquestioningly a movement for the negation of the world. The world it negates, however, is the world of scientific forestry and of politicians, technicians, and contractors within whose knowledge nature is reduced to a commodity in a system of economic exchange that leaves the people destitute and dispossessed, that discounts their material needs and the religious life that supports them. The asceticism of Chipko is a renunciation of this world and its promises. It is also certainly correct that Hinduism inspired and grounded the Chipko movement. But the Hinduism of the Chipko activist differs widely from Callicott's characterization of Hinduism as a religion that views the empirical world as morally negligible and judges it as contemptible, because it deludes the soul into crediting appearance and pursuing false ends. For the Chipko movement, the false ends are the ends of scientific forestry: resin, timber, and foreign exchange; those of the Chipko agitation are soil, water, and pure air. The Hinduism of Chipko hears the claims of this world [of development] and, like the jivanmukta, knows that they are false.[59]

The world of change must be quelled to reveal the also-real luminous silence.

As Ortega y Gasset so beautifully articulated, we live in a world invented by our ancestors.[60] The world of Yoga, as articulated by Patañjali, has shaped many of the values and assumptions of South Asian life. For too long, without carefully examining the text, Yoga has been characterized as a form of world-rejecting asceticism. Yoga does not reject the reality of the world, nor does it condemn the world, only the human propensity to misidentify with the more base aspects of the world. The path of Yoga, like the Chipko movement, seeks not to deny the beauty of nature but seeks to purify our relationship with it by correcting mistaken notions and usurping damaging attachments. Rather than seeking to condemn the world to a state of irredeemable darkness, Yoga seeks to bring the world and, most important, the seers of the world, to a state of luminosity.

7 *Living Liberation in Sāṃkhya and Yoga*

INTRODUCTION

The notion of being liberated while alive has come to be closely associated with the Vedānta, Yoga, and Sāṃkhya schools, among others. In this chapter, I will explore metaphors for liberation in the *Sāṃkhya Kārikā*, and then turn to some later Sāṃkhya texts that make mention of the term *jīvan-mukta*. The second portion of the chapter will examine notions related to living liberation in the *Yoga Sūtra*. Both traditions emphasize the importance of nonattachment, identified with the cultivation and actualization of a knowledge or discernment (*jñāna* in Sāṃkhya and *viveka khyāti* in Yoga) that frees one from compulsive thought and action. In the concluding section I explore differences in the liberated state as described in each text, especially on the issue of purification, with comparative reference to the Jaina tradition, which contains many parallel concepts.

The *Sāṃkhya Kārikā* of Īśvarakṛṣṇa and the *Yoga Sūtra* of Patañjali, both of which probably appeared by the fourth or fifth centuries of the common era,[1] provide extensive categorizations of the nature of bondage and, in the case of Yoga, numerous means of escape from that bondage. In these root texts of Yoga and Sāṃkhya, the terms *jīvan* and *mukta* are not used, separately or in tandem, though the *Sāṃkhya Kārikā* does use verbal forms derived from the root *muc*, to liberate. Neither text waxes eloquent on the qualities one exhibits after the escape has taken place. The Sāṃkhya states rather cryptically that the "wheel keeps spinning" after release;[2] Yoga claims that one dwells without impurity in a "cloud of dharma."[3]

One possible reason for this brevity of description is that the genre in which these texts were written does not allow for the sort of narrative and poetic embellishment found in the epics and *purāṇas*. Another reason might be that a deliberate attempt has been made to guarantee that the recognition of a liberated person remains in the hands of a spiritual preceptor. The teachings of Yoga and Sāṃkhya traditionally have taken place in the context of an ashram, a community closely regulated by its guru. The largely oral and highly personalized lineage tradition maintained by the guru helps to ensure the authenticity and integrity of the tradition. Without the authority of the main teacher, whose task it is to discern the spiritual progress of an ashram's inhabitants, it would be relatively easy for impure persons to claim advanced spiritual status based on their misinterpretation of written texts. A third reason for brevity could hinge on the logical contradiction that arises due to the fact that the notion of self is so closely identified with *ahaṃkāra*, the mistaken ego sense that is fraught with impure residues of karma. It would be an oxymoron for a person to say, "I am liberated." According to the *Yoga Sūtra*, it is impossible for the Self to see itself.[4] The liberative experience is by definition ineffable, with no content, no activity, no mark.

Despite the brevity of their descriptions, both texts present an ideal state in which a person has uprooted the causes of bondage, and hence embodies a perspective that lies beyond attachment. Though the *Yoga Sūtra* and *Sāṃkhya Kārikā* speak sparingly and metaphorically of what later is called "living liberation," their definitions are indeed helpful for understanding subsequent discussions.

SĀṂKHYA

Sāṃkhya is quite often associated with the term *dualism*, a label applied to the system that perhaps has lead to some fundamental misconceptions regarding its intent. In Greek and later European thought, the mind and/or spirit has been discussed as opposed to one's body, with the latter often denigrated as inferior to the former. As these notions became absorbed within the Christian tradition, the body became seen as something to be disdained and transcended because it distracts and pollutes one's spiritual nature. This dichotomy at first glance seems resonant with the Sāṃkhya system, whose terminology is often translated in terms of "spirit" or *puruṣa* overcoming "material nature" or *prakṛti*. The system could be seen as a cosmic cosmological dualism, with the physical realm held in low esteem. However, a closer look at the Sāṃkhya system reveals that this interpretation is not accurate. The text states that the only means to liberation is knowledge of the distinction between not two but *three* constituents of reality: the unseen seer or pure consciousness (*puruṣa*), the realm of manifestation (*prakṛti*), and the realm of the unmanifest (*pradhāna*), which is *prakṛti* in a state of quiescence but with potential for further activity.[5]

The Sāṃkhya system affirms the manifestations of *prakṛti* as providing experience to be enjoyed by pure consciousness. Although deemed to be fraught with threefold suffering (*duḥkha*),[6] the purpose of experience is to provide both enjoyment and liberation for *puruṣa*. The Sāṃkhya path to liberation emphasizes that through release from mental conditionings, one becomes free. However, this can only take place through *prakṛti*; there is no escape *from prakṛti* until the point of death.

PURUṢA'S RELEASE FROM *PRAKṚTI*

Sāṃkhya describes human experience as an interplay between an unconscious realm of manifestation as expressed through the many constituents (*tattva*) of *prakṛti* and a silent witness (*puruṣa*) for whom all this is performed. Anything that can be spoken of in concrete terms is in the realm of *prakṛti*, which is pervaded and instigated by the three *guṇas*. By definition, *puruṣa* is inactive and is not creative; hence *puruṣa* cannot strive for liberation, nor is it responsible for the created world. *All* experience, including the drive to become liberated, is performed for *puruṣa*, yet *puruṣa* remains aloof. Activity is performed by *prakṛti*, and it is *prakṛti* only that can claim, "I am free," though, as we will see, she does this negatively by stating, "I am not, this is not mine, there is no self of me." By seeing how and why she operates, she paradoxically undoes herself, allowing for liberation.

To describe this function, Īśvarakṛṣṇa writes that "as the unknowing milk flows to nourish the calf, so the *pradhāna* (*prakṛti*) functions for the sake of *puruṣa*'s liberation."[7] The association of *puruṣa* and *prakṛti* is also compared to the relationship between a blind person and a lame person: *puruṣa* cannot act or move, and *prakṛti* cannot see; hence *puruṣa* climbs on the back of the blind person (*prakṛti*), and the two together operate within the world, with *prakṛti* clearly doing all the work for *puruṣa*.[8] Liberation takes place when knowledge (*jñāna*) arises, the unique modality (*bhāva*) within *prakṛti* that allows the mind to realize its actions are not for itself but for the unseen master. At this point, *prakṛti* ceases her yearning, and the pure consciousness attains a state of repose.

In order for living liberation to be attained, the nature of bondage due to desire must clearly be discerned and then eliminated. Īśvarakṛṣṇa states that *prakṛti* operates so that desires may be fulfilled, hence releasing *puruṣa*.[9] Once this has transpired, and *prakṛti* has done her job, so to speak, *puruṣa* loses interest, the dancer ceases to dance. The lame one who sees no longer needs the blind one because the desire to "get around" has ceased. The cessation of *prakṛti* and the loss of interest on the part of *puruṣa* constitute the raw liberating event that suspends compulsive attachment driven by desire.

Verses 64 through 68 summarize the process of liberation as follows:

> From the study of the constituents of manifest reality (*tattvas*), the knowledge arises that "I do not exist, nothing is mine, I am not." This [knowledge] leaves no residue, is free from ignorance, pure, and is singular (*kevala*).
>
> Then *puruṣa*, with the repose of a spectator, sees *prakṛti*, whose activity has ceased since her task has been fulfilled and who has abandoned her seven modes [that perpetuate bondage: ignorance, virtue, nonvirtue, attachment, indifference, power, and weakness].
>
> The seer (*puruṣa*) says "I have seen her." The seen (*prakṛti*) says "I have been seen." Though there is closeness of the two, there is no incentive for further creation.
>
> Upon gaining this singular knowledge (*kevalajñāna*), virtue (*dharma*) and the other [modes of bondage or *bhāvas*] no longer constitute reasons [for action]. Yet the body abides due to the force of saṃskāras like the spinning of a potter's wheel.
>
> When separation from the body is attained, and when *prakṛti* ceases, her task fulfilled, then complete and unending isolation (*kaivalyam*) is attained.[10]

The negation of self, the abandonment of all modalities (*bhāvas*) except for discriminative knowledge (*jñāna*), and the image of the wheel that continues to spin, all indicate that the liberation in Sāṃkhya hinges on nonattachment.

KNOWLEDGE AND NONATTACHMENT IN *SĀṂKHYA*

In an uncharacteristically personal and poignant verse, Īśvarakṛṣṇa states, "In my opinion, there is nothing as delicate as *prakṛti* who says, 'I have been seen' and then does not again come into the view of *puruṣa*."[11] The sentiment conveyed here is that *prakṛti* undergoes a dignified form of embarrassment and that her retreat clearly results from the dawning of the knowledge that any further action would be utterly inappropriate. This transformation is perhaps comparable to a scenario wherein a person with a harmful or irrational behavioral habit continues to perform this behavior until stopped in his or her tracks in an embarrassing moment. Such a jolt, which certainly need not be experienced as pleasant, can carry with it enough impetus to reshape future actions.

In his commentary, Gauḍapāda describes this process as follows: "As people being influenced by some favorite desire engage in actions of various kinds like going and coming for the gratification and fulfilment of that desire and stop from their activity when that is accomplished, so Prakṛti too, active for the purpose of liberating Puruṣa, ceases from its activity, after having accomplished its twofold purpose for Puruṣa."[12] Once this reordering has taken place—that is, once the dance of *prakṛti* has been arrested by knowledge (*jñāna*)—the manifestations of *prakṛti* no longer hold any interest for the witness (*puruṣa*). The motivating intent has been eradicated. The text states that "though the two are still in proximity, no creation (emerges),"[13] indicating that the propensity to enter again into attachment has been rendered sterile. This is perhaps the closest direct acknowledgment of "living liberation" in the *Sāṃkhya Kārikā*. The text strongly implies that the compulsive activities dominated by the residue of past impulses no longer gnaw at one's being, though the body remains. Knowledge (*jñāna*) prevents a resubmersion in that which has proven futile. The body and mind and so forth go on, but due to the direct knowledge that the Self has nothing it can call its own,[14] not even *dharma* obtains as a compulsive call for action. The individual moves on through life in a detached manner, until the moment of death when final separation takes place.[15]

In this phenomenological or process reading of Sāṃkhya, *puruṣa* is not a soul or thing, and *prakṛti* is not dead materiality. *Puruṣa* is defined by Īśvarakṛṣṇa as "consciousness, inactive, noncreative, witness, nonreactive, neutral, not created, free."[16] It is not mind in the conventional sense: mind is governed by past impulses and is inseparable from the world that it first construes and then conceives and then perceives. Residues of past action contained in the intellect (*buddhi*) congeal into a fixed notion of self that then defines and construes the world. Suffering results because the world does not cooperate with one's notions of the way it should be. The world is not at fault; the source of discomfort is to be found in firmly held expectations and anticipations (*saṃskāras* or *vāsanās*), which are far removed from a pure consciousness that merely witnesses the unfolding of things.

Sāṃkhya invites the reexamination of the notion of self in such a way that the patina of inappropriate, self-generating interpretation is stripped away, leaving one free. Gauḍapāda employs a business analogy in describing this state of freedom: "An analogy is of the debtor and creditor, between whom a contract exists for receiving [payment back on a] loan; but after the repayment of the loan, there is no money transaction between them, even if their contract continues. In a similar manner, Puruṣa and Prakṛti have no motive."[17] Any necessity or compulsion for further action has been eliminated.

This intermediary state between becoming established in the mode of spiritual knowledge (*jñāna bhāva*) and final liberation (*kaivalyam*) is very similar to what the Jainas refer to as the thirteenth of the fourteen stages (*guṇasthānas*) of spiritual development (which will be discussed briefly at the end of this chapter) and what the Vedāntins refer to as "knowledge of Brahman." However, the intratraditional commentators make scant reference to this transitional state, leaving its full discussion to later Vedāntins. Various questions remain unanswered if one looks solely at the Sāṃkhya system. What sorts of action does a person engage in as the "wheel goes on spinning?" Can a "backsliding" into ignorance and the other seven detrimental modes occur? If so, what can be done to prevent it?

LATER VEDĀNTIC INTERPRETATIONS OF *SĀṂKHYA*

By the time of both the major and minor commentaries on the *Sāṃkhya Kārikā*, Vedānta had gained ground as the pre-eminent basis for philosophical discourse, eclipsing the other major schools of thought.[18] Hence, the views analyzed below show evidence of syncretism that automatically draws from assumptions established by Vedāntins. For instance, though the *Sāṃkhya Kārikā* does not mention the phrase *jīvan-mukta*, several authors discuss it as if it were part of Īśvarakṛṣṇa's system. In his commentarial gloss on the *Sāṃkhya Sūtra*, Aniruddha, who probably flourished in the early sixteenth century, describes *jīvan-mukta* as a "middle-level" accomplishment prior to the total dissolution of *prakṛti* at the time of death. He claims that *jīvan-mukta* "allows for the teaching of the tradition" and that it is supported in the Vedas. Without persons in the status of *jīvan-mukta*, there would be no standard for liberation; any spiritual quest would be the blind leading the blind.[19]

The descriptions of the *jīvan-mukta* given in Vijñānabhikṣu's *Sāṃkhyasāra* (ca. late sixteenth century) seem to have been influenced by the *Bhagavad Gītā* and the *Yogavāsiṣṭha*: "[Such a one] neither rejoices nor hates . . . never fails to remember the existence of the transcending self . . . possesses an even and unshaken mind and acts without any attachment . . . devoid of passion and aversion . . . being free from duties, attains liberation . . . [T]he same in honor and dishonour . . . lust, greed, anger, etc., have dwindled and erroneous awareness has come to an end forever . . . [H]e abides in the fourth state."[20] In commenting on Aniruddha's gloss cited above, Pramathanātha Tarkabhūṣana (1865–1941) has provided an interesting description of how *saṃskāras* or karmic influences operate for a *jīvan-mukta*, saying they are "without sting."[21] Another modern Sāṃkhya commentator, Rāmeśacandra Tarkatīrtha (1881–1960), underscores that liberative knowledge (*jñāna*) provides both liberation while living and liberation from rebirth after death.[22] These later commentarial traditions clearly have embraced the vocabulary of "living liberation" and seemingly presume that the *saṃskāras* that remain active for bodily maintenance no longer sway the liberated one from the transcendent state of *puruṣa*, defined by Īśvarakṛṣṇa as a "free, nonaligned witnessing, a state of nonreactive looking on."[23]

In summary, the *Sāṃkhya Kārikā* provides a philosophical basis for the discussion of liberation within life, although it is not extensively described, and later commentaries seem to pattern their descriptions on other sources. The text clearly states that the force of past impressions will cause one to continue to live. Does this mean that defilement remains but that the liberated one is nonattached within the defilement? When Vijñānabhikṣu and others wax eloquent about the personal qualities of the *jīvan-mukta*, is the perdurance of *saṃskāra* being whitewashed? Or are they assuming that the only remaining *saṃskāras* would be those cultivated during the course of achieving *jñāna*? For a more complete perspective on the difficult issue of the influence of past impressions, we need to look at statements in Patañjali's *Yoga Sūtra* regarding the diminution of karmic effects and its descriptions of what may be considered the state of *jīvanmukta*.

YOGA

In this section, we will examine the discussion of liberation as found in the *Yoga Sūtra* of Patañjali, which relies upon the view of reality asserted in the Sāṃkhya system but augments Sāṃkhya by articulating in greater detail the nature of suffering and offering several alternative paths to liberation.

The Yoga system places greater emphasis than Sāṃkhya on the processes of purification that accompany the cultivation of liberative knowledge. The term that perhaps best describes the yogic path to liberation is *subtilization* (*pratiprasava*): the aspiring yogi strives to lessen his or her attachment first to the gross world, then to the subliminal influences that shape perception of the gross, and finally enters a liberated state wherein all obscurations are burned away. In order to understand the context for this state of liberation, we will briefly discuss Patañjali's view on the nature of afflicted action and then turn to three of the means by which it is purified: concentration, eightfold Yoga, and the reversal of the mind's going forth (*pariṇāma*). Each of these culminates in *samādhi* and, as T. S. Rukmani has noted, "*Samādhi* is not only a means to the end but is also the end itself. For it is in *samādhi* that the final truth is realized."[24]

The path to *samādhi* requires that the yogic practitioner overcome the influences of past action that are fraught with impurity or affliction. The *Yoga Sūtra* identifies five afflictions (*kleśa*) as the root causes of bondage that must be overcome in order for living liberation to take place. These afflictions, listed as ignorance, egoism, attachment, revulsion, and clinging to life (*avidyā, asmitā, rāga, dveṣa*, and *abhiniveśa*), according to Patañjali, are inextricably linked to *karma* and are to be avoided through meditation.[25] Whenever *karma* occurs, it is fraught with one of these five. With the suppression of these five through the process of meditation and purification, the practitioner attains a state of equilibrium. In the *Bhagavad Gītā*, Krishna states, "Supreme bliss comes to the yogi whose mind is peaceful, whose passions are calmed, who is free from sin."[26] The discriminating one sees the sorrow and difficulty (*duḥkha*) inherent in worldly involvement[27] and seeks to avoid the difficulty in the future[28] through understanding the world-generating process of the seen.[29] As in the Sāṃkhya system, once the yogi sees that all activity is only performed for the sake of the seer, then the need to perpetuate that action is quelled. At this point, the culmination of the subtilization process, a state of liberating wisdom is achieved: "From following the limbs of Yoga, on the destruction of impurity there is a light of knowledge, leading to discriminative discernment."[30] This discernment (*viveka khyāti*) provides a way to prevent the predominance of ignorance and the other four afflictions (*kleśas*) and its application indicates a state of living liberation.

The hierarchy of concentrations (*samāpatti* and *samādhi*) given in *YS* I:44–51 is ordered according to increasing levels of subtlety designed to progressively minimize attachment. The concentration process begins with focus on gross objects, first with the object present (*savitarkā*) and then using the mind alone (*nirvitarkā*). One then focuses on subtle objects, first with imagery (*savicārā*) and then without imagery (*nirvicārā*). At each stage, a greater degree of purification and refinement is attained, finally culminating in *nirbīja*, or seedless, *samādhi*, which reverses and replaces the impulses of prior *saṃskāras*.[31] This hierarchy of concentrations progressively purifies the mind of the practitioner.

The eightfold Yoga path[32] outlines a more detailed program for the attainment of liberation through overcoming the influences of afflicted past action (*kliṣṭa-karma*). The first phase is a series of vows of abstinence (*yama*) that involve a conscious retreat from the habits of violence, lying, stealing, lust, and possessiveness. Each of these involves turning away from attachment to the gross. Next, in the practice of observances (*niyama*), one cultivates new interactions in the world based on purity, contentment, austerity, self-study, and dedication to Īśvara (the lord). Having thus stabilized one's social intercourse, one then focuses on the outer layer of one's immediate self, the body. Through postures (*āsana*), comfort and steadiness are gained (II:46); through breath control, the internal and external are appeased.[33] This then allows, in the final four phases of Yoga, the taking on of the most subtle aspects of the *citta*. *Pratyāhāra*, the first of these four, is specifically defined as the withdrawal from objects of sense; it is followed by the inner limbs of concentration, meditation, and *samādhi* as mentioned above.

The path to liberation is also discussed by Patañjali in yet another way that emphasizes subtilization (*pratiprasava*) as the means but using a terminology focused more directly on mental processes. This approach hinges on the notion that the source of ignorance and suffering is to be found in the sullied going forth or transformation of the mind (*citta-pariṇāma*) and that this process can be stopped. Patañjali states that the powers of mind can be either directed outward toward manifestation[34] or called back to the point of restraint or *nirodha*,[35] which, when applied consistently, leads to the mental state identified with liberation or *samādhi*.[36] In going outward and involving and identifying oneself with objectivizing processes, the *saṃskāras* fraught with impurity or affliction (*kleśa*) that bind one to compulsive action are strengthened. The reversal of this process through its transformation (*pariṇāma*) into a state of *samādhi* causes seeds of deleterious action to diminish and eventually vanish. Things arise because of the solidification of mind processes;[37] Yoga reverses the process. At the conclusion of *pariṇāma*,[38] wherein the compulsive generation of the world ceases, one becomes liberated.

Sāṃkhya and Yoga can be read in tandem. Both systems bring one to the point of overcoming ignorance, associated with the modes (*bhāvas*) of Sāṃkhya and the residues of afflicted action (*kliṣṭa karma* or *saṃskāra*) in Yoga. No further binding action is created once this state has been achieved; in later traditions, such an adept would be referred to as a "*jīvan-mukta*." However, whereas Sāṃkhya almost fatalistically states that the "wheel continues to turn" after the initial liberating experience, Yoga develops and advances a "postgraduate" course for eradicating *saṃskāras* through the continued application of *samādhi*, leading to a state known as seedless.[39] Through the subtilizing techniques of Yoga, one can steady and deepen the detachment that originally arises with knowledge. In the practice of Yoga, the karmic residues or *saṃskāras* that cause bondage become subtilized: first they are meditated upon in external form; next they are internalized; and finally, according to Vyāsa's commentary of the seventh or eighth century, they become roasted (*dagdham*) like a seed of winter rice.[40] Such a seed, once burned, is rendered sterile; it can produce no sprout. Analogously, a specific *saṃskāra* can no longer exert influence that would cause further action after it is burned through meditation and *samādhi*; one becomes freed of its sway, and, according to the modern Yoga commentator Hariharananda Aranya, one enters into the state of *jīvan-mukta*.[41]

Although this description of liberation in many ways can be seen as parallel to the description of liberation given in the *Sāṃkhya Kārikā*, it could be argued that the emphasis on dissolution of *saṃskāra* in Yoga allows for the emergence of the *jīvan-mukta* state, while in Sāṃkhya, the persistence of *saṃskāra* until death seems to provide for a more provisional form of liberation. In Sāṃkhya, there seems to be an almost "fatalistic" unfolding of *saṃskāras* until the point of death; Yoga advocates an active path to their dissolution. Both systems emphasize knowledge, though Sāṃkhya does not specify the outcome of this knowledge in as much detail as does Yoga.

YOGIC LIBERATION AS THE END OF AFFLICTED ACTION

Of particular interest is the notion that in the practice of Yoga, afflicted action (*kleṣá-karma*) ceases (*nivṛtti*)[42] and an active, clarified mode of perception (*citi śakti*) emerges.[43] Patañjali does not state that all action comes to an end, but that action becomes devoid of afflicted impulses. Impure motives and results cease, and presumably only purified action can be performed. The seventh-century commentator Vyāsa states that "when afflicted action ceases, that wise person is liberated, even while living."[44] This sentence is the earliest extant account of the notion of *jīvan-mukta* in the classical Yoga tradition and is specifically linked to how action is performed. One is reminded that the performer of such activity is described in the *Bhagavad Gītā* as one who has "cast away desire, fear and anger,"[45] has renounced attachment, and knows "I am not doing anything at all."[46]

The quality of being free from afflicted action is also associated with Patañjali's description of Īśvara or God, defined as "a distinct *puruṣa* untouched by afflicted action, fruitions, or their residue."[47] Patañjali states that Īśvara is the teacher or *guru* or all that are wise[48] and associates the deity with the sacred syllable *oṃ*.[49] By devoting oneself to the ideal put forth by Īśvara, the paradigm for what is later described by Vyāsa as *jīvan-mukta*, success in *samādhi* is guaranteed.[50] In the *Yoga Sūtra*, what the two have in common is the absence of afflicted actions. The difference is that Īśvara has never been associated with afflicted action, whereas the liberated one has struggled to undo the afflictions.

The state of liberation is achieved when the generation and identification of the false self mired in afflicted activities ceases and one enters into association with the highest *sattva*, or purity.[51] In this state, the five afflictions (*kleśas*) of ignorance, egoism, attachment, revulsion, and clinging to life cease. The very definition of Yoga as "restraint of the fluctuations of the mind"[52] indicates that these five have been quelled; the thought process is driven by past impressions linked to impure *karma*. Patañjali offers other definitions of yogic accomplishment that also imply freedom from afflicted *karma*, such as "clarity of authentic self."[53] Actions that proceed from this modality are said to be "seedless"[54] or nonproductive of further compulsory, afflicted action. In this state of purification, the purpose of the manifest world (*prakṛti*) has been fulfilled, and the seen no longer is compelled to spin forth her manifestations in the previous sullied manner. The seen as characterized and determined by the afflictions disappears,[55] leaving the seer pure.[56] Patañjali describes this final state of isolation (*kaivalyam*) as seeing the distinction between the purity of *sattva* and the *puruṣa*.[57] Simultaneous with this liberated moment, "discriminative discernment" and "cloud of *dharma samādhi*"[58] are said to arise, along with the "cessation of afflicted action,"[59] which, as noted above, is the one instance directly characterized by Vyāsa as the state of living liberation. The culmination of Yoga is given in the final *sūtra* as follows:

> The return to the origin of the *guṇas*,
> emptied of their purpose for *puruṣa*,
> is *kaivalyam*, the steadfastness in own form,
> and the power of higher awareness.[60]

This final description echoes the original definition of Yoga, indicating that the dance of the manifested mind has ceased with "the return to the origin of the *guṇas*" and that the seer or pure witness has prevailed, exhibiting both "steadfastness in own form" and the "power of higher awareness."[61] These descriptions seem to equate living liberation with quiescence and nonattachment but not total negation. "Higher awareness" indicates that some life endures but that this life is lived within an ongoing path of discernment (*viveka khyātir*) and lightness (*sattva*).

The action of the accomplished yogi is free from affliction; the *Yoga Sūtra* states that such a person enters into a form of *samādhi* characterized as "cloud of dharma" (*dharma megha*). Does this phrase mean that the undertakings of the yogi are permeated with duty or have the form of virtuous actions? Patañjali does not clearly define the meaning of *dharma megha samādhi*, and the commentators do little to resolve this question. Sixteenth-century commentator Vijñānabhikṣu writes that the one who is "established in the state of *dharma megha samādhi* is called a *jīvan-mukta*,"[62]

Perhaps Patañjali's use of this obscure term might have been inspired by Mahāyāna Buddhism.[63] In the *Daśabhūmika Sūtra*, a Mahāyāna Buddhist text from the early third century (and hence within a century or so of Patañjali), *dharma megha* is the name of the tenth and highest level of attainment for the bodhisattva. At this phase, the bodhisattva "acquires a glorious body . . . [H]e emits some rays which destroy the pain and misery of all living beings . . . He especially cultivates the perfection of knowledge (*jñāna*) without neglecting others."[64] Although the texts of Yoga and Sāṃkhya do not include the Mahāyāna Buddhist term *bodhisattva*, all three traditions emphasize knowledge (usually referred to as "*vidyā*" in Buddhism), and Patañjali speaks of both compassion and bodily perfection. Another similarity can be found in the fact that both the *bodhisattva* and the *jīvan-mukta* attain the stage of *dharma megha* within the realm of human birth.

In summary, the commentator Vyāsa states that the person freed of afflicted action (*kliṣṭa-karma*) is liberated while living. Vijñānabhikṣu states that such a person dwells in a state of *dharma megha samādhi*. Both require the overthrow of impure, afflicted activities, as advocated by the practices presented by Patañjali. Whereas Sāṃkhya places sole emphasis on the cultivation of knowledge and nonattachment for liberation, Yoga places additional emphasis on several practices designed to reverse the influence of afflicted tendencies, replacing them with purified modes of behavior.

A COMPARATIVE ANALYSIS OF LIVING LIBERATION IN SĀṂKHYA AND YOGA

The various descriptions of yogic liberation offer an interesting complement to the Sāṃkhya notion of liberation. As we saw above, Yoga claims that afflicted past impressions (*saṃskāras*) are sequentially attenuated and replaced by unafflicted *saṃskāras* generated by *samādhi* experiences. This process starts with the arising of knowledge (*jñāna*) or discriminative discernment (*viveka khyāti*), accompanied by the performance of purified action. For Sāṃkhya, it seems acceptable that past *saṃskāras* will continue to operate; according to the potter's wheel analogy, the world spins on, but one's investment in it has ceased. In Yoga, discernment results in the cessation of afflicted action.[65] Sāṃkhya states that the embarrassed *prakṛti* runs away but that life somehow goes on, perhaps unaltered, save for the new, detached perspective. In Yoga there is said in liberation to be a cloud of *dharma* (*dharma megha*); in Sāṃkhya, it is said that there is no longer any further reason for *dharma* and the like to operate or exert their influence.[66] Yoga appears to be somewhat more rigorous in its definition of the liberated state, demanding its adherents to follow any one of a number of paths of purification and asserting that only unafflicted action can remain for the truly liberated. Sāṃkhya, however, does not specifically address the question of performing action following the knowledge event, except to imply that one develops a sense of detachment.

This difference between the two systems, whether seen as contrasting or complementary, can be found in many aspects of the traditions. The adept within Sāṃkhya is said to have achieved a state of knowledge (*jñāna*) that results in a sublime detachment from things of the world. Knowledge allows one to watch life go by without becoming invested or interested in life's affairs. The relative absence of emphasis on purity and virtue within the Sāṃkhya system,[67] though not highlighted by prior commentators and scholars, seems striking. In Yoga, the liberated being also displays discriminative discernment that seemingly results not only in a detached perspective but also involves the cultivation of virtue and the elimination of deleterious activity. In Sāṃkhya, one knows that one is not the doer, regardless of what is done; in Yoga, only virtuous actions remain as possibilities. Sāṃkhya seems to emphasize only one moment of knowledge that brings about the destruction of the seven modes (*bhāvas*) and a state of liberation. In this living state, the wheel turns due to past momentum; the body persists, and *saṃskāras* continue to operate to produce life experience until death. Nothing is said in Sāṃkhya about this, though it is stated that the individual remains detached from it all. Yoga provides a program for ongoing purification.

Another key to understanding the differences between Sāṃkhya and Yoga might be gleaned from the nature of the texts to which each tradition is tied. Though both systems are concerned with the prospect of human liberation, the *Sāṃkhya Kārikā* of Īśvarakṛṣṇa is a brief philosophical poem that clearly conveys the centrality of knowledge as the means to release. The *Yoga Sūtra* of Patañjali comes from another literary genre, serving as a catalogue of methods designed to attenuate the effects of afflicted action and to promote the adoption of a lifestyle that is conducive to a purified way of life. Sāṃkhya clearly communicates the excitement of liberation on a theoretical level, whereas Yoga meticulously outlines how the sort of knowledge gained in moments of insight can be applied in an ongoing manner. One is reminded of the encounter near the end of the *Mahābhārata*, where Krishna is asked what happened to Arjuna following his enlightenment in the *Bhagavad Gītā*. Krishna replies that Arjuna forgot the knowledge he had gained and as a result suffered the consequences of attachment in his later life. It might be that the practice of Yoga as outlined by Patañjali is needed to help people remember and cultivate moments of insight.

Some of the contrast between Sāṃkhya and Yoga can perhaps be understood by juxtaposing certain aspects of Vedānta and Jainism. When one reads the texts of Vedānta such as the *Ātmabodha*, the metaphysical tidiness of the author's system makes one almost able to taste the experience of liberation; by gaining knowledge that all this is merely illusion, dialectically one becomes free.[68] This reading of Vedānta in some ways resembles our discussion of Sāṃkhya above, which emphasizes the cultivation of knowledge alone as the path to release. When one studies Jainism, the path appears much more rigorous, requiring monasticism and in some instances total renunciation of all possessions, even one's clothes. Bondage is taken much more seriously, and the path to release seems much more arduous. Knowledge alone is merely the beginning of true liberation. All afflicted *karma* must be exhausted, and the job cannot be finally finished until the body is left behind.

POSSIBLE JAINA INFLUENCE ON THE YOGA TRADITION

Possible Jaina influence on the Yoga tradition might provide an explanation for the greater emphasis on purity within the Yoga tradition. The first practices within the eightfold path of Yoga—nonviolence, truthfulness, not stealing, chastity, and nonpossession (*ahiṃsā*, *satya*, *asteya*, *brahmacarya*, and *aparigraha*)—are the same as the Jaina teachings of Mahāvīra.[69] This emphasis on the observance of vows indicates that yogis take moral behavior and worldly renunciation very seriously. In the Jaina system, these practices are undertaken to purge (*nirjarā*) the accumulated (*āsrava*) karma that has attached itself to one's life force or *jīva*. This *jīva* in its pure state is characterized as possessing boundless consciousness, energy, and bliss. However, due to having committed countless acts of violence throughout repeated births in the four realms of elemental/botanical/animal, demonic, divine, and human life forms, the *jīva* has become clouded over and unable to experience or express its highest nature. Only in the human realm (*gati*) can the *jīva* hope to proceed in the process of purging fettering karma accrued by violence and ultimately enter the state of freedom or enlightenment. This final state of perfect aloneness (*kevala*) is referred to metaphorically as the vantage point one assumes when sitting in solitude on the top of a great mountain.

In Jainism, the karmas that bind one to ignorance are found in eight fundamental species (*mūla-prakṛti*). Five karmas obscure knowledge; four karmas obscure insight; five cause different forms of sleep; two cause feelings of pain and pleasure; three pervert religious views; twenty-five disrupt proper conduct, subdivided into sixteen passions, six "non-passions," and three forms of sexual desire; four karmas determine the nature of one's birth; ninety-three karmas determine the composition of one's body; two establish one's family status; and five hinder one's energy. In total, Jainism analyzes 148 *karma-prakṛtis*[70] that must be overcome in order to gain liberation.[71]

Unlike Sāṃkhya but similar to Yoga, the process that leads to Jaina liberation is progressive. In Jainism, fourteen levels or *guṇasthānas* are said to comprise the path to liberation.[72] In the first stage (*mithyā-dṛṣṭi*), one dwells in ignorance, disbelieving any statements of a spiritual nature. One is said then to proceed directly to the fourth level (*saṃyag-dṛṣṭi*), a state of liberating insight that is said to last from one instant in duration up to forty-eight minutes (see figure 3).[73] In this state, vast numbers of binding karmas are said to depart. P. S. Jaini comments that the fourth state "allows the soul to progress quickly . . . It withdraws attention from the possessions, body, and psychological states with which it had formerly identified itself; gaining thereby a certain distance or detachment from passions, it attains the pure and peaceful state called *viśuddhi*."[74] However, this experience, though an important rite of passage, is clearly temporary: one might fall back to the second or third level, or even to the first level of utter ignorance (*mithyā-dṛṣṭi*).

The path to final liberation in Jainism truly "gets started" after one experiences the fourth *guṇasthāna*. The insight gained in *samyag-darśana* is said

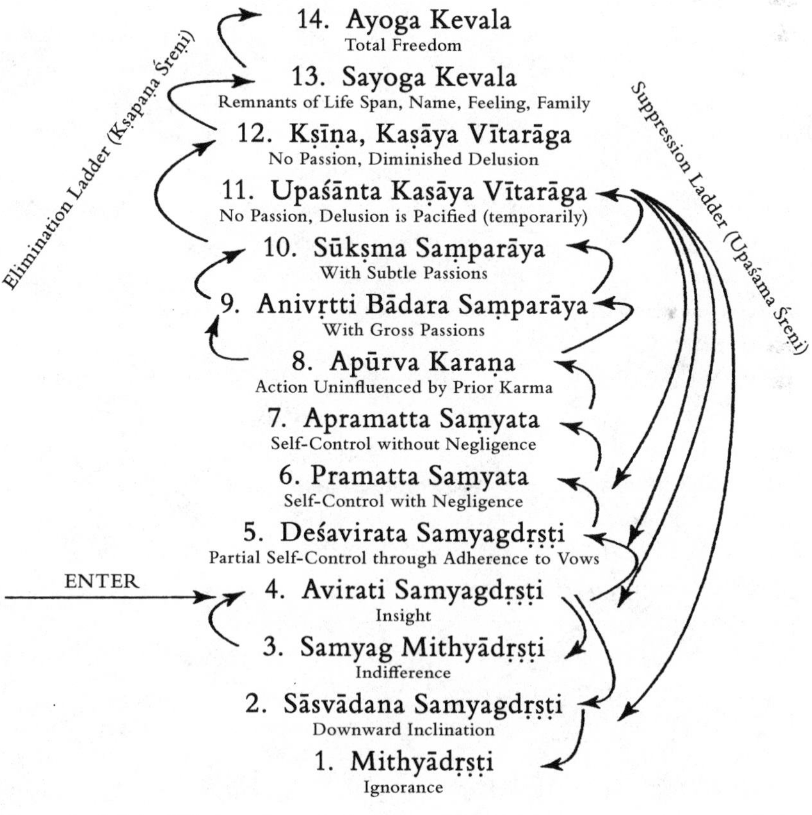

Figure 3. Spiritual Ascent through the Guṇasthāna(s)

to prompt in some souls the purposeful adoption of the five basic vows of Jaina religious life: *ahiṃsā*, *satya*, *asteya*, *brahmacarya*, and *aparigraha*. This occurs in the fifth *guṇasthāna*. In the sixth stage, one eliminates anger, pride, deceit, and greed. In the seventh, one quells all forms of carelessness. In the eighth, ninth, and tenth stages, one banishes such sentiments as laughter, pleasure, displeasure, sorrow, fear, disgust, and sexual cravings. If one reaches the eleventh stage, one falls back to a lower rung on the ladder. If one proceeds directly from the tenth to the twelfth stage, one has climbed the Elimination ladder (*kṣapaṇa-śreni*) and attained "complete restraint with elminated passions."[75]

The critical phase for the purposes of our discussion of *jīvan-mukta* is found in the thirteenth stage (*sayoga-kevali-guṇasthāna*). P. S. Jaini summarizes this state as follows: "This is the state of enlightenment, where the aspirant will become an *Arhat* or *Kevalin*, endowed with infinite knowledge, infinite perception, infinite bliss, and infinite energy . . . The *Kevalin* because of his omniscience has no use of the senses or the mind that coordinates their functions; but he still is not free from the vocal and physical activities such as moving place to place."[76] In terms of the Sāṃkhya and Yoga systems, this would mean that all eight or fifty *bhāvas* and all five *kleśas* have been destroyed. All three traditions refer to this state with terminology that resembles the Jaina state *kevala-jñāna*. One is released from all psychological fetters; only the body remains. The *kevalin* or *jina*, the Jaina equivalent of a *jīvan-mukta*, is one who has achieved the level of the thirteenth *guṇasthāna*, free of all passions, carelessness, and obscurations. This person is referred to as "*sayoga-kevalin*," which in the Jaina tradition means that although liberated from destructive karmas, one is still joined (*sayoga*) to the body.

For the Jainas, karmas cannot be entirely eliminated until the moment of death, at which point one moves into the state of *ayoga*. The final and fourteenth level is said to occur at the moment just prior to death; at this point all karmas that have kept a person alive but are not necessarily deleterious (feeling, name, life span, and family identity) now dissolve. With the dissolution of these four, the drive to continue with life[77] ceases and death follows, often preceded with a ritual final fast. As an interesting sidenote to this discussion, both the Digambara and the Śvetāmbara schools of Jainism teach that the last person to achieve liberation was the monk Jambū, who died in 463 BCE, 64 years after the death of Mahavira.[78]

I would like to discuss some of the implications of the phase in which religious insight first dawns, the state known as *saṃyag-dṛṣṭi*, the fourth *guṇasthāna*. The entry into this fourth level is compared to the experience of a blind man who is suddenly able to see. It perhaps is not unlike that critical moment in *Sāṃkhya Kārikā* 64 when the seer's consciousness realizes, "I am not, nothing is mine." In Jainism, this moment of first insight is preliminary to a long and arduous path of purification, along which many pitfalls and setbacks are expected.

This contrasts with the state described in the Sāṃkhya system, which considers this insight to be final and does not discuss any possibility of falling back. Sāṃkhya states that the modes (*bhāvas*) no longer have any effect, though the body continues to live, due to the force of prior *karma*. The difficulty here is that Sāṃkhya does not specify which type of karma continues. Is it the *karma* of personality? Or is it merely the breath and body that lives on, perpetually unattached? Sāṃkhya does state that one *bhāva* persists, that of knowledge (*jñāna*). The persistence of knowledge implies that a disciplined form of discrimination continues to be applied. If, as I suggested earlier, this results in a constant state of psychological awareness that prevents one from entering into attachment and repeating old patterns, then some forms of *karma* would in fact appear to be present. If this hypothesis stands, then the moment of liberation described in the *Sāṃkhya Kārikā* would be followed with a life of mindfulness until the point of death, during which *karmas* would continue to be encountered but would be disassembled by the modality of knowledge.

In many ways, this seems that it could be parallel to the ongoing path described in Jainism. If only innocuous forms of *karma* remain, then the liberation described in Sāṃkhya would be equivalent to the thirteenth stage of the Jaina path, as described below. However, due to nonspecificity of the nature of *karma* in Sāṃkhya, this point remains somewhat ambiguous. By contrast, in the Jaina tradition, as well as in Yoga as noted above, the varieties and potencies of various *karmas* are well described, along with methods through which they can be uprooted.

The long and detailed process of purifying the various destructive *karmas* in Jainism raises many questions when compared with the Sāṃkhya and Yoga traditions. Are these the same as the *saṃskāras* mentioned by Patañjali and Īśvarakṛṣṇa? In Sāṃkhya, remnants of karma do remain after the experience of liberation, and the wheel of *prakṛtic* existence does turn, implying the presence of some action, though, as noted above, this *karma* is neutralized by the application of knowledge. In Yoga, the seeds of karma are countered by the repeated practice of *samādhi* until, in the words of Vyāsa, the seeds all become burned up and hence incapable of bearing fruit. At this point one's actions become unafflicted, which for Vyāsa qualifies one for liberated status.[79] One gets the sense that these *karmas* that continue to unfold until the point of death are a bit more "weighty" than the nondestructive *karmas* mentioned in Jainism that determine feeling, type of birth, family, and lifespan.

Sāṃkhya emphasizes the insight experience; Yoga augments this by explicating various paths to reduce the effects of afflicted action (*kliṣṭa-karma*); and Jainism provides a complete catalogue of the 148 forms through which karma becomes manifest. Both the Jaina and the Yoga systems emphasize a commitment to the purification of karma through taking on vows; both acknowledge a sequenced hierarchy of spiritual attainment, and both claim that the true adept cannot engage in afflicted or harmful action.

LIBERATED INTO THE ETHICAL LIFE

Perhaps at variance with both traditional commentators and modern scholars, I would suggest that Sāṃkhya and Yoga might be read sequentially as well as in tandem. Sāṃkhya describes a life-reordering, liberating breakthrough, perhaps corresponding to the fourth *guṇasthāna* of Jainism. Yoga, beginning with the Jaina-inspired practice of nonviolence or *ahiṃsā*, provides tools for this insight wisdom to be cultivated and applied to quell attachments within *prakṛti*. Living liberation as hinted at in Sāṃkhya begins with a moment of transformative insight. This insight as described in Yoga can lead one to restructure and purify one's actions through the application of various yogic ethical disciplines designed to bring about the progressive elimination of residual karmic influences. Stemming from the critical insight that "this is not the self of me," one important practice to sustain living liberation is common to both systems: discriminative discernment (*viveka khyāti*) or knowledge (*jñāna*), which are to be applied until the moment of death, when even the desire to live ceases.

The *jīvan-mukta* concept provides inspiration for one to seek knowledge. Although the qualities of this person are not discussed as such in the root texts of Sāṃkhya and Yoga, both systems are designed to lessen the effects of bondage and lead one to a knowledge that allows living liberation. Sāṃkhya offers a single method, described in terms of one single metaphor: the allures of manifestation (*prakṛti*) cease when the knowledge dawns that "I am not really this, nothing really is mine," allowing entry into the highest mode of human consciousness (*puruṣa*), a "free, nonaligned witnessing, a state of non-reactive looking on."[80] Yoga offers multiple paths to the unafflicted action of *dharma megha samādhi*, emphasizing the cultivation of dispassion and virtue. Although it does not contradict Sāṃkhya, it does emphasize the need for ongoing purification both on the path and at the penultimate phase of the quest for liberation.

III *Patañjali's Yoga Sūtra*

8 *Approaching the Yoga Sūtra*

The *Yoga Sūtra* of Patañjali, which was most likely composed more than 1,500 years ago, concatenates a range of philosophical, theological, ethical, psychological, and prescriptive materials designed to effect a transformation of the individual. The text, divided into four sections or *pādas* opens with an analysis of human knowing, summarizes twenty yogic practices, examines the root causes of human despair, prescribes a threefold and an eightfold practice, itemizes powers that arise in their application, and advances a philosophy of reflective inwardness that liberates one's true self or being from its mistaken identity with the realm of change. Composed and even today transmitted as an oral document, the *Yoga Sūtra* provides a mental map for restructuring the influences of past habituations (*saṃskāras*).

WAYS OF YOGA

The *Yoga Sūtra* serves as a catalogue of various meditative and ascetic practices. Each of these aims at producing a state of Yoga, defined variously as restraint of mental fluctuations (*citta-vṛtti nirodha*), discernment (*viveka khyāti*), aloneness (*kaivalyam*), or one of the various *samādhis*. The *Yoga Sūtra* emphasizes practices; it discusses process, giving little attention to doctrine or belief. As an ascetic handbook, the *Yoga Sūtra* is comprehensive. In the first two sections (*pāda*), "*Samādhi*" and "*Sādhana*," numerous means are suggested for accomplishing Yoga, the results of which are explained in the concluding sections, "*Vibhūti*" and "*Kaivalya*."

The first *pāda* alone lists ten sets of ways to do Yoga. The first method mentioned by Patañjali in *Yoga Sūtra* I:12–16 is practice and release from desire (*abhyāsa* and *vairāgya*). Another, found in *Yoga Sūtra* I:20, is to apply faith, energy, mindfulness, concentration, and wisdom (*śraddhā*, *vīrya*, *smṛti*, *samādhi*, *prajñā*). Yet another method is found in *Yoga Sūtra* I:23–32 and II:1, 32, 45: to dedicate one's meditation to the primal teacher, Īśvara, who remains untainted by the ravages of change inflicted by association with *prakṛti*. Appropriate behavior in interpersonal relationships is seen to be another tool for achieving Yoga. *Yoga Sūtra* I:33 states: "One should cultivate friendship with the joyful, compassion for the sorrowful, gladness for those who are virtuous, and equanimity in regard to the non-virtuous; through this, the mind is pacified." In gaining control over the breath, the yogin masters the senses, including the thinking process, as illustrated in *Yoga Sūtra* I:34 and II:49–53. Other practices in the first *pāda* include directing one's consciousness to one who is free from being attracted, meditating on an auspicious dream experience, centering the mind in activity, cultivating thoughts that are sorrowless and illuminating, or by any other means desired.[1]

In the second *pāda*, two main forms of practice are prescribed, one set of three and one set of eight. The first, Kriyā Yoga, involves austerity, self-study, and dedication to Īśvara with the express purpose of uprooting the influence of impurity (*kleśa*).[2] The second, Aṣṭāṅga Yoga, contains the eight limbs of Yoga, each of which may be considered as a distinct form of practice: restraint (*yama*), observance (*niyama*), postures (*āsana*), control of breath (*prāṇāyāma*), inwardness (*prayāhāra*), concentration (*dhāraṇā*), meditation (*dhyāna*), and *samādhi*.[3]

In all, we have listed more than twenty techniques, many of which may be subdivided into component parts. These methods are juxtaposed by Patañjali but not integrated into a comprehensive, sequential scheme. This approach reflects a flexibility and openness in regard to the methods of Yoga to be used in the pursuit of spiritual experience. Rather than asserting the primacy of a single practice, Patañjali proposes multiple paths, without condemning or praising any one particular method. This attitude evokes a spirit of tolerance characteristic of a fundamental internalization of India's preeminent ethical standard of nonviolence or *ahiṃsā*

PATAÑJALI'S CENTRAL THEME: SUBTILIZATION

There are three principal concerns in the *Yoga Sūtra*: practice (*sādhana*), return to the origin or subtilization (*pratiprasava*), and *samādhi*. The three are interrelated and at times synchronic. The application of yogic practices causes a progressive subtilization of one's focus, which is directed away from the gross manifestations of *citta-vṛtti* to the most sublime aspect of *prakṛti*, the state of *sattva*. When this is achieved, the resulting equipoise is defined as a state where distinctions of grasped, grasping, and grasper dissolve (see I:41).

Procedurally and ultimately, Yoga takes an array of approaches, offering myriad paths to the goal and several descriptions of the goal once it has been achieved. Furthermore, mention of the goal is found in each of the four sections of the text. The descriptions of each are diverse, and one could possibly choose a "favorite" description of yogic attainment whether it be jewel-like, cloud of *dharma*, or seedless. However, despite the plurality of practices and culminations, the significance of which will be discussed later, there is one matter in Yoga about which there is no choice: the necessity for the practitioner to recall the *guṇas* back to a condition of equilibrium (*pratiprasava*), mentioned in II:10 and IV:34. Yoga empowers one to regulate and pacify the drama of the ever-changing *guṇas*. Lethargy (*tamas*), passionate activity (*rajas*), and lightness (*sattva*) comprise the *guṇas*.

To understand this critical process, the link between Sāṃkhya and Yoga must be acknowledged. With a few exceptions the vocabulary of Yoga and Sāṃkhya is shared. Like Sāṃkhya, Yoga unequivocally asserts the reality of *prakṛti*. Like Sāṃkhya, Yoga extols discriminative knowledge as the means to liberation. Yoga, however, prescribes several more disciplines to achieve this elevated state and describes the results in various ways. Nonetheless, each of the disciplines of Yoga serves a common purpose: to lessen attachment, first to the gross world, and then to the subtle influences that shape one's perception of the gross. Ultimately, when the final state is attained, all the obscurations are burned away, the *citta* is purified, and one dwells in a state of pure *sattva* that allows one to reflect pure consciousness. This *kaivalyam* or *samādhi* is not a catatonic state, nor does it require death; it is the power of higher awareness (*citi śakti*) through which one continues to observe the play of life.[4]

The technical procedure for the subtilization of the *citta* serves as the thread that binds together the *Yoga Sūtra*. In a sense, the entire Yoga system is designed to accomplish and perfect this process. It is first hinted at in the opening definition of Yoga: "Yoga is the restraint of fluctuations in the mind" (I:2). It is explicitly described in the section on dispassion (I:13–16). A hierarchy of accomplishment seems to be described in I:19–22, with the mild ones ready to return to the manifestations of *prakṛti*, the medium well established in skills that keep one from bondage, and the ardent close to the vision of *puruṣa*. The progressively subtle hierarchy of concentrations (*samāpatti* and *samādhi*) given in I:44–51 (which have been commented upon earlier) further establish the nature of Yoga as requiring the gathering back of the mind from its obfuscated involvements with the world.

The beginning of the second section ("Sādhana-pāda") of the text clearly outlines that which is to be overcome by the practice of Yoga. The fluctuations of the mind, inextricably linked to karma and the afflictions, are to be avoided through meditation (II:11), which returns the practitioner to a state of equilibrium. The discriminating one sees the dissatisfaction (*duḥkha*) inherent in worldly involvement (II:15) and seeks to avoid the dissatisfaction of the future (II:16) through understanding the world-generating process of the seen (II:18). Once it is seen that all activity is only performed for the sake of the seer, then it is in fact called back to its origin, reminiscent of the *Sāṃkhya Kārikā* when *prakṛti* ceases her dance. At this point, the culmination of the subtilization process, a state of wisdom is achieved: "From following the limbs of Yoga, on the destruction of impurity there is a light of knowledge, leading to discriminative discernment" (II:28).

The eightfold Yoga path, described in II:29 through III:3 similarly follows a process of increasing subtilization. The first phase, *yama*, involves a conscious displacement of the habits of violence, lying, stealing, lust, and possessiveness. Each of these involves turning away from attachment to the gross. Next, in the practice of *niyama*, one cultivates new interactions in the world based on purity, contentment, austerity, self-study, and dedication to Īśvara.

Having thus stabilized one's social intercourse, one then focuses directly on the outer layer of one's immediate self, the body. Through *āsana*, comfort and steadiness are gained (II:46); through breath, control, the internal and external conditions of breath are transcended (II:51). This then allows, in the final four phases of Yoga, the taking on of the most subtle aspects of the *citta*. The first of these four, *prayāhāra*, specifically is defined as inwardness or the withdrawal from objects of sense; it is followed by the inner limbs of concentration, meditation, and *samādhi*, which are taken up in the third section of the text.

Throughout the third section ("Vibhūti-pāda"), the powers resulting from progressive subtilization are detailed. All are seen to stem from a mind that is disciplined by the inner limbs of concentration, meditation, and *samādhi*, a mind that is no longer directed to the outer world (see III:9–11). Numerous skills arise, but none are necessarily seen by another (III:20) because the transformation takes place within the experience of the yogin.

Some of the more fantastic *sūtras* in this section can perhaps be reread in light of the subtilization process. For instance, the discussion in III:39–41 implies the ascension through the *tattvas* advocated in Sāṃkhya. The yogin is first able to rise above the grossest elements of water and mud (III:39) and through fire (III:40) using the breath (air) to the subtlest of elements, space (III:41). *Sūtra* III:44 summarizes the initial attainment of mastery over the elements, stating their dependence on that which is more subtle; III:47 takes this a stage higher stating that mastery of the sense organs is gained by knowledge of the sense of self. Yet even higher than this, again following the course of *pratiprasava*, a steady, dispassionate vision is revealed. This progression, from mastery of the elements, to mastery of the senses, to mastery of the mind, and finally, the stilling of the mind, reaffirms the emphasis placed by Patañjali on subtilization, a concern also found in the *Bhagavad Gītā*: "The senses are great, they say, but the mind is above the senses, and intellect above the mind. And above the intellect is He" (II:42).

The fourth section ("Kaivalya-pāda") continues the theme of return to the origin, again using a highly Sāṃkhyan terminology. The concept of the '*pariṇāma* of *citta*' can either be directed outward toward manifestation (III:13) or called back to the point of restraint or *nirodha* (III:9), which, when applied consistently, leads to the *pariṇāma* of *samādhi* (III:11). In the fourth section, again we find the same themes echoed. Things arise because of the stabilization of *pariṇāma* (IV:2, 14); the goal of Yoga is the reversal of this process, the conclusion of *pariṇāma* (IV:32, 33) wherein the compulsive generation of the world ceases.

In his interpretation of the discussion of *citta pariṇāma* in the fourth section, Vyāsa, the fifth-century commentator, interprets Patañjali as arguing against the Buddhist Yogācāra school, which has been seen by some as pure idealism, negating the reality of the manifest world. However, in our reading of the text, we do not see Patañjali explicitly polemicizing against such a view but merely advancing the Sāṃkhya perspective that all things stem from *prakṛti* through *pariṇāma*, that *pariṇāma* can be directed to increasingly subtle levels through *pratiprasava*, and that the culmination of this process results in the total purification of the *citta*. This yields a state of *sattva* that is characterized as higher awareness, steadfastness in own form, *kaivalyam* (III:34).

As in Sāṃkhya, it is noted that *prakṛti* cannot operate without *puruṣa* (IV:3); it needs a witness for whom to perform. The performance is played out through a mistaken self-identity (IV:4) but is only possible because of the unchanging witness (IV:18). Both are necessary; neither is sufficient unto itself, as stated in the Sāṃkhya analogy of the lame assisting the blind. Though they work together, they remain essentially separate.

Despite any attempts to limit or claim the power of consciousness by way of identification, the Self can never be seen (IV:21). It is only through the suspension of all identification by the process of *pratiprasava* that *kaivalyam* takes place. The process of identification is inseparable from that of afflicted action; identity is the second of the five afflictions that bind one to action. Both stem from residues in the *citta* that cause repeated manifestation. The explanation of karma in this section (IV:7–11) asserts that experience is dependent on the *citta's* structures. When the mind is returned to its origin in *prakṛti*, and when highest *sattva* is achieved (IV:25), the generation of the false sense of self ceases. This purity guarantees nonafflicted action (IV:30), with the culmination of Yoga given in the final *sūtra* as:

> The return to the origin of the *guṇas*,
> emptied of their purpose for *puruṣa*,
> is *kaivalyam*, the steadfastness in own form,
> and the power of higher awareness.

OBSERVATIONS ON THE STRUCTURE OF THE TEXT

Having examined the thread that in our reading binds the text together, we will now note those aspects of the text that scholars have found particularly noncohesive. These issues may be divided as follows: (1) the date of the text, (2) the plurality of practices included, (3) the various descriptions of the goal, (4) the presence of Buddhist and Jaina elements, (5) the position of some that there are multiple texts contained in the *Yoga Sūtra*.

First, let us begin with the dating of the text. Two contemporary scholars of Yoga vary by as much as five hundred years in their placing of the date. Georg Feuerstein claims it "is a product of the third century A.D.,"[5] while T. S. Rukmani, following S. N. Dasgupta, states that the date "can be accepted as between the second century B.C. and the first century A.D.,"[6] thus allowing for a possible identification between the composer of the *Yoga Sūtra* and the grammarian of the same name. The early scholars Jacobi, Keith, and Poussin assent to the later date; Dasgupta thinks that the first three sections were early and that the last one is a later accretion.[7] From my reading of the text, as noted earlier in the discussion of subtilization, I see continuity throughout. However, for reasons detailed below, I would support the notion that Patañjali flourished after the popularization of various Yoga techniques practiced by diverse schools, Buddhist, Brahmanical, and Jaina. As Eliade has stated, "they are not his discoveries, not those of his time; they had been first tested many centuries before him."[8] Gerald Larson, in the Yoga volume of the *Encyclopedia of Indian Philosophies*, states that Yoga is "India's intellectual chameleon" and that it "arises out of an older Sāṃkhya environment . . . in direct polemical dialogue with the Abhidharma Buddhist[s]."[9]

In addition to the plurality of practices mentioned in the *Yoga Sūtra*, Yoga is described in various places throughout the text with often quite different characteristics. In the first section, it is described as "restraint of the fluctuations of the mind" (I:2), as "a jewel assuming the color of any near object, with unity among grasper, grasping, and grasped" (I:41), as "clarity of authentic self" (I:47), and as "seedless" (I:51). In the second section, it is described as the disappearance of the seen (II:21, 22), leaving the pure seer (II:20). Mention is made in the third section of the purity of *sattva* as equal to that of the *puruṣa* (III: 35, 49, 55), which is said to be the same as *kaivalyam*. And in the fourth and final section, several descriptions of yogic attainments are found: "discriminative discernment" and "cloud of *dharma samādhi*" (IV:29), "cessation of afflicted action" (IV:30), "the end of *parniṇāma*" (IV:33), and "the return to the origin of the *guṇas*" "steadfastness in own form," and "power of higher awareness" (IV:34). As is evident, concern for the culmination of Yoga pervades the text; this is not a narrative where the climax is saved and not revealed until the conclusion. Furthermore, it is difficult to reconcile the technically precise requirement that all things be restrained (*nirodha*) with the more poetic proclamation of cloud of *dharma samādhi* and higher awareness (*citi śakti*). Are these competing goals or different descriptions of the same experience? Are they contradictory? Or perhaps, as we will explore at the end of this introduction, Patañjali has purposefully presented an artful array of possibilities.

Traces of both Buddhism and Jainism are found in the *Yoga Sūtra* as noted in prior chapters. Many of the practices mentioned undoubtedly have their roots in the classical Hindu, specifically Upaniṣadic-Brahmanical, tradition, reflecting prescriptions from the *Kaṭha* and *Śvetāśvatara Upaniṣads*, the *Mahābhārata*, and other texts. However, while retaining a Sāṃkhya-oriented philosophical position, the *Yoga Sūtra* does incorporate practices that must have been identifiably associated with Buddhism and Jainism at the time of Patañjali. Several scholars have pointed out the parallels between Buddhist Yoga and the Yoga of Patañjali, including Sénart, Lindquist, la Vallée Poussin, Eliade, and others. Eliade accepts Sénart's assessment that Buddhism arose "on the terrain of Yoga."[10] However, this "terrain" must refer to the pre-Patañjali prototradition, probably older than any institutionalized religion for which we have historical records, since the earliest date that scholars have advanced for the *Yoga Sūtra* is 200 BCE to 100 CE, and even after, postdating Buddhism by at least three and possibly eight centuries.

The parallels cited by Poussin and others are so pervasive in Buddhist literature and so absent from the traditional "Hindu" literature that it cannot be denied that Patañjali chose to include yogic practices from Buddhist manuals. The most obvious of these include the five practices listed in I:20 of *śraddhā, vīrya, smṛti, samādhi, prajñā*; the four *brahmavihāra* widely applied by Buddhists cited in *sūtra* I:33, and the parallel definitions of ignorance (*avidyā*) and suffering (*duḥkha*) in II:5 and II:15, respectively. Similarities can also be seen between the four *dhyānas* in Buddhism and the *samādhis* listed by Patañjali, the reference to seven *prajñās* [II:27], and so forth.[11] Keith even goes so far as to state that "it is only the light of the Mahāyāna (Buddhist) doctrine of *tathāgatagarbha* and the Yogācāra use of the term *bīja* in this connection, that we can understand the statement of *īśvara* in *Yoga Sūtra* I:25. In him the germ of the omniscient reaches its highest state!"[12]

The scholarship about the relationship between Buddhism and the *Yoga Sūtras* has been extensive. Less attention has been given to Jaina influence in the various analytical studies of the text. Three teachings closely associated with Jainism appear in Yoga: the doctrine of *karma*, described as colorful in both traditions; the *telos* of isolation (*kevala* in Jainism, *kaivalyam* in Yoga); and the practice of nonviolence (*ahiṃsā*). In fact, the entire list of the five *yamas* (II:30) is identical with the ethical precepts taught by Mahāvira, the contemporary of the Buddha who established the foundations of modern Jainism.

The various pieces of evidence given above have caused modern Western scholars to speculate that the text as it now appears is in fact a patchwork. The absence of a perceived architectonic has led to many attempts to dissect the text into the original sections that had been sewn together by Patañjali. Georg Feuerstein sees two yogic texts melded together: a "Kriyā Yoga Text" extending from I:1 to II:27 and from III:3 or 4 to IV:34, interrupted by an "Aṣṭāṅga Yoga Text," which extends from II:28 to III:2 or 3 and also picks up *sūtra* III:55. Hence, he would include all the practices of the first *pāda* as part of Kriyā Yoga, along with the discussion of *kaivalyam* in the fourth *pāda*.[13] Deussen claims that the *Yoga Sūtra* was patched together from five different texts, dividing the first *pāda* into two sections, isolating the Kriyā Yoga section of the second *pāda*, extending Aṣṭāṅga Yoga through the third *pāda*, and regarding the material in the Kaivalyam *pāda* as an independent text.[14] Hauer similarly postulates five texts, which he dubs *Nirodha* (I:1–22), *Īśvarapraṇidhāna* (I:23–51), *Kriyā-Yoga* (II:1–27), *Yoga-aṅga* (II:28–III:55), and *Nirmāṇa-citta* (IV:1–34).[15] Frauwallner sees a distinctive difference between the *nirodha* form of Yoga described in *pāda* 1 which he claims calls for the suppression of "every mental activity" and the eight-limbed Yoga of *pāda* 2, which he asserts "seeks to raise the capacity for knowledge to the highest."[16] Dasgupta, however, remains unperturbed by what might be considered inconsistencies in the text, referring to it as a "masterly and systematic compilation."[17] In any case, it is clear from purely internal evidence that the text involves the overly and interweaving of various yogic traditions which became harmonized not by inherent consistency but through their joint appearance in Patañjali.

NONVIOLENT PHILOSOPHY AND THE *YOGA SŪTRA*

The Vedic and early Upaniṣadic texts do not emphasize *ahiṃsā*. The *Ṛg Veda* uses the word only to implore the gods, specifically Indra, not to hurt the people.[18] The *Chāndogya Upaniṣad* lists nonviolence (*ahiṃsā*) as a gift to be presented to the priests, along with austerity, alms-giving, uprightness, and truthfulness;[19] this early Upaniṣad also mentions "harmlessness" (*ahimsant*) toward all things elsewhere than at holy places (*tīrtha*)" as one of the prerequisites for not being born again.[20] It is not until the later *Dharma Śāstra* material that we find specific references to *ahiṃsā* similar to those mentioned in the *Yoga Sūtra*[21]: Gonda dates these materials at between 600 BCE and the second century BCE, contemporary with the rise of Buddhism and the later Upaniṣads, but not older than Jainism.[22]

Ahiṃsā is referred to in the *Yoga Sūtra* in two places: once, in II:30, as the first of the *yamas* and again in II:35, when it is stated that when one is established in *ahiṃsā* then all surrounding enmity ceases. Vyāsa, however, emphasizes that all other disciplines are based in *ahiṃsā* and that noninjuriousness (*anabhidroha*) is to be practiced toward all living beings (*sarva-bhūta*) in all respects (*sarvathā*) and for all times (*sarvadā*). Patañjali himself uses the Jaina term *mahāvrata* (from the *Ācārāṅga Sūtra*) to further describe the practice of the *yamas*, stating that they are to be unrestricted by caste (*jāti*), place (*deśa*), time (*kāla*), or circumstance (*samaya*) (II:31). This *sūtra* undeniably places the yogin outside of the sacrificial Brahmanical framework and further strengthens the evidence of "exterior" influence on the text.

At this juncture, I wish to turn to a discussion of the methodology employed by Patañjali. We have seen that the *Yoga Sūtra* consists of a concatenation of distinct schools of Yoga that can be variously designated as *Nirodha Yoga*, *Samādhi Yoga*, *Kriyā Yoga*, *Aṣṭāṅga Yoga*, and so on, along with practices drawn from the Buddhists, Jainas, and perhaps others. However, I hesitate to describe Patañjali's process with the term *syncretism*, defined by Berling as a "borrowing, affirmation, or integration of the concepts, symbols or practices of one religious tradition into another by a process of selection and reconciliation."[23] Patañjali simply does not reconcile or mathematically "total out" the diverse practices he mentions; as Frauwallner has written, "The *Yoga Sūtra* of Patañjali is composed of different constituents or elements which, in no way, give a uniform homogenous picture."[24] However, the text has been immensely successful, surviving nearly two millennia.

To understand Patañjali's success, we return to our opening statement that the text is one not of positions but of practices. The *telos* of the various practices, whether described as *nirodha*, *samādhi*, or *kaivalyam*, lies beyond language, beyond intellectual speculation, and this experience, which is itself beyond syncretism or synthesis, holds the text together. Patañjali does not advance one practice above another. The practice that is effective is the one to be used, as indicated in *sūtra* II:39, *yathā abhimatadhyānād vā* (or from meditation as desired). Patañjali provides us with an important clue regarding his method in the first *pāda*. When listing all the practices to be undertaken, he uses the connecting particle *vā*, which can be construed as "or," rather than *ca*, which means "and." Like the terms used to describe an electron vacillate according to context from wave to particle, so the practices expounded by Patañjali stand in juxtaposition and in complementarity; although they ultimately refer to the same experience, they cannot be said to be identical.

Max Mueller talked about a similar process when trying to cope with the multiplicity of gods in the *Ṛg Veda*, and invented a term, *henotheism*, described as follows: "To identify Indra, Agni, and Varuna is one thing, it is syncretism; to address either Indra or Agni or Varuna, as for the time being the only god in existence with an entire forgetfulness of all other gods, is quite another; and it was this phase so fully developed in the hymns of the Veda, which I wished to mark definitely by a name of its own, calling it henotheism."[25] This method is similar to that employed in the *Bhagavad Gītā* where again and again Arjuna asks Krishna for one truth, and again and again Krishna offers Arjuna yet another perspective, another chapter, another Yoga. Each view, whether that of a god being sacrificed to or a yogic discipline being practiced, is given life as long as it proves effective. Multiplicity is the rule, without one perspective, one god, or one Yoga gaining ascendancy. The culmination of Yoga comes when all differentiations are obliterated in *nirodha* or *samādhi*. This is not to say that all life ends but that a state of being is attained wherein, quoting *sūtra* I:41, "like a clear jewel, one has unity among the grasper, grasping, and grasped," a state of Yoga wherein totality is embraced without denying multiplicity.

This returns us again to the practice of *ahiṃsā*. In the *Mahābhārata*, *ahiṃsā* is extolled as the highest *dharma* and explained in terms of "not doing to another which one regards as injurious to one's own self."[26] If *ahiṃsā* is to be truly practiced, one must see others as no different than oneself, a state alluded to in the jewel metaphor used to describe the *samādhi* experience. The question may be raised, is it possible to be a philosopher, a text-maker like Patañjali, and still be a practitioner of *ahiṃsā*? Does rigorous thinking require that positions be held in opposition to those of others, a premise that violates the spirit of *ahiṃsā*? The Jainas avoided this problem from the onset by admitting that all non-Jaina positions are possibly the case (*syādvāda*) and that no words are ever totally adequate to experience (*avaktavya eva*). The *Yoga Sūtra* does not hint that Patañjali had accepted or even considered such ground rules. However, in his own fashion, the format he uses is in accord with *ahiṃsā*. Contradictions are seemingly present in the text, but judgments are not pronounced; no teaching is said to be higher or better. Differences between systems are not denied, nor are they even discussed. The method by which Patañjali presents the various Yogas is as if he becomes established in *kaivalyam*, surveying them with a dispassionate eye, seeing the possibility of each. Moreover, his method is consistent with the goal of all the various practices: a vision of noninterference wherein techniques exist in complementarity, not competition. Some have said that Patañjali has made no specific philosophical contribution in this presentation of the Yoga school. To the contrary, I suggest that his is a masterful contribution, communicated through nonjudgmentally presenting diverse practices, a methodology rooted in *ahiṃsā*, an important aspect of the culture and traditions of India.

9 *The Yoga Sūtra of Patañjali*

Continuous Text and Translation

I. SAMĀDHI PĀDA

I.1 अथ योगानुशासनम् ॥१॥
atha yogānuśāsanam
Attend to these teachings on Yoga.

I.2 योगश्चित्त वृत्ति निरोधः ॥२॥
yogaś citta vṛtti nirodhaḥ
Yoga is the restraint of the fluctuations of the mind.

I.3 तदा द्रष्टुः स्वरूपे ऽवस्थानम् ॥३॥
tadā draṣṭuḥ svarūpe 'vasthānam
Then, the Seer abides in its own form.

I.4 वृत्ति सारूप्यमितरत्र ॥४॥
vṛtti sārūpyam itaratra
Otherwise there is conformity with the fluctuations.

I.5 वृत्तयः पञ्चतय्यः क्लिष्टाक्लिष्टाः ॥५॥
vṛttayaḥ pañcatay yaḥ kliṣṭākliṣṭāḥ
Five [types of] fluctuations exist, afflicted or nonafflicted.

I.6 प्रमाण विपर्यय विकल्प निद्रा स्मृतयः ॥६॥
pramāṇa viparyaya vikalpa nidrā smṛtayaḥ
Correct cognition, error, imagining, sleep, and memory.

I.7 प्रत्यक्षानुमानागमाः प्रमाणानि ॥७॥
pratyakṣānumānāgamāḥ pramāṇāni
Correct cognitions arise from perception, inference, and truthful testimony.

I.8 विपर्ययो मिथ्या ज्ञानमतद्रूप प्रतिष्ठम् ॥८॥
viparyayo mithyā jñānam atad rūpa pratiṣṭham
Error, or false knowledge, has no foundation in form.

I.9 शब्द ज्ञानानुपाती वस्तु शून्यो विकल्पः ॥९॥
śabda jñānānupātī vastu śūnyo vikalpaḥ
Imagining is the result of words and knowledge that are empty of an object.

I.10 अभाव प्रत्ययालम्बना वृत्तिर्निद्रा ॥१०॥
abhāva pratyayālambanā vṛttir nidrā
The sleep fluctuation depends on an intention of non-becoming.

I.11 अनुभूत विषयासंप्रमोषः स्मृतिः ॥११॥
anubhūta viṣayāsaṁpramoṣaḥ smṛtiḥ
Memory recalls previously experienced conditions.

I.12 अभ्यास वैराग्याभ्यां तन्निरोधः ॥१२॥
abhyāsa vairāgyābhyāṁ tan nirodhaḥ
Restraint arises through practice and release from desire.

I.13 तत्र स्थितौ यत्नो ऽभ्यासः ॥१३॥
tatra sthitau yatno 'bhyāsaḥ
Practice requires effort and stability.

I.14 स तु दीर्घ काल नैरन्तर्य सत्कारासेवितो दृढभूमिः ॥१४॥
sa tu dīrgha kāla nairantarya satkārāsevito dṛḍha bhūmiḥ
It becomes firmly grounded when carefully attended to for a long period of time without interruption.

I.15 दृष्टानुश्रविक विषय वितृष्णस्य वशीकार संज्ञा वैराग्यम् ॥१५॥
dṛṣṭānuśravika viṣaya vitṛṣṇasya vaśīkāra saṁjñā vairāgyam
Release from desire results in the harmony of mastery in one who thirsts not for conditions seen or heard.

I.16 तत्परं पुरुष ख्यातेर्गुण वैतृष्ण्यम् ॥१६॥
tat paraṃ puruṣa khyāter guṇa vaitṛṣṇyam
That highest [release]—thirstlessness for the *guṇas*—proceeds from the discernment of *puruṣa*.

I.17 वितर्क विचारानन्दास्मितानुगमात्संप्रज्ञातः ॥१७॥
vitarka vicārānandāsmitānugamāt saṁprajñātaḥ
Awareness arises from association with deliberation, reflection, bliss, and I-am-ness.

I.18 विराम प्रत्ययाभ्यास पूर्वः संस्कार शेषो ऽन्यः ॥१८॥
virāma pratyayābhyāsa pūrvaḥ saṁskāra śeṣo 'nyaḥ
[On a more subtle level] the other [state] has *saṁskāra* only and is preceded by practice and the intention of cessation.

I.19 भव प्रत्ययो विदेह प्रकृति लयानाम् ॥१९॥
bhava pratyayo videha prakṛti layānām
The ones absorbed in *prakṛti* and free from the body still have an intention of becoming.

I.20 श्रद्धा वीर्य स्मृति समाधि प्रज्ञा पूर्वक इतरेषाम् ॥२०॥
śraddhā vīrya smṛti samādhi prajñā pūrvaka itareṣām
Of the others it is preceded by faith, energy, mindfulness, *samādhi*, and wisdom.

I.21 तीव्र संवेगानामासन्नः ॥२१॥
tīvra saṃvegānām āsannaḥ
The strongly intense ones are near.

I.22 मृदु मध्याधिमात्रत्वात्ततो ऽपि विशेषः ॥२२॥
mṛdu madhyādhimātratvāt tato 'pi viśeṣaḥ
Hence, the distinctions of mild, moderate, and ardent.

I.23 ईश्वर प्रणिधानाद्वा ॥२३॥
īśvara praṇidhānād vā
Or from dedication to *Īśvara*.

I.24 क्लेश कर्म विपाकाशयैरपरामृष्टः पुरुष विशेष ईश्वरः ॥२४॥
kleśa karma vipākāśayair aparāmṛṣṭaḥ puruṣa viśeṣa īśvaraḥ
Īśvara is a distinct *puruṣa* untouched by afflictions, actions, fruitions, or their residue.

I.25 तत्र निरतिशयम्सर्वज्ञ बीजम् ॥२५॥
tatra niratiśayam sarvajña bījam
There the seed of omniscience is unsurpassed.

I.26 स पूर्वेषामपि गुरुः कालेनानवच्छेदात् ॥२६॥
sa pūrveṣām api guruḥ kālenānavacchedāt
Due to its being unlimited by time, it is the teacher of the prior ones.

I.27 तस्य वाचकः प्रणवः ॥२७॥
tasya vācakaḥ praṇavaḥ
Its expression is *praṇava* (*oṁ*).

I.28 तज्जपस्तदर्थ भावनम् ॥२८॥
taj japas tad artha bhāvanam
Repetition of it [results in] cultivation of its purpose.

I.29 ततः प्रत्यक्चेतनाधिगमो ऽप्यन्तराया भावश्च ॥२९॥
tataḥ pratyak cetanādhigamo 'pyantarāyā bhāvaś ca
Thus, inward-consciousness is attained and obstacles do not arise.

I.30 व्याधि स्त्यान संशय प्रमादालस्याविरति भ्रान्ति दर्शनालब्ध भूमि कत्वानवस्थि तत्वानि चित्त विक्षेपास्ते ऽन्तरायाः ॥३०॥
vyādhi styāna saṃśaya pramādālasyāvirati bhrānti darśanālabdha bhūmi katvānavasthitatvāni citta vikṣepās te 'ntarāyāḥ
These obstacles, distractions of the mind, are: sickness, dullness, doubt, carelessness, laziness, sense addiction, false view, losing ground, and instability.

I.31 दुःख दौर्मनस्याङ्गमेजयत्व श्वास प्रश्वासा विक्षेप सहभुवः ॥३१॥
duḥkha daurmanasyāṅgamejayatva śvāsa praśvāsā vikṣepa sahabhuvaḥ
A suffering, despairing body and unsteady inhalation and exhalation accompany the distractions.

I.32 तत्प्रतिषेधार्थमेक तत्त्वाभ्यासः ॥३२॥
tat pratiṣedhārtham eka tattvābhyāsaḥ
For the purpose of counteracting them, there is one principle: practice.

I.33 मैत्री करुणा मुदितोपेक्षाणां सुख दुःख पुण्यापुण्य विषयाणां भावनातश्चित्त प्रसादनम् ॥३३॥
maitrī karuṇā muditopekṣāṇāṃ sukha duḥkha puṇyāpuṇya viṣayāṇāṃ bhāvanātaś citta prasādanam
Clarification of the mind [results] from the cultivation of friendliness toward the happy, compassion for those who suffer, sympathetic joy for the good, and equanimity toward those who lack goodness.

I.34 प्रच्छर्दन विधारणाभ्यां वा प्राणस्य ॥३४॥
pracchardana vidhāraṇābhyāṃ vā prāṇasya
Or by expulsion and retention of breath.

I.35 विषयवती वा प्रवृत्तिरुत्पन्ना मनसः स्थिति निबन्धनी ॥३५॥
viṣayavatī vā pravṛttir utpannā manasaḥ sthiti nibandhanī
Or steady binding of the mind-power arises in the activity of being absorbed with a condition.

I.36 विशोका वा ज्योतिष्मती ॥३६॥
viśokā vā jyotiṣmatī
Or having sorrowless illumination.

I.37 वीत राग विषयं वा चित्तम् ॥३७॥
vīta rāga viṣayaṃ vā cittam
Or [in a] mind in a condition free from attachment.

I.38 स्वप्न निद्रा ज्ञानालम्बनं वा ॥३८॥
svapna nidrā jñānālambanaṃ vā
Or resting on a knowledge [derived] from dream or sleep.

I.39 यथाभिमत ध्यानाद्वा ॥३९॥
yathābhimata dhyānād vā
Or from meditation as desired.

I.40 परमाणु परम महत्त्वान्तो ऽस्य वशीकारः ॥४०॥
paramāṇu parama mahattvānto 'sya vaśīkāraḥ
Mastery of it extends from the smallest to the greatest.

I.41 क्षीण वृत्तेरभिजातस्येव मणेर्ग्रहीतृ ग्रहण ग्राह्येषु तत्स्थ तदञ्जनता समापत्तिः ॥४१॥
kṣīṇa vṛtter abhijātasyeva maṇer grahītṛ grahaṇa grāhyeṣu tat stha tad añjanatā samāpattiḥ
[The accomplished mind] of diminished fluctuations, like a precious (or clear) jewel assuming the color of any near object, has unity among grasper, grasping, and grasped.

I.42 तत्र शब्दार्थ ज्ञान विकल्पैः संकीर्णा सवितर्का समापत्तिः ॥४२॥
tatra śabdārtha jñāna vikalpaiḥ saṁkīrṇā savitarkā samāpattiḥ
Savitarkā unity is the commingling by imagining of word, purpose and knowledge.

I.43 स्मृति परिशुद्धौ स्वरूप शून्येवार्थ मात्र निर्भासा निर्वितर्का ॥४३॥
smṛti pariśuddhau svarūpa śūnyevārtha mātra nirbhāsā nirvitarkā
Nirvitarkā is when memory is purified, as if emptied of its own form and the purpose alone shines forth.

I.44 एतयैव सविचारा निर्विचारा च सूक्ष्म विषया व्याख्याता ॥४४॥
etayaiva savicārā nirvicārā ca sūkṣma viṣayā vyākhyātā
Similarly explained are *savicārā* and *nirvicārā*, which are subtle conditions,

I.45 सूक्ष्म विषयत्वं चालिङ्ग पर्यवसानम् ॥४५॥
sūkṣma viṣayatvaṁ cāliṅga paryavasānam
And the subtle condition terminates in the undesignated.

I.46 ता एव सबीजः समाधिः ॥४६॥
tā eva sabījaḥ samādhiḥ
These are *samādhi* with seed.

I.47 निर्विचार वैशारद्ये ऽध्यात्म प्रसादः ॥४७॥
nirvicāra vaiśāradye 'dhyātma prasādaḥ
In skill with *nirvicārā*, clarity of authentic self arises.

I.48 ऋतम्भरा तत्र प्रज्ञा ॥४८॥
ṛtambharā tatra prajñā
There the wisdom is *ṛtaṃ*-bearing.

I.49 श्रुतानुमान प्रज्ञाभ्यामन्य विषया विशेषार्थत्वात् ॥४९॥
śrutānumāna prajñābhyām anya viṣayā viśeṣārthatvāt
Its condition is different from heard or inferred knowledge because of its distinct purpose.

I.50 तज्जः संस्कारो ऽन्य संस्कार प्रतिबन्धी ॥५०॥
taj jaḥ saṃskāro 'nya saṃskāra pratibandhī
The *saṃskāra* born of it restricts other *saṃskāras*.

I.51 तस्यापि निरोधे सर्व निरोधान्निर्बीजः समाधिः ॥५१॥
tasyāpi nirodhe sarva nirodhān nirbījaḥ samādhiḥ
With even that restricted, everything is restricted and that is seedless *samādhi*.

II. Sādhana Pāda

II.1 तपः स्वाध्यायेश्वर प्रणिधानानि क्रिया योगः ॥१॥
tapaḥ svādhyāyeśvara praṇidhānāni kriyā yogaḥ
Austerity, self-study, and dedication to *Īśvara* are Kriyā Yoga.

II.2 समाधि भावनार्थः क्लेश तनूकरणार्थश्च ॥२॥
samādhi bhāvanārthaḥ kleśa tanūkaraṇārthaś ca
[One engages in Kriyā Yoga] for the purpose of cultivating *samādhi* and diminishing the afflictions.

II.3 अविद्यास्मिता राग द्वेषाभिनिवेशाः क्लेशाः ॥३॥
avidyāsmitā rāga dveṣābhiniveśāḥ kleśāḥ
Ignorance, I-am-ness, attraction, aversion, and desire for continuity are the afflictions.

II.4 अविद्या क्षेत्रमुत्तरेषां प्रसुप्त तनु विच्छिन्नोदाराणाम् ॥४॥
avidyā kṣetram uttareṣāṁ prasupta tanu vicchinnodārāṇām
Ignorance is the cause of the others, whether dormant, diminished, interrupted, or fully active.

II.5 अनित्याशुचि दुःखानात्मसु नित्य शुचि सुखात्मख्यातिरविद्या ॥५॥
anityāśuci duḥkhānātmasu nitya śuci sukhātmakhyātir avidyā
Ignorance is seeing the non-eternal as eternal, the impure as pure, suffering as pleasure, and the non-self as self.

II.6 दृग्दर्शन शक्त्योरेकात्मतेवास्मिता ॥६॥
dṛg darśana śaktyor ekātmatevāsmitā
I-am-ness is when the two powers of Seer and Seen [appear] as a single self.

II.7 सुखानुशयी रागः ॥७॥
sukhānuśayī rāgaḥ
Attraction is clinging to pleasure.

II.8 दुःखानुशयी द्वेषः ॥८॥
duḥkhānuśayī dveṣaḥ
Aversion is clinging to suffering.

II.9 स्वरसवाही विदुषो ऽपि तथा रूढो ऽभिनिवेशः ॥९॥
svarasavāhī viduṣo 'pi tathā rūḍho 'bhiniveśaḥ
Desire for continuity, arising even among the wise, is sustained by self-essence.

II.10 ते प्रतिप्रसव हेयाः सूक्ष्माः ॥१०॥
te pratiprasava heyāḥ sūkṣmāḥ
These subtle [afflictions] are to be avoided by a return to the origin.

II.11 ध्यान हेयास्तद् वृत्तयः ॥११॥
dhyāna heyās tad vṛttayaḥ
The fluctuations [generated by those afflictions] are to be avoided by meditation.

II.12 क्लेश मूलः कर्माशयो दृष्टादृष्ट जन्म वेदनीयः ॥१२॥
kleśa mūlaḥ karmāśayo dṛṣṭādṛṣṭa janma vedanīyaḥ
The residue of karma, rooted in affliction, is felt in seen or unseen existence.

II.13 सति मूले तद्विपाको जात्यायुर्भोगाः ॥१३॥
sati mūle tad vipāko jāty āyur bhogāḥ
While the root exists, there is fruition of it as birth, duration, and experience.

II.14 ते ह्लाद परिताप फलाः पुण्यापुण्य हेतुत्वात् ॥१४॥
te hlāda paritāpa phalāḥ puṇyāpuṇya hetutvāt
These fruits are joyful or painful according to whether the causes are meritorious or demeritorious.

II.15 परिणाम ताप संस्कार दुःखैर्गुण वृत्ति विरोधाच्च दुःखमेव सर्वं विवेकिनः ॥१५॥
pariṇāma tāpa saṁskāra duḥkhair guṇa vṛtti virodhāc ca duḥkhaṁ eva sarvaṁ vivekinaḥ
For the discriminating one, all is suffering, due to the conflict of the fluctuations of the *guṇas* and by the sufferings due to *pariṇāma*, sorrow, and *saṃskāra*.

II.16 हेयं दुःखमनागतम् ॥१६॥
heyaṁ duḥkham anāgatam
The suffering yet to come is to be avoided.

II.17 द्रष्टृ दृश्ययोः संयोगो हेय हेतुः ॥१७॥
draṣṭṛ dṛśyayoḥ saṁyogo heya hetuḥ
The cause of what is to be avoided is the confusion of the Seer with the Seen.

II.18 प्रकाश क्रिया स्थिति शीलं भूतेन्द्रियात्मकं भोगापवर्गार्थं दृश्यम् ॥१८॥
prakāśa kriyā sthiti śīlaṁ bhūtendriyātmakaṁ bhogāpavargārthaṁ dṛśyam
The Seen has the qualities of light, activity, and inertia, consists of the elements and the senses, and has the purposes of experience and liberation.

II.19 विशेषाविशेष लिङ्ग मात्रालिङ्गानि गुण पर्वाणि ॥१९॥
viśeṣāviśeṣa liṅga mātrāliṅgāni guṇa parvāṇi
The distinct, the indistinct, the designator, and the unmanifest are the divisions of the *guṇas*.

II.20 द्रष्टा दृशिमात्रः शुद्धो ऽपि प्रत्ययानुपश्यः ॥२०॥
draṣṭā dṛśimātraḥ śuddho 'pi pratyayānupaśyaḥ
The Seer only sees; though pure, it appears intentional.

II.21 तदर्थ एव दृश्यस्यात्मा ॥२१॥
tad artha eva dṛśyasyātmā
The nature of the Seen is only for the purpose of that (*puruṣa*).

II.22 कृतार्थं प्रति नष्टमप्यनष्टं तदन्य साधारणत्वात् ॥२२॥
kṛtārthaṁ prati naṣṭam apy anaṣṭaṁ tad anya sādhāraṇatvāt
When [its] purpose is done, [the Seen] disappears; otherwise it does not disappear due to being common to others.

II.23 स्व स्वामि शक्त्योः स्वरूपोपलब्धि हेतुः संयोगः ॥२३॥
sva svāmi śaktyoḥ svarūpopalabdhi hetuḥ saṁyogaḥ
Confusion (*saṃyoga*) results when one perceives the two powers of owner [*puruṣa*] and owned [*prakṛti*] as (one) self form.

II.24 तस्य हेतुरविद्या ॥२४॥
tasya hetur avidyā
The cause of it is ignorance.

II.25 तदभावात्संयोगाभावो हानं तद् दृशेः कैवल्यम् ॥२५॥
tad abhāvāt saṁyogābhāvo hānaṁ tad dṛśeḥ kaivalyam
From the absence [of ignorance], confusion ceases; [this is] the escape, the isolation from the Seen.

II.26 विवेक ख्यातिरविप्लवा हानोपायः ॥२६॥
viveka khyātir aviplavā hānopāyaḥ
The means of escape is unfaltering discriminative discernment.

II.27 तस्य सप्तधा प्रान्त भूमिः प्रज्ञा ॥२७॥
tasya saptadhā prānta bhūmiḥ prajñā
The preparatory ground for this wisdom is sevenfold.

II.28 योगाङ्गानुष्ठानादशुद्धि क्षये ज्ञान दीप्तिरा विवेक ख्यातेः ॥२८॥
yogāṅgānuṣṭhānād aśuddhi kṣaye jñāna dīptir ā viveka khyāteḥ
From following the limbs of Yoga, which destroy impurity, the light of knowledge arises, leading to discriminative discernment.

II.29 यम नियमासन प्राणायाम प्रत्याहार धारणा ध्यान समाधयो ऽष्टावङ्गानि ॥२९॥
yama niyamāsana prāṇāyāma pratyāhāra dhāraṇā dhyāna samādhayo 'ṣṭāv aṅgāni
Precepts, observances, postures, control of breath, inwardness, concentration, meditation, and *samādhi* are the eight limbs.

II.30 अहिंसा सत्यास्तेय ब्रह्मचर्यापरिग्रहा यमाः ॥३०॥
ahiṁsā satyāsteya brahmacaryāparigrahā yamāḥ
The precepts are non-violence, truthfulness, not stealing, sexual restraint, and non-possession.

II.31 जाति देश काल समयानवच्छिन्नाः सार्व भौमा महाव्रतम् ॥३१॥
jāti deśa kāla samayānavacchinnāḥ sārva bhaumā mahāvratam
When not limited by birth, place, time, or circumstance in all occasions [these constitute] the great vow.

II.32 शौच सन्तोष तपः स्वाध्यायेश्वर प्रणिधानानि नियमाः ॥३२॥
śauca santoṣa tapaḥ svādhyāyeśvara praṇidhānāni niyamāḥ
Purity, contentment, austerity, self-study, and dedication to *Īśvara* are the observances.

II.33 वितर्क बाधने प्रतिपक्ष भावनम् ॥३३॥
vitarka bādhane pratipakṣa bhāvanam
When there is bondage due to deliberation, the cultivation of the opposite [is prescribed].

II.34 वितर्का हिंसादयः कृत कारितानुमोदिता लोभ क्रोध मोह पूर्वका मृदु मध्याधिमात्रा दुःखाज्ञानानन्त फला इति प्रतिपक्ष भावनम् ॥३४॥
vitarkā hiṁsādayaḥ kṛta kāritānumoditā lobha krodha moha pūrvakā mṛdu madhyādhimātrā duḥkhājñānānanta phalā iti pratipakṣa bhāvanam
Deliberations about violence and so forth, whether done, caused, or approved, consisting in lust, anger, or delusion, and whether mild, medium, or intense, have as their endless fruits suffering and ignorance; thus cultivation of opposites [is prescribed].

II.35 अहिंसा प्रतिष्ठायां तत्संनिधौ वैर त्यागः ॥३५॥
ahiṁsā pratiṣṭhāyāṁ tat saṁnidhau vaira tyāgaḥ
When in the presence of one established in non-violence, there is the abandonment of hostility.

II.36 सत्य प्रतिष्ठायां क्रिया फलाश्रयत्वम् ॥३६॥
satya pratiṣṭhāyāṁ kriyā phalāśrayatvam
When established in truthfulness, [there is] correspondence between action and fruit.

II.37 अस्तेय प्रतिष्ठायां सर्व रत्नोपस्थानम् ॥३७॥
asteya pratiṣṭhāyāṁ sarva ratnopasthānam
When established in nonstealing, [whatever is] present is all jewels.

II.38 ब्रह्मचर्य प्रतिष्ठायां वीर्य लाभः ॥३८॥
brahmacarya pratiṣṭhāyāṃ vīrya lābhaḥ
When established in sexual restraint, vigor is obtained.

II.39 अपरिग्रह स्थैर्ये जन्म कथंता संबोधः ॥३९॥
aparigraha sthairye janma kathaṁtā saṃbodhaḥ
When steadfast in non-possession, there is knowledge of "the how" of existence.

II.40 शौचात्स्वाङ्ग जुगुप्सा परैरसंसर्गः ॥४०॥
śaucāt svāṅga jugupsā parair asaṁsargaḥ
From purity arises dislike for one's own body and non-contact with others.

II.41 सत्त्व शुद्धि सौमनस्यैकाग्र्येन्द्रिय जयात्म दर्शन योग्यत्वानि च ॥४१॥
sattva śuddhi saumanasyaikāgryendriya jayātma darśana yogyatvāni ca
And purity of *sattva*, cheerfulness, one-pointedness, mastery of the senses, and fitness for the vision of the self [arise].

II.42 सन्तोषादनुत्तमः सुख लाभः ॥४२॥
santoṣād anuttamaḥ sukha lābhaḥ
From contentment, unsurpassed happiness is obtained.

II.43 कायेन्द्रिय सिद्धिरशुद्धि क्षयात्तपसः ॥४३॥
kāyendriya siddhir aśuddhi kṣayāt tapasaḥ
From austerity arises the destruction of impurity and the perfection of the body and the senses.

II.44 स्वाध्यायादिष्ट देवता संप्रयोगः ॥४४॥
svādhyāyād iṣṭa devatā saṁprayogaḥ
From self-study arises union with the desired deity.

II.45 समाधि सिद्धिरीश्वर प्रणिधानात् ॥४५॥
samādhi siddhir īśvara praṇidhānāt
Perfection in *samādhi* [arises] from dedication to *Īśvara*.

II.46 स्थिर सुखमासनम् ॥४६॥
sthira sukham āsanam
Āsana is steadiness and ease.

II.47 प्रयत्न शैथिल्यानन्त समापत्तिभ्याम् ॥४७॥
prayatna śaithilyānanta samāpattibhyām
From [it arises] relaxation of effort and endless unity.

II.48 ततो द्वन्द्वानभिघातः ॥४८॥
tato dvandvānabhighātaḥ
Thus, there is no assault by the pairs of opposites.

II.49 तस्मिन्सति श्वास प्रश्वासयोर्गति विच्छेदः प्राणायामः ॥४९॥
tasmin sati śvāsa praśvāsayor gati vicchedaḥ prāṇāyāmaḥ
Being in this, there is control of breath, which is the cutting off of the motion of inbreath and outbreath.

II.50 बाह्याभ्यन्तर स्तम्भ वृत्तिर्देश काल संख्याभिः परिदृष्टो दीर्घ सूक्ष्मः ॥५०॥
bāhyābhyantara stambha vṛttir deśa kāla saṁkhyābhiḥ paridṛṣṭo dīrgha sūkṣmaḥ
Its fluctuations are external, internal, and suppressed; it is observed according to time, place, number, and becomes long and subtle.

II.51 बाह्याभ्यन्तर विषयाक्षेपी चतुर्थः ॥५१॥
bāhyābhyantara viṣayākṣepī caturthaḥ
The fourth is withdrawal from external and internal conditions [of breath].

II.52 ततः क्षीयते प्रकाशावरणम् ॥५२॥
tataḥ kṣīyate prakāśāvaraṇam
Thus, the covering of light is dissolved.

II.53 धारणासु च योग्यता मनसः ॥५३॥
dhāraṇāsu ca yogyatā manasaḥ
And there is fitness of the mind-power for concentrations.

II.54 स्वविषयासंप्रयोगे चित्त स्वरूपानुकार इवेन्द्रियाणाम्प्रत्याहारः ॥५४॥
svaviṣayāsaṁprayoge citta svarūpānukāra ivendriyāṇām pratyāhāraḥ
Inwardness of the senses is the disengagement from conditions, as if in imitation of the own-form of the mind.

II.55 ततः परमा वश्यतेन्द्रियाणाम् ॥५५॥
tataḥ paramā vaśyatendriyāṇām
Then arises utmost command of the senses.

III. VIBHŪTI PĀDA

III.1 देश बन्धश्चित्तस्य धारणा ॥१॥
deśa bandhaś cittasya dhāraṇā
Concentration of the mind is [its] binding to a place.

III.2 तत्र प्रत्ययैक तानता ध्यानम् ॥२॥
tatra pratyayaika tānatā dhyānam
There, the extension of one intention is meditation.

III.3 तदेवार्थ मात्र निर्भासं स्वरूप शून्यमिव समाधिः ॥३॥
tad evārtha mātra nirbhāsaṃ svarūpa śūnyam iva samādhiḥ
When the purpose alone shines forth, as if empty of own form, that indeed is *samādhi.*

III.4 त्रयमेकत्र संयमः ॥४॥
trayam ekatra saṁyamaḥ
The unity of these three is *saṁyama.*

III.5 तज्जयात्प्रज्ञालोकः ॥५॥
taj jayāt prajñālokaḥ
From mastery of that, the splendor of wisdom.

III.6 तस्य भूमिषु विनियोगः ॥६॥
tasya bhūmiṣu viniyogaḥ
Its application [occurs] in [various stages or] grounds.

III.7 त्रयमन्तरङ्गं पूर्वेभ्यः ॥७॥
trayam antar aṅgaṁ pūrvebhyaḥ
These three inner limbs are [distinct] from the prior ones.

III.8 तदपि बहिरङ्गं निर्बीजस्य ॥८॥
tad api bahir aṅgaṁ nirbījasya
These indeed are outer limbs [in regard to] the seedless.

III.9 व्युत्थान निरोध संस्कारयोरभिभव प्रादुर्भावौ निरोध क्षण चित्तान्वयो निरोध परिणामः ॥९॥
vyutthāna nirodha saṁskārayor abhibhava prādurbhāvau nirodha kṣaṇa cittānvayo nirodha pariṇāmaḥ
[In regard to] the two *saṁskāras* of emergence and restraint, when that of appearance (emergence) is overpowered, there follows a moment of restraint in the mind; this is the *pariṇāma* of restraint.

III.10 तस्य प्रशान्त वाहिता संस्कारात् ॥१०॥
tasya praśānta vāhitā saṁskārāt
From the *saṁskāra* of this there is calm flow.

III.11 सर्वार्थतैकाग्रतयोः क्षयोदयौ चित्तस्य समाधि परिणामः ॥११॥
sarvārthataikāgratayoḥ kṣayodayau cittasya samādhi pariṇāmaḥ
When there is destruction of all objectivity and the arising of one-pointedness, the mind [has] the *pariṇāma* of *samādhi*.

III.12 ततः पुनः शान्तोदितौ तुल्य प्रत्ययौ चित्तस्यैकाग्रता परिणामः ॥१२॥
tataḥ punaḥ śāntoditau tulya pratyayau cittasyaikāgratā pariṇāmaḥ
Hence again, when there is equality between arising and quieted intentions, there is the *pariṇāma* of one-pointedness of the mind.

III.13 एतेन भूतेन्द्रियेषु धर्म लक्षणावस्था परिणामा व्याख्याताः ॥१३॥
etena bhūtendriyeṣu dharma lakṣaṇāvasthā pariṇāmā vyākhyātāḥ
By this are similarly explained the *pariṇāmas* of state, characteristic, and *dharma* amongst the elements and the senses.

III.14 शान्तोदिताव्यपदेश्य धर्मानुपाती धर्मी ॥१४॥
śāntoditāvyapadeśya dharmānupātī dharmī
The *dharma*-holder corresponds to the *dharma*, whether quieted, arisen, or undetermined (past, present, or future).

III.15 क्रमान्यत्वं परिणामान्यत्वे हेतुः ॥१५॥
kramānyatvaṁ pariṇāmānyatve hetuḥ
The cause of difference between *pariṇāmas* is the difference in the succession.

III.16 परिणाम त्रय संयमादतीतानागत ज्ञानम् ॥१६॥
pariṇāma traya saṁyamād atītānāgata jñānam
From *saṁyama* on the threefold *pariṇāmas* [there is] knowledge of past and future.

III.17 शब्दार्थ प्रत्ययानामितरेतराध्यासात्संकरस्तत्प्रविभाग संयमात्सर्व भूत रुत ज्ञानम् ॥१७॥
śabdārtha pratyayānām itaretarādhyāsāt saṁkaras tat pravibhāga saṁyamāt sarva bhūta rūta jñānam
From the overlapping here and there of word, purposes, and intentions, there is confusion. From *saṁyama* on the distinctions of them, there is knowledge of the [way of] utterance of all beings.

III.18 संस्कार साक्षात्करणात्पूर्व जाति ज्ञानम् ॥१८॥
saṁskāra sākṣāt karaṇāt pūrva jāti jñānam
From effecting perception of *saṃskāra*, there arises knowledge of previous births.

III.19 प्रत्ययस्य पर चित्त ज्ञानम् ॥१९॥
pratyayasya para citta jñānam
[Similarly, from perception of another's] intention, there is knowledge of another mind.

III.20 न च तत्सालम्बनं तस्याविषयी भूतत्वात् ॥२०॥
na ca tat sālambanaṁ tasyāviṣayī bhūtatvāt
But this is not with support because there is no condition of it in the elements.

III.21 काय रूप संयमात्तद्ग्राह्य शक्ति स्तम्भे चक्षुः प्रकाशासंप्रयोगे ऽन्तर्धानम् ॥२१॥
kāya rūpa saṁyamāt tad grāhya śakti stambhe cakṣuḥ prakāśāsaṁprayoge 'ntardhānam
From *saṁyama* on the form (*rūpa*) of the body, [there arises] the suspension of the power of what is to be grasped and the disjunction of light and the eye, resulting in concealment.

III.22 सोपक्रमं निरुपक्रमं च कर्म तत्संयमादपरान्त ज्ञानमरिष्टेभ्यो वा ॥२२॥
sopakramaṁ nirupakramaṁ ca karma tat saṁyamād aparānta jñānam ariṣṭebhyo vā
Karma is either in motion or not in motion. From *saṁyama* on this, or from natural phenomena boding misfortune, there is knowledge of death.

III.23 मैत्र्यादिषु बलानि ॥२३॥
maitry ādiṣu balāni
[By *saṁyama*] on friendliness and so forth, [corresponding] powers.

III.24 बलेषु हस्ति बलादीनि ॥२४॥
baleṣu hasti balādīni
[By *saṁyama*] on powers, the powers arise like those of an elephant, and so forth.

III.25 प्रवृत्त्यालोक न्यासात्सूक्ष्म व्यवहित विप्रकृष्ट ज्ञानम् ॥२५॥
pravṛtty āloka nyāsāt sūkṣma vyavahita viprakṛṣṭa jñānam
Due to the casting of light on a [sense] activity, there is knowledge of the subtle, concealed, and distant.

III.26 भुवन ज्ञानं सूर्ये संयमात् ॥२६॥
bhuvana jñānaṁ sūrye saṁyamāt
From *saṁyama* on the sun, [arises] knowledge of the world.

III.27 चन्द्रे तारा व्यूह ज्ञानम् ॥२७॥
candre tārā vyūha jñānam
On the moon, knowledge of the ordering of the stars.

III.28 ध्रुवे तद्गति ज्ञानम् ॥२८॥
dhruve tad gati jñānam
On the polar star, knowledge of their movement.

III.29 नाभि चक्रे काय व्यूह ज्ञानम् ॥२९॥
nābhi cakre kāya vyūha jñānam
On the navel *cakra*, knowledge of the ordering of the body.

III.30 कण्ठ कूपे क्षुत्पिपासा निवृत्तिः ॥३०॥
kaṇṭha kūpe kṣut pipāsā nivṛttiḥ
On the hollow of the throat, cessation of hunger and thirst.

III.31 कूर्म नाड्यांस्थैर्यम् ॥३१॥
kūrma nāḍyāṁ sthairyam
On the tortoise *nāḍī*, stability.

III.32 मूर्ध ज्योतिषि सिद्ध दर्शनम् ॥३२॥
mūrdha jyotiṣi siddha darśanam
On the light in the head, vision of perfected ones.

III.33 प्रातिभाद्वा सर्वम् ॥३३॥
prātibhād vā sarvam
Or from intuition, everything.

III.34 हृदये चित्त संवित् ॥३४॥
hṛdaye citta saṁvit
On the heart, understanding of the mind.

III.35 सत्त्व पुरुषयोरत्यन्तासंकीर्णयोः प्रत्ययाविशेषो भोगः परार्थत्वात्स्वार्थ संयमात्पुरुष ज्ञानम् ॥३५॥
sattva puruṣayor atyantāsaṁkīrṇayoḥ pratyayāviśeṣo bhogaḥ parārthatvāt svārtha saṁyamāt puruṣa jñānam
When there is no distinction of intention between the pure *puruṣa* and the perfect *sattva*, there is experience for the purpose of the other [*puruṣa*]; from *saṁyama* on purpose being for the self, there is knowledge of *puruṣa*.

III.36 ततः प्रातिभ श्रावण वेदनादर्शास्वाद वार्ता जायन्ते ॥३६॥
tataḥ prātibha śrāvaṇa vedanādarśāsvāda vārtā jāyante
Hence are born intuitive hearing, touching, seeing, tasting, and smelling.

III.37 ते समाधावुपसर्गा व्युत्थाने सिद्धयः ॥३७॥
te samādhāv upasargā vyutthāne siddhayaḥ
These are impediments to *samādhi*; in emergence (world production), they are perfections.

III.38 बन्ध कारण शैथिल्यात्प्रचार संवेदनाच्च चित्तस्य पर शरीरावेशः ॥३८॥
bandha kāraṇa śaithilyāt pracāra saṁvedanāc ca cittasya para śarīrāveśaḥ
From the relaxation of the cause of bondage and from the perception of a manifestation, there is an entering of mind into another embodiment.

III.39 उदान जयाज्जल पङ्क कण्टकादिष्वसङ्गः उत्क्रान्तिश्च ॥३९॥
udāna jayāj jala paṅka kaṇṭakādiṣv asaṅga utkrāntiś ca
From mastery of the upbreath, there is nonattachment among water, mud, and thorns, etc., and a rising above.

III.40 समान जयाज्ज्वलनम् ॥४०॥
samāna jayāj jvalanam
From mastery of the *samāna*, there is radiance.

III.41 श्रोत्राकाशयोः संबन्ध संयमाद्दिव्यम्श्रोत्रम् ॥४१॥
śrotrākāśayoḥ saṁbandha saṁyamād divyam śrotram
From *saṁyama* on the connection between the ear and space, [there arises] the divine ear.

III.42 कायाकाशयोः संबन्ध संयमाल्लघु तूल समापत्तेश्चाकाश गमनम् ॥४२॥
kāyākāśayoḥ saṁbandha saṁyamāl laghu tūla samāpatteś cākāśa gamanam
From *saṁyama* on the connection between the body and space, and from unity with the lightness of cotton, there is movement through space.

III.43 बहिरकल्पितावृत्तिर्महाविदेहा ततः प्रकाशावरण क्षयः ॥४३॥
bahir akalpitā vṛttir mahā videhā tataḥ prakāśāvaraṇa kṣayaḥ
An outer, genuine fluctuation results in freedom from the body; hence the covering of light is destroyed.

III.44 स्थूल स्वरूप सूक्ष्मान्वयार्थवत्त्व संयमाद् भूत जयः ॥४४॥
sthūla svarūpa sūkṣmānvayārthavattva saṁyamād bhūta jayaḥ
From *saṁyama* on the significance and connection of the subtle and the own form of the gross, there is mastery over the elements.

III.45 ततो ऽणिमादि प्रादुर्भावः काय संपत्तद्धर्मानभिघातश्च ॥४५॥
tato 'ṇimādi prādurbhāvaḥ kāya saṁpat tad dharmānabhighātaś ca
Hence arises the appearance of minuteness and so forth, perfection of the body, and unassailability of its *dharma*.

III.46 रूप लावण्य बल वज्र संहननत्वानि काय संपत् ॥४६॥
rūpa lāvaṇya bala vajra saṁhananatvāni kāya saṁpat
Perfection of the body is beauty of form, strength, and adamantine stability.

III.47 ग्रहण स्वरूपास्मितान्वयार्थवत्त्व संयमादिन्द्रिय जयः ॥४७॥
grahaṇa svarūpāsmitānvayārthavattva saṁyamād indriya jayaḥ
From *saṁyama* on grasping, own form, I-am-ness, their connection, and their significance, there is mastery over the sense organs.

III.48 ततो मनो जवित्वं विकरण भावः प्रधान जयश्च ॥४८॥
tato mano javitvaṁ vikaraṇa bhāvaḥ pradhāna jayaś ca
Hence, there is swiftness of the mind-power, a state of being beyond the senses, and mastery over the *pradhāna*.

III.49 सत्त्व पुरुषान्यता ख्याति मात्रस्य सर्व भावाधिष्ठातृत्वं सर्व ज्ञातृत्वं च ॥४९॥
sattva puruṣānyatā khyāti mātrasya sarva bhāvādhiṣṭhātṛtvaṁ sarva jñātṛtvaṁ ca
Only from the discernment of the difference between *sattva* and *puruṣa*, there is sovereignty over all states of being and knowledge of all.

III.50 तद्वैराग्यादपि दोष बीज क्षये कैवल्यम् ॥५०॥
tad vairāgyād api doṣa bīja kṣaye kaivalyam
Due to release from even this, in the destruction of the seed of this impediment, arises *kaivalyam*.

III.51 स्थान्युपनिमन्त्रणे सङ्गस्मयाकरणम्पुनरनिष्ट प्रसङ्गात् ॥५१॥
sthāny upanimantraṇe saṅga smayā karaṇaṃ punar aniṣṭa prasaṅgāt
There is no cause for attachment and pride upon the invitation of those well established, because of repeated association with the undesirable.

III.52 क्षण तत्क्रमयोः संयमाद्विवेकजं ज्ञानम् ॥५२॥
kṣaṇa tat kramayoḥ saṁyamād vivekajaṁ jñānam
From *saṁyama* on the moment and its succession, there is knowledge born of discrimination.

III.53 जाति लक्षण देशैरन्यतानवच्छेदात्तुल्ययोस्ततः प्रतिपत्तिः ॥५३॥
jāti lakṣaṇa deśair anyatānavacchedāt tulyayos tataḥ pratipattiḥ
Hence, there is the ascertainment of two things that are similar, due to their not being limited (made separate) by differences of birth, designation, and place.

III.54 तारकं सर्व विषयं सर्वथा विषयमक्रमं चेति विवेकजं ज्ञानम् ॥५४॥
tārakaṁ sarva viṣayaṁ sarvathā viṣayam akramaṁ ceti vivekajaṁ jñānam
The knowledge born of discrimination is said to be liberating, [inclusive of] all conditions and all times, and nonsuccessive.

III.55 सत्त्व पुरुषयोः शुद्धि साम्ये कैवल्यम् ॥५५॥
sattva puruṣayoḥ śuddhi sāmye kaivalyam
In the sameness of purity between *sattva* and the *puruṣa*, there is *kaivalyam*.

IV. KAIVALYA PĀDA

IV.1 जन्मौषधि मन्त्र तपः समाधि जाः सिद्धयः ॥१॥
janmauṣadhi mantra tapaḥ samādhi jāḥ siddhayaḥ
Perfections are born due to birth, drugs, mantra, austerity, or *samādhi*.

IV.2 जात्यन्तर परिणामः प्रकृत्यापूरात् ॥२॥
jāty antara pariṇāmaḥ prakṛty āpūrāt
From the flooding of *prakṛti*, arises *pariṇāma* into other births.

IV.3 निमित्तमप्रयोजकं प्रकृतीनां वरण भेदस्तु ततः क्षेत्रिकवत् ॥३॥
nimittam aprayojakaṁ prakṛtīnāṁ varaṇa bhedas tu tataḥ kṣetrikavat
The cause [of this flooding that results in experiences] is breakage in the enclosure of *prakṛtis*, as when a farmer [irrigates his fields]. [Experience] is not caused by the "initiator."

IV.4 निर्माण चित्तान्यस्मिता मात्रात् ॥४॥
nirmāṇa cittāny asmitā mātrāt
The fabricating minds arise only from I-am-ness.

IV.5 प्रवृत्ति भेदे प्रयोजकं चित्तं एकमनेकेषाम् ॥५॥
pravṛtti bhede prayojakaṁ cittaṁ ekam anekeṣām
The "initiator" is the one mind among many that is distinct from activity.

IV.6 तत्र ध्यान जमनाशयम् ॥६॥
tatra dhyāna jam anāśayam
Therein, what is born of meditation is without residue.

IV.7 कर्माशुक्लाकृष्णं योगिनस्त्रिविधमितरेषाम् ॥७॥
karmāśuklākṛṣṇaṁ yoginas trividham itareṣām
The action of a yogi is neither white nor black; that of others is threefold.

IV.8 ततस्तद्विपाकानुगुणानामेवाभिव्यक्तिर्वासनानाम् ॥८॥
tatas tad vipākānuguṇānām evābhivyaktir vāsanānām
Hence, the manifestation of habit patterns thus corresponds to the fruition of that (*karma*).

IV.9 जाति देश काल व्यवहितानामप्यानन्तर्यं स्मृति संस्कारयोरेक रूपत्वात् ॥९॥
jāti deśa kāla vyavahitānāṁ apy ānantaryaṁ smṛti saṁskārayor eka rūpatvāt
Because memory and *saṁskāra* are of one form, there is a link even among births, places, and times that are concealed.

IV.10 तासामनादित्वं चाशिषो नित्यत्वात् ॥१०॥
tāsām anāditvaṁ cāśiṣo nityatvāt
And there is no beginning of these, due to the perpetuity of desire.

IV.11 हेतु फलाश्रयालम्बनैः संगृहीतत्वादेषामभावे तदभावः ॥११॥
hetu phalāśrayālambanaiḥ saṁgṛhītatvād eṣām abhāve tad abhāvaḥ
Because they are held together by causes, results, correspondences, and supports, when these [go into] nonbeing, [there is the] nonbeing of them (*saṁskāras*).

IV.12 अतीतानागतं स्वरूपतो ऽस्त्यध्व भेदाद्धर्माणाम् ॥१२॥
atītānāgataṁ svarūpato 'sty adhva bhedād dharmāṇām
In their forms, the past and future exist, due to distinctions between paths of *dharmas*.

IV.13 ते व्यक्त सूक्ष्मा गुणात्मानः ॥१३॥
te vyakta sūkṣmā guṇātmānaḥ
These have manifest and subtle *guṇa* natures.

IV.14 परिणामैकत्वाद्वस्तु तत्त्वम् ॥१४॥
pariṇāmaikatvād vastu tattvam
From the uniformity of its *pariṇāma*, there is the principle of an object.

IV.15 वस्तु साम्ये चित्त भेदात्तयोर्विभक्तः पन्थाः ॥१५॥
vastu sāmye citta bhedāt tayor vibhaktaḥ panthāḥ
In the sameness of an object, because of its distinctness from the mind, there is a separate path of each.

IV.16 न चैक चित्त तन्त्रं वस्तु तदप्रमाणकं तदा किं स्यात् ॥१६॥
na caika citta tantraṁ vastu tad apramāṇakaṁ tadā kiṁ syāt
An object does not depend on one mind; there is no proof of this: how could it be?

IV.17 तदुपरागापेक्षित्वाच्चित्तस्य वस्तु ज्ञाताज्ञातं ॥१७॥
tad uparāgāpekṣitvāc cittasya vastu jñātājñātaṁ
An object of the mind is known or not known due to the anticipation that colors it (the mind).

IV.18 सदा ज्ञाताश्चित्त वृत्तयस्तत्प्रभोः पुरुषस्यापरिणामित्वात् ॥१८॥
sadā jñātāś citta vṛttayas tat prabhoḥ puruṣasyāpariṇāmitvāt
The fluctuations of the mind are always known due to the changelessness of their master, *puruṣa*.

IV.19 न तत्स्वाभासं दृश्यत्वात् ॥१९॥
na tat svābhāsaṁ dṛśyatvāt
There is no self-illuminosity of that (*citta-vṛtti*), because of the nature of the Seen.

IV.20 एक समये चोभयानवधारणम् ॥२०॥
eka samaye cobhayānavadhāraṇam
In one circumstance, there is no ascertainment of both (*vṛtti* and *puruṣa* together).

IV.21 चित्तान्तर दृश्ये बुद्धि बुद्धेरतिप्रसङ्गः स्मृति संकरश्च ॥२१॥
cittāntara dṛśye buddhi buddher atiprasaṅgaḥ smṛti saṁkaraś ca
In trying to see another higher mind there is an overstretching of the intellect from the intellect and a confusion of memory.

IV.22 चितेरप्रतिसंक्रमायास्तदाकारापत्तौ स्वबुद्धि संवेदनम् ॥२२॥
citer apratisaṁkramāyās tad ākārāpattau svabuddhi saṃvedanam
Due to the non-mixing of higher consciousness, entering into that form is [in fact] the perception of one's own intellect.

IV.23 द्रष्टृ दृश्योपरक्तं चित्तं सर्वार्थम् ॥२३॥
draṣṭṛ dṛśyoparaktaṁ cittaṁ sarvārtham
All purposes [are known due to] the mind being tinted with Seer and Seen.

IV.24 तदसंख्येय वासनाभिश्चित्रमपि परार्थं संहत्य कारित्वात् ॥२४॥
tad asaṁkhyeya vāsanābhiś citram api parārthaṁ saṁhatya kāritvāt
From action having been done conjointly for the purpose of another, it is speckled with innumerable habit patterns.

IV.25 विशेष दर्शिन आत्म भाव भावना विनिवृत्तिः ॥२५॥
viśeṣa darśina ātma bhāva bhāvanā vinivṛttiḥ
The one who sees the distinction discontinues the cultivation of self-becoming.

IV.26 तदा विवेक निम्नं कैवल्य प्राग्भारं चित्तम् ॥२६॥
tadā viveka nimnaṁ kaivalya prāgbhāraṁ cittam
Then, inclined towards discrimination, the mind has a propensity for *kaivalyam*.

IV.27 तच्छिद्रेषु प्रत्ययान्तराणि संस्कारेभ्यः ॥२७॥
tac chidreṣu pratyayāntarāṇi saṃskārebhyaḥ
In the intervening spaces of that, there are also other intentions, due to *saṁskāras.*

IV.28 हानमेषां क्लेशवदुक्तम् ॥२८॥
hānam eṣāṁ kleśavad uktam
The cessation of them is said to be like that of the afflictions.

IV.29 प्रसंख्याने ऽप्यकुसीदस्य सर्वथा विवेक ख्यातेर्धर्म मेघः समाधिः ॥२९॥
prasaṁkhyāne 'py akusīdasya sarvathā viveka khyāter dharma meghaḥ samādhiḥ
Indeed, in [that state of] reflection for the one who has discriminative discernment and always takes no interest, there is the cloud of *dharma samādhi.*

IV.30 ततः क्लेश कर्म निवृत्तिः ॥३०॥
tataḥ kleśa karma nivṛttiḥ
From that, there is the cessation of afflicted action.

IV.31 तदा सर्वावरण मलापेतस्य ज्ञानस्यानन्त्याज्ज्ञेयमल्पम् ॥३१॥
tadā sarvāvaraṇa malāpetasya jñānasyānantyāj jñeyam alpam
Then, little is to be known due to the eternality of knowledge which is free from all impure covering.

IV.32 ततः कृतार्थानां परिणाम क्रम समाप्तिर्गुणानाम् ॥३२॥
tataḥ kṛtārthānāṁ pariṇāma krama samāptir guṇānām
From that, the purpose of the *guṇas* is done and the succession of *pariṇāma* is concluded.

IV.33 क्षण प्रतियोगी परिणामापरान्त निर्ग्राह्यः क्रमः ॥३३॥
kṣaṇa pratiyogī pariṇāmāparānta nirgrāhyaḥ kramaḥ
Succession and its correlate, the moment, are terminated by the end of *pariṇāma.*

IV.34 पुरुषार्थ शून्यानां गुणानां प्रतिप्रसवः कैवल्यं स्वरूप प्रतिष्ठा वा चिति शक्तिरिति ॥३४॥
puruṣārtha śūnyānāṃ guṇānāṁ pratiprasavaḥ kaivalyaṃ svarūpa pratiṣṭhā vā citi śaktir iti
The return to the origin of the *guṇas*, emptied of their purpose for *puruṣa*, is *kaivalyam*, the steadfastness in own form, and the power of higher consciousness.

10 *Translation Methodology and Grammatical Analysis*

TECHNICAL FEATURES OF THIS TRANSLATION

This translation of the *Yoga Sūtra* is designed for those interested in making direct contact with the Sanskrit text attributed to Patañjali. Although the *Yoga Sūtra* is perhaps two thousand years more recent than the earliest Sanskrit literatures, this text in many ways is more difficult to decipher than the Vedic hymns, owing to their epigrammatic form. Each *sūtra* was designed as a mnemonic device to bring into focus specific and involved meditation practices and experiences. To explain the import of these, later scholars of Yoga provided extensive written commentaries on the text including Vyāsa (fifth century CE), and Vijñāna Bhīkṣu (sixteenth century CE).

The present work includes a grammatical explication of Patañjali's text. Vyāsa and other commentators have been consulted, as well as the dozen or more English translations listed at the end. This translation provides the reader with a comprehensive analysis of the words used by Patañjali and how they interrelate. One need know no Sanskrit in order to use this analysis. However, if one studies it carefully, a working knowledge of *sūtra* Sanskrit will be gained. With few exceptions, no verbs are used by Patañjali, immensely simplifying the task. The Romanization is given for each *sūtra* of the text, with each word separated. In general, consonants in their combining form are retained, whereas vowels are rendered separately, according to rules of euphonic combination (*sandhi*). Compounded words are connected with a hyphen. Then, each word is isolated and analyzed separately. Words within compounds are identified by gender, grammatical case, and number. Each word is then followed by various possible translations, references to other *sūtras*, and/or a detailed analysis of prefixes and verb roots. The analysis (*vigraha*) of compounds (*samāsa*) is given in brackets at the end of the compound. Our translation of the *sūtra* then follows, sometimes accompanied by additional comments.

The single feature that most distinguishes this translation from the prior ones is that we have also used a single English word to translate Sanskrit terms and have left a handful of terms in the Sanskrit, either because they are referring to specialized states for which there is no English equivalent (such as *guṇa, puruṣa, prakṛti, pariṇāma, saṃyama, kaivalyam*) or because the usage of a term in Sanskrit is loaded with numerous meanings, some of which would be eliminated by translation with a single term. For instance, *dharma* seems to refer to both a discrete nature and larger order of things.

In a couple of instances, we have employed terms in English that equal the Sanskrit terms in their elasticity. For instance, the term *viṣaya*, translated by others as "object," also is used in a more general, process-oriented sense. We have used the word *condition*, which conveys both meanings and use the word object to translate *vastu*. Another term for which we offer a new translation is *pratyaya*, which refers to the significance or content of a *vṛtti* or mental fluctuation. This has been rendered "presented ideas" by Woods and "knowledge" or "cause producing effect" by Araṇya. Drawing from the phenomenological language of Husserl and others, we have used the single word *intention*, capturing the directionality that is evident in its verbal root *i* (go), prefixed with *prati* (against, toward).

The word *citta* is one of the most difficult terms to adequately translate in the *Yoga Sūtras*. Patañjali offers no definition of the term within the text. Some scholars have equated the term with the inner organ (*antaḥkaraṇa*), said in the *Sāṃkhya Kārikā* to be comprised of the intellect (*buddhi*), I-maker (*ahaṃkāra*), and mind organs (*manas*). These translators have used such terms as "mind-stuff" for *citta*. Others have chosen to translate the term as "consciousness." Although this may be correct etymologically (the root *cit* means "perceive"), consciousness in the Indian context generally refers to the pure consciousness or witnessing mode of *puruṣa*. Interestingly, *citta* can go either way. It can bind one through consciousness of things as typified in the five forms of its fluctuations (I:5–11), or it can, through its onepointedness, bring one to *sattva* and *kaivalyam* (III:55). It is through the purification of the *citta* that the nonattached state that is the goal of Yoga is achieved. Because of the ambivalence of the term, the more neutral "mind" will be used for *citta*, with *manas*, which appears only thrice, translated as "mind power."

Artha we have translated uniformly as "purpose." Originally, following Vyāsa and other translators, we thought that at least two meanings pertained: in some instances *artha* seemed to refer to meaning, in other instances to objects. However, keeping in mind that all objects, as manifestations of *prakṛti*, are for the enjoyment of *puruṣa*, we have found that the word "purpose" fits consistently.

Throughout our translation we have attempted to be sensitive to various clues offered by Patañjali in the areas of style and flow that seemingly lend a greater coherence to the text than previously discerned. At variance with some earlier interpretations, we see the categorization of yogis in *sūtra* I:22 as a summary verse describing the "types" described in the three prior *sūtras*; we interpret I:41 as providing a foundational definition for the states of *samādhi* that are later described; we see a hierarchy evident in the descriptions of powers (*vibhūti*), thus linking this section to Patañjali's central theme of subtilization; we suggest that the discernment of "two things" in III:53 refers to the perception of the distinction between the purest form of *sattva* and *puruṣa*; we see the theme of *pariṇāma* as a logical extension of earlier statements and not an appended afterthought, as some have surmised; and finally, we see a complementarity (if not a continuity) evident in the various descriptions of Yoga that Patañjali proposes.

GRAMMATICAL ABBREVIATIONS

abl.	ablative case
adj.	adjective
acc.	accusative case
adv.	adverb
BV cpd.	*bahuvṛhi samāsa* (descriptive compound)
du.	Dual
f.	feminine
gen.	genitive case
ind.	indeclinable
instr.	instrumental
KD cpd.	*karmadharya samāsa* (adjectival compound)
loc.	locative case
m.	masculine
n.	neuter
nom.	nominative case
pl.	plural
p.p.p.	past passive participle
pron.	pronoun
sg.	singular
TP cpd.	*tat puruṣa samāsa* (compound that indicates case relationship between members, generally followed by Sanskrit case number [see below])

Grammatical cases:

1. nominative
2. accusative
3. instrumental
4. dative
5. ablative
6. genitive
7. locative

11 "Samādhi pāda"

I.1 ***atha yoga-anuśāsanam***

atha (adv.) now

yoga (m.) union, connection, joining; from √*yuj* (unite, join, connect, employ, use)

anuśāsanam (n. nom. sg.) instruction, direction, teaching; *anu* (after, with) + *śāsana* from √*śas* (chastise, correct, restrain, teach) [end of TP7 cpd.]

Attend to these teachings on Yoga.

I.2 ***yogaś citta-vṛtti-nirodhaḥ***

yogaś (m. nom. sg) yoga (see above)

citta (n.) mind, reason, intelligence; from √*cit* (perceive, observe, know)

vṛtti (f.) modification, turning, fluctuations; from √*vṛt* (turn, resolve, roll, move) [end of TP6 cpd.]

nirodhaḥ (m. nom. sg.) restraint, control, suppression; *ni* (down, into) + *rodha*, from √*rudh* (obstruct, arrest, avert) [end of TP6 cpd.]

Yoga is the restraint of the fluctuations of the mind.

I.3 ***tadā draṣṭuḥ sva rūpe'vasthānam***

tadā (ind.) then

draṣṭuḥ (m. gen. sg.) of the seer; from √*dṛś* (see, perceive, understand)

svarūpe (n. loc. sg.) in own form; *sva* (own, self) + *rūpa* (form, shape, figure)

avasthānam (n. loc. sg.) abiding, standing, dwelling; *ava* (off, away) + *sthāna*, from √*sthā* (stand, endure, continue)

Then, the Seer abides in its own form.

I.4 ***vṛtti-sārūpyam itaratra***

vṛtti (f.) fluctuation (see I.2)

sārūpyam (n. nom. sg.) with form, likeness, conformity with, similarity of form; *sā* (with) + *rūpya* (stamped, impression, in the possession of), from *rūpa* (see I.3) [end of TP6 cpd.]

itaratra (ind.) at other times, otherwise

Otherwise, there is conformity with the fluctuations.

I.5 ***vṛttayaḥ pañcatayaḥ kliṣṭa akliṣṭāḥ***

vṛttayaḥ (f. nom. pl.) fluctuations (see I.2)

pañcatayaḥ (m. mon. sg.) fivefold, having five parts; from *pañca* (five)

kliṣṭa (m.) afflicted, painful, troubling; from √*kliś* (torment, distress)

akliṣṭāḥ (m. or f. nom. pl.) not afflicted, untroubled, undisturbed; a (not) + *kliṣṭa* (see above) [end of DV cpd.]

Five [types of] fluctuations exist, afflicted or nonafflicted.

I.6 ***pramāṇa-viparyaya-vikalpa-nidrā-smṛtayaḥ***

pramāna (n.) correct cognition, valid notion, right perception; *pra* (before, forward) + *māna* (means of proof, demonstrating) from √*mā* (measure, prepare, display)

viparyaya (m.) misconception, error misapprehension; *vi* (asunder, away) + *pari* (around) + *aya, from* √*i* (go, flow, get about)

vikalpa (m.) conceptualization, imagination; *vi* (asunder, away) + *kalpa*, from √*kḷp* (correspond, in accordance with, suitable to)

nidrā (f.) sleep, slumber, *ni* (down, into) + √*drā* (sleep)

smṛtayaḥ (m. nom. pl.) memory; from √*smṛ* (remember) [end of DV cpd.]

Correct cognition, error, imagining, sleep, and memory.

I.7 ***pratyakṣa-anumāna-āgamāḥ pramāṇāni***

pratyakṣa (m.) direct perception, apprehension by the senses; *prati* (against, back) + *akṣa* (organ of sense, eye) from √*akṣ* (reach, penetrate, embrace)

anumāna (m.) inference, consideration, reflection; *anu* (along, after) +*māna* (means of proof, demonstration) from √*mā* (measure, prepare, display)

āgamāḥ (m. nom. pl.) a traditional doctrine or precept, a sacred work *ā* (hither, unto) + *gama* (going), from √*gam* (go, move) [end of DV cpd.]

pramāṇāṇi (n. nom.pl) correct cognitions (see I.6).

Correct cognitions arise from perception, inference, and truthful testimony.

I.8 ***viparyayo mithyā-jñānam atad rūpa-pratiṣṭham***

viparyayo (m.) error (see I.6)

mithyā (ind.) false, untrue, incorrect; from √*mith* (altercate, dispute angrily)

jñānam (n. nom. sg.) knowledge, understanding; from √*jñā* (know, be acquainted with)

atad (n.) nom. sg. pronoun) not that

rūpa (n.) form, outward appearance, shape (see I.3)

prastiṣṭham (n. nom. sg.) resting place, base, foundation; *prati* (against, back) + √*sthā* (stand, take position) [end of TP7 cpd.]

Error, or false knowledge, has no foundation in form.

I.9 ***śabda-jñāna-anupātī vastu-śūnyo vikalpaḥ***

śabda (m.) word, sound, voice, tone, speech

jñāna (n.) knowledge (see I.8)

anupātī (m. nom. sg.) following as a consequence or result; *anu* (along, after) + *pātin* (falling, rising, appearing), from √*pat* (fly, fall) [end of TP3 cpd.]

vastu (n.) thing, object, matter, article; from √*vas* (live, dwell, remain, abide)

śūnyaḥ (m. nom. sg.) empty, void, possessing nothing; from √*śū*, *śvā*, *śvi* (swell) [end of TP6 cpd.]

vikalpaḥ (m. nom. sg.) imagining (see I.6).

Imagining is the result of words and knowledge that are empty of an object.

I.10 ***abhāva-pratyaya-ālambanā vṛttir nidrā***

abhāva (m.) nonbecoming, not appearing; *a* (not) + *bhāva* (becoming, being, existing); from √*bhū* (be, become, exist)

pratyaya (m.) intention, firm conviction, basis; *prati* (against, back) + *aya* (going), from √*i* (go) [first part of cpd.; TP6]
ālambanā (f. nom. sg) based or depending on, supporting; *ā* (hither, unto) + *lambana* (having down), from √*lamb* (hang down) [end of cpd.; TP7]
vṛttiḥ (f. nom. sg.) fluctuation (see I.2)
nidrā (f. nom. sg.) sleep (see I.6)

The sleep fluctuation depends on an intention of nonbecoming.

I.11 ***anubhūta-viṣaya-asaṃpramoṣaḥ smṛtiḥ***
anubhūta (m.) experienced, perceived, understood; *anu* (along, after) + *bhūta* (become, existing, present), from √*bhū* (be, become, exist)
viṣaya (m.) condition, dominion, sphere of activity or concern, an object of senses; probably from √*viṣ* (be active) or *vi* (asunder, away) + √*si* (extend)([first part of cpd., KD]
asaṃpramoṣaḥ (m. nom. sg.) recollection, not letting drop or be set free; a (not) + *sam* (together) + *pra* (before, forward) + *moṣa* (robbery, theft, stealing), from √*muṣ* (steal) [end of cpd.; TP6]
smṛtiḥ (f. nom. sg.) memory (see I.6)

Memory recalls previously experienced conditions.

I.12 ***abhyāsa-vairāgyābhyāṃ tan nirodhaḥ***
abhyāsa (m.) practice, repeated exercise, discipline, study; *abhi* (to, unto, toward) + *āsa* (seat), from √*ās* (sit quietly)
vairāgyābhyām (n. instr. du.) dispassion, release, freedom from worldly desires; from *virāga*, *vi* (asunder, away) + *rāga* (passion, love, desire), from √*rañj* (be reddened, be attracted) [end of DV cpd.]
tad (ind.) there, in that place
nirodhaḥ (m. nom. sg.) restraint, control, suppression (see I.2)

Restraint arises through practice and release [from desire].

I.13 ***tatra sthitau yatno' bhyāsaḥ***
tatra (ind.) there
sthitau (f. loc. sg.) remaining in a state, continued existence, steadiness; from √*sthā* (stand)
yatnaḥ (m. nom. sg.) effort, activity of will, zeal; from √*yat* (place in order)

abhyāsaḥ (m. nom. sg.) practice (see I.12)

Practice requires effort and stability.

I.14 ***sa tu dīrgha-kāla-nairantarya-satkāra-āsevito dṛḍha-bhūmiḥ***

saḥ (m. nom. sg. pron.) it, this, that

tu (ind.) but, now, then

dīrgha (adj.) long

kāla (m.) time; from √*kal* (drive, produce) [first part of cpd., KD]

nairantarya (n.) uninterruptedness, continuousness; *nair* (*vṛddhi* form of *nir*, away from) + *antarya*, from *antara* (interior, near, intimate) [second part of TP3 cpd.]

sat kāra (m.) care, attention, consideration; from *sat* (being), from √*as* (is); + *kāra* (making, doing, working), from √*kṛ* (do, make, perform) [third part of TP3 cpd.]

āsevitaḥ (m. nom, sg,) frequent, practiced assiduously; *ā* (hither, unto) + *sevita* (dwelt in visited, frequented), from √*sev* (stay, dwell) [end of KD cpd.]

dṛḍha (m.) fixed, firm, hard, strong; p.p.p. from √*dṛṃh* (be firm or strong)

bhūmiḥ (f. nom. sg.) situation, place, ground, earth; from √*bhū* (be, exist) [end of KD cpd.]

It becomes firmly grounded when carefully attended to for a long period of time without interruption.

I.15 ***dṛṣṭa-ānuśravika-viṣaya-vitṛṣṇasya vaśīkāra-samjñā vairāgyam***

dṛṣṭa (m.) seen, observed, perceived; p.p.p. from *dṛś* (see, apprehend)

ānuśravika (m.) according to hearing, based on tradition; from *anu* (along, after) +*śravik*, from √*śru* (hear) [first part of DV cpd.]

viṣaya (m.) condition, object of sense (see I.11) [second part of KD cpd.]

vitṛṣṇasya (m. gen. sg.) of one free from thirst, desirelessness; *vi* (asunder, away) + √*tṛṣ* (be thirsty or desirous) [end of TP4 cpd.]

vaśīkāra (m.) mastery, subjugating, bringing into subjection; *vaśī* (will, desire), from √*vaś* (command, desire) + *kāra* (making), from √*kṛ* (do, act)

saṃjñā (f. nom. sg.) harmony, knowledge, clear conception; *sam* (together) + *jñā* (know, understand) [end of TP6 cpd.]

vairāgyam (n. nom. sg.) release from desire, dispassion (see I.12)

Release [from desire] results in the harmony of mastery in one who thirsts not for conditions seen or heard.

I.16 ***tat paraṃ puruṣa-khyāter guṇa-vaitṛṣṇyam***

tad (n. nom. sg. pron.) that, this

param (n. nom sg.) highest, best, supreme; from √*pṛ* (surpass, excel)

puruṣa (m.) man, human, primeval man as source of everything, highest self; sometimes translated as soul or spirit; in Sāṃkhya, defined as inactive, witness; probably from √*pṝ* (fill, make complete)

khyāteḥ (f. abl. sg.) from discernment, perception, knowledge; from √*khyā* (see, make known, procalim) [end of TP6 cpd.]

guṇa (m.) thread or strand; quality, attribute; in Sāṃkhya, the three *guṇas* (*sattva*, lightness; *rajas*, activity; *tamas*, darkness) constitute *prakṛti* and hence all created things

vaitṛṣṇyam (n. nom. sg) freedom from desire; strengthened form of *vitṛṣṇa* (see I:15) [end of TP4 cpd.]

That highest [release]—thirstlessness for the *guṇas*—proceeds from the discernment of *puruṣa*.

I.17 ***vitarka-vicāra-ānanda-asmitā-anugamāt-saṃprajñātaḥ***

vitarka (m.) discursive thought, deliberation, consideration, doubt; conjecture, supposition; from *vi* (asunder, away) + *tarka* (conjecture, supposition), from √*tark* (conjecture, reason, reflect)

vicāra (m.) mode of proceeding; reflection; 'clear vision" (Bengali Baba), from *vi* (asunder, away) + *cāra* (going, motion), from √*car* (go, move)

ānanda (m.) bliss, happiness, enjoyment; from *ā* (hither, unto) + *nanda* (joy, delight), from √*nand* (rejoice, be glad)

asmitā (f.) I-am-ness, egotism; from *asmi* (first-person singular indicative of √*as* (be)) + *tā*, (feminine suffix denoting "having the quality of") [end of series of DV cpds.]

anugamāt (m. abl. sg.) following, going after; association; from *anu* (along, after) + *gama* (going), from √*gam* (go) [end of TP3 cpd.]

saṃprajñātaḥ (m. nom. sg.) with consciousness, awareness; cognitive; distinguished, discerned, known accurately; *sam* (together)

+ *pra* (before, forward) + *jñāta* (known, understood, percieved), from √*jñā* (known)

Awareness arises from association with deliberation, reflection, bliss, and I-am-ness.

I.18 ***virāma-pratyaya-abhyāsa-pūrvaḥ saṃskāra-śeṣo'nyaḥ***

virāma (m.) cesation, termination, end; *vi* (asunder, away) + *rāma*, from √*ram* (stop, set, at rest)

pratyaya (m.) intention (see I.10) [end of TP6 cpd.]

abhyāsa (m.) practice (see I.12) [end of DV cpd.]

pūrvaḥ (m. nom. sg.) former, prior, preceding [end of TP3 cpd.]

saṃskāra (m.) impression left by action done in the past, which conditions future action; "subliminal activator" (Feuerstein); "habitual potency" (Baba); latency; from *sam* (together) + *kāra* (doing,) from √*kṛ* (do)

śeṣaḥ (m. nom. sg.) remainder, residue; here translated as only; from √*śiṣ* (leave, leave remaining) [end of BV cpd.]

anyaḥ (m. nom. sg.) other, different

[On a more subtle level], the other [state*] has *saṃskāra* only and is preceded by practice and the intention of cessation.

*Referred to by Vyāsa as *"asaṃprajñāta samādhi"*

I.19 ***bhava-pratyayo videha-prakṛti-layānām***

bhava (m.) becoming, coming into existence; from √*bhū* (be, exist)

pratyayaḥ (m. nom, sg.) intention, (see I.10) [end of TP6 cpd.]

videha (m.) discarnate, bodiless, incorporeal; *vi* (asunder, away) + *deha* (body), from √*dih* (smear, annoint) [first part of DV cpd.]

prakṛti (f.) creative, active aspect of reality; sometimes translated as nature or primary matter; composed of and inseparable from the three *guṇas* (see I.16); *pra* (before, forward) + *kṛti* (act of doing or creating), from √*kṛ* (do, make)

layānām (m. gen. pl.) absorption in melting; clinging to; from √*lī* (melt, cling) [end of BV cpd.]

The ones absorbed in *prakṛti* and free from the body still have an intention of becoming.

(These are deemed mild practitioners [see I.22].)

I.20 ***śraddhā vīrya-smṛti-samādhi-prajñā-pūrvaka itareṣām***

śraddhā (f.) faith, confidence, trust

vīrya (n.) energy, strength, power, from *vīra* (brave or eminent man, hero)
smṛti (f.) mindfulness (see I.6)
samādhi (m.) absorption, concentration, putting together, completion, intense absorption; from *sam* (together) + *ā* (hither, unto) + *dhi*, from √*dhā* (put, place)
prajñā (f.) wisdom, knowledge, insight; from *pra* (before, forward) + √*jña* (know, understand) [end of series of DV cpds.]
pūrvakaḥ (m. nom. sg.) preceded or accompanied by; from *pūrva* (see I.8) + *ka*, suffix indicating possession [end of TP3 cpd.]
itareṣām (m. gen. pl.) of the others

Of the others it is preceded by faith, energy, mindfulness, *Samādhi*, and wisdom.

(These may be seen as medium practitioners.)

I.21 ***tīvra-saṃvegānām āsannaḥ***
tīvra (m.) strong, intense, acute
saṃvegānām (m. gen. pl.) of the intense or vehement ones; *sam* (together) + *vega* (impetuosity, excitement) from √*vij* (be agitated, tremble) [end of KD cpd,]; related to Pali word for "shock" or "thrill"
āsannaḥ (m. nom. sg.) near, proximate; from *ā* (hither, unto) + *sanna* (set down), from √*sad* (sit)

The strongly intense ones are near. (These may be seen as ardent.)

I.22 ***mṛdu-madhya-adhimātratvāt tato'pi viśeṣaḥ***
mṛdu (m.) mild, soft, weak; from √*mṛd* (trample, down)
madhya (m.) moderate, standing between two, middle
adhimātratvāt (m. abl. sg.) above measure, more than usual, ardent; *adhi* (over, on) + *mātra* (measure, quantity), from √*mā* (measure) + *tva*, suffix meaning "having the quality of"
tataḥ (ind.) hence, from that
api (ind.) also, indeed, very
viśeṣaḥ (m. nom. sg.) distinction, difference, peculiarity; *vi* (asunder, away) + *śeṣa* (remainder), from √*śiṣ* (leave)

Hence, the distinctions of mild, moderate, and ardent.

I.23 ***īśvara-praṇidhānād vā***
īśvara (m.) master, lord, king; able to do, capable; from √*īś* (command, rule) + *vara* (valuable, eminent, choicest), from √*vṛ* (choose)

praṇidhānāt (m. abl. sg.) dedication, attention paid to, respectful conduct; *pra* (before, forward)+ *ni* (down, into) + *dhāna* (containing, holding) from √*dhā* (put, place) [end of TP7 cpd.]
vā (ind.) or

Or from dedication to *Īśvara*.

I.24 ***kleśa-karma-vipākāśayair aparāmṛṣṭaḥ puruṣa-viśeṣa īśvaraḥ***
kleśa (m.) affliction, pain, distress; from √*kliś* (trouble, afflict)
karma (n.) action, work; from √*kṛ* (to make)
vipāka (m.) fruition, ripening; effect, result; *vi* (away) + *pāka* (cooking), from √*pac* (cook)
āśayair (m. instr. pl.) residue, stock, balance of fruits from past actions; *ā* (hither, unto) + √*śaya* (lying, resting, abiding), from √*śī* (rest, lie) [end of DV cpd.]
aparāmṛṣṭaḥ (m. nom. sg.) untouched; *a* (not) + *parā* (away, off, aside) + *mṛṣṭa* (touched), from √*mṛś* (touch, feel)
puruṣa (m.) (see I.16)
viśesaḥ (m. nom. sg.) distinct (see I.22) [end of TP6]
īśvaraḥ (m. nom. sg.) (see I.23)

Īśvara is a distinct *puruṣa* untouched by afflictions, actions, fruitions, or their residue.

I.25 ***tatra niratiśayaṃ sarva-jña bījam***
tatra (ind.) there
niratiśayaṃ (n. nom. sg.) unsurpassed, unexcelled; *nir* (out, away from) +*ati* (over, beyond, past) + *śaya* (lying, resting), from √*śī* (rest, lie)
sarva (n.) all, every, whole, entire
jña (m.) knowing, knowledge; from √*jñā* (know, understand) [end of KD cpd.]
bījam (n. nom. sg.) seed, germ, origin [end of TP6 cpd.]

There the seed of omniscience is unsurpassed.

I.26 ***pūrveṣām api guruḥ kālena anavacchedāt***
pūrveṣām (m. gen. pl.) of the prior ones (see I.18)
api (ind.) also, even
guruḥ (m. nom. sg.) teacher, venerable person, preceptor
kālena (m. instr. sg.) by time; from √*kal* (drive forward, produce)

anavacchedāt (m. abl. sg.) from not being cut or limited or separated; from *an* (not) + *ava* (down, from, away) + *cheda* (cutting off, interrupting) from √*chid* (cut, amputate)

Due to its being unlimited by time, it is the teacher of the prior ones.

I.27 ***tasya vācakaḥ praṇavaḥ***

tasya (m. gen. sg.)

vācakaḥ (m. nom. sg.) expression; from √*vac* (speak)

praṇavaḥ (m. nom. sg.) the sacred syllable "*oṃ*"; from *pra* (before, forward) + *nava*, from √*nu* (sound, shout, exult)

Its expression is *praṇava* (*oṃ*).

I.28 ***taj japas tad artha-bhāvanam***

tat (n. nom. sg. pron.) that

japas (m. nom. sg.) repetition, repeating in a low voice; from √*jap* (whisper, mutter)

tad (n. nom. sg. pron.) that

artha (m. or n.) meaning, aim, purpose

bhāvanam (n. nom. sg.) realization, causing to be, effecting, cultivating, manifesting; from causative form of √*bhū* (be, exist) [end of TP6 cpd.]

Repetition of it [results in] cultivation of its purpose.

I.29 ***tataḥ pratyak-cetanā-adhigamo'py-antarāya-abhāvaś-ca***

tataḥ (ind.) thence, from it

pratyak (m.) combining form of *pratyañc*, inward, in opposite direction

cetanā (f.) consciousness, understanding, sense; from √*cit* (perceive, know, appear) [end of KD cpd.]

adhigamo (m. nom. sg.) attainment, mastery, acquirement; *adhi* (over, on) + *gama* (going), from √*gam* (go) [end of TP6 cpd.]

api (ind.) also, even

antarāya (m.) obstacle, intervention; *antar* (between) + *āya*, from √*i* (go)

abhāvaḥ (m. nom. sg.) nonarising, disappearance, absence; *a* (not) + *bhāva* (being), from √*bhū* (be, exist)

ca (ind.) and

Thus, inward-consciousness is attained and obstacles do not arise.

I.30 ***vyādhi-styāna-saṃśaya-pramāda-ālasya-avirati-bhrānti-darśana-alabdha-bhūmikatva-anavasthitatvāni citta-vikṣepās te'ntarāyāḥ***

vyādhi (m.) sickness, disorder, ailment; *vi* (asunder, away) +*ā* (hither, unto) + *dhi*, from √*dhā* (put, place)

styāna (m.) dullness, thickness, rigidity; from √*styā* (stiffen)

saṃśaya (m.) doubt, hesitation, uncertainty; *sam* (together) + *śaya* (lying, sleeping), from √*śī* (rest, lie)

pramāda (m.) carelessness, negligence; intoxication, madness; *pra* (before, forward) + *māda* (drunkenness), from √*mad* (be intoxicated, revel, or delight in)

ālasya (n.) laziness, idleness, sloth; derived from *alasa*, *ā* (hither, unto) + *a* (not) + *lasa* (lively, shining, moving about), from √*las* (shine, flash; play, frolic)

avirati (f.) sense indulgence, intemperance; sensuality (Baba); worldliness (Woods); lack of detachment (Rukmani); *a* (not) + *vi* (asunder, away) + *rati* (pleasure, enjoyment) from √*ram* (delight, enjoy carnally) [end of series DV cpds.]

bhrānti (f.) false, confusing, erroneous; from √*bhram* (wander, about, waver)

darśana (m.) view, observation, understanding; from √*dṛś* (see, perceive) [end of KD cpd.]

alabdha (m.) unobtained, not having attained; *a* (not) + *labdha*, p.p.p. from √*labh* (obtain, take)

bhūmikatva (n.) stage, place, step; from *bhūmi* (earth, position, stage) + *ka* (suffix meaning "having") + *tva* (suffix meaning "quality") [end of KD cpd.]

anavasthitatvāni (n. nom. pl.) instability, unsteadiness; from *an* (not) + *ava* (down, from, away) + *sthita* (standing, established), from √*sthā* (stand) + *tva* (suffix meaning quality) [end of DV cpds.]

citta (n.) mind (see I.2)

vikṣepāḥ (m. nom. pl.) distraction, scattering, dispersion; *vi* (away, asunder) + *kṣepa* (throwing, casting), from √*kṣip* (throw, send) [end of TP6 cpd.]

te (m. nom. pl.) these

antarāyāḥ (m. nom. pl.) obstacles (see I.29)

These obstacles, distractions of the mind, are sickness, dullness, doubt, carelessness, laziness, sense addiction, false view, losing ground, and instability.

I.31 ***duḥkha-daurmanasya-aṅgam ejayatva-śvāsa-praśvāsā vikṣepa-sahabhuvaḥ***

duḥkha (n.) suffering, dissatisfaction, pain, uneasiness, sorrow, trouble, difficulty; from √*duṣ* (spoil) + *kha* (axle hole, cavity, hollow, cave)

daurmanasya (n.) despair, depression, dejectedness; *daur* (strong form of √*duṣ*; see above) + *manasya* (have in mind, think), from √*man* (think, conjecture) [end of DV cpd.]

aṅgam (n. nom. sg.) body, limb, member [end of KD cpd.]

ejayatva (m.) unsteadiness, trembling, shaking; causative derivation of √*ej* (stir, move, tremble) + *tva* suffix indicating quality [Note: Vyāsa links this word with *aṅgam*, though grammatically it is part of a *karmadharya* compound describing *śvāsa* and *praśvāsa*.]

śvāsa (m.) inhalation, breathing; from √*śvas* (breathe, respire)

praśvāsāḥ (m. nom. pl.) breathing out, exhaling; *pra* (before, forward) + *śvāsa* (see above)

vikṣepa (m.) distraction (see I.30)

sahabhuvaḥ (m. nom. sg.) appearing together, counterpart of; *saha* (together with) + *bhuva*, from √*bhū* (be, exist) [end of TP6 cpd.]

A suffering, despairing body and unsteady inhalation and exhalation accompany the distractions.

I.32 ***tat pratiṣedha-artham eka-tattva-abhyāsaḥ***

tat (usually, n. nom. sg.; here, ind.) it, that; these, them

pratiṣedha (m.) countering, preventing, keeping back; *prati* (against, back) + *sedha*, driving away, from √*sidh* (repel)

artham (n. nom. sg.) purpose (see I.28)

eka (m.) one; alone, solitary, single

tattva (n.) thing; literally "that-ness," sometimes translated as principle, essence; elementary property; "entity" (Woods, Rukmani)

abhyāsaḥ (m. nom. sg.) practice (see I.12)

For the purpose of counteracting them, there is one principle: practice.

Various practices are listed below.

I.33 ***maitrī-karuṇā-muditā-upekṣāṇāṃ sukha-duḥkha-puṇya-apuṇya-viṣayāṇāṃ bhāvanātaś citta prasādanam***

maitrī (f.) friendliness, good will, benevolence

karuṇā (f.) compassion, pity; from 1st √*kṛ* (do make) or 2nd √*kṛ* (pour out, scatter)

muditā (f.) happiness, gladness, joy; from √*mud* (be happy, rejoice)
upekṣāṇāṃ (f. gen. pl.) equanimity, indifference; literally, overlooking; *upa* (to, unto) + *īkṣa* from √*īkṣ* (see, look) [end of DV cpds.]
sukha (n.) pleasure, happiness, comfort, ease, virtue; *su* (good) + *kha* (axle-hole)
duḥkha (n.) dissatisfaction, pain, suffering (see I.31)
puṇya (n.) merit, virtue, righteousness, goodness, auspicious, propitious; from √*puṇ* (act virtuously) or √*puṣ* (thrive, cause to prosper)
apuṇya (n.) absence of merit, evil, nonvirtuous; from *a* (not) + √*puṇ or* √*puṣ* (see above) [end of DV cpd.]
viṣayāṇāṃ (m. gen. pl.) of conditions, spheres of activity (see I.11) [end of TP6 cpd.; genitive absolute construction]
bhāvanātaś (ind.) from cultivation; producing, effecting, projecting; *bhāvanā* (f.) causative form of √*bhū* (be, exist) + *tas*, indeclinable ablative suffix meaning "from"
citta (n.) consciousness, mind (see I.2)
prasādanam (n. nom. sg.) clarification, calmness, tranquility, clearness; *pra* (before, forward) + *sādana* (causing to settle down), from √*sad* (sit) [end of TP6 cpd.]

Clarification of the mind [results] from the cultivation of friendliness toward the happy, compassion for those who suffer, sympathetic joy for the good, and equanimity toward those who lack goodness.

I.34 ***pracchardana-vidhāraṇābhyām vā prāṇasya***
pracchardana (n.) expulsion, exhalation, emitting; from *pra* (before, forward) + *cchardana*, from √*chṛd* (spew, eject)
vidhāraṇābhyāṃ (m. instr. du.) of the retention, holding, checking; from *vi* (asunder, away) + *dhāraṇā* (holding, bearing keeping), from √*dhṛ* (hold, keep)
vā (ind.) or
prāṇasya (m. gen. sg.) of breath; life; *pra* (before, forward) + *ana* (breath, respiration), from √*an* (breathe)

Or by expulsion and retention of breath.

I.35 ***viṣaya-vatī vā pravṛttir utpannā manasaḥ sthiti-nibandhanī***
viṣayavatī (f. non. sg.) having a condition; involved in a sphere of sense activity; taking up an object of desire; *viṣaya* (see I.11 and I.23) + *vatī*, feminine form of suffix indicating possessive adjective

vā (ind.) or
pravṛttir (f. nom. sg.) activity, moving onward, "cognition" in regard to *Y.S.* according to Monier-Williams; *pra* (before, forward) + *vṛtti* (see I.2), from √*vṛt* (turn, revolve, move)
utpannā (f. non. sg.) risen, born, produced; *ut* (up, forth) + *pannā* (fallen, gone), from √*pad* (fall)
manasaḥ (n. gen. sg.) of the mind, organ of perception and cognition; from √*man* (think, believe, conjecture)
sthiti (f.) steadiness, standing upright, staying; from √*sthā* (stand, take up a position)
nibandhanī (m. nom. sg.) holding, binding, causing; *ni* (down, into) + *bandha*, from √*bandh* (bind) + *in* (possessive suffix) [end of BV cpd.]

Or steady binding of the mind-power arises in the activity of being absorbed with a condition.

[Vyāsa gives examples of directly perceived sensations as stabilizers of the mind.]

I.36 ***viśokā vā jyotiṣmatī***
viśokā (f. nom. sg.) sorrowless, without pain or affliction; *vi* (away, asunder) + *śoka* (sorrow, anguish, trouble), from √*śuc* (suffer violent heat or pain, be afflicted)
vā (ind.) or
jyotiṣmatī (f. nom. sg.) having illumination, light, brightness; *jyotis*, from √*jyut* (shine upon, illuminate) + *matī*, feminine form of suffix indicating possessive adjective.

Or having sorrowless illumination.

I.37 ***vīta-rāga-viṣayaṃ vā cittam***
vīta (m.) free; released, gone away, departed, disappeared; *vi* (asunder, away) + *ita*, from √*i* (go)
rāga (m.) attachment, passion, love, desire; from √*rañj* (be reddened, be attracted) (see I.12) [end of KD cpd.]
viṣayaṃ (n. nom. sg.) condition (see I.11)
vā (ind.) or
cittam (n. nom. sg.) mind (see I.2)

Or [in a] mind in a condition free from attachment.

I.38 ***svapna-nidrā-jñāna-ālambanaṃ vā***
svapna (m.) dream, sleep; from √*svap* (sleep)

nidrā (f.) sleep, sleepiness; *ni* (down, into) + √*dra* (sleep) [end of DV cpd.]
jñāna (n.) knowledge (see I.8) [end of TP5 cpd.]
ālambanaṃ (n. nom. sg.) resting or depending on, hanging from; *ā* (hither, unto) + *lambana* (hanging down), from √*lamb* (hang, dangle, sink) [end of TP7 cpd.]
vā (ind.) or

Or resting on knowledge [derived] from dream or sleep.

I.39 ***yathā abhimata-dhyānād-vā***
yathā (ind.) as
abhimata (m.) desired, longed for, wished; *abhi* (to, toward) + mata (thought, sentiment), from √*man* (think, believe, conjecture)
dhyānād (m. abl. sg.) from meditation or contemplation; derived from √*dhyai* (meditate, think of, contemplate) [end of KD cpd.]
vā (ind.) or

Or from meditation as desired.

I.40 ***parama-aṇu-parama-mahattva-anto'sya vaśīkāraḥ***
parama (m.) most; extreme limit; superlative form of *para* (more or better), derived from √*pṛ* (surpass)
aṇu (m.) small, fine, minute [end of KD cpd.]
parama (m.) most (see above)
mahattva (n.) greatness, great size or extent, magnitude; *maha* (great, mighty, strong), from √*mah* (magnify) + *tva* (suffix indicating "ness" or essence) [end of KD cpd.]
antaḥ (m. nom. sg.) end, conclusion; indicates from . . . to [end of TP6 cpd.]
asya (m. gen. sg. pron.) his, of him
vaśīkāraḥ (m. nom. sg.) mastery (see I.15)

Mastery of it extends from the smallest to the greatest.

I.41 ***kṣīṇa-vṛtter abhijātasya-iva maṇer grahītṛ-grahaṇa-grāhyeṣu tat-stha-tad-añjanatā samāpattiḥ***
kṣīṇa (m.) diminished, expended, worn away, waning; from √*kṣi* (destroy, make an end to)
vṛtteḥ (f. gen. sg.) fluctuation (see I.1) [end of BV cpd.]
abhijātasya (m. gen. sg.) precious, noble, handsome, well-born; *abhi* (to, toward) + *jāta* (born), from √*jan* (be born)

iva (ind.) like
maṇeḥ (m. gen. sg.) of a jewel, gem
grahītṛ (m.) grasper, taker, experiencer; from √*grabh* (grab, seize) + *tṛ* suffix indicating agency
grahaṇa (m.) grasping, seizing, holding, act of experiencing, from √*grabh* (see above)
grahyeṣu (m. loc. pl.) in the grasped (lit., to be grasped, seized, or taken); that which is experienced, gerundive derived from √*grabh* (see above) [end of DV cpd.]
tat (ind.) that, it
stha (m.) standing, staying, abiding; from √*sthā* (stand, remain)
tad (ind.) that, it
añjanatā (f. nom. sg.) made clear, annointed, caused to appear; *añjana*, from √*añj* (annoint) + *tā* (feminine suffix indicating quality) [*tat-stha-tad-añjana-tā*, literally "there standing, there annointed-ness" is translated by Monier Williams as "assuming the color of any near object"]
samāpattiḥ (f. nom. sg.) unity, coming together; *sam* (together) + *ā* (hither, unto) + *patti*, from √*pat* (fall, fly)

[The accomplished mind] of diminished fluctuations, like a precious (or clear) jewel assuming the color of any near object, has unity among grasper, grasping, and grasped.

This translation is at variance with Vyāsa's interpretation. Vyāsa posits three types of unity; we posit one form of unity wherein distinctions among grasping, grasper, and grasped collapse.

I.42 ***tatra śabda-artha-jñāna-vikalpaiḥ saṃkīrṇā savitarkā samāpattiḥ***
tatra (ind.) there, in that
śabda (m.) word (see I.9)
artha (m. or n.) purpose (see I.28)
jñāna (n.) knowledge (see I.8) [end of DV cpd.]
vikalpaiḥ (m. inst. pl.) conceptualization (see I.6) [end of TP6 cpd.]
saṃkīrṇā (f. nom. sg.) commingling, mixed, interspersed; confusion; *sam* (together) + *kīrṇa* (scattered, thrown), from √*kṛ* (scatter)
savitarkā (f. nom. sg.) with thought, cognition, or deliberation; *sa* (with) + *vi* (asunder, away) + *tarka* (conjecture, reasoning)
samāpattiḥ (f. nom. sg.) unity (see I.41)

Savitarkā unity is the commingling by imagining of word, purpose, and knowledge.

I.43 ***smṛti-pariśuddhau sva rūpa-śūnyā iva-arth-mātra-nirbhāsā nirvitarkā***

smṛti (f.) memory (see I.6)

pariśuddhau (m. loc. sg.) purified, clean; *pari* (around) + *śuddhi*, from √*śudh* (purify, cleanse) [end of TP6 cpd.]

sva rūpa (n.) own-form (see I.3)

śūnyā (f. nom. sg.) empty (see I.9) [end of TP6 cpd.]

iva (ind.) like, as if

artha (m. or n.) purpose; meaning (see I.28)

mātra (m.) only, nothing but, entirely; also means measure, quantity, element; from √*mā* (measure) [end of TP6 cpd.]

nirbhāsā (f. nom. sg.) shines forth, is apparent or illumined; *nir* (asunder, away) + *bhāsa* (light, lustre, brightness), from √*bhās* (illuminate, shine) [end of KD cpd.]

nirvitarkā (f. nom. sg.) beyond thought or cognition; *nir* (out, away from) + *vi* (asunder, away) + *tarka* (conjecture, reasoning)

Nirvitarkā is when memory is purified, as if emptied of its own form, and the purpose alone shines forth.

When the memory is purified, the superimposition of karmic deposits is halted, and the purpose, in this case the object of perceptions, is not tinged with the past. See III.3.

I.44 ***etayaiva savicārā nirvicārā ca sūkṣma-viṣayā vyākhyātā***

etayā (f. instr. sg.) by this

eva (ind.) thus

savicārā (f. nom. sg.) with reflection, consideration; *sa* (with) + *vi* (asunder, away) + *cāra* (going, motion, progression), from √*car* (go, wander)

nirvicārā (f. nom. sg.) beyond reflection or consideration; *nir* (asunder, away) + *vicārā* (see above)

ca (ind.) and

sūkṣma (m.) subtle, fine, thin; probably related to √*siv* (sew)

viṣayā (f. nom. sg.) condition (see I.11) [end of BV cpd.]

vyākhyātā (f. nom. sg.) explained, fully detailed; *vi* (asunder, away) + *ā* (unto) + *khyātā* (named, known), from √*khyā* (name, declare)

Similarly explained are *savicārā* and *nirvicārā* which are subtle conditions.

The levels of unity (*samāpatti*) are explained as four fold: *savitarkā* (with gross object); *nirvitarkā* (free of gross object); *savicārā* (with subtle object); *nirvicārā* (free of subtle object).

I.45 ***sūkṣma-viṣayatvaṃ ca aliṅga-paryavasānam***

sūkṣma (m.) subtle (see I.44)

viṣayatvaṃ (n. nom. sg.) condition; nature of condition; *viṣaya* (see I.11) + *tva*, suffix indicating "ness" or nature of [end of KD cpd.]

ca (ind.) and

aliṅga (n.) undesignated, bearing no marks, undifferentiated, unmanifest; said by Vyāsa to refer to *prakṛti*, the most subtle cause; *a* (not) + *linga* (sign, mark), from √*ling* (paint, change)

paryavasānam (n. nom. sg.) termination, end, conclusion; *pari* (around) + *ava* (down) + *sāna*, from √*sā* (bind) [end of TP7 cpd.]

And the subtle condition terminates in the undesignated.

I.46 ***tā eva sabījaḥ samādhiḥ***

tāḥ (f. nom. pl.) these

eva (ind.) indeed

sabījaḥ (m. nom. sg.) with seed or source; *sa* (with) + *bīja* (seed, germ, primary cause)

samādhiḥ (m. nom. sg.) absorption (see I.20)

These are *Samādhi* with seed.

I.47 ***nirvicāra-vaiśāradye 'dhyātma-prasādaḥ***

nirvicāra (m.) beyond reflection (see I.44)

vaiśāradye (n. loc. sg.) skill in, expertness, clearness of intellect; strengthened form of *viśārada* (experienced, skilled), *vi* (away) + *śārada* (autumn) [end of TP3 cpd.]

adhyātma (n.) authentic self, inner-being; *adhi* (over, on) + *ātma* (self, sometimes translated as soul), from √*an* (breathe) or √*at* (move)

prasādaḥ (m. nom. sg.) clarity, brightness, purity (see I.33)

In skill with *nirvicārā*, clarity of authentic self arises.

I.48 ***ṛtaṃ bharā tatra prajñā***

ṛtaṃ (n. nom. sg.) truth, righteousness, *dharma*, order, norm; cognates in English include art, ritual, and rhythm; refers to the order established by sacrifice or the movement of life, from √*ṛ* (go towards, obtain, reach)

bharā (f. nom. sg.) bearing, carrying; from √*bhṛ* (bear)
tatra (adv.) there
prajñā (f. nom. sg.) wisdom, knowledge, intelligence; from *pra* (before, forward) + √*jña* (know)

There the wisdom is *ṛtaṃ* bearing.

This wisdom sustains the movement of life. Ignorance causes one to fall from this order.

I.49 ***śruta-anumāna-prajñābhyām anya-viṣayā viśeṣa-arthatvāt***
śruta (m.) tradition, that which is heard; from √*śru* (hear)
anumāna (m.) inference (see I.7) [end of DV cpd.]
prajñābhyām (f. abl. du.) from wisdom (see I.48) [end of TP5 cpd.]
anya (m.) different, other
viṣayā (f. nom. sg.) condition (see I.11) [end of KD cpd.; agrees with *prajñā* of prior *sūtra*]
viṣeṣa (m.) distinct (see I:22) due to purpose, because of its aim; from *arthatvāt* (m. abl. sg.) (see I.28) + *tva*, suffix indicating quality [end of KD cpd.]

Its condition is different from heard or inferred knowledge because of its distinct purpose.

As in I.43 the purpose is to enable the perception of *puruṣa*.

I.50 ***taj-jaḥ saṃskāro 'nya saṃskāra-pratibandhī***
taj (n.) that
jaḥ (m. nom. sg.) born, arisen, sprung; from √*jan* (generate, produce) [end of TP5 cpd.]
saṃskāraḥ (m. nom. sg.) (see I.18)
anya (m.) other
saṃskāra (m.) (see I.18) [end of KD cpd.]
pratibandhī (m. nom. sg.) obstructing, preventing, impeding; *prati* (against, back) + *bandhin*, from √*bandh* (bind) + *in*, suffix indicating possession [end of TP2 cpd.]

The *saṃskāra* born of it obstructs other *saṃskāras*.

I.51 ***tasya api nirodhe sarva-nirodhān nirbījaḥ samādhiḥ***
tasya (m. gen. sg.) of it
api (ind.) also even
nirodhe (m. loc. sg.) in being restricted, suppressed (see I.2)
sarva (m.) all

nirodhāt (m. abl. sg.) from being restricted (see I.2)
nirbījaḥ (m. nom. sg.) without seed; *nir* (away from, out) + *bīja* (see I.46)
samādhiḥ (m. nom. sg.) (see I.20)

With even that restricted, everything is restricted and that is seedless *samādhi*.

12 "Śādhana pāda"

II.1 ***tapaḥ-svādhyāya-Īśvara-praṇidhānāni Kriyā Yogaḥ***

tapaḥ (n.) austerity, self discipline, creative heat from √*tap* (make hot)
svādhyāya (m.) self study; study of the sacred texts; *sva* (own) + *adhi* (over, on) + *a* (hither, unto) + *ya*, from √*i* (*go*)
Īśvara (m.) (see I.23)
praṇidhānāni (n. nom. pl.) dedication (see I.23) [end of DV cpd.]
kriyā (f.) doing, performing, work, action; from √*kṛ* (do, make)
yogaḥ (m. nom. sg.) (see I.1) [end of KD cpd.)

Austerity, self-study, and dedication to īśvara are Kriyā Yoga.

II.2 ***samādhi-bhāvana-arthaḥ kleśa-tanū-karaṇa-arthaś ca***

samādhi (m.) (see I:20)
bhāvana (m.) cultivating, causing to be, manifested; causative form of √*bhū* (be)
arthaḥ (m. nom. sg.) purpose (see I:28) [end of TP6 cpd.]
kleśa (m.) affliction (see I:24)
tanū (f.) lessened, diminished, weakened, attenuated; from √*tan* (stretch, spin, out)
karaṇa (m.) doing, making, causing, effecting; from √*kṛ* (do)
arthaḥ (m. nom. sg.) purpose (see I:28) [end of TP6 cpd.]
ca (ind.) and

[It is] for the purpose of cultivating *samādhi* and diminishing the afflictions.

II.3 ***avidyā-asmitā-rāga-dveṣa-abhiniveśāḥ kleśaḥ***

avidyā (f.) ignorance, nonwisdom, delusion; *a* (not) + *vidyā*, wisdom, from √*vid* (known)

asmitā (f.) I-am-ness (see I:17)
rāga (m.) attraction (see I:37)
dveṣa (m) aversion, repulsion, hatred, dislike; from √*dviṣ* (hate)
abhiniveśāḥ (m. nom. pl.) desire for continuity, clinging to life, will to live, tenacity; *abhi* (to, toward) +*ni* (down, into) + *veśa* from √*viś* (enter) [end of DV cpd.]
kleśāḥ (m. nom. pl.) affliction (see I:24)

Ignorance, I-am-ness, attraction, aversion, and desire for continuity are the aflictions.

II.4 ***avidyā-kṣetraṃ uttareṣāṃ prasupta-tanu-vicchina-udārāṇām***
avidyā (f. nom. sg.) ignorance (see II:3)
kṣetraṃ (n. nom. sg.) origin, field, ground; from √*kṣi* (possess)
uttareṣāṃ (m. gen. pl.) of the others
prasupta (m.) dormant, fallen, asleep, inactive, latent; *pra* (before, forward) + *supta*, from √*svap* (sleep)
tanu (m.) suppressed, lessened, diminished; from √*tan* (stretch, spin out)
vicchinna (m.) supressed, overpowered, interupted; *vi* (asunder, away) + *chinna*, from √*chid* (cut)
udārāṇām (m. gen. pl) fully active or engaged, aroused; *ud* (up, forth, out) + *ara*, from √*ṛ* (go) [end of DV cpd.]

Ignorance is the origin of the others, whether dormant, diminished, interrupted, or fully active.

II.5 ***anitya-aśuci-duḥkha-anātmasu nitya-śuci-sukha-ātma-khyātir avidyā***
anitya (m.) noneternal, temporal, fleeting, transient; *a* (not) + *nitya* (eternal) from √*nī* (lead)
aśuci (m.) impure, defiled; *a* (not) +*śuci* (pure), from √*śuc* (gleam)
duḥkha (n.) difficulty, dissatisfaction, sorrow (see I:31)
anātmasu (m. loc pl.) nonself; *an* (not) + *ātman*, self, probably from √*an* (breath) [end of DV cpd.]
nitya (m.) eternal (see above)
śuci (m.) pure, undefiled, untainted (see above)
sukha (n.) pleasure, happiness, joy, well-being (see I:33)
ātma (m.) self (see above) [end of DV]
khyātir (f. nom. sg.) seeing, ascertainment; from √*khyā* (see I:16)
avidyā (f. nom. sg.) ignorance (see II:3)

Ignorance is seeing the non-eternal as eternal, the impure as pure, suffering as pleasure, and the non-self as self.

Alternate translation: Ignorance is seeing the transient as intransigent, a sullied thing as pure, a painful experience as pleasure, and the ego as one's true self.

II.6 ***dṛg-darśana-śaktyor eka ātmatā iva asmitā***

dṛg (*dṛś*) (m.) seeing, looking, discerning: from √*dṛś* (see)

darśana (m.) what is seen (see I:30)

śaktyor (f.gen.du) power, ability; from √*śak* (be able) [end of TP6 cpd.]

eka (m.) one

ātmatā (f. nom. sg.) self-ness, nature, from *ātma* (self) + *tā*, feminine suffix denoting "having the quality of" [end of KD cpd.]

iva (ind.) as if

asmitā (f. nom. sg.) I-am-ness (see I:17)

I-am-ness is when the two powers of Seer and Seen [appear] as a single self.

II.7 ***sukha-anuśayī rāgaḥ***

sukha (n.) pleasant (see I:33)

anuśayī (m. nom. sg.) clinging to, resting on: *anu* (along, after) + *śaya*, from √*śī* (rest) + *in*, possessive suffix [end of TP7 cpd.]

rāgaḥ (m. nom. sg.) attraction (see I:37)

Attraction is clinging to pleasure.

II.8 ***duḥkha-anuśayī dveṣaḥ***

duḥkha (n.) suffering (see I:31)

anuśayī (m. nom. sg.) clinging to (see above) [end of TP7 cpd.]

dveṣaḥ (m. nom. sg) aversion (see II:8)

Aversion is clinging to dissatisfaction.

II.9 ***svarasa-vāhī viduṣo' pi tathā rūḍho' bhiniveśaḥ***

svarasa (m.) own inclination: literally own juice or essence; *sva* (self) + *rasa*, from √ras (taste)

vāhī (m. nom. sg.) sustained, borne, carried: from √*vah* (carry, flow, sustain)

viduṣaḥ (m. gen. sg.) wise person, sage, one who knows; from √*vid* (know)

api (ind.) even, also

tathā (ind.) thus

rūḍhaḥ (m. nom. sg.) arisen, sprung up, produced from, from √*ruh* (rise, spring up)
abhiniveśaḥ (m. nom. sg.) desire for continuity (see II:3)

Desire for continuity, arising even among the wise, is sustained by self-essence.

II.10 ***te pratiprasava-heyāḥ sūkṣmāḥ***
te (m. nom. pl.) they (refers to afflictions)
pratiprasava (m.) disassociation from the creation process, counter-order, return to the original state, inverse propagation; *prati* (against, back) + *prasava* (creation, begetting), from *pra* (before, forward) + *sava* (pressing out), from √*sū* (generate, impel)
heyāḥ (m. nom. pl.) to be avoided, overcome, abandoned, from √*ha* (leave, abandon) [end of TP3 cpd.]
sūkṣmāḥ (m. nom pl.) subtle (see I:44)

These subtle ones are to be avoided by a return to the origin.

II.11 ***dhyāna-heyās tad-vṛttayaḥ***
dhyāna (m.) meditation (see I:39)
heyāḥ (m. nom. pl.) (see above)
tad (n.) that, those
vṛttayaḥ (m. nom. pl.) fluctuations (see I:22) [end of TP6 cpd.]

The fluctuations [generated by these afflictions] are to be avoided by meditation.

II.12 ***kleśa-mūlaḥ karma-āśayo dṛṣṭa-adṛṣṭa-janma-vedanīyaḥ***
kleśa (m.) affliction (see I:24)
mūlaḥ (m. nom. sg) root, foundation, from √*mūl* (be rooted) [end of TP6 cpd.]
karma (n.) action (see I:24)
āśayaḥ (m. nom. sg.) residue (see I.24) [end of TP6 cpd.]
dṛṣṭa (m.) seen (see I.15)
adṛṣṭa (m.) unseen (see I.15)
janma (n.) existence, life, birth; from √*jan* (be born, come into existence)
vedanīyaḥ (m. nom. sg.) to be felt or experienced; gerundive form of √*vid* (know) [end of TP6 cpd.]

The residue of karma, rooted in affliction, is felt in seen or unseen existence.

II.13 ***sati mūle tad-vipāko jāty-āyur-bhogāḥ***

sati (m. loc. sg.) being, existing, occurring

mūle (m. loc. sg.) root (see II:12) [end of locative absolute construction]

tad (n.) that

vipākaḥ (m. nom. sg.) fruition (see I.24)

jāti (f.) birth, production, position assigned by caste or rank; from √*jan* (be born)

āyuḥ (n.) life, vital power, span of life; *ā* (hither, unto) + *yuḥ*, from √*i* (go)

bhogāḥ (m. nom. pl.) experience, enjoyment, eating; from √*bhuj* (enjoy) [end of DV cpd.]

While the root exists, there is fruition of it as birth, duration, and experience.

II.14 ***te hlāda-paritāpa-phalāḥ puṇya-apuṇya-hetutvāt***

te (m. nom. pl.) they, these

hlāda (m.) joyful, delightful, pleasurable; from √*hlād* (rejoice)

paritāpa (m.) pain, agony, grief, sorrow; *pari* (around) + *tāpa*, from √*tap* (be hot) [end of DV cpd.]

phalāḥ (m. nom. pl.) fruits, consequences, result (used adjectivally to describe the three life states in II:13) [end of BV cpd.]

puṇya (n.) meritorious, auspicious, propitious, pure, holy, sacred; from √*puṇ* (do good)

apuṇya (n.) opposite of above; *a* (not) +√*puṇ* (do good)

hetutvāt (m. abl. sg.) cause, motive, reason, *hetu*, from √*hi* (impel, incite) + *tva*, suffix indicating quality [end of KD cpd.]

These fruits are joyful or painful according to whether the causes are meritorious or demeritorious.

II.15 ***pariṇāma-tāpa-saṃskāra-duḥkhair guṇa-vṛtti-virodhāc ca duḥkham eva sarvaṃ vivekinaḥ***

pariṇāma (m.) change, alteration, transformation, evolution, development, ripeness, result; *pari* (around) + √*nam* (bow)

tāpa (m.) sorrow, anxiety, pain, angst, anguish; √*tap* (be hot)

saṃskāra (m.) impression left by past action (see I:14) [end of TP5 cpd.]

duḥkhair (n. instr. pl.) by sufferings (see I:31) [end of TP5 cpd.]

guṇa (m.) strand, thread, quality (see I:16)

vṛtti (f.) fluctuation (see I:2)

vīrodhāt (m. abl. sg.) conflict, opposition, hostility, adversity; *vi* (asunder, away) + *rodha* (obstruct, arrest) [end of TP6 cpd.]
ca (ind.) and
duḥkham (n. nom. sg.) suffering (see I:31)
eva (ind.) indeed, thus
sarvaṃ (n. nom. sg.) all, everything
vivekinaḥ (m. gen. sg) the discriminating, discerning one; *vi* (asunder, away) +*vekin*, from √*vic* (divide asunder, distinguish, sift) + *in*, possessive suffix

For the discriminating one, all is suffering, due to the conflict of the fluctuations of the *guṇas* and by the sufferings due to *pariṇāma*, sorrow, and *saṃskāra*.

II.16 ***heyaṃ duḥkham anāgataṃ***
heyaṃ (n. nom. sg.) to be avoided (see II:20)
duḥkham (n. nom. sg.) dissatisfaction (see I:31)
anāgataṃ (n. nom. sg.) not yet come; *an* (not) + *ā* (unto) + *gata* (gone), from √*gam* (go)
The suffering yet to come is to be avoided.

II.17 ***draṣṭṛ-dṛśyayoḥ saṃyogo heya-hetuḥ***
draṣṭṛ (m.) seer (see I:3)
dṛśyayoḥ (m. gen. du.) seen, that which is visible; from √*dṛś* (see) [end of DV cpd.]
saṃyogaḥ (m. nom sg.) union, correlation, joining, confusion, conjunction; *sam* (together) + *yoga* (union, from √*yuj* (unite, yoke)
heya (n.) to be avoided (see II:20)
hetuḥ (m. nom. sg.) cause, motive, reason; from √*hi* (impel, incite) [end of KD cpd.]

The cause of what is to be avoided is the confusion of the Seer with the Seen.

II.18 ***prakāśa-kriyā-sthiti-śīlaṃ bhūta-indriya-ātmakaṃ bhoga-apavargārthaṃ dṛśyaṃ***
prakāśa (m.) light, luster, splendor, brightness; *pra* (before, forward) + *kāśa*, from √*kāś* (shine, appear)
kriyā (f.) activity (see I:1)
sthiti (f.) remaining inert, standing (see I:13) [end of DV cpd.]

śīlaṃ (n. nom. sg.) quality, character, nature; from √*śīl* (serve, act) [end of TP6 cpd.]
bhūta (m.) elements: earth, water, fire, air, space; constituent of the manifest world; from √*bhū* (be)
indriya (n.) sense organ, power; derived from the name *Indra* [end of DV cpd.]
ātmakaṃ (n. nom. sg.) having the self-nature of; *ātma* (self) + *ka*, possessive suffix
bhoga (m.) experience, enjoyment (see II.13)
apavarga (m.) liberation, emancipation; *apa* (away, off) + *varga*, from √*vṛj* (twist, bend, turn) [end of DV cpd.]
arthaṃ (n. nom. sg.) purpose (see I:28) [end of TP6 cpd.]
dṛśyam (n. nom. sg.) seen (see II:17)

The Seen has the qualities of light, activity, and inertia*, consists of the elements and senses, and has the purposes of experience and liberation.

*These correspond to the three *guṇas*: *sattva*, *rajas*, *tamas*, respectively.

II.19 ***viśeṣa-aviśeṣa-liṅga-mātra-aliṅgāni guṇa-parvāṇi***
viśeṣa (m.) distinct (see I:22)
aviśeṣa (m.) indistinct; *a* (not) + *viśeṣa* (see I:22)
liṅga (n.) designator, signifier, indicator, from √*ling* (paint, mark)
mātra (n.) suffix designating measure or quantity; entirely, only; from √*mā* (measure)
aliṅgāni (n. nom. pl.) literally, without mark; unmanifest; *a* (not) + *liṅga* (see above) [end of DV cpd.]
guṇa (m.) thread or strand (see I:16)
parvāṇi (n. nom. pl.) division, level; from √*pṛ* (fill) [end of TP6 cpd.]

The distinct, the indistinct, the designator, and the unmanifest are the divisions of the *guṇas*.

According to Vyāsa these four divisions are as follows: The distinct (*viśeṣa*) has sixteen parts: five gross elements (space, air, fire, water, earth), the five sense organs (ears, skin, eyes, tongue, nose), the five action organs (mouth, hands, feet, and organs of evacuation and generation), and the mind. The indistinct (*aviśeṣa*) includes six parts: the five subtle elements (hearing, touching, seeing, tasting, smelling) and the sense of self (*ahaṃkāra*). The designator (*liṅgamātra*) is the intellect (*buddhi*), and the unmanifest *aliṅga* is *mūlaprakṛti*.

II.20 ***draṣṭā dṛśi-mātraḥ śuddho'pi pratyaya-anupaśyaḥ***

draṣṭā (m. nom. sg) seer (see I:3)

dṛśi (f.) seeing, power of seeing; from √*dṛś* (see)

mātraḥ (m. nom. sg.) only (see II:20)

śuddhaḥ (m. nom. sg.) pure, correct, cleansed; from √*śūdh* (purify, clean)

api (ind.) also, even, although

pratyaya (m.) intention (see I:10)

anupaśyaḥ (m. nom. sg.) to appear, to be looked upon, to be taken as; *anu* (along, after) + *paśya* from √*paś* (see) [end of T6 cpd.]

The Seer only sees; though pure, it appears intentional.

II.21 ***tad-artha eva dṛśyasya-ātmā***

tad (n.) that, this; in this case refers to the seer (*puruṣa*)

arthaḥ (m. nom. sg.) purpose (see I:28) [end of TP6 cpd.]

eva (ind.) indeed, only

dṛśyasya (m. gen. sg.) seen (see II:17)

ātmā (m. nom. sg.) nature, self, essence (see II:5)

The nature of the Seen is only for the purpose of that (*puruṣa*).

II.22 ***kṛta-arthaṃ prati naṣṭam apy anaṣṭam tad anya-sādhāraṇatvāt***

kṛta (m.) done, made; from √*kṛ* (do, make)

arthaṃ (n. nom. sg.) purpose (see I:28) [end of KD cpd.]

prati (ind.) towards, for

naṣṭaṃ (n. nom. sg.) disappeared, lost, destroyed, expelled, wasted; from √*naś* (perish)

api (ind.) even, also

anaṣṭam (n. nom. sg.) not destroyed; *a* (not) + *naṣṭaṃ* (see above)

tad (n.) that

anya (n.) other

sādhāraṇatvāt (n. abl. sg.) commonality, universality; *sā* (with) + *dhāraṇa* (holding); from √*dhṛ* (hold) [end of TP6 cpd.]

When (its) purpose is done, it disappears; otherwise it does not disappear due to being common to others.

II.23 ***sva-svāmi-śaktyoḥ sva-rūpa-upalabdhi-hetuḥ saṃyogaḥ***

sva (m.) owned

svāmi (m.) owner, lord, chief

śaktyoḥ (f. gen. du.) power (see II:6)

svarūpa (n.) own form (see I:3)
upalabdhi (f.) apprehension, perception; *upa* (to unto) *labdhi*, from √*labh* (obtain)
hetuḥ (m. nom. sg.) cause (see II:17)
saṃyogaḥ (m. nom. sg.) union (see II:17)

Confusion (*saṃyogaḥ*) results when one perceives the two powers of owner and owned as (one) self form.

II.24 ***tasya hetur avidyā***

tasya (m. gen. sg.) of it
hetuḥ (m. nom. sg.) cause (see II:17)
avidyā (f. nom. sg.) ignorance (see II:3)

The cause of it is ignorance.

II.25 ***tad-abhāvāt saṃyoga-abhāvo hānaṃ tad-dṛśeḥ kaivalyaṃ***

tad (n.) that (refers to ignorance)
abhāvāt (m. abl. sg.) absence, nonexistence, negation; *a* (not) + *bhāva* (being), from √*bhū* (be); see I:10
saṃyoga (m.) confusion (see II:17)
abhāvaḥ (m. nom. sg.) see above [end of TP6 cpd.]
hānaṃ (n. nom. sg.) escape, giving up, relinquishment, abandoning, cessation; from √*hā* (depart)
tad (n.) that
dṛśeḥ (f. abl. sg.) from the seen (see II:20)
kaivalyam (n. nom. sg.) isolation, aloneness; single, unitary, uncompounded; from the noun *kevala*, meaning alone, not connected to anything

From the absence [of ignorance], confusion (*saṃyoga*) ceases; [this is] the escape, the isolation from the Seen.

II.26 ***viveka-khyātir aviplavā hānopāyaḥ***

viveka (m.) discrimination, discerning (see II:15)
khyātiḥ (f. nom. sg.) discernment, perception, knowledge (see I:16) [end of KD cpd.]
aviplavā (f. nom. sg.) unfaltering, unbroken, unwavering; *a* (not) + *vi* (asunder, away) + *plava*, from √*plu* (float)
hāna (n.) escape (see I:25)
upāyaḥ (m. nom sg.) means, method, that by which one reaches a goal; *upa* (to, unto), + *aya*, from √*i* (go)

The means of escape is unfaltering discriminative discernment.

II.27 ***tasya saptadhā prānta-bhūmiḥ prajñā***

tasya (m. gen. sg.) of him (the accomplished Yogin)

saptadhā (f. nom. sg) sevenfold; *sapta* (seven) +*dhā*, suffix meaning "fold"

prānta (m.) last, edge, boundary; *pra* (before, foward) + *anta* (end, limit)

bhūmiḥ (f. nom. sg) stage, place, ground (see I:14) [end of KD cpd.]

prajñā (f. nom. sg.) wisdom (see I:20)

The preparatory ground for this wisdom is seven-fold.

According to Vyāsa, the seven stages are (1) that which is to be known has been known; (2) that which is to be avoided has been avoided; (3) that which is to be attained has been attained; (4) the means (discriminative discernment) has been realized; (5) the intellect has completed its purpose of providing experience and liberation; (6) the activities of the *guṇas* have ceased; (7) *puruṣa* abides in isolation. For an alternate reading, see chapter 15.

II.28 ***yoga-aṅga-anuṣṭhānād aśuddhi-kṣaye jñāna-dīptir ā viveka-khyāteḥ***

yoga (m.) (see I:1)

aṅga (n.) limb, member, division, body (see I:31)

anuṣṭhānād (n. abl. sg.) following, carrying out and undertaking, doing; *anu* (along, after) + *sthāna*, from √*sthā* (stand) [end of TP6 cpd.]

aśuddhi (f.) impure, sullied; *a* (not) + *śuddhi*, from √*śudh* (purify)

kṣaye (m. loc. sg.) destruction, loss, wearing away; from √*kṣi* (destroy)

jñāna (m.) knowledge (see I:8)

diptiḥ (f. nom. sg.) light, splendor, radiance; from √*dīp* (to light)

ā (ind.) up to, as far as

viveka (m.) discrimination (see II:15)

khyāteḥ (f. abl. sg.) discernment (see I:16)

From following the limbs of Yoga, which destroy impurity, the light of knowledge arises, leading to discriminative discernment.

II.29 ***yama-niyama-āsana-prāṇāyāma-pratyāhāra-dhāraṇā-dhyāna-samādhayo 'ṣṭāv-aṅgāni***

yama (m.) restraint, self-control, precept, holding back; from √*yam* (restrain)

niyama (m.) observance; *ni* (down, into) + √*yam* (restrain)

āsana (n.) posture, position, sitting down; from √*ās* (sit, be)
prāṇāyāma (m.) control of breath; *prāṇa* (breath) from *pra* (before, forward) + √*an* (breathe) +*yāma*, from √*yam* (see above)
pratyāhāra (m.) withdrawal, retreat, holding back (especially of senses); *prati* (against, back) + *ā* (unto) + *hāra*, from √*hṛ* (take, hold)
dhāraṇā (f.) concentration, act of holding, retaining; from √*dhṛ* (hold, maintain)
dhyāna (n.) meditation (see I:39)
samādhayaḥ (m. nom. pl.) absorption, concentration, unified state of awareness (see I:20) [end of DV cpd.]
aṣṭau (m.) eight
aṅgāni (n. nom. pl.) limb (see II: 28)

Precepts, observances, postures, control of breath, inwardness, concentration, meditation, and *samādhi* are the eight limbs.

II.30 ***ahiṃsā-satya-asteya-brahmacarya-aparigrahā yamāḥ***
ahiṃsā (f.) nonviolence, absence of desire to kill or injure, *a* (not) + *hiṃsā*, desiderative derivative from √*han* (strike, kill)
satya (n.) authenticity, truthfulness, sincerity, veracity; from *sat* (real, actual), present participle of √*as* (be, exist)
asteya (n.) not stealing; *a* (not) + *steya*, from √*stai* (steal)
brahmacarya (n.) sexual restraint, chastity continence; *brahma* (one versed in sacred knowledge) + *carya*, engaged in, from √*car* (move, walk)
aparigrahāḥ (m. nom. pl.) nonpossession, renunciation of nonessentials; *a* (not) + *pari* (around) + *graha* (holding), from √*grabh* (grasp, hold) [end of DV cpd.]
yamāḥ (m. nom. pl.) precepts (see II:29)

The precepts are nonviolence, truthfulness, nonstealing, sexual restraint, and nonpossession.

II.31 ***jāti-deśa-kāla-samaya-anavacchinnāḥ sārva-bhaumā mahāvratam***
jāti (f.) birth (see II:13)
deśa (m.) place, region, location; from √*diś* (point out)
kāla (m.) time (see: I:26)
samaya (m.) circumstances, coming together; *sam* (together) + *aya*, from √*i* (go) [end of DV cpd.]
anavacchināḥ (m. nom. pl.) unlimited, unbounded, not delineated; *an* (not) + *ava* (down) + *chinna*, from √*chid* (cut) [end of TP3 cpd.]

sārva (m.) all, every; strengthened form of *sarva*
bhaumāḥ (m. nom. pl.) occasion, anything related to the world or earth; strengthened form of *bhūmi* (earth) [end of BV cpd.]
mahā (m.) great, large, extensive
vratam (n. nom. sg.) vow, resolve, conduct, decision; from √*vṛ* (choose, decide) [end of KD cpd.]

When not limited by birth, place, time, or circumstance in all occasions [these constitute] the great vow.

II.32 ***śauca-santoṣa-tapaḥ-svādhyāya-īśvara-praṇidhānāni niyamāḥ***
śauca (n.) purity, cleanliness; strengthened form of *śuci* (see II:5)
santoṣa (m.) contentment, satisfaction; *sam* (together) + *toṣa* from √*tuṣ* (enjoy)
tapaḥ (n.) austerity (see II:1)
svādhyāya (m.) (see II:1)
īśvara (m.) (see I.23)
praṇidhānāni (n. nom. pl.) dedication (see I:23)
niyamāḥ (m. nom. pl.) observance (see II:29)

Purity, contentment, austerity, self-study, and dedication to Īśvara are the observances.

II.33 ***vitarka-bādhane pratipakṣa-bhāvanam***
vitarka (m.) discursive thought (see I:17)
bādhane (m. loc. sg.) bondage, inhibiting, binding; from √*bādh* (harass, oppress, trouble) [end of TP5 cpd.]
pratipaskṣa (m.) opposite, *prati* (against, back) +*pakṣa* (wing)
bhāvanam (n. nom. sg.) cultivation (see I:28) [end of TP6 cpd.]

When there is bondage due to deliberation, the cultivation of the opposite [is prescribed.]

II.34 ***vitarkā hiṃsā-ādayaḥ kṛta-kārita-anumoditā lobha-krodha-moha-pūrvakā mṛdu-madhya-adhimātrā duḥkha-ajñāna-ananta-phalā iti pratipakṣa-bhāvanam***
vitarkāḥ (n. nom. pl.) deliberations (see I:17)
hiṃsā (f.) violence (see II:30)
ādayaḥ (m. nom. pl.) and the rest, starting with, etcetera; from *ādi*
kṛta (m.) done, make (see II:22)
kārita (m.) caused to be done; from √*kṛ* (do)
anumoditāḥ (m. nom. pl.) approved, permitted; *anu* (along, after) + *modita*, from √*mud* (rejoice, celebrate) [end of DV cpd.]

lobha (m.) lust, greed, cupidity; from √*lubh* (entice, allure)
krodha (m.) anger, wrath, passion; from √*krudh* (be angry)
moha (m.) delusion, bewilderment, perplexity; from √*muh* (be stupefied)
pūrvakāḥ (m. nom. pl.) consisting of, accompanied by, connected with; *pūrva* (prior) + *ka* (nominalizing suffix) [end of TP3 cpd.]
mṛdu (m.) mild (see I:22)
madhya (m.) medium (see I:22)
adhimātrāḥ (m. nom. pl.) intense (see I:22) [end of DV cpd.]
duḥkha (n.) dissatisfaction (see I:31)
ajñāna (n.) ignorance; *a* (not) +*jñāna* (see I:8)
ananta (m.) boundless, endless, eternal, infinite
phalāḥ (m. nom. pl.) fruits (see II:14) [end of BV cpd.]
iti (ind.) thus, so
pratipakṣa (m.) opposite (see II:33)
bhāvanam (n. nom. sg.) cultivation (see I:28) [end of TP6 cpd.]

Deliberations about violence and so forth, whether done, caused, or approved, consisting of lust, anger, or delusion, and whether mild, medium or intense, have as their endless fruits suffering and ignorance; thus, cultivation of opposites [is prescribed].

II.35 ***ahiṃsā-pratiṣṭhāyāṃ tat-saṃnidhau vaira-tyāgaḥ***
ahiṃsā (f.) nonviolence (see II:30)
pratiṣṭhāyāṃ (f. loc. sg.) established, abiding, standing; *prati* (against, back) + *ṣṭhāyam*, from √*sthā* (stand) [end of TP7 cpd.]
tat (n.) that
saṃnidhau (m. loc. sg.) presence, nearness, proximity; *sam* (together) + *ni* (down, into) +*dhi*, from √*dhā* (put, place) [end of TP6 cpd.]
vaira (m.) hostility, animosity, enmity; from *vīra* (vehemence)
tyāgaḥ (m. nom. sg.) abandonment, leaving behind, giving up; from √*tyaj* (renounce) [end of TP6 cpd.]

When in the presence of one established in nonviolence, there is the abandonment of hostility.

II.36 ***satya-pratiṣṭhāyāṃ kriyā-phala āśrayatvam***
satya (n.) truthfulness (see II:30)
pratiṣṭhāyāṃ (f. loc. sg.) established (see II:35) [end of TP7 cpd.]
kriyā (f.) action (see II:1)

phala (n.) fruit (see II:14)
āśrayatvam (n. nom. sg.) correspondence; dwelling in, depending on, following; *ā* (hither, unto) + *śraya* protection, refuge; from √*śri* (rest on) +*tva*, suffix denoting "ness" [end of TP3 cpd.]

When established in truthfulness, [there is] correspondence between action and fruit.

II.37 ***asteya-pratiṣṭhāyāṃ sarva-ratna-upasthānam***
asteya (n.) not stealing (see II:30)
pratiṣṭhāyām (f. loc. sg.) established (see II:34)
sarva (n.) all
ratna (n.) jewel, gem
upasthānam (n. nom. sg.) presence, appearance; *upa* (to, unto) + *sthāna*, from √*sthā* (stand) [end of TP6 cpd.]

When established in nonstealing, [whatever is] present is all jewels.

II.38 ***brahmacarya-pratiṣṭhāyāṃ vīrya-lābhaḥ***
brahmacarya (n.) sexual restraint (see II:30)
pratiṣṭhāyāṃ (f. loc. sg.) established (see II:34) [end of TP7 cpd.]
vīrya (n.) vigor, strength, power, energy; from √*vīr* (be powerful)
lābhaḥ (m. nom. sg.) obtained, gotten; from √*labh* (obtain) [end of TP6 cpd.]

When established in sexual restraint, vigor is obtained.

II.39 ***aparigraha-sthairye janma-kathaṃtā saṃbodhaḥ***
aparigraha (m.) nonpossession (see II:30)
sthairye (n. loc sg.) steadfastness, firmness, stability; from √*sthā* (stand) [end of TP7 cpd.]
janma (n.) existence, birth, origin (see II:12)
kathaṃtā (f. nom. sg.) the how or what, whatness; *katham* (how) + *tā*, feminine suffix denoting quality
saṃbodhaḥ (m. nom. sg) knowledge, understanding; *saṃ* (together) + *bodha*, from √budh (awaken)

When steadfast in nonpossession, there is knowledge of "the how" of existence.

II.40 ***śaucāt sva-aṅga-jugupsā parair asaṃsargaḥ***
śauca (n.) purity (see II:32)
sva (m.) own

aṅga (n.) body, limb, member (see I:31)
jugupsā (f. nom. sg.) dislike, disgust; reduplicated desiderative form of √*gup* (shun, avoid)
parair (m. instr. pl.) others
asaṃsargaḥ (m. nom. sg) noncontact, nonassociation; *a* (not) + *sam* (together) +*sarga*, from √*sṛj* (emit)

From purity arises dislike for one's own body and noncontact with others.

II.41 ***sattva-śuddhi-saumanasya-eka-indriya-agrya-jaya-ātma-darśana-yogyatvāni ca***
sattva (n.) lightness, "being-ness," existence; *sat* (existence) + *tva*, suffix indicating quality
śuddhi (f.) purity (see II:28) [end of KD cpd.]
saumanasya (m.) cheerfulness, gladness, satisfaction of mind; *sau*, strengthened form of *su* (goodness) + *manasya* (to have in mind)
eka (m.) one
agrya (m.) intent, closely attentive; from *agra* (foremost) [end of TP6 cpd.], with *eka*, one pointedness
indriya (n.) sense organ (see II:18)
jaya (m.) mastery, conquering, being victorious; from √*ji* (conquer) [end of TP cpd.]
ātman (m.) self (see II:5)
darśana (m.) vision, view (see I:30) [end of TP6 cpd.]
yogyatvāni (n. nom. pl.) fitness, suitability, ability; *yoga*, from √*yuj* (join) + *tva*, suffix indicating quality [end of DV cpd.]
ca (ind.) and

And purity of *sattva*, cheerfulness, one-pointedness, mastery of the senses, and fitness for the vision of the self [arise].

II.42 ***santoṣād anuttamaḥ sukha-lābhaḥ***
santoṣād (m. abl. sg.) contentment (see II:32)
anuttamaḥ (m. nom. sg.) unsurpasssed, excellent; *an* (not) + *ud* (up) + *tama*, suffix forming superlative
sukha (n.) happiness, joy (see I:33)
lābhaḥ (m. nom. sg) obtained, gained (see II:38)

From contentment, unsurpassed happiness is obtained.

II.43 ***kāya-indriya-siddhir aśuddhi-kṣayāt tapasaḥ***
kāya (m.) body, assemblage; from √*ci* (gather)
indriya (n.) sense organ (see II:18)
siddhiḥ (f. nom. sg.) perfection, accomplishment, attainment from √*sidh* (accomplish) [end of TP7 cpd.]
aśuddhi (f.) impure (see II:28)
kṣayāt (m. abl. sg) destruction (see II:28)
tapasaḥ (n. abl. sg.) austerity (see II:1)

From austerity arises the destruction of impurity and the perfection of the body and senses.

II.44 ***svādhyāyād iṣṭa-devatā-saṃprayogaḥ***
svādhyāyād (m. abl. sg.) self-study (see II:1)
iṣṭa (m.) intended, sought, desired, liked; from √*iṣ* (wish)
devatā (f.) god, divinity; *deva* (god) +*tā* feminine suffix denoting quality [end of KD cpd.]
saṃprayogaḥ (m. nom. sg.) union, joining together; *sam* (together) + *pra* (before) + *yoga*, from √*yuj* (join) [end of TP3 cpd.]

From self-study (arises) union with the desired deity.

II.45 ***samādhi-siddhir īśvara-praṇidhānāt***
samādhi (f.) absorption (see I:20)
siddhiḥ (f. nom. sg.) perfection (see II:43) [end of TP6 cpd.]
īśvara (m.) (see I:23)
praṇidhānāt (m. abl. sg.) devotion (see I:23) [end of TP4 cpd.]

Perfection in *Samādhi* (arises) from dedication to *Īśvara*.

II.46 ***sthira-sukhaṃ āsanam***
sthira (m.) steadiness, firmness; from √*sthā* (stand)
sukhaṃ (n. nom. sg.) ease (see I:33)
āsanam (n, nom sg.) posture (see II:29)

Āsana is steadiness and ease.

II.47 ***prayatna-śaithilya-ananta-samāpattibhyām***
prayatna (m.) effort, striving, extertion; *pra* (before, forward) + *yatna*, from √*yat* (strive)
śaithilya (n.) relaxation, looseness; from √*śithila*, loose, slack)
ananta (m.) endless (see II:34)
samāpattibhyām (f. abl. du.) unity (see I:41)

From [it arises] relaxation of effort and endless unity.

II.48 ***tato dvandva-anabhighātāḥ***

tataḥ (ind.) thus, from that

dvandva (n.) pair of opposites; literally, "two-two"

anabhighātāḥ (n. nom. pl.) assault, attacking, assailing; *an* (not) + *abhi* (to, unto) *ghāta*, from √*han* (strike, kill) [end of TP3 cpd.]

Thus, there is no assault by the pairs of opposites.

II.49 ***tasmin sati śvāsa-praśvāsayor gati-vicchedaḥ prāṇāyāmaḥ***

tasmin (m. loc. sg.) in this

sati (m. loc. sg.) being (see II:13)

śvāsa (m.) breath, inbreath; from √*śvas* (breathe)

praśvāsayoḥ (m. gen. du.) outbreath, exhalation; *pra* (before, forward) + *śvāsa* (see above) [end of DV cpd.]

gati (f.) motion, procession; from √*gam* (go)

vicchedaḥ (m. nom. sg.) cutting off, breaking; *vi* (away, asunder) + *cheda*, from √*chid* (cut) [end of TP6 cpd.]

prāṇāyāmaḥ (m. nom. sg.) control of breath (see II:29)

Being in this, there is control of breath, which is the cutting off of the motion of inbreath and outbreath.

II.50 ***bāhya-abhyantara-stambha-vṛttir deśa-kāla-saṃkhyābhiḥ paridṛṣṭo dīrgha-sūkṣmaḥ***

bāhya (m.) external, outer; from *bahis* (outside)

abhyantara (m.) internal, inside; *abhi* (to, unto) + *antar* (interior, inside)

stambha (m.) suppressed, stopped, obstructed; from √*stambh* (hold up) [end of DV cpd.]

vṛttiḥ (f. nom. sg.) fluctuation (see I:2) [end of KD cpd.)

deśa (m.) place (see II:31)

kāla (m.) time (see I:4)

saṃkhyābhis (f. instr. pl.) observation, calculation; *sam* (together) + √*khyā* (count) [end of TP6 cpd.]

paridṛṣto (m. nom. sg.) seen, beheld, perceived; *pari* (around) + *dṛṣta* from √*dṛś* (see)

dīrgha (m.) long, loftly, tall

sūkṣmaḥ (m. nom. sg.) subtle (see I:44) [end of DV cpd.]

Its fluctuations are external, internal, and suppressed; it is observed according to time, place, and number, and becomes long and subtle.

II.51 ***bāhya-abhyantara-viṣaya-ākṣepī caturthaḥ***

bāhya (m.) external (see II:50)

abhyantara (m.) internal (see II:50) [end of DV cpd.]

viṣaya (m.) condition (see I:11) [end of KD cpd.]

ākṣepī (n. nom. sg.) withdrawal, casting aside; *ā* (hither, unto) + *kṣepin*, from √*kṣip* (throw, cast) + possessive suffix *in* [end of TP cpd.]

caturthaḥ (m. nom. sg.) fourth

The fourth is withdrawal from external and internal conditions [of breath].

II.52 ***tataḥ kṣīyate prakāśa-āvaraṇam***

tataḥ (ind.) then

kṣīyate (3rd pers. sg. pass.) is dissolved, destroyed, diminished; from √*kṣi* (destroy)

prakāśa (m.) light, clearness, brightness, splendor; *pra* (before, forward) + *kāśa*, (shine) (see II:18)

āvaraṇam (n. nom. sg.) covering, concealing; *ā* (hither, unto) + *varaṇa*, from √*vṛ* (cover) [end of TP6 cpd.]

Thus, the covering of light is dissolved.

II.53 ***dhāraṇāsu ca yogyatāmanasaḥ***

dhāraṇāsu (f. loc. pl.) in concentrations (see II:29)

ca (ind.) and

yogyatā (f. nom. sg.) fitness (see II:41)

manasaḥ (n. gen. sg.) of the mind (see I:35)

And there is fitness of the mind-power for concentrations.

II.54 ***sva-viṣaya-asaṃprayoge cittasya sva-rūpa-anukāra iva indriyāṇāṃ pratyāhāraḥ***

sva (m.) own (see I:3)

viṣaya (m.) circumstance, object (see I:11)

asaṃprayoge (n. loc. sg.) disengagement; *a* (not) + *saṃprayoga* (see II:44)

cittasya (n. gen. sg.) of mind (see I:2)

sva (m.) own (see I:3)

rūpa (n.) form (see I:3)

anukāraḥ (n. nom. sg.) imitation, resemblance; *anu* (along, after) +*kāra*, from √*kṛ* (do)

iva (ind.) as if, just as
indriyāṇām (n. gen. pl.) of the senses (see II:18)
pratyāhāraḥ (m. nom. sg.) withdrawal (see II:29)

Inwardness of the senses is the disengagement from conditions as if in imitation of the own-form of the mind.

> The senses follow the course of the mind (*citta*). When the mind withdraws from sensory activity the senses also withdraw.

II.55 ***tataḥ paramā vaśyatā indriyāṇām***
tataḥ (ind.) then
paramā (f. nom. sg.) utmost, best; superlative from of *para*
vaśyatā (f. nom. sg.) command, control, being subdued or subjected; *vaśya*, from √*vaś* (will, command) +*tā*, feminine suffix meaning quality
indriyāṇām (n. gen. pl.) senses (see II:18)

Then arises utmost command of the senses.

13 "Vibhūti pāda"

III.1 ***deśa-bandhaś cittasya dhāraṇā***

deśa (m.) place (see I:31)

bandhaḥ (m. nom. sg.) binding, holding; from √*bandh* (bind) [end of TP7 cpd.]

cittasya (n. gen. sg.) mind (see I:2)

dhāraṇā (f. nom. sg.) concentration (see II:29)

Concentration of the mind is (its) binding to a place.

III.2 ***tatra pratyaya-eka-tānatā dhyānam***

tatra (ind.) there (see I:13)

pratyaya (m.) intention (see I:10)

eka (m.) one (see I:32)

tānatā (f. nom. sg.) extension, stretching; *tāna*, from √*tan* (extend) + *tā* (feminine suffix denoting "having the quality of")

dhyānam (n. nom. sg.) meditation (see I:39)

The extension of one intention there is meditation.

III.3 ***tad eva-artha-mātra-nirbhāsaṃ svarūpa-śūnyam iva samādhiḥ***

tad (n. nom. sg.) that

eva (ind.) indeed

artha (m. or n.) purpose, meaning (see I:28)

mātra (m.) only (see I:43)

nirbhāsaṃ (n. nom. sg.) shining forth (see I:43)

svarūpa (n.) own form (see I:3)

śūnyaṃ (n. nom. sg.) empty (see I:9)

iva (ind.) as if

samādhiḥ (f. nom. sg.) absorption (see I:20)

When the purpose alone shines forth as if empty of own form, that indeed is *samādhi.*

When one realizes through meditation that all objects and conditions are presented for the sake of *puruṣa*, *samādhi* arises. In this *sūtra*, purpose refers to any intended object (see I:43).

III.4 ***trayam ekatra saṃyamaḥ***

trayam (n. nom. sg.) threesome

ekatra (ind.) in one, in one and the same together; from *eka* (one)

saṃyamaḥ (m. nom. sg.) binding together, holding, restraint, control; *sam* (together) + *yama*, from √*yam* (restrain)

The unity of these three is *saṃyama.*

III.5 ***taj-jayāt prajñā ālokaḥ***

tad (n.) that

jayāt (m. abl. sg.) mastery (see II:41) (end of TP6 cpd.)

prajñā (f. nom. sg.) wisdom (see I:20)

ālokaḥ (m. nom. sg.) light, lustre, splendor; *ā* (hither, unto) + *lokaḥ* (world), from √*lok* (see, behold) (end of TP6 cpd.)

From the mastery of that, the splendor of wisdom.

III.6 ***tasya bhūmiṣu viniyogaḥ***

tasya (m. gen. sg.) of it

bhūmiṣu (f. loc. pl.) stage, ground (see I:14)

viniyogaḥ (m. nom. sg.) application, progression; *vi* (asunder, away) + *ni* (down, into) + *yoga* (see I:1)

Its application [occurs] in [various stages or] grounds.

III.7 ***trayam-antar-aṅgaṃ pūrvebhyaḥ***

trayam (n. nom. sg.) threesome (see III:4)

antar (ind.) inner

aṅgaṃ (n. nom. sg.) limb (see I:31)

pūrvebhyaḥ (m. abl. pl.) prior (see I:18)

These three inner limbs are (distinct) from the prior ones.

III.8 ***tad api bahir-aṅgaṃ nirbījasya***

tad (n. nom. sg.) that

api (ind.) indeed, also

bahir (ind.) outer, external

aṅgaṃ (n. nom. sg.) limb (see I:31)

nirbījasya (m. gen. sg.) seedless (see I:51)

These indeed are outer limbs [in regard to] the seedless.

III.9 ***vyutthāna-nirodha-saṃskārayor abhibhava-prādurbhāvau nirodha-kṣaṇa-citta-anvayo nirodha-pariṇāmaḥ***

vyutthāna (m.) emergence, state of being turned outward; *vi* (away, asunder) + *ut* (up) + *thāna*, from √*sthā* (stand)

nirodha (m.) restraint (see I:2)

saṃskārayoḥ (m. gen. du.) (see I:18) [end of TP6 cpd.]

abhibhava (m.) overpowering, powerful; *abhi* (to, toward) + *bhāva*, from √*bhū* (be)

prādurbhāvau (m. nom. du.) appearance, manifestation; from *prādur* (bring to light, make manifest or visible) + *bhāva*, from √*bhū* (be)

nirodha (m.) restraint (see I:2)

kṣaṇa (n.) moment, instant

citta (n.) mind (see I:2)

anvayoḥ (m. nom. sg.) following, succession, connection; *anu* (along, after) + *aya*, from √*i* (go)

nirodha (m.) restraint (see I:2)

pariṇāmaḥ (m. nom. sg.) engagement, transformation (see II:15)

[In regard to] the two *saṃskāras* of emergence and restraint, when that of appearance (emergence) is overpowered, there follows a moment of restraint in the mind; this is the *pariṇāma* of restraint.

III.10 ***tasya praśānta vāhitā saṃskārāt***

tasya (m. gen. sg.) of this

praśānta (m.) pacified, calm, quiet, composed; *pra* (before, forward) + *śānta*, from √*śam* (be quiet)

vāhitā (f. nom. sg.) flow, exertion, endeavor; from √*vah* (press) [end of KD cpd.]

saṃskārāt (m. abl. sg.) (see I:18)

From the *saṃskāra* of this there is a calm flow.

III.11 ***sarva-arthatā-ekāgratayoḥ kṣaya-udayau cittasya samādhi-pariṇāmaḥ***

sarva (n.) all

arthatā (f.) thingness, objectivity; from *artha* (possession, wealth; see also I:28) + *tā* (feminine suffix denoting "having the quality of")

ekāgratayoḥ (f. loc. du.) one-pointedness (see II:41) [end of DV cpd.]

kṣaya (m.) destruction (see II:28)
udayau (m. loc. du.) arisen; *ud* (up) + *aya* from √*i* (go) [end of DV cpd.] (end of locative absolute construction)
cittasya (n. gen. sg.) mind, consciousness (see I:2)
samādhi (f.) (see I:20)
pariṇāmaḥ (m. nom. sg.) engagement, modification (see II:15) [end of TP6 cpd.]

When there is destruction of all objectivity and the arising of onepointedness, the mind has the *pariṇāma* of *samādhi*.

III.12 ***tataḥ punaḥ śānta-uditau tulya-pratyayau cittasya-ekāgratā-pariṇāmaḥ***
tataḥ (ind.) hence
punaḥ (ind.) again, repeated
śānta (m.) quieted, appeased, pacified, calm, undisturbed; from √*śam* (be quiet)
uditau (m. nom. du.) uprisen, apparent, visible; *ud* (up) + *ita*, from √*i* (go) [end of DV cpd.]
tulya (m.) same, equal, of the same kind, similar; from √*tul* (weigh)
pratyayau (m. nom. du.) intention (see I:10) [end of KD cpd.]
cittasya (n. gen. sg.) mind (see I:2)
ekāgratā (f.) one-pointedness (see II:41)
pariṇāmaḥ (m. nom. sg.) engagement, modification, transformation (see II:15) [end of TP6 cpd.]

Hence again, when there is equality between arising and quieted intentions, there is the *pariṇāma* of onepointedness of the mind.

III.13 ***etena bhūta-indriyeṣu dharma-lakṣaṇa-avasthā-pariṇāmā vyākhyātāḥ***
etena (m. instr. sg.) through this (from *etad*)
bhūta (m.) elements (see II:18)
indriyeṣu (m. loc. pl.) senses (see II:18) [end of DV cpd.]
dharma (m.) nature, character, essential quality; that which is established or held; virtue, religion; from √*dhṛ* (hold)
lakṣaṇa (m.) designation, mark, sign, symbol, definition; from √*lakṣ* (recognize)
avasthā (f.) stability; state, condition; *ava* (down) + √*stha* (stand)
pariṇāmāḥ (m. nom. pl.) engagement (see II:15)
vyākhyātāḥ (m. nom. pl.) explained (see I:44)

By this are similarly explained the *pariṇāmas* of state, designation, and *dharma* among the elements and the senses.

These appear to be categorizations of the movements (*pariṇāma*) of the three *guṇas* (see I:15). In other words, these three *pariṇāmas* embody the *guṇa pariṇāma.*

III.14 ***śānta-udita-avyapadeśya-dharma-anupātī-dharmī***

śānta (m.) quieted (see III:12)

udita (m.) arising (see III:12)

avyapadeśya (m.) undetermined, undefined; *a* (not) + *vi* (asunder, away) + *apa* (away, off) + *deśya*, from √*diś* (point out) [end of DV cpd.]

dharma (m.) (see III:13) [end of KD cpd.]

anupātī (m. nom. sg.) following, corresponds to (see I:9) [end of TP7 cpd.]

dharmī (m. nom. sg.) holder of *dharma* (see III:13); *dharma* + *in* (possessive suffix)

The *dharma*-holder corresponds to the *dharma* whether quieted, arisen, or undetermined (past, present, or future).

III.15 ***krama-anyatvaṃ pariṇāma-anyatve hetuḥ***

krama (m.) series, succession, order; from √*kram* (go, walk, step)

anyatvam (n. nom. sg.) otherness; *anya* (other) + *tvam*, neuter suffix denoting having the quality of [end of TP7 cpd.]

pariṇāma (m.) (see II:15)

anyatve (n. loc. sg.) in the otherness or difference (see above) [end of TP6 cpd.]

hetuḥ (n. nom. sg.) cause (see II:17)

The cause of the difference between *pariṇāmas* is the difference in the succession.

III.16 ***pariṇāma-traya-saṃyamād atīta-anāgata-jñānam***

pariṇāma (m.) (see II:15)

traya (m.) threefold (see III:4)

saṃyamād (m. abl. sg.) binding together (see III:4) [end of TP7 cpd.]

atīta (m.) past, from *ati* (over, beyond) + *ita*, past perfect participle of √*i* (go)

anāgata (m.) future, yet to happen; *an* (not) + *ā* (hither,unto) + *gata*, past perfect participle of √*gam* (go)

jñānam (n. nom. sg.) knowledge (see I:8) [end of TP7 cpd.]

From *saṃyama* on the threefold *pariṇāmas* (there is) knowledge of past and future.

III.17 ***śabda-artha-pratyayānām itara-itara adhyāsāt saṃkaras tat pravibhāga saṃyamāt sarva-bhūta-rūta-jñānam***

śabda (m.) word, sound, noise, voice, speech, language

artha (m. or n.) thing, meaning, aim, purpose (see I:2)

pratyayānām (m. gen. pl.) of the intentions (see I:10) [end of TP7 cpd.]

itara (ind.) whereas

itara (ind.) whereas; when appearing together, they mean "this contrasts with that"

adhyāsāt (m. abl. sg.) imposition, overlapping; *adhi* (over, on) + *asa*, from √*as* (be)

saṃkaraḥ (m. nom. sg.) confusion, mixing together, commingling; *sam* (together) + *kara* from √*kṛ* (scatter)

tat (n. nom. sg.) that

pravibhāga (m.) distinction, separation, division; *pra* (before) + *vi* (asunder) + *bhāga*, from √*bhaj* (divide)

saṃyamāt (m. abl. sg.) from *saṃyama* (see III:4) [end of TP7 cpd.]

sarva (n.) all (see I:25)

bhūta (m.) being (see II:8)

rūta (n.) utterance, cry, noise, roar, yell, sound; from √*ru* (roar) [end of TP6 cpd.]

jñānam (n. nom. sg.) knowledge (see I:8) [end of TP6 cpd.]

From the overlapping here and there of words, purposes, and intentions, there is confusion. From *saṃyama* on the distinctions of them, there is knowledge of the (way of) utterance of all beings.

> This *sūtra* refers to the way language is generated and understood (see III:3).

III.18 ***saṃskāra-sākṣāt karaṇāt pūrva-jāti-jñānam***

saṃskāra (m.) (see I:18)

sākṣāt (m. abl. sg.) from the perception of, with one's own eyes, evident to the senses; *sa* (with) + *akṣa* (eye) [end of TP7 cpd.]

karaṇāt (m. abl. sg.) doing, making, effecting; from √*kṛ* (made, do)

pūrva (ind.) previous (see I:18)

jāti (f.) birth (see II:13)

jñānam (n. nom. sg.) knowledge (see I:18) [end of TP6 cpd.]

From effecting the perception of *saṃskāra*, there is knowledge of previous births.

III.19 ***pratyayasya para-citta-jñānam***

pratyayasya (m. gen. sg.) intention (see I:10)

para (m.) another, different from; from √*pṛ* (rescue, protect)
citta (n.) mind, thought (see I:2) [end of TP7 cpd.]
jñānam (n. nom. sg.) knowledge (see I:8) [end of TP7 cpd.]

[Similarly, from perception of another's] intention, there is knowledge of another mind.

III.20 ***na ca tat sālambanaṃ tasya aviṣayī bhūtatvāt***
na (ind.) not
ca (ind.) and or but
tad (n. nom. sg.) that (see I:12)
sālambanaṃ (n. nom. sg.) with support, with basis; *sa* (with) + *ālambana* (see I:10)
tasya (m. nom. sg.) of it (see I:27)
aviṣayī (m. nom. sg.) without having an object or condition; *a* (not) + *viṣayin*, from *viṣaya* (condition), see I:11 + *in*, possessive suffix
bhūtatvāt (n. abl. sg.) element, constituent of the manifest world; from *bhūta* (see II:18) + *tva*, suffix denoting "having the quality of"

But this is not with support because there is no condition of it in the elements.

The knowledge residing at the subtle level has no corresponding form in the manifest realm of the elements.

III.21 ***kāya-rūpa-saṃyamāt tad grāhya-śakti-stambhe cakṣuḥ prakāśa-asaṃyoge antardhānam***
kāya (m.) body (see II:43)
rūpa (n.) form, one of the *tanmātras* (see I:3) [end of TP6 cpd.]
saṃyamāt (m. abl. sg.) from *saṃyama* (see III:4) [end of TP7 cpd.]
tad (n.) that (see I:12)
grāhya (m.) to be grasped (see I:41)
śakti (f.) power (see II:6) [end of TP6 cpd.]
stambhe (m. loc. sg.) suspension, supression, stoppage (see II:50) [end of TP7 cpd.]
cakṣuḥ (m. nom. sg.) eye, from √*cakṣ* (see)
prakāśa (m.) light (see II:18) [end of TP6 cpd.]
asaṃyoge (m. loc. sg.) disjunction, disunion; *a* (not) +*saṃyoga* (union), see II:18; [end of TP6 cpd.] (end of locative absolute construction)
antardhānam (n. nom. sg.) hidden, concealed, invisible; from *antar* (between) + *dhāna*, from √*dhā* (put)

From *saṃyama* on the form (*rūpa*) of the body, [there arises] the suspension of the power of what is to be grasped and the disjunction of light and the eye, resulting in concealment.

Most interpretations have read this *sūtra* as stating that a yogi has the power of invisibility. In understanding how light reflected off a body allows a person to be seen, the yogi is able to avoid being observed. This could refer also to the yogi's ability to suspend the grasping of the world through control over the *tanmātras*; he or she is able to render things hidden or invisible due to the nonactivation of the power of grasping.

III.22 ***sopakramaṃ nirupakramaṃ ca karma tat saṃyamād aparānta-jñānam ariṣṭebhyo vā***

sopakramaṃ (n. nom. sg.) set in motion, undertaken; *sa* (with) + *upa* (to, unto) + *krama*, from √*kram* (step)

nirupakramaṃ (n. nom. sg.) not in motion, not taken up, not pursued; *nir* (away from) + *upakrama* (see above)

ca (ind.) and

karma (n. nom. sg.) action (see I:24)

tad (n.) that

saṃyamāt (m. abl. sg.) from *saṃyama* (see III:4) [end of TP7 cpd.]

aparānta (m.) literally, the "Western extremity"; the latter end, conclusion, death

jñānam (n. nom. sg) knowledge (see I:18)

ariṣṭebhyaḥ (m. abl. pl.) from natural phenomena boding misfortune, ill omens, signs of approaching death; *a* (not) + *riṣṭa*, from √*riṣ* (be hurt)

vā (ind.) or

Karma is either in motion or not in motion. From *saṃyama* on this, or from natural phenomena boding misfortune, there is knowledge of death.

III.23 ***maitrī ādiṣu balāni***

maitrī (f.) friendliness (see I:33)

ādiṣu (m. loc. pl.) and so forth, etc.

balāni (n. nom. pl.) powers, strengths; from √*bal* (breathe, live)

(By *saṃyama*) on friendliness and so forth, (corresponding) powers.

This appears to be a reference to the Brahma Vihāra (see I:33).

III.24 ***baleṣu hasti-bala-ādīni***

baleṣu (n. loc. pl.) in powers (see III:23)
hasti (m.) elephant
bala (n.) power (see III:23) [end of KD cpd.]
ādīni (n. nom. pl.) and so forth, etc.

[By *saṃyama*] on powers, the powers arise like those of the elephant, and so forth.

III.25 ***pravṛtti-āloka-nyāsāt sūkṣma-vyavahita-viprakṛṣṭa-jñānam***

pravṛtti (f.) activity (see I:35)
āloka (m.) light (see III:5) [end of TP7 cpd.]
nyāsāt (m. abl. sg.) placing down or setting down, applying, casting; *ni* (down, into) + √*ās* (sit) [end of TP6 cpd.]
sūkṣma (m.) subtle (see I:44)
vyavahita (m.) concealed, obstructed; *vi* (asunder, away) + *ava* (down) + *hita*, from √*dhā* (place, put)
viprakṛṣṭa (m.) distant, remote; *vi* (asunder, away) + *pra* (before) + *kṛṣṭa*, from √*kṛṣ* (drag, plough) [end of DV cpd.]
jñānam (n. nom. sg.) knowledge (see I:8) [end of TP6 cpd.]

Due to the casting of light on a [sense] activity, there is knowledge of the subtle, concealed, and distant.

III.26 ***bhuvana-jñānaṃ sūrye saṃyamāt***

bhuvana (n.) world, cosmic region; from √*bhū* (be)
jñānaṃ (n. nom. sg.) knowledge (see I:8) [end of TP6 cpd.]
sūrye (m. loc. sg.) on the sun
saṃyamāt (m. abl. sg.) from *saṃyama* (see III:4)

From *saṃyama* on the sun, [arises] knowledge of the world.

III.27 ***candre tārā-vyūha-jñānam***

candre (m. loc. sg.) on the moon, from √*cand* (shine)
tārā (f.) star, from √*tṛ* (pass beyond)
vyūha (m.) ordering, arrangement, distribution; from *vi* (asunder, away) + √*ūh* (remove)
jñānam (n. nom. sg.) knowledge (see I:8) [end of TP6 cpd.]

On the moon, knowledge of the ordering of the stars.

III.28 ***dhruve tad gati-jñānam***

dhruve (m. loc. sg.) on the polar star

tad (n.) that (refers to stars in prior *sūtra*)
gati (f.) motion (see II:14)
jñānam (n. nom. sg.) knowledge (see I:8) [end of TP6 cpd.]

On the polar star, knowledge of their movement.

III.29 ***nābhi-cakre kāya-vyūha-jñānam***
nābhi (f.) central point, navel
cakre (n. loc. sg.) a center of energy in the body; wheel, circle; reduplicated derivative of √*kṛ* (do) [end of KD cpd.]
kāya (m.) body (see II:43)
vyūha (m.) arrangement (see III:127) [end of TP6 cpd.]
jñānam (n. nom. sg.) knowledge (see I:8) [end of TP6 cpd.]

On the navel *cakra*, knowledge of the ordering of the body.

III.30 ***kaṇṭha-kūpe kṣut-pipāsā-nivṛttiḥ***
kaṇṭha (m.) throat, neck
kūpe (m. loc. sg.) hollow, cavity, well [end of TP6 cpd.]
kṣudh (f.) hunger, from √*kṣudh* (to hunger)
pipāsā (f.) thirst, wishing to drink; desiderative form of √*pā* (drink) [end of DV cpd.]
nivṛttiḥ (f. nom. sg.) cessation, disappearance; from *ni* (down, into) + *vṛtti* (see I:2) [end of TP6 cpd.]

On the hollow of the throat, cessation of hunger and thirst.

III.31 ***kūrma-nāḍyām sthairyam***
kūrma (m.) tortoise, turtle
nāḍyām (f. loc. sg.) pathway of *prāṇa* (energy); vein or artery [end of KD cpd.]
sthairyam (n. nom. sg.) firmness, stability, steadfastness; from √*sthā* (stand)

On the tortoise *nāḍī*, stability.

III.32 ***mūrdha-jyotiṣi siddha-darśanam***
mūrdha (m.) head
jyotiṣi (n. loc. sg.) light, brightness; from √*jyut* (shine) [end of TP7 cpd.]
siddha (m.) perfected one, accomplished one, sacred, powerful (see II:43)
darśanam (n. nom. sg.) vision (see I:30) [end of TP6 cpd.]

On the light in the head, vision of perfected ones.

III.33 ***prātibhād vā sarvam***

prātibhād (m. abl. sg.) intuition, vividness; from *pra* (before) + *ati* (over, beyond) + √*bhā* (shine)
vā (ind.) or, and
sarvam (n. nom. sg.) all, everything (see I:25)

Or from intuition, everything.

III.34 ***hṛdaye citta-saṃvit***

hṛdaye (n. loc. sg.) heart; the seat of the feelings and sensations
citta (n.) mind (see I:2)
saṃvid (f. nom. sg.) understanding, knowledge; from *sam* (together) + √*vid* (know)

On the heart, understanding of the mind.

III.35 ***sattva-puruṣayor atyanta-asaṃkīrṇayoḥ pratyaya-aviśeṣa bhogaḥ para-arthatvāt svārtha-saṃyamāt puruṣa-jñānam***

sattva (n.) lightness, beingness (see II:41)
puruṣayor (m. loc. du.) (see I:16) [end of DV cpd.]
atyanta (m.) perfect, endless, unbroken, perpetual, very great; *ati* (over, beyond) + *anta* (end)
asaṃkīṛnayoḥ (m. gen. du.) unmixed, not unclean, not confused, pure, distinct; *a* (not) + *saṃkīrṇa* (see I:42) [end of DV cpd.]
pratyaya (m.) intention (see I:10)
aviśeṣaḥ (m. nom. sg.) indistinct (see II:19) [end of TP6 cpd.]
bhogaḥ (m. nom. sg.) experience (see II:13)
para (m.) other (see III:19)
arthavāt (m. abl. sg.) due to purpose (see I:49) [end of TP4 cpd.]
svārtha (m. or n.) purpose for the self; *sva* (own) + *artha* (purpose) (see I:28)
saṃyamāt (m. abl. sg.) from *saṃyama* (see III:4) (end of TP7 cpd.)
puruṣa (m.) (see I:16)
jñānam (n. nom. sg.) knowledge (see I:8) (end of TP6 cpd.]

When there is no distinction of intention between the pure *puruṣa* and the perfect *sattva*, there is experience for the purpose of the other [*puruṣa*]; from *saṃyama* on purpose being for the self, there is knowledge of *puruṣa*.

See *Sāṃkhya Kārikā* 17.

III.36 ***tataḥ prātibha-śrāvaṇa-vedanā-ādarśa-āsvāda-vārtā jāyante***

tataḥ (ind.) hence (see I:22)

prātibha (m.) intuition, vividness (see III:33)
śrāvaṇa (m.) hearing, relating to or perceived by the ear; from √*śru* (hear)
vedanā (f.) touching, feeling, sensing; from √*vid* (know)
ādarśa (m.) seeing, act of perceiving by the eyes; *ā* (hither, unto) + *darśa*, from √*dṛś* (see)
āsvāda (m.) tasting, enjoying, eating; from *ā* (hither, unto) + *svāda*, from √*svad* (eat)
vārtāḥ (m. nom. pl.) smelling [end of five part DV cpd., each member of which is modified by the term *prātibha*, hence forming an extended KD cpd.]
jāyante (third-person plural, present middle) are born or produced; from √*jan* (be born)

Hence are born intuitive hearing, touching, seeing, tasting, and smelling.

These five enhanced abilities allow one to observe the subtle elements (*tanmātras*) giving birth to the gross elements. It is clear that Patañjali is closely following Sāṃkhya.

III.37 ***te samādhau upasargā vyutthāne siddhayaḥ***
te (m. nom. pl.) these (see I:30)
samādhau (f. loc. sg.) in *samādhi* (see I:20)
upasargāḥ (m. nom. pl.) impediment, obstacle, trouble; *upa* (to, unto) + *sarga*, from √*sṛj* (create)
vyutthāne (m. loc. sg.) in emergence (see III:9)
siddhayaḥ (f. nom. pl.) perfections (see II:43)

These are impediments to *samādhi*; in emergence (world production), they are perfections.

III.38 ***bandha-kāraṇa-śaithilyāt pracāra-saṃvedanāc ca cittasya para-śarīra-āveśaḥ***
bandha (m.) binding, holding, bondage (see III:1)
kāraṇa (n.) reason, cause, motive, origin; from √*kṛ* (do)
śaithilyāt (m. abl. sg.) relaxation (see II:47)
pracāra (m.) coming forth, showing oneself, manifestation, appearance; *pra* (before, forward) + *cāra*, from √*car* (move)
saṃvedanāt (n. abl. sg.) the act of perceiving or feeling; perception, sensation; *sam* (together) + *vedana*, from √*vid* (know)
ca (ind.) and

cittasya (n. gen. sg.) of the mind or consciousness (see I:2)
para (m.) other (see III:19)
śarīra (n.) body, that which is subject to decay, from √*śṛ* (crush)
āveśaḥ (m. nom. sg.) entrance, taking possession of, entering; *ā* (hither, unto) + *veśa*, from √*viś* (enter)

From the relaxation of the cause of bondage and from the perception of a manifestation, there is an entering of the mind into another embodiment.

> In loosening the bonds of karma, the yogi realizes how karma is assembled and disassembled and thereby can move from one assemblage to another. Also, by focusing on perfected beings (as in Tantra), those qualities of perfection are embodied (see II:44). Compare this to verses in the *Bhagavad Gītā* where Krishna advises Arjuna to surrender to him, saying the yogin "goes to union with me" (*yogi . . . matsaṃsthām adhigacchati*) VI:15, an event that takes place in chapter 11.

III.39 ***udāna-jayāj jala-paṅka-kaṇṭaka-ādiṣu asaṅga ukrāntiś ca***

udāna (m.) upbreath, one of the five vital breaths; *ud* (up) + *āna*, from √*an* (breathe)
jayāt (m. abl. sg.) from mastery (see II:41) [end of TP6 cpd.]
jala (n.) water
paṅka (m.) mud
kaṇṭaka (m.) thorn
ādiṣu (m. loc. pl.) and so forth, etc. [end of DV cpd.]
asaṅgaḥ (m. nom. sg.) unattached, free from ties, independent; *a* (not) + *saṅga*, from √*sañj* (cling)
utkrāntiḥ (f. nom. sg.) rising, stepping up, passing away, dying; *ud* (up) + *krānti*, from √*kram* (stride)
ca (ind.) and

From mastery of the upbreath, there is nonattachment among water, mud, and thorns, etc., and a rising above.

> Compare with *Bhagavad Gītā* II:23: "Weapons do not pierce this, fire does not burn this, waters do not wet this, nor does wind dry it."

III.40 ***samāna-jayāj jvalanam***

samāna (m.) breath of the middle region; *sam* (together) + *āna*, from √*an* (breath)

jayāt (m. abl. sg.) mastery (see II:41) [end of TP6 cpd.]
jvalanam (n. nom. sg.) radiance, effulgence, shining; from √*jval* (burn, flame)

From mastery of the *samāna*, there is radiance.

III.41 ***śrotra-ākāśayoḥ saṃbandha-saṃyamād divyam śrotram***
śrotra (n.) ear; from √*śrū* (hear)
ākāśayoḥ (n. gen. du.) space, ether; *ā* (to, unto) + *kāśa*, from √*kāś* (appear, make a show)
saṃbandha (m.) connection, union, association; *sam* (together) + *bandha*, from √*bandh* (bind)
saṃyamāt (m. abl. sg.) from *saṃyama* (see III:4)
divyam (n. nom. sg.) divine, heavenly, wonderful
śrotram (n. nom. sg.) ear

From *saṃyama* on the connection between the ear and space, [there arises] the divine ear.

The last and most subtle of the gross elements is mastered here.

III.42 ***kāya-ākāśayoḥ saṃbandha-saṃyamāl laghu-tūla-samāpatteś ca ākāśa-gamanam***
kāya (m.) body (see II:43)
ākāśayoḥ (n. gen. du.) space (see III:41)
saṃbandha (m.) connection (see III:41)
saṃyamāt (m. abl. sg.) from *saṃyama* (see III:4)
laghu (m.) light, easy, not difficult
tūla (n.) cotton, tuft of grass or reeds
samāpatteḥ (f. abl. sg.) unity (see I:41) [end of TP6 cpd.]
ca (ind.) and
ākāśa (n.) space (see III:41)
gamanam (n. nom. sg.) movement, going; from √*gam* (go) [end of KD cpd.]

From *saṃyama* on the connection between the body and space, and from unity with the lightness of cotton, there is movement through space.

Through meditation on the lightness of cotton, the mind (*citta*), which pervades the whole body, takes on its qualities (see III:38).

III.43 ***bahir akalpitā vṛttir mahā-videhā tataḥ prakāśa-āvaraṇa-kṣayaḥ***
bahir (ind.) outer, external (see III:8)

akalpitā (f. nom. sg.) genuine, not artificial; *a* (not) + *kalpitā* from √*kḷp* (be adapted)
vṛttiḥ (f. nom. sg.) fluctuation (see I:2)
mahā (m.) great (see II: 31)
videhā (f. nom. sg.) discarnate (see I:19) [end of KD cpd.]
tataḥ (ind.) hence (see I:22)
prakāśa (m.) light (see II:18)
āvaraṇa (n.) covering (see II:18)
kṣayaḥ (m. nom. sg.) destruction; from √*kṣi* (see II:28) [end TP6 cpd.]

An outer, genuine fluctuation results in freedom from the body; hence the covering of light is destroyed.

In this state, the yogi experiences bodiless absorption. (See I:19, as well as II:52 and III:38.)

III.44 ***sthūla-svarūpa-sūkṣma-anvaya-arthavattva-saṃyamād bhūta-jayaḥ***
sthūla (m.) gross, coarse, solid, material; from √*sthā* (stand)
svarūpa (n.) own, form (see I:3) [end of TP6 cpd.]
sūkṣma (m.) subtle (see I:44) [end of TP6 cpd.]
anvaya (m.) connection (see III:9)
arthavattva (n.) significance, importance; from *artha* (purpose) + *vat* (suffix indicating possession) + *tva* (suffix indicating "having the quality of" [end of DV cpd.]
saṃyamāt (m. abl. sg.) (see III:4) [end of TP7 cpd.]
bhūta (m.) element (see II:18)
jayaḥ (m. nom. sg.) mastery (see II:41) [end of TP6 cpd.]

From *saṃyama* on the significance and connection of the subtle and the own form of the gross, there is mastery over the elements.

The arisal of the gross stems from the subtle; by investigating the relationship between the two, mastery over the gross is achieved. See III:47, which links sensing, the approach to the gross, with the sense of self, which is more subtle.

III.45 ***tato'ṇima-ādi-prādurbhāvaḥ kāya-saṃpat tad-dharma-anabhighātaś ca***
tatas (ind.) hence
aṇima (m.) minuteness, fineness, thinness
ādi (ind.) and so forth, etc.

prādurbhāvaḥ (m. nom. sg.) appearance, that which is visible (see III:9) [end of TP6 cpd.]
kāya (m.) body (see II:43)
saṃpad (f. nom. sg.) perfection, success, accomplishment, fulfilment; *sam* (together)+ √*pad* (go) [end of TP6 cpd.]
tad (n.) that
dharma (m.) (see III:13) [end of TP6 cpd.]
anabhighātaḥ (m. nom. sg.) unassailability (see II:48) [end of TP6 cpd.]
ca (ind.) and

Hence arises the appearance of minuteness and so forth, perfection of the body, and unassailability of its *dharma*.

Perfection of the body does not arise in regard to a standard of health, but proceeds from a comprehension of the operation of the *tattvas*. See *Bhagavad Gītā* XIII:2–5. Also, "unassailability of its *dharma*" refers to the yogi's ability to maintain a particular embodiment without the normal limits imposed by one's experience of the elements.

III.46 ***rūpa-lāvaṇya-bala-vajra-saṃhananatvāni kāya-saṃpat***
rūpa (n.) form (see I:8)
lāvaṇya (n.) beauty, loveliness [end of TP6 cpd.]
bala (n.) strength, power, might, vigor; from √*bal* (breathe, live)
vajra (m.) thunderbolt; hard, mighty, adamantine; from √*vaj* (be strong)
saṃhananatvāni (n. nom. pl.) solidity, robustness, firmness, steadfastness; *sam* (together)+ *hanana*, from √*han* (strike) + *tva*, suffix denoting "having the quality of" [end of DV cpd.]
kāya (m.) body (see II:43)
saṃpad (f. nom. sg.) perfection (see III:45) [end of TP6 cpd.]

Perfection of the body is beauty of form, strength, and admantine stability.

III.47 ***grahaṇa-svarūpa-asmitā-anvaya-arthavattva-saṃyamād indriya-jayaḥ***
grahaṇa (m.) grasping (see I:41)
svarūpa (n.) own-form (see I:3)
asmitā (f.) I-am-ness (see I:17)
anvaya (m.) connection (see III:9)
arthavattva (n.) significance (see III:44)
saṃyamād (m. abl. sg.) (see III:4) [end of TP7 cpd.]

indriya (n.) sense organ (see II:18)
jayaḥ (m. nom. sg.) mastery (see II:41) [end of TP6 cpd.]

From *saṃyama* on grasping, own form, I-am-ness, their connection, and their significance, there is mastery over the sense organs.

This parallels III:44 above. In the earlier *sūtra*, the gross is linked to the elements. In this *sūtra*, the subtle sense of I-am-ness is linked to the sense organs.

III.48 ***tato mano-javitvaṃ vikaraṇa-bhāvaḥ pradhāna-jayaś ca***
tataḥ (ind.) hence (see I:22)
manas (n.) mind organ (see I:22)
javitvam (n. nom. sg.) swiftness, speed; from √*jā* (be born)
vikaraṇa (m.) deprived of organs of sense; *vi* (asunder, away) + *karaṇa* (organ of sense), from √*kṛ* (do)
bhāvaḥ (m. nom. sg.) state of becoming, being, existing; true state or condition; temperament, nature; way of thinking, disposition; from √*bhū* (be) [end of KD cpd.]
pradhāna (n.) originator, original source of the manifest; *prakṛti*; *pra* (before, forward) +*dhāna*, from √*dhā* (put)
jayaḥ (m. nom. sg.) mastery (see II: 41) [end of TP6 cpd.]
ca (ind.) and

Hence, there is swiftness of the mind-power, a state of being beyond the senses, and mastery over the *pradhāna*.

III.49 ***sattva-puruṣa-anyatā-khyāti-mātrasya sarva-bhāva-adhiṣṭhā-tṛtvaṃ sarva-jñātṛtvaṃ ca***
sattva (n.) (see II:41)
puruṣa (m.) (see I:16) [end of DV cpd.]
anyatā (f.) difference, distinction; *anya* (other) + *tā* (feminine suffix denoting "having the power of") [end of TP6 cpd.]
khyāti (f.) discernment (see I:16) [end of TP6 cpd.]
mātrasya (m. g. sg.) only (see I:43)
sarva (n.) all (see I:25)
bhāva (m.) state of being (see III:48)
adhiṣṭhātṛtvaṃ (n. nom. sg.) sovereignty, ruleship, supremacy; *adhi* (over, on) +*ṣṭhātṛ*, stander, from √*sthā* (stand) + *tṛ* (agentive suffix) +*tvam* (neuter suffix denoting "having the quality of")
sarva (n.) all (see I:25)

jñātṛtvaṃ (n. nom. sg.) knowledge; literally, the quality stemming from being a knower; √*jnā* (know) + *tṛ* (agentive suffix) + *tvam* (see above)

ca (ind.) and

Only from the discernment of the difference between *sattva* and *puruṣa*, there is sovereignty over all states of being and knowledge of all.

At the most subtle levels, the distinction is seen between the finest aspects of *prakṛti* and the inactive *puruṣa*. From this ability proceeds supreme knowledge and power.

III.50 ***tad-vairāgyād api doṣa-bīja-kṣaye kaivalyaṃ***

tad (n.) this

vairāgyāt (n. abl. sg.) release, dispassion (see I:12) [end of TP4 cpd.]

api (ind.) even (see I:22)

doṣa (m.) impediment, detriment, fault, want; from √*duṣ* (spoil)

bīja (n.) seed (see I:25)

kṣaye (m. loc. sg.) destruction (see II:28) [end of TP6 cpd.]

kaivalyaṃ (m. loc. sg.) isolation (see II:25)

Due to release from even this, in the destruction of the seed of this impediment, arises *kaivalyam*.

III.51 ***sthāny-upanimantraṇe saṅga-smaya-akaraṇa punar aniṣṭa-prasaṅgāt***

sthāni (m.) well-established, having a place, being in the right place; original form; from √*sthā* (stand) +*in* (possessive suffix)

upanimantraṇe (n. loc. sg.) invitation, offer; from *upa* (to, unto) + *mantraṇa* (consultation), from *mantra* (sacred speech), from √*man* (think) [end of TP5 cpd.]

saṅga (m.) attachment (see III:39)

smaya (m.) pride, arrogance; smiling from √*smi*; (smile) [end of DV cpd.]

akaraṇam (n. nom. sg.) no cause (see III:38)

punar (ind.) again (see III:12)

aniṣṭa (m.) unwanted, undesirable; *an* (not) + *iṣṭa*, from √*iṣ* (wish)

prasaṅgāt (m. abl. sg.) association, devotion to, attachment, adherence; from *pra* (before, forward) + *saṅga* from √*sañj* (cling)

There is no cause for attachment and pride upon the invitation of those well established, because of repeated association with the undesirable.

Even if one is tempted to reenter the realm of attachment, the momentum to do so has ceased, because one is constantly aware of the undesirable outcome of such a return. See I:15.

III.52 ***kṣaṇa-tat-kramayoḥ saṃyamād viveka-jaṃ jñānaṃ***
kṣaṇa (n.) moment (see III:9)
tad (n.) this
kramayoḥ (m. loc. du.) succession (see III:15) [end of DV cpd.]
saṃyamāt (m. abl. sg.) (see III:4)
viveka (m.) discrimination (see II:15)
jam (n. nom. sg.) born of (see I:50) [end of TP5 cpd.]
jñānaṃ (n. nom. sg.) knowledge (see I:8)

From *saṃyama* on the moment and its succession, there is knowledge born of discrimination.

III.53 ***jāti-lakṣaṇa-deśair anyatā anavacchedāt tulyayos tataḥ pratipattiḥ***
jāti (f.) birth (see II:13)
lakṣaṇa (m.) designation (see III:13)
deśaiḥ (m. instr. pl.) place (see II:31) [end of DV cpd.]
anyatā (f. nom. sg.) difference (see III:49)
anavacchedāt (m. abl. sg.) unlimited, not separated (see I:26)
tulyayoḥ (m. gen. du.) sameness (see III:12)
tataḥ (ind.) hence (see I:22)
pratipattiḥ (f. nom. sg.) perception, observation, ascertainment, acknowledgment; from *prati* (against, back) + *patti*, from √*pad* (go)

Hence, there is the ascertainment of two things that are similar, due to their not being limited (made separate) by differences of birth, designation, and place.

The traditional reading of Vyāsa states that a yogi is able to tell two identical items apart despite their occupying the same space but at different times. This signifies that all things are in a state of flux.

As a variant reading, this *sūtra* probably refers to the similarity between the *sattva* or unmanifest form of *prakṛti* and the *puruṣa*. For a list of their similarities, see *Sāṃkhya Kārikā* XI. The key to liberation is to be able to see the difference between these two; this is the highest *siddhi* of *kaivalyam*. This interpretation is borne out by the context before and after this passage. See III:49 and III:55.

III.54 ***tārakaṃ sarva-viṣayaṃ sarvathā viṣayaṃ akramaṃ ca iti viveka-jaṃ jñānam***

tārakaṃ (n. nom. sg.) enabling one to cross over, rescuing, liberation, saving; from *tāra* (protector), from √*tṛ* (pass)

sarva (n.) all (see I:25)

viṣayam (n. nom. sg.) condition (see I:11) [end of BV cpd.]

sarvathā (ind.) in every way or respect, at all times; from *sarva* (all) + *thā* (temporal suffix)

viṣayaṃ (n. nom. sg.) object (see I:11)

akramaṃ (n. nom. sg.) nonsuccessive (see III:15)

ca (ind.) and

iti (ind.) thus

viveka (m.) discrimination (see II:15)

jaṃ (n. nom. sg.) born of (see I:50) [end of TP5 cpd.]

jñānam (n. nom. sg.) knowledge (see I:8)

The knowledge born of discrimination is said to be liberating, (inclusive of) all conditions and all times and nonsuccessive.

III.55 ***sattva-puruṣayoḥ śuddhi-sāmye kaivalyaṃ iti***

sattva (n.) (see II:41)

puruṣayoḥ (m. gen. du.) (see I:16) [end of DV cpd.]

śuddhi (f.) purity (see II:28)

sāmye (n. loc. sg.) evenness, sameness; from *sama* (same) [end of TP6 cpd.]

kaivalyaṃ (n. nom. sg.) isolation (see II:25)

iti (ind.) thus

In the sameness of purity between the *sattva* and the *puruṣa*, there is *kaivalyam*.

14 "*Kaivalya pāda*"

IV.1 ***janma-oṣadhi-mantra-tapaḥ-samādhi-jāḥ siddhayaḥ***

janma (n.) birth, existence (see II.12)

oṣadhi (f.) medicinal herb, remedy, drug

mantra (m.) sacred formula or speech, prayer, song of praise, mystical verse; from √*man* (think)

tapaḥ (n.) austerity (see II:1)

samādhi (f.) absorption (see I:20) [end of DV cpd.]

jāḥ (n. nom. pl.) born (see I:50) [end of TP5 cpd.]

siddhayaḥ (f. nom. pl.) perfection (see II:43)

Perfections are born due to birth, drugs, *mantra*, austerity, or *samādhi*.

IV.2 ***jāti-antara-pariṇāmaḥ prakṛti-āpūrāt***

jāti (f.) birth (see II:13)

antara (m.) different, other, another [end of TP6 cpd.]

pariṇāmaḥ (m. nom. sg.) (see II:15) [end of TP7 cpd.]

prakṛti (f.) (see I:19)

āpūrāt (m. abl. sg.) excess, abundance, flooding; *ā* (to, unto) + *pūra*, from √*pṛ* (fill) [end of TP6 cpd.]

From the flooding of *prakṛti*, arises *pariṇāma* into other births.

Whatever *saṃskāras* remain cause future experiences to unfold.

IV.3 ***nimittam aprayojakaṃ prakṛtīnāṃ varaṇa-bhedas tu tataḥ kṣetrikavat***

nimittam (n. nom. sg.) cause, motive, ground, reason, instrumental cause; *ni* (down, into) + *mitta*, from √*mā* (measure)

aprayojakaṃ (n. nom. sg.) not causing or effecting; not initiating, prompting or instigating; *a* (not) + *pra* (before) + *yojaka*, from √*yuj* (join)

prakṛtīnām (f. gen. pl.) manifestations (see I:19)
varaṇa (n.) surrounding, enclosing so as to limit; from √*vṛ* (cover)
bhedaḥ (m. nom. sg.) separation, divison, distinction; from √*bhid* (split) [end of BV cpd.]
tu (ind.) but
tataḥ (ind.) but
kṣetrikavat (m. nom. sg.) like a farmer, like the owner of a field; *kṣetra* (field) + *ika* (possessive suffix) + *vat* (suffix indicating likeness)

The cause [of this flooding that results in experiences] is breakage in the enclosure of the *prakṛtis*, as when a farmer [irrigates his fields]. [Experience] is not caused by the "initiator."

The initiator remains aloof from activity. See IV 5–6.

IV.4 ***nirmāṇa-cittāni asmitā-mātrāt***
nirmāṇa (m.) creating, making, forming, fabricating; *nir* (out, away from) + *māna*, from √*mā* (measure)
cittāni (n. nom. pl.) minds, (see I:2) [end of KD cpd.]
asmitā (f.) I-am-ness (see I:17, II:3, II:6)
mātrāt (m. abl. sg.) only (see I:43) [end of KD cpd.]

The fabricating minds arise only from I-am-ness.

IV.5 ***pravṛtti-bhede prayojakaṃ cittaṃ ekaṃ anekeṣāṃ***
pravṛtti (f.) activity (see I:35)
bhede (m. loc. sg.) distinction (see IV:3) [end of TP5 cpd.]
prayojakaṃ (n. nom. sg.) initiator (see IV:3)
cittaṃ (n. nom. sg.) mind (see IV:3)
ekaṃ (n. nom. sg.) one (see I:26)
anekeṣām (n. gen. pl.) many; *an* (not) + *eka* (one)

The "inititator" is the one mind among many that is distinct from activity.

This most probably would be the intellect in its most subtle form of *sattva*, which we saw earlier (III:55) as associated with *kaivalyam*. All mind is in some sense active, but this "one mind" is like *puruṣa* and hence pure. The following verse seems to confirm this position.

IV.6 ***tatra dhyāna-jaṃ anāśayam***
tatra (ind.) there (see I:3)
dhyāna (m.) meditation (see I:39)

jaṃ (n. nom. sg.) born (see I:50) [end of TP5 cpd.]
anāśayam (n. nom. sg.) without residue; *an* (not) + *āśaya* (residue), see I:24

There, what is born of meditation is without residue.

IV.7 ***karma-aśukla-akṛṣṇaṃ yoginas trividhaṃ itareṣām***
karma (m. nom. sg.) action (see I:24)
aśukla (n.) not white; *a* (not) + *śukla* (white, pure, stainless), from √*sūc* (gleam)
akṛṣṇaṃ (n. nom. sg.) not black; *a* (not) + *kṛṣṇa* (black, dark)
yoginas (m. gen. sg.) yogin, one who has yoga; yoga (see I:1) + *in*, possessive suffix
trividhaṃ (n. nom. sg.) threefold; *tri* (three) *vidha* (division, part), from *vi* (asunder, away) + *dha*, from √*dhā* (put)
itareṣām (m. gen. pl.) others (see I:20)

The action of a yogi is neither white nor black; that of others is threefold.

(Black, white, and mixed.)

IV.8 ***tatas tad-vipāka-anuguṇānāṃ eva abhivyaktir vāsanānām***
tatas (ind.) hence (see I:22)
tad (n.) that
vipāka (m.) fruition (see I:24)
anuguṇānāṃ (m. gen. pl.) having similar qualities; *anu* (along, after) + *guṇa* (see I:16)
eva (ind.) thus, only (see I:44)
abhivyaktiḥ (f. nom. sg.) manifestation, distinction; *abhi* (to, unto) + *vyakti*, from *vi* (asunder, away) + *akti*, from √*añj* (annoint)
vāsanānām (f. gen. pl.) habit pattern, impression of anything remaining unconsciously in the mind, inclination; from √*vas* (dwell)

Hence, the manifestation of habit patterns thus corresponds to the fruition of that (*karma*).

This *sūtra* states that action one performs proceeds according to the residue of past action (*saṃskāra* or *vāsanā*).

IV.9 ***jāti-deśa-kāla-vyavahitānāṃ api ānantaryaṃ smṛti-saṃskārayor eka rūpatvāt***
jāti (f.) life state, birth (see II:13)

deśa (m.) place (see II:31)
kāla (m.) time (see I:4) [end of DV cpd.]
vyavhitānāṃ (m. gen. pl.) concealed (see III:25) [end of KD cpd.]
api (ind.) though, even
ānantaryaṃ (n. nom. sg.) link, immediate sequence or succesion; from *an* (not) + *antara* (different, see IV:2)
smṛti (f.) memory (see I:16)
saṃskārayor (m. gen. du.) (see I:18) [end of DV cpd.]
eka (n.) one (see I:32)
rūpatvāt (n. abl. sg.) formness; *rūpa* (form, see I:3) + *tva* (suffix denoting possession of quality)

Because memory and *saṃskāra* are of one form, there is a link even among births, places, and times that are concealed.

Past actions, even if not remembered, continue to affect present actions.

IV.10 ***tāsāṃ anāditvaṃ ca āśiṣo nityatvāt***

tāsāṃ (m. gen. pl.) of these
anāditvaṃ (n. nom. sg.) state of having no beginning; *an* (not) + *ādi* (and so forth) + *tvam* (suffix denoting quality possessed)
ca (ind.) and
āśiṣaḥ (f. gen. sg.) asking for, prayer, wish, desire; *ā* (hither, unto) + *śis*, from √*śās* (order)
nityatvāt (m. abl. sg.) perpetuity, continuance; *nitya* (eternal, see II:5) + *tva* (see above)

And there is no beginning of these due to the perpetuity of desire.

IV.11 ***hetu-phala-āśraya-ālambanaiḥ samgṛhītatvād eṣām abhāve tad abhāvaḥ***

hetu (m.) cause (see II:17)
phala (n.) fruit (see II:14)
āśraya (n.) correspondence (see II:36)
ālambanaiḥ (m. instr. pl.) based on, supporting (see I:10) [end of DV cpd.]
samgṛhītatvāt (m. abl. pl.) that which is grasped, seized, caught, gathered; *sam* (together) + *gṛhīta*, from √*grabh* (grasp) + *tva* (suffix indicating possession of a quality)
eṣāṃ (m. gen. pl.) of these
abhāve (m. loc. sg.) nonbecoming (see I:10)

tad (n.) that
abhāvaḥ (m. nom. sg.) nonbecoming (see I:10) [end of TP6 cpd.]

Because they are held together by causes, results, correspondences, and supports, when these (go into) nonbeing, (there is the) nonbeing of them (*saṃskāras*).

IV.12 ***atīta-anāgataṃ svarūpato 'asty adhva-bhedād dharmāṇām***
atīta (m.) past (see III:16)
anāgatam (n. nom. sg.) yet to come, future (see II:16) [end of DV cpd.]
svarūpataḥ (ind.) in reality, from own form, according to own form; *svarūpa* (see I:3) + *tas* (indeclinable ablative suffix)
asti (pres. ind. 3rd pers. sg.) exist, is; from √*as* (be)
adhva (m.) path, road, way, course
bhedhāt (m. abl. sg.) distinction (see IV:3) [end of TP6 cpd.]
dharmāṇām (m. gen. pl.) (see III:13)

In their forms, the past and future exist, due to distinctions between paths of *dharmas*.

IV.13 ***te vyakta-sūkṣmā guṇa ātmānaḥ***
te (m. nom. pl.) these
vyakta (n.) manifest, apparent, visible, developed, evolved; *vi* (asunder, away) + *akta* from √*añj* (annoint)
sūkṣmāḥ (m. nom. pl.) subtle (see I:44) [end of DV cpd.]
guṇa (m.) (see I:16)
ātmānaḥ (m. nom. pl.) nature (see II:21 and II:5) [end of TP6 cpd.]

These have manifest and subtle *guṇa* natures.

IV.14 ***pariṇāma-ekatvād vastu-tattvaṃ***
pariṇāma (m.) (see II:15)
ekatvāt (m. abl. sg.) oneness, uniformity; *eka* (one) + *tva*, suffix denoting "having the quality of" [end of TP6 cpd.]
vastu (n.) object, matter (see I:9)
tattvam (n. nom. sg.) thatness, essence, principle (see I:32) [end of TP6 cpd.]

From the uniformity of its *pariṇāma*, there is the principle of an object.

IV.15 ***vastu-sāmye citta-bhedāt tayor vibhaktaḥ panthāḥ***
vastu (n.) object, matter (see I:9)
sāmye (n. loc. sg.) equality (see III:55) [end of TP4 cpd.]

citta (n.) mind (see I:2)
bhedāt (m. abl. sg.) distinction (see IV:3) [end of TP6 cpd.]
tayoḥ (m. gen. du.) of both, each
vibhaktaḥ (m. nom. sg.) divided, separate; *vi* (asunder, away) + *bhakta*, from √*bhaj* (divide)
panthāḥ (m. nom. sg.) path, way, course; from √*path* (go, move)

In the sameness of an object, because of its distinctness from the mind, there is a separate path of each.

IV.16 ***na ca eka-citta tantraṃ vastu tad-apramāṇakaṃ tadā kiṃ syāt***
na (ind.) not
ca (ind.) and
eka (m.) one
citta (n.) mind (see I:2)
tantraṃ (n. nom. sg.) thread, essential part, main point, teaching; from √*tan* (extend)
vastu (n. nom. sg.) object, matter (see I:9)
tad (ind.) that
apramāṇakaṃ (n. nom. sg.) not provable, not demonstrated; *a* (not) + *pra* (before) + *māṇaka*, (measure)
tadā (ind.) then
kiṃ (n. nom. sg.) interrogative pronoun
syāt (3rd pers. optative. sg.) could be; from √*as* (be)

An object does not depend on one mind; there is no proof of this: how could it be?

> All objects are made of the *guṇas* of *prakṛti* and are not the product of a single mind. See IV:14.

IV.17 ***tad-uparāga-apekṣitvāc cittasya vastu jñāta-ajñātaṃ***
tad (n.) that
uparāga (m.) coloring, dyeing, darkening, influence; *upa* (to) + *rāga*, from √*rañj* (color) [end of TP6 cpd.]
apekṣitvāt (m. abl. sg.) anticipation, expectation, wished, looked for; *apa* (away) + *īkṣitva*, from √*īkṣ* (see) + *tva*, suffix denoting possession of a quality [end of KD cpd.]
cittasya (n. gen. sg.) mind (see 1:2)
vastu (n. nom. sg.) object, matter (see 1:9)
jñāta (n.) known; from √*jñā* (know)
ajñātaṃ (n. nom. sg.) not known (see above) [end of DV cpd.]

An object of the mind is known or not known due to the anticipation that colors it (the mind).

IV.18 ***sadā jñātāś citta-vṛttayas tat-prabhoḥ puruṣasya apariṇāmitvāt***
sadā (ind.) always; *sa* (with) + *dā* (temporal indicator)
jñātāḥ (m. nom. pl.) known (see IV:17)
citta (n.) mind (see I:2)
vṛttayas (f. nom. pl.) fluctuations (see I:2)
tad (n.) that
prabhoḥ (m. gen. sg.) master (see I:16)
puruṣasya (m. gen. sg.) of the *puruṣa* (see I:16)
apariṇāmitvāt (m. abl. sg.) nontransformative, not changing; *a* (not) + *pariṇāmas* see II:15) + *tva*, suffix denoting possession of a quality

The fluctuations of the mind are always known due to the changelessness of their master, *puruṣa*.

See *Sāṃkhya Kārikā* 17 for proofs establishing *puruṣa*.

IV.19 ***na tat-svābhāsaṃ dṛśyatvāt***
na (ind.) not
tad (n.) that
svābhāsaṃ (n. nom. sg.) self-luminosity, own light; *sva* (self) + *ābhāsa*, from *ā* (to) + *bhāsa*, from √*bhās* (shine)
dṛśyatvāt (m. abl. sg.) nature of the seen; *dṛśya* (see II:17) + *tva*, suffix denoting possession of quality

There is no self-luminosity of that (*citta-vṛtti*) because of the nature of the Seen.

The seen is nonconscious. See *Sāṃkhya Kārikā* 20.

IV.20 ***eka-samaye ca ubhaya-anavadhāraṇam***
eka (m.) one (see I:32)
samaye (m. loc. sg.) circumstance (see II:31)
ca (ind.) and
ubhaya (m.) both
anavadhāraṇam (n. nom. sg.) nondiscernment, not ascertaining; *an* (not) + *ava* (down) + *dhāraṇa*, from √*dhṛ* (hold) [end of TP6 cpd.]

In one circumstance, there is no ascertainment of both (*vṛtti* and *puruṣa* together).

The *puruṣa* always remains distinct from circumstance (*prakṛti*).

IV.21 ***citta-antara-dṛśye buddhi-buddher atiprasaṅgaḥ smṛti-saṃkaraś ca***

citta (n.) mind (see I:2)

antara (m.) different (see IV:2)

dṛśye (m. loc. sg.) seen (see II:17) [end of TP6 cpd.]

buddhi (f.) intellect repository for *saṃskāras*; in Sāṃkhya, first *tattva* to emerge from *prakṛti*; from √*budh* (awaken)

buddheḥ (f. gen. sg.) intellect (see above) [end of TP5 cpd.]

atiprasaṅgaḥ (m. nom. sg.) excessive attachment, unwarranted stretch of a rule; *ati* (beyond) + *pra* (before) + *saṅga*, from √*sañj* (adhere)

smṛti (f.) memory (see I:6)

saṃkaraḥ (m. nom. sg.) confusion (see III:17) [end of DV cpd.]

ca (ind.) and

In trying to see another higher mind there is an overstretching of the intellect from the intellect and a confusion of memory.

Reflecting on the existential implications of this *sūtra*, it seems that this is a warning against trying to get behind your "Self," that is, against trying to find the truly "spiritual" identity, which according to this system is impossible: there is no one there to find; the witness cannot be witnessed. See *Bṛhadāraṇyaka Upaniṣad* III:7:23.

IV.22 ***citer apratisaṃkramāyās tad-ākāra-āpattau svabuddhi-saṃvedanam***

citeḥ (m. gen. sg.) higher consciousness; from √*cit* (think)

apratisaṃkramāyāḥ (f. abl. sg.) no intermixture, nondissolution, nonreabsorption; *a* (not) + *prati* (against) + *sam* (together) + *krama*, from √*kram* (step)

tad (n.) that

ākāra (m.) form, figure, shape, appearance; *ā* (hither, unto) + *kāra*, from √*kṛ* (do)

āpattau (f. loc. sg.) happening, occurence, arising, entering into a state or condition; *ā* (hither, unto) + *patti*, from √*pat* (fall, fly) [end of TP6 cpd.]

svabuddhi (f.) own intellect; *sva* (own) + *buddhi* (see IV:21)

saṃvedanam (n. nom. sg.) perception (see III:38) [end of TP6 cpd.]

Due to the nonmixing of higher consciousness, entering into that form is [in fact] the perception of one's own intellect.

IV.23 ***draṣṭṛ-dṛśya-uparaktaṃ cittaṃ sarva-arthaṃ***

draṣṭṛ (m.) seer (see I:3)

dṛśya (m.) seen (see II:7) [end of DV cpd.]
uparaktaṃ (n. nom. sg.) tinted, colored, dyed; *upa* (to, unto) + *rakta*, from √*rañj* (color) [end of TP3 cpd.]
cittaṃ (n. nom. sg.) mind (see I:2)
sarva (n.) all (see I:25)
arthaṃ (n. nom. sg.) meaning, purpose (see I:28) [end of KD cpd.]

All purposes [are known due to] the mind being tinted with Seer and Seen.

The purpose of all things is to provide experience and liberation, the former through the joining of the Seer and Seen, the latter through their distinction. See II:18.

IV.24 ***tad-asaṃkhyeya-vāsanābhiś-citraṃ api para-arthaṃ saṃhatya kāritvāt***
tad (n.) that
asaṃkhyeya (m.) innumerable, countless, multitude; *a* (not) + *saṃkhyeya*, gerundive form of *saṃkhyā*, *sam* (together) + √*khyā* (see)
vāsanābhiḥ (f. instr. pl.) habit pattern (see IV:8) [end of TP3 cpd.]
citraṃ (n. nom. sg.) variegated, spotted, speckled, various, manifold; from √*cit* (perceive)
api (ind.) also
para (m.) other (see II:40)
arthaṃ (n. nom. sg.) purpose (see I:28) [end of TP6 cpd.]
saṃhatya (ind.) having stuck or put together, joined, combined; gerund form of *sam* (together) + *hati*, from √*han* (strike)
kāritvāt (n. abl. sg.) action, activity; *kāri*, from √*kṛ* (do) + *tva*, suffix denoting possession of a quality

From action having been done conjointly for the purpose of another, it is speckled with innumerable habit patterns.

Compare with the statement in *Sāṃkhya Kārikā* 36 and 37 that all activities of *prakṛti* are done for the sake of *puruṣa*. See also *Yoga Sūtra* III:35 and IV:34.

IV.25 ***viśeṣa-darśina ātma-bhāva-bhāvanā-vinivṛttiḥ***
viśeṣa (m.) distinction (see I:22)
darśinaḥ (m. gen. sg.) seer, one who has sight; *darśa*, from √*dṛś* (see) + *in* (progressive suffix) [end of TP6 cpd.]
ātma (m.) self (see II:15)

bhāva (m.) state of being, becoming, existing; condition; intention (see III:9) [end of Kd cpd.]
bhāvanā (f. nom. sg.) cultivation (see I:33)
vinivṛttiḥ (f. nom. sg.) turned back, withdrawn, abandoned, cessation, coming to an end, discontinuance; *vi* (asunder, away) + *ni* (down, into) + *vṛtti*, from √*vṛt* (turn) [end of TP6 cpd.]

The one who sees the distinction discontinues the cultivation of self-becoming.

IV.26 ***tadā viveka-nimnaṃ kaivalya-prāgbhāraṃ cittaṃ***
tadā (ind.) then
viveka (m.) discrimination (see II:15)
nimnaṃ (n. nom. sg.) inclined towards, bending into; from *ni* (down, into) + *na*, from √*nam* (bend) [end of TP7 cpd.]
kaivalya (n.) isolation (see II:25)
prāgbhāraṃ (n. nom. sg.) propensity, inclination, being not far from; from *prāk* (directed towards) + *bhāra*, from √*bhṛ* (bear)
cittaṃ (n.) mind (see I:2)

Then, inclined toward discrimination, the mind has a propensity for *kaivalyam*.

IV.27 ***tac-chidreṣu pratyaya-antarāṇi saṃskārebhyaḥ***
tad (n.) that
chidreṣu (m. loc. pl.) torn asunder, containing holes, pierced; defect, fault; from √*chid* (cut)
pratyaya (m.) intention (see I:10)
antarāṇi (n. nom. pl.) other (see IV:2)
saṃskārebhyaḥ (m. abl. pl.) from *saṃskāras* (see I:18)

In the intervening spaces of that, there are also other intentions, due to *saṃskāras*.

IV.28 ***hānaṃ eṣāṃ kleśavad uktaṃ***
hānaṃ (n. nom. sg.) cessation, relinquishment (see II:25)
eṣāṃ (n. gen. pl.) of those
kleśavat (ind.) like affliction; *kleśa* (see I:24) + *vat* (suffix indicating analogy)
uktaṃ (n. nom. sg.) spoken; past passive participle of √*vac* (speak)

The cessation of them is said to be like that of the afflictions.

This process is described in II:10 and II:11 as *pratiprasava* or subtilization.

IV.29 ***prasaṃkhyāne'pi akusīdasya sarvathā viveka-khyāter dharma-meghaḥ samādhiḥ***

prasaṃkhyāne (m. loc. sg.) payment, liquidation; (n. loc. sg.), enumeration; reflection, meditation; *pra* (before, forward) + *saṃ* (together) + *khyāna*, from √*khyā* (see)
api (ind.) also, even, indeed
akusīdasya (m. nom. sg.) taking no interest, without gain, without usury; *a* (not) + *kusīda* (loan to be repaid with interest)
sarvathā (ind.) at all times, always (see III:54)
viveka (m.) discrimination (see II:26)
khyāteḥ (m. gen. sg.) discernment (see I:16) [end of BV cpd.]
dharma (m.) (see III:13)
meghaḥ (m. nom. sg.) cloud; from √*mih* (sprinkle) [end of KD cpd.]
saṃādhiḥ (f. nom. sg.) absorption (see I:20)

Indeed, for the one who has discriminative discernment in [that state of] reflection and always takes no interest, there is the cloud of *dharma samādhi.*

An interesting double entendre occurs here; the term *prasaṃkhyāne* can be interpreted either as reflection or as payment. In the latter sense, a financial analogy is used to describe the balancing of the karmic accounts. Once the debts accured due to past action have been paid off, and no interest remains, then one becomes established in the state of *samādhi* that allows all things to proceed as seen through the liberating knowledge of discriminative discernment.

IV.30 ***tataḥ kleśa-karma-nivṛttiḥ***

tataḥ (ind.) from that, thence (see I:22)
kleśa (m.) affliction (see I:24)
karma (n.) action (see I:24) [end of KD cpd.]
nivṛttiḥ (f. nom. sg.) cessation (see III:30) [end of TP6 cpd.]

From that, there is the cessation of afflicted action.

IV.31 ***tadā sarva-āvaraṇa-mala-apetasya jñānasya ānantyāj jñeyam alpam***

tadā (ind.) then
sarva (n.) all (see II:25)

āvaraṇa (n.) covering (see II:52)
mala (n.) impurity, dirt, filth, dust
apetasya (m. gen. sg.) departed, gone, departed, free from; *apa* (away, off) + *ita*, from √*i* (go)
jñānasya (n. gen. sg.) knowledge (see I:8)
ānantyāt (m. abl. sg.) infinite, eternal; from *ananta* (see II:34)
jñeyaṃ (n. nom. sg.) to be known; gerundive form of *jñā* (known)
alpaṃ (n. nom. sg.) little, small

Then, little is to be known due to the eternality of knowledge which is free from all impure covering.

IV.32 ***tataḥ kṛta-arthānāṃ pariṇāma-krama-samāptir guṇānāṃ***
tataḥ (ind.) from that, thence (see I:22)
kṛta (m.) done (see II:22)
arthānāṃ (n. gen. pl.) purpose (see I:22) [end of KD cpd.]
pariṇāma (m.) (see III:15)
krama (m.) succession (see III:15) [end of TP6 cpd.]
samāptiḥ (f. nom. sg.) conclusion, completion, accomplishment; *sam* (together) + *āpti*, from √*āp* (obtain) [end of TP6 cpd.]
guṇānāṃ (m. gen. pl.) (see I:16)

From that, the purpose of the *guṇas* is done and the succession of *pariṇāma* is concluded.

IV.33 ***kṣana-pratiyogī pariṇāma-aparānta-nigrāhyaḥ kramaḥ***
kṣana (n.) moment (see III:9)
pratiyogī (m. nom. sg.) correlate, counterpart, match; *prati* (against, back) + *yogin*, from √*yuj* (join) [end of KD cpd.]
pariṇāma (m.) (see II:15)
aparānta (m.) end (see III:22) [end of TP6 cpd.]
nigrāhyaḥ (m. nom. sg.) terminated, to be suppressed; *ni* (down, into) + *grāhya*, gerundive form of √*grabh* (grasp) [end of TP3 cpd.]
kramaḥ (m. nom. sg.) succession (see III:15)

Succesion and its correlate, the moment, are terminated by the end of *pariṇāma*.

IV.34 ***puruṣa-artha-śūnyānāṃ guṇānāṃ pratiprasavaḥ kaivalyaṃ svarūpa-pratiṣṭhā vā citi- śaktir iti***
puruṣa (m.) (see I:16)

artha (m.) purpose (see I:28) [end of TP4 cpd.]
śūnyānām (m. gen. pl.) empty (see I:9) [end of TP6 cpd.]
guṇānāṃ (m. gen. pl.) (see I:16)
pratiprasavaḥ (m. nom. sg.) (see I:16)
kaivalyaṃ (n. nom. sg.) isolation (see II:25)
svarūpa (n.) own form (see I:3)
pratiṣṭhā (f. nom. sg.) steadfastness, perserverence; preeminence; *prati* (agaisnt, back) + √*sthā* (stand) [end of TP7 cpd.]
vā (ind.) or, and
citi (m.) higher awareness, consciousness (see IV:22)
śaktiḥ (f. nom. sg.) power (see II:6) [end of TP6 cpd.]
iti (ind.) thus

The return to the origin of the *guṇas*, emptied of their purpose for *puruṣa*, is *kaivalyam*, the steadfastness in own form, and the power of higher consciousness.

> The concluding *sūtra* completes the definition of Yoga as an embodied experience given in I:3: "Then there is abiding in the Seer's own form."

IV *Interpreting Yoga*

15 *Reading Patañjali without Vyāsa*

A Critique of Four *Yoga Sūtra* Passages

Textual criticism is not a branch of mathematics, nor indeed an exact science at all. It deals with a matter not rigid and constant, like lines and numbers, but fluid and variable . . . It is therefore not susceptible to hard-and-fast rules.

—A. E. Houseman, "The Application of Thought to Textual Criticism"

In discussing oral literature . . . , it must be understood that we are discussing a large body of material which can have its total integrity, impact, and realisation only within the scope of performance, transmission, and occasion. The performer of oral literature gives body to the material, formulates it, and realises it, within regulated and specified occasions.

—Kofi Awoonar, *Breast of the Earth*

The *Yoga Sūtra* of Patañjali was commented upon by various authors, most notably in Vyāsa's *Bhāṣya* (fifth century CE). In this chapter, I propose that the standard interpretation given by Vyāsa needs to be reconsidered, particularly regarding his analysis of Patañjali's mention of three types of yogis,[1] his definition of concentration,[2] his interpretation of the Sāṃkhya system,[3] and his assertion that the yogi can detect the difference between two apparently identical objects.[4]

The *Yoga Sūtra* was undoubtedly intended primarily as an oral text. It was composed within a genre designed to be memorized; as with most teachings of the South Asian tradition, to "learn" a tradition meant that its key text or texts would be memorized. Its mere 195 *sūtras*, far briefer than text of the Vedas or Upaniṣads, made it relatively easy to commit to memory. It pulses with an internal rhythm conducive to memorization. Like other forms of oral literature, it uses the cadence of language clearly to introduce new topics, emphasize important points, and bring closure when needed, exhibiting formulaic patterns and devices of oral literature. Although the bulk of studies on oral literature focus on the classical Greek tradition,[5] some modern Indologists have examined the oral nature of Hindu texts. Harold Coward has noted "In the Hindu tradition, language is thought to be truly and most fully experienced only in its oral form. The written word is a secondary thing developed only for heuristic teaching purposes and as an aid for those too dull to remember the important texts by heart. For the Indian, the form of language that is used as the criterion is not written but oral."[6] Likewise, William A. Graham has written, "The teacher who knows the sacred text by heart and has devoted his or her life to studying and explicating it is the one and only reliable guarantor of the sacred truth . . . one telling Hindu term that indicates that a text has been memorized is *kanthastha*, which means literally 'situated in the throat.' Knowing a text means also to 'place it in the heart' (Hindi: *hrdya mem dharana karna*)."[7] The construction of oral texts can differ significantly from that of written texts. Oral texts tend to use literary devices that enhance memorization, and to be more attuned to the medium of the ear. Kofi Awoonar, a scholar of African literature, describes some basic characteristics of oral literature as follows: "The chant's basic poetic qualities include repetition of lines, digression, word-picture painting-use of ideophones and parallelism-comparison, simile, metaphor, metonymy, allusions, and epigrams."[8] Though not filled with all these literary devices, Patañjali's *Yoga Sūtra* does establish internal patterns through parallel structure, repetition of key terms, and a distinctive though sparing use of simile and metaphor. Devices such as rhythm and repetition not only assist in memorization but also delineate transitions and emphasis. For instance, particularly long *sūtras* tend to indicate a greater degree of importance, and exceptionally short *sūtras* often hold palpable poignancy.[9]

The traditional scholarly approach to studying the *Yoga Sūtra*, in addition to the method mentioned above, also includes reading the text with its accompanying commentary by Vyāsa and subcommentaries by Vācaspati Miśra (ninth century) and Vijñāna Bhikṣu (sixteenth century). However, this method if used exclusively has several drawbacks. First, the oral aspects of the text, including much of the rhythm, assonance, and alliteration, are lost. The memory is not engaged to the extent as when reciting a text, and insights derived from hearing "echoes" within the recited text cannot be gleaned. Additionally, the format of the commentary literally stands between the *sūtras* of Patañjali. In nearly all cases, the commentary is several times longer than the *sūtra* itself, and by the time one reads through it, the continuity or flow from one *sūtra* to the next is lost. The commentarial tradition focuses primarily on *sūtras* in isolation from one another. Although Vyāsa occasionally provides philosophical summaries of the Yoga system, and although he sometimes introduces an individual *sūtra* with some reference to the prior *sūtra*, he does not, for the most part, identify key themes over a sequence of *sūtras* or cross-reference *sūtras* to one another. For instance, although the term *īśvara* is used in three different places,[10] Vyāsa does not refer to the various other usages in any of the three places. Furthermore, he does not refer to Patañjali's sources, such as the *Sāṃkhya Kārikā*, Buddhism, or Jainism.

Insight into Patañjali's original intent can arise when the text is heard or recited in sequence rather than being read with the intervention of one or more commentators. Using this technique, I will reconnect four thematic sequences that in my reading (or hearing) of the text have been interrupted by Vyāsa's atomistic approach. Following leads stemming from the style and vocabulary of Patañjali and the immediate context of specific *sūtras*, I am engaging in what biblical scholars refer to as "rational criticism."[11] Categories of style and context are used by biblical scholars when they seek to determine a particular author's true intent. My purpose in employing this method is to suggest that Vyāsa overlooked important aspects of Patañjali's system. What I propose is a form of conjectural emendation, improving our understanding of Patañjali based on evidence internal to the root text itself and thereby moving away from four select interpretations of Vyāsa.

Several scholars have claimed that Patañjali compiled his *Yoga Sūtra* from a number of different texts. Georg Feuerstein parses the text into two, a "Kriyā Yoga Text" extending from I:1 to II:27 and from III:3 or 4 to IV:34, interrupted by an "Aṣṭānga Yoga Text" from II:28 to III:2 or 3, which also picks up III:55. Deussen and Hauer posit that the text was pieced together from five different texts, and each proposes his own grouping of subtexts. These speculations are possible. However, Vyāsa does not in his commentary mention subtexts or refer to different traditions or authors. Nor does the style of Patañjali indicate that he in fact is borrowing texts from others. With one or two notable exceptions in the form of purposeful stylistic variations,[12] Patañjali is consistently terse. Although it is certainly the case that Patañjali summarizes a number of different practices and philosophical perspectives, it seems that he does so in his own voice. As I have noted earlier, although he describes Yoga practice and the goal in a number of different ways and does not provide a conclusive definition of what way is best or which goal is highest, his major themes and vocabulary are largely consistent throughout the text.

I suggest that we leave aside the notion that he pieced together existing texts and agree to the premise that Patañjali presents a concatenation of summaries based on earlier and extant contemporaneous systems. The issue I address hinges on an investigation of consistent units within Patañjali that seem to have been overlooked by Vyāsa and hence ignored by later commentators and translators, who seemingly without exception rely heavily upon Vyāsa for guidance. Since Vyāsa concentrated on explicating individual verses and not groupings of verses, these units or subtexts have been neglected. Although I am suggesting four such units or pericopes, others might also exist.

THE THREE TYPES OF YOGIS

The first case involves verses I:9–22, a pericope or set of verses that discusses different practitioners of Yoga:

19. The ones who are absorbed in *prakṛti* and free from the body still have an intention of becoming.
20. Of the others it is preceded by faith, energy, mindfulness, *samādhi*, and wisdom.
21. The strongly intense ones are near.
22. Hence the distinctions of mild, moderate and ardent.

These verses are found directly following the description of two types of concentration (*saṃprajñāta*). The first type of *saṃprajñāta* is described as being associated with thought, reflection, bliss, and I-am-ness; the second type is said to have "*saṃskāra*-only," following the application of "practice and the intention of cessation." The first verse of the above pericope introduces the concept that even if one is not fully involved in worldly activity, there still can linger the possibility of future action. This contrasts sharply with the prior two verses, which describe states of concentration. No vocabulary is shared with the verse immediately prior, and it seems that a new idea is being introduced. This first verse clearly refers to an inferior state that can lead to "backsliding."

The next verse in this pericope mentions more steadfast practitioners who adhere to disciplines familiar within the Buddhist tradition: faith, energy, mindfulness, *samādhi*, and wisdom. These five are called the "five cardinal virtues" of Buddhism,[13] though Vyāsa does not in his commentary acknowledge any Buddhist parallel. Facility at these five indicates that a person has entered the spiritual path in a serious way, in contrast to the people mentioned earlier who intend to return to worldly ways. Hence, these verses present a contrast between two groups of practitioners. The former group intends to return to the realm of active involvement with things worldly; the latter group exhibits qualities associated with renunciation.

The next *sūtra* speaks of a seemingly even higher type of yogi, the "strongly intense ones" who are deemed "near." This completes a hierarchic triad of yogic practitioners, as indicated in the final piece of the pericope: "Hence, the distinctions of mild, moderate, and ardent." Given the clear break between verse 18 and verse 19, and given the obvious threefold progression, it stands to reason that verse 22 completes a discrete theme. The following verse (I:23) takes up a new, unrelated topic pertaining to devotion to Īśvara.

Vyāsa does not indicate any relationship among these verses, and he treats each of them individually. Rather than explaining the meaning of the terms *mild*, *moderate*, and *ardent*, his commentary on I:22 merely asserts that yogis are of nine classes, with mild, moderate, and ardent variations of each of three categories, and that similarly subdividing these three categories yields eighty-one varieties of yogis. He does not explain the meaning of "strongly intense," though one might surmise that the strongly intense practitioner would be least inclined to involve himself or herself with worldly or afflicted activity. In verse 22 Patañjali uses "hence" (*tataḥ*), which would indicate that this *sūtra* follows from ones immediately prior as a sort of conclusion. Because he lists three qualities in this *sūtra* and the three prior *sūtras* described advancing states of attainment, it stands to reason that the "mild" yogi holds the potential to reenter the world, that the "moderate" yogi diligently follows the five practices of "faith, energy, mindfulness, *saṃādhi*, and wisdom," and that the ardent yogi is near, due to his or her intensity of practice.

Vyāsa does not acknowledge such an association, nor do the later commentators. Yet the evidence seems clear that Patañjali intended for verse 22 to refer to the prior three verses. My contention here is that the commentarial style interrupted the flow of the text and that Vyāsa overlooks two important clues: the use of the number 3 and the use of the qualifying particle *tataḥ* (hence).

A SINGULAR STATE OF UNITY

The next issue that I wish to take up stems from the verse in which Patañjali describes the state of absorption using the metaphor of the clear jewel that takes on the color of an object in close proximity.[14] This verse appears at the end of a long section beginning seventeen verses prior that describes alternate means of achieving the state of Yoga. Having defined the distinctions of mild, moderate, and ardent, Patañjali lists ten ways in addition to dispassion and practice that may be applied to achieve Yoga, beginning with verse 23. These include dedication to Īśvara, repetition of mantra, stabilization of breath, the practice of *eka tattva*, the application of the Brahma Vihāra of the Buddhists (through Patañjali does not acknowledge the Buddhist parallel), steady binding of the mind, sorrowless illumination, freedom from attachment, reflection on dream knowledge, or "meditation as desired."[15] This section is set apart from the preceding and following discussions by repeated use of the word *vā*, a conjunction that usually is translated as "or," and a verse that provides closure: "Mastery of it extends from the smallest to the greatest."[16] The "*vā*" sequence has concluded, and the interruption of the text's flow prepares the reader for a new section.

Verse I:41 comprises one of the most lengthy and descriptive passages in Patañjali's *Yoga Sūtra*. Its length and striking use of imagery indicate its importance: "[That state] of diminished fluctuations, like a precious (or clear) jewel assuming the color of any near object, has unity among grasper, grasping, and grasped."[17] This passage can be seen as describing the culmination achieved when one has completed one of the ten forms of Yoga. It also serves to introduce the discussion of various forms of trance (*samādhi* or *samāpatti*) that arise with the practice of Yoga. As T. S. Rukmani has noted, the accomplishment of Yoga posits no distinctions between the process and the goal; success at technique fulfils the goal of Yoga.

Patañjali states that the goal of Yoga is the diminishment of fluctuations in the mind,[18] resulting in "abiding in the seer's own form."[19] Various practices, starting with practice and dispassion[20] and including the ten cited above, are listed by which this can be achieved. It stands to reason that I:41 describes in generic fashion the distinguishing characteristics of that state, using the metaphor of the clear jewel and a phenomenological analysis of trance experience.

In the *Laṅkāvatāra Sūtra*, which is roughly contemporaneous with Patañjali's text and hence predates Vyāsa by at least two hundred years, we see the metaphor of the clear jewel being used to describe the elevated state of the bodhisattva. The text states that the bodhisattva "will become thoroughly conversant with the noble truth of self-realization, will become a perfect master of his own mind, will conduct himself without effort, will be like a gem reflecting a variety of colors."[21] The image of the reflecting gem is used to describe an advanced state of attainment. The control of mind and effortlessness of the bodhisattva seem to indicate a close relationship between the ideals of the Yoga school generally associated with Hinduism and the Yogācāra school of Buddhism.

The parallel use of the phenomenological terms *grasping* and *grasped* in the *Laṅkāvatāra Sūtra* can also help illuminate our understanding of *Yoga Sūtra* I:41. Repeatedly, the author makes reference to grasping (*grahaṇa*) and grasped (*grāhya*), which Suzuki also translates as subject and object:

> If the Bodhisattva should wish to understand fully that an external world to be consumed under categories of discrimination, such as the grasping (subject) and the grasped (objects), is of the mind itself, let him be kept away from such hindrance as turmoil, social intercourse, and sleep.[22]
>
> In my teaching, Mahamati, discrimination does not take place because I teach to stand above grasped and grasping . . . those who are addicted to grasped and grasping . . . do not have a thorough understanding of the world, which is not more that what is seen of the Mind itself.[23]
>
> You will cast off discrimination such as grasped and grasping.[24]
>
> I do not belong to the school of causation, nor to the school of no-causation, except that I teach the chain of origination as far as the thought-constructed world of grasped and grasping exists depending upon discrimination.[25]

In each of these passages, the author advocates the collapse of both grasping and grasped.

In the *Madhyāntavibhāgabhāṣya*, another text associated with Yogācāra Buddhist tradition, Vasubandhu states that imagination (*parikalpa*) of what is unreal (*abhūta*) is none other than the conceptualization (*vikalpa*) of the object (*grāhya*) and subject (*grāhaka*). Emptiness, the goal of Buddhism, is the "absence of the subject-object relationship in the Imagination of what is unreal." Vasubandhu writes that

> 1.4: Consciousness arises as the appearance (*pratibhāsa*) of objects, sentient beings, the self, and ideation. Its object (*artha*) does not exist; and because [the object] does not exist, [the subject] also does not exist.
>
> 1.5a–c: Thus it is proved that [consciousness] is Imagination, for [consciousness] is not as [it appears], but it is not utterly non-existent.
>
> 1.5d: From its extinction is thought to come liberation (*mokṣa*).
>
> 1.14ab: Emptiness is characterized as the absence of the duality of subject and object and as the existence (*bhāva*) of the absence (*abhāva*). . . .
>
> [1.14c]: it is neither an existence (*bhāva*) nor an absence (*abhāva*).[26]

In the Buddhist tradition, the highest state (emptiness) arises when distinctions of grasping and grasped dissolve. Buddhism does not recognize the notions of seer (*draṣṭṛ*), or grasper (*grahītr*), or self (*ātman or puruṣa*); the enlightened view is alluded to through the careful avoidance of such positive statements.

However, despite this foundational theological difference, the analysis of perceptual processes bears an interesting similarity. In both Yoga and Yogācāra Buddhism, the separation of grasper and grasped must be overcome. In Yoga, this involves the unity (*samāpatti*) of these two with the seer, resulting in a state compared to the clear jewel, indicating a state of purified awareness in which the distinctions among grasper, grasping, and grasped disappear. In Buddhism, there is said to be emptiness of the subject-object relationship, again indicating that it has been overcome. Each of these discussions of grasping and grasped emphasizes their transcendence or dissolution.

However, Vyāsa's analysis of the text places emphasis not on unity or transcendence. Instead, he digresses into a prolonged discussion about the differences among grasper, grasping, and grasped. Vyāsa outlines three different forms of trance (*samāpanna*): one that hooks onto a gross element (the grasped), one that hooks into a subtle element (grasping), and one that transforms one into the seer (grasper). In his reading, only the final form would truly be a state of Yoga. In the first and second, where emphasis is placed in the grasped and the grasping, mental fluctuations are not restrained and hence are clearly operative, a state contrary of the goal of Yoga. However, Patañjali states that this *sūtra* is describing a state wherein the fluctuations have been restrained (*kṣīṇa-vṛtti*) and that a unity (*samāpatti*) arises among the three components of perception. The word *samāpatti* appears in the singular; if Patañjali intended to indicate three separate forms of *samāpatti*, he would have used the plural, to correspond with the locative plural ending attached to the compound "among grasper, grasping and grasped." With the word *samāpatti* being singular, it is clear that one state of unity is being discussed by Patañjali. This single state arises when all three aspects of perception appear as one.

Furthermore, there is no indication of threeness in the jewel metaphor. The jewel takes on the color of an object that stands near. The jewel itself could be seen as the seer, the color of the object could be seen as the seen, but in the way they are described, there is a complete transformation of the jewel; it takes on the quality of the object in such a way that one cannot be distinguished from the other. In this metaphor, no mention is made of the third process emphasized by Vyāsa, the process of grasping. Hence, it would stand to reason that the metaphor itself supports the singular reading of *saṃāpatti* and does not advance Vyāsa's theory of three forms.

If the case is made that these three distinctions made by Vyāsa relate to other listings of *samādhi*, no support can be found. Four types of *saṃprajñāta* (discursive thought, reflection, bliss, and I-am-ness) are listed in I:17, not three. The *sūtras* following I:41 also delineate four distinct ways in which *samāpatti* takes place. In *savitarkā*, the object or *grāhya* is gross and then is transcended in *nirvitarkā*; in *savicārā*, the object is subtle and yet again transcended in *nirvicārā*. In this state of transcendence, the distinctions among seer, seeing, and seen disappear. In this discussion as well as in the discussion of *saṃprajñāta* in I:17, Patañjali mentions four, not three, distinct aspects or paths.

It seems evident both from the grammar and imagery of the *sūtra* and from the usage of parallel terms in the Buddhist tradition that the *sūtra* is describing the collapse of distinctions that transpires when the fluctuations of the mind cease and not suggesting different states pertaining to each of the three. Recalling again the Buddhist usage of 'grasping' and 'grasped' in the *Laṅkāvatāra Sūtra* and the *Madhyātavibhāgabhāṣya*, there ultimately is no grasping and nothing that is grasped. This negation indicates that the Bodhisattva has gone beyond the conventional realm (*samvṛtti*) into the realm of enlightenment (*paramārtha*), where in there is no attachment. The Yoga system does not negate perceptual process in its description of higher states of consciousness, due to its assent of the presence of pure consciousness, referred to as "*puruṣa*" or "*ātman*," but asserts a state of unity in which no distinction can be found among grasper, grasping, and grasped.

This state of unity can also be interpreted shamanistically. In shamanistic traditions, as explained by Mircea Eliade, the shaman "takes on" the qualities of a particular totem animal in order to gain power. Vestiges of this tradition can be found in those Yoga postures that imitate animals: in doing the *siṅgha āsana*, one strives to take on the ferocity and strength of a lion. In a sense, one enters into a bodily felt state other than that of the human person, thereby extending and enhancing one's self-definition. "Unity," which often has been regarded in Yoga as indicating unity with higher consciousness, does not make higher consciousness an object with which one merges but rather refers to the process by which one's consciousness is transformed by immersion into the object of one's attention, whatever that may be.

In summary, there seems to be little or no support for Vyāsa's interpretation that Patañjali intended to discuss three types of *saṃāpatti*: one pertaining to unity achieved with the gross object, another with process of perception, and yet another pertaining to the unity with the seer. This *sūtra* seems to discuss what happens when a state of Yoga has been achieved after applying any one of a number of different techniques. There would be no purpose, according to Yoga, to gaining a state of unity with a gross object or with sensory activity, because mental fluctuations would remain. Given the metaphor of the clear jewel and the unmistakably singular reference to unity, it does not make sense, grammatical or otherwise, to posit a three-fold analysis of *samāpatti* based on this *sūtra*. As with the listing of eighty-one different types of yogis, Vyāsa seems overly concerned with adding enumerative speculations to Patañjali's text where it perhaps is not necessary or helpful.

SĀṂKHYA, YOGA, AND THE NUMBER SEVEN

Another aspect of the text that I wish to discuss that is not mentioned explicitly by Vyāsa is the direct parallel between verses II:15–27 and the *Sāṃkhya Kārikā* of Īśvarakṛṣṇa. By tying these thirteen verses of Patañjali to the text of Īśvarakṛṣṇa, I suggest an alternate interpretation of verse II:27, to which Vyāsa ascribes seven stages of accomplishment. The "Sāṃkhya Pericope" follows:

15. For the discriminating one, all is suffering, due to the conflict of the fluctuations of the *guṇas*, and by the sufferings due to *pariṇāma*, sorrow, and *saṃskāra*.
16. The suffering yet to come is to be avoided.
17. The cause of what is to be avoided is the confusion of the Seer with the Seen.
18. The Seen has the qualities of light, activity, and inertia, consists of the element and the senses, and has the purposes of experience and liberation.
19. The distinct, the indistinct, the designator, and the unmanifest are the division of the *guṇas*.
20. The Seer only sees; though pure, it appears intentional.
21. The nature of the Seen is only for the purpose of that (*puruṣa*).
22. When [its] purpose is done, [the Seen] disappears; otherwise it does not disappear due to being common to others.
23. Confusion (*saṃyoga*) results when one perceives the two powers of owner [*puruṣa*] and owned [*prakṛti*] as (one) self form.
24. The cause of it is ignorance.
25. From the absence [of ignorance], confusion (*saṃyoga*) ceases; [this is] the escape, the isolation from the Seen.
26. The means of escape is unfaltering discriminative discernment.
27. The preparatory ground for this wisdom is sevenfold.

To match the two systems, we begin with II:15 and 16. These assert that all is suffering and that this suffering can be overcome, the point of departure indicated in *Sāṃkhya Kārikā* I and II.

I. From torment by three-fold misery arises the inquiry into the means of terminating it; if it is said that it is fruitless, the means being known by perception, no [we reply], since in them there is no certainty or finality.

II. The scriptural means of terminating misery is also like the perceptible; it is verily linked with impurity, destruction, and surpassability; different therefrom and superior thereto is that means derived from the discriminative knowledge of the evolved, the unevolved, and the knower.[27]

Reference to the *guṇas*, a hallmark feature of Sāṃkhya is included in II:15, reflecting the definition of the *guṇas* given in *SK* XII. "The attributes are of the nature of pleasure, pain, and delusion; they serve the purpose of illumination, action and restraint; and they are mutually subjugative, and supporting, and productive and co-operative." In II:17, the confusion of *prakṛti* and *puruṣa*, Seen and Seer, is regarded to be the cause of suffering, reflecting *SK* XX. "Thus, from this union, the insentient 'evolute' appears as if 'sentient'; and similarly, from the activity really belonging to the attributes, the spirit, which is neutral, appears as if it were active." The constituents of the manifested *prakṛti* are listed in II:18 and 19, summarizing the contents of *SK* XXII up through XXXVIII. "From *prakṛti* (primordial nature, Nature) issues *mahat* (*buddhi*, the Great Principle); from this issue *ahaṃkārā* (I-principle); from which proceed the 'set of sixteen'; from five of this 'set of sixteen' proceed the five elementary substances." *YS* II:20 then defines the Seer, reflecting the discussion of *puruṣa* in *SK* XI, XVII, XVIII and XIX.

XI. The manifest is "with the three attributes" (*guṇas*), "undistinguishable," "objective," "common," "insentient," and "productive." So also is Nature. The spirit is the reverse, and yet also [in some respect] similar.

XVII. (a) Because all composite objects are for another's use, (b) because there must absence of the three attributes and other properties, (c) because there must be control, (d) because there must be someone to experience, and (e) because there is a tendency towards "isolation" or final beatitude, therefore, the spirit must be there.

XVIII. The plurality of spirits certainly follows from the distributive nature of the incidence of birth and death and of the endowment of the instruments of cognition and action, from bodies engaging in action, not all at the same time, and also from difference in the proportion of the three constituents.

XIX. And from the contrast it follows that the spirit is "witness," and has "isolation," "neutrality," and is the "seer," and "inactive."

YS II:21, "The nature of the Seen is only for the purpose of that (*puruṣa*)," echoes the following *Sāṃkhya Kārikā* passages that describe the purpose of the Seen:

> XLII. For the purpose of the Spirit, the subtle body, through its connections with the means and their results, and with the aid of the might of Nature, acts like an actor.
>
> LVI. Thus, this effort in the activity of Nature, beginning from the Mahat down to the gross elements, is for the liberation of each Spirit; although it is for another's benefit, yet it seems as if it were for itself.
>
> LVII. As non-intelligent milk functions for the nourishment of the calf, so does Nature function for the liberation of the Spirit.
>
> LVIII. As people engage in action for relieving desires, so does the Unmanifest (function) for liberating the Spirit.

When this purpose has been fulfilled, *YS* II:22 states that the Seen disappears; *SK* LIX declares that "Nature desists after showing herself to the spirit, as a dancer desists from dancing after showing herself to the audience." With a poetic flourish, *SK* LXI proclaims there is nothing more modest than Nature who "never again exposes herself to the view of the Spirit." The author emphasizes that the Spirit is never bound or touched in any way:

> LXII. Therefore, no Spirit is bound or liberated not does any migrate. It is Nature, abiding in manifest forms, that migrates, bounds, and is liberated.

Patañjali states that the confusion between Spirit and Nature, the Seer and the Seen, is caused by ignorance and is the root of suffering.[28] When this association stops, the goal of *kaivalyam* is achieved.[29] He emphasizes the need for discriminative discernment (*viveka khyāti*)[30] to take place, which corresponds to Īśvarakṛṣṇa's emphasis on knowledge (*jñāna*).[31]

At this point, though Patañjali has summarized most of the Sāṃkhya system, he has not fully explained the subtle body. Īśvarakṛṣṇa is very specific on this topic, devoting fifteen verses[32] to a discussion of the subtle body. It includes the *buddhi*, *ahaṃkāra*, and *manas*, as well as two complementary groupings of *bhāvas* or states of existence. One group lists eight *bhāvas*; the other group lists fifty *bhāvas*. Perhaps for reasons of brevity, or perhaps because he substitutes his own philosophy of *kleśas*, *saṃskāras*, and *vāsanās*, Patañjali does not go into great detail regarding the nature of the subtle body, though he does use the term *sūkṣma* in each of the sections of the text.[33] However, both authors acknowledge the key role played by knowledge in the quest for liberation: Sāṃkhya uses the term *jñāna*, and Yoga uses the term discriminative discernment (*viveka khyāti*).

The number seven figures prominently in Īśvarakṛṣṇa's discussion of the process of liberation. He states in *SK* LXIII that "Nature binds herself by herself by seven forms alone and for the purpose of the Spirit, liberates herself through one form, knowledge." At the point where knowledge predominates, *prakṛti* turns her back on the other seven *bhāvas*:

> From the study of the constituents of manifest reality (*tattvas*), the knowledge arises that "I do not exist, nothing is mine, I am not." This [knowledge] leaves no residue, is free from ignorance, pure and is singular (*kevala*).
>
> Then *puruṣa* with the repose of a spectator, sees *prakṛti*, whose activity has ceased since her task has been fulfilled and who has abandoned her seven modes [that perpetuate bondage: ignorance, virtue, nonvirtue, attachment, indifference, power, and weakness].[34]

In this sequence the process of liberation is explained as the turning back from the seven modes or *bhāvas* that stem from ignorance and dwelling in a state of knowledge.

Vyāsa claims that the number seven in *Yoga Sūtra* II:27, which similarly appears adjacent to a discussion of liberation, refers to seven attainments:

1. that which is to be known has been known
2. that which is to be avoided has been avoided
3. that which is to be attained has been attained
4. the means (discriminative discernment) has been attained
5. the intellect has completed its purpose of proving experience and liberation
6. the activities of the *guṇas* have ceased
7. *puruṣa* abides in isolation.[35]

Conversely, I would like to suggest that the mention of the number seven in verse II:27 can hold numerous meanings, as it often does in Indian art and literature.[36] This may include an oblique reference to the part of the *Sāṃkhya Kārikā* cited above wherein one turns away from the seven *bhāvas* that perpetuated bondage.

The term *prānta-bhūmi*, interpreted by Vyāsa as referring to the final goal, could refer to the sequence of stages leading to the eighth stage. *Prānta* combines the prefix *pra*, which means "up to," with *anta*, which means "end." Hence, it would refer to that which precedes the final stage or eighth-level attainment, the stages that are preparatory for the achievement of *samādhi*. Each of these seven must be ultimately transcended, just as the seven *bhāvas* are rejected by *prakṛti* at her moment of liberating knowledge. Given the placement of the *sūtras* within the summary discussion of Sāṃkhya, and just prior to the exposition of eightfold Yoga, I think it is plausible that '*prānta-bhūmi*' refers to stages prior to the attainment of the goal and not to the goal itself, as Vyāsa asserts.

Eightfold analyses of spiritual disciplines and stages are common in yogic traditions. Patañjali lists eight limbs of Yoga, culminating in *samādhi*, in *sūtras* II:29–55 and III:1–3. The *Laṅkāvatāra Sūtra* lists seven preliminary stages in the path of Bodhisattva that lead to an eighth stage, the description of which is analogous to the eighth stage of Yoga:

> At the seventh stage, Mahāmatī, the Bodhisattva properly examines the nature of the Citta, Manas, and Manovijñāna; he examines ego-soul and what belongs to it, grasped and grasping, the egolessness of presence and things, rising and disappearing, individuality and generally, etc.[37]

> Of the Bodhisattva-Mahāsattvas of the eighth stage of Bodhisattvahood . . . there is the cessation of all things as to grasped and grasping which rise from one's ardent desire for things.[38]

The *Yogadṛṣṭisamuccaya* of Haribhadra outlines four systems of eightfold Yoga.[39] If we look at the placement of *Yoga Sūtra* II:27 at the end of the Sāṃkhya system summary, the term *prānta-bhūmi* could refer to the seven *bhāvas* other than *jñāna*. If we look at it in terms of the discussion of eightfold Yoga that follows, it could refer to the seven stages prior to the attainment of *samādhi*. But for Vyāsa to equate the number seven with his lists of seven final accomplishments seems at odds with usage of the number seven in parallel traditions and at variance with the meaning of '*prānta-bhūmi*.'

TWO OBJECTS OR DISCRIMINATIVE DISCERNMENT?

The final area that I wish to discuss revolves around Vyāsa's commentary on verse III:53. Patañjali states, "Hence, there is the ascertainment of two things that are similar, due to their not being limited (made separate) by differences of birth, designation, and place." Vyāsa's commentary interprets this to mean that the yogi is able to tell apart two identical items despite their occupying the same place but at different times. He uses the example of a cow, stating that the yogi can tell the difference between two similar cows even if their position is switched, due to the yogi's keen abilities of discernment. As with the above examples, this interpretation is universally accepted by the later commentators, such as Vācaspati Miśra, Vijñānabhikṣu, and Rāmānanda. However I would like to suggest that the yogi's power would not be directed to such as mundane task, and I prefer to interpret this *sūtra* in light of its context within the third chapter and within the overall intent of the system.

The *sūtra* states that, due to birth, marking, and place (*jāti*, *lakṣaṇa*, *deśa*), a difference (*anyatā*) can be perceived (*pratipatti*) between two things that are similar (*tulyayoḥ*). I would like to argue that the number two holds particular philosophical significance consistently for Patañjali throughout the text. In other places, the number two refers to the Seer and the Seen. In I:3, the Seer is contrasted with the realm of mental fluctuations. In II:17, Patañjali states that "[t]he cause of what is to be avoided is the union of the Seer with the Seen." This sentiment is echoed later in the fourth section of the text, when Patañjali states that "[a]ll things are known due to the mind being tinged with Seer and Seen."[40] The Seer and Seen are contrasted in II:20 and 21, and the liberated state is said to hinge on being able to separate these two, which are seen to be one due to ignorance, as explained in II:22–26 above. The key to overcoming the pain inherent in involvement with and attachment to the manifested realm of *prakṛti* is to be able clearly to discern the difference between the two realms. Just as the *jñāna bhāva* is the modality by which Sāṃkhya claims one achieves *kevala*, so in the *Yoga Sūtra*, Patañjali places great emphasis on discriminative discernment (*viveka-khyāti*) as the "means of escape" (*hāna-upāya*).

In the fourth and final part of the text, Patañjali again emphasizes the need for distinguishing between the Seer and Seen as preliminary to *kaivalyam* and *dharma-megha-samādhi*, the highest states of Yoga. Patañjali states: "The one who sees the distinction discontinues the cultivation of self-becoming. Then, inclined toward discrimination, the mind has a propensity for *kaivalyam*."[41] The application of discriminative discernment allows one to enter the state of *samādhi* known as *dharma megha*, through which all afflicted action ceases: "Indeed, in [that state of] reflection, for the one who has discriminative discernment and always takes no interest, there is the cloud of *dharma samādhi*."[42] From these *sūtras*, we detect a close link between the Sāṃkhya system and its emphasis on the separation of the two great principles *puruṣa* and *prakṛti* and the process of liberation of Yoga. When Patañjali refers to things in twos, he consistently alludes to Sāṃkhya and concomitantly insists that a distinction be made between these two.

One point that needs clarification in regard to III:53 is the reason why Patañjali would refer to two things that are similar. To understand this similarity, I suggest that we turn to one of the *sūtras* mentioned earlier. In I:19 he mentions those who are "absorbed in *prakṛti* and free from the body" (*videha prakṛti-laya*) as potentially entering again into existence (*bhāva-pratyaya*). In this state, the outward manifestation of *prakṛti* has been stilled, but the desire to become active once more has not been quelled. The fully accomplished yogi has the ability to see the difference between the true uprooting of desire and its deceptive form of latency, which some might mistake for true purity (*akliṣta*) and isolation (*kaivalyam*). The *Sāṃkhya Kārikā* also lists various ways in which *puruṣa* and *prakṛti* in its unmanifest form are similar; both are said to be uncaused, infinite, all-pervasive, inactive, singular, without support, nondistinct, without parts, and independent.[43]

If we look at the immediate context of *sūtra* III:53, we can see a continuity of thought that is interrupted if, as Vyasa reads it, the yogi cultivates a power to discern difference between two similar cows or pieces of fruit. Starting at *sūtra* III:47 and continuing to the end of the *pāda*, we can see that Patañjali in *sūtra* III:53 is referring to a distinction similar to that suggested above and not in accord with Vyāsa's interpretation. Earlier in this section, Patañjali has discussed in sequence the cultivation of mastery over the body and gross elements. He states that one can master the sense organs: "From *saṃyama* on grasping, own-form, I-am-ness, their connection, and their significance, there is mastery over the sense organs." He also states that one can gain control over the source of all these forms of manifestations, clearly referring to the ability to placate the urges of *prakṛti*: "Hence, there is swiftness of the mind organ, a state of being beyond the senses, and mastery over the *pradhāna*."[44] However, this accomplishment itself is not sufficient for liberation; there must be an even higher form of discernment that sees the difference between this quiescent, *sattvika* form of *prakṛti* and the *puruṣa*: "Only from the discernment of the difference between *sattva* and *puruṣa*, there is sovereignty over all states of being and knowledge of all."[45]

When one exhibits dispassion even toward this state of sovereignty, the goal of Yoga is achieved: "Due to release from even this, in the destruction of the seed of this impediment, arises *kaivalyam*."[46]

The next verse further explains the depth of such dispassion, stating that such a yogi will not be tempted to rekindle a relationship with *prakṛti* due to his or her memory of the undesirable results of such a union: "There is no cause for attachment and pride upon the invitation of those well established, because of repeated association with the undesirable."[47] Hence, knowing the consequences of such action, one then abides in a state of discriminative knowledge (*viveka-jñānam*): "From *saṃyama* on the moment and its succession, there is knowledge born of discrimination."[48]

The next verse, to which Vyāsa mistakenly ascribes the power of seeing the difference between two manifested objects, in fact restates and reemphasizes the need to discern the difference between *prakṛti* in a state of quiescence and the *puruṣa*: "Hence, there is the ascertainment of two things that are similar, due to their not being limited (made separate) by differences of birth, designation, and place."[49]

The "two things that are similar" refer to the dormant or latent form of *prakṛti* and the purity of *puruṣa*, whose differences must be discriminated. The verses immediately following underscore the importance of this discrimination as central to the process of achieving liberation: "The knowledge born of discrimination is said to be liberating, (inclusive of) all conditions and all times, and nonsuccessive.[50] In the sameness of purity between the *sattva* and the *puruṣa*, there is *kaivalyam*."[51]

Consequently, if we read these *sūtras* sequentially, *sūtra* III:53, rather than being a digression referring to a mundane power, in fact is part of a sequence building up to a description of the goal of Yoga practice.

In conclusion, the *Yoga Sūtra* of Patañjali has been read traditionally through the prism of Vyāsa's commentary. None of the commentators on the text have taken issue with Vyāsa's interpretation of the *sūtras* listed above. However, even the most casual reader of the text can be somewhat confused by Vyāsa's insistence on eighty-one yogis, three forms of *samāpatti*, seven states of Yoga, and the yogi's purported ability to distinguish between two seemingly identical objects. None of these interpretations has internal linguistic or philosophical confirmation within Patañjali's root text. By staying close to the philosophical premises of the Sāṃkhya and Yoga traditions, by heeding clues from parallel Buddhist ideas, and by simply being sensitive to the flow of the text as indicated by its symmetry and sound, I am suggesting that these four critical areas be reinterpreted.

16 The Use of the Feminine Gender in Patañjali's Description of Yogic Practices

This chapter will examine the presence of terminology in the feminine gender in the *Yoga Sūtra* of Patañjali. The usage of the feminine appears to be not accidental. In Patañjali, it can be linked to the explicitly gendered philosophical language of the Sāṃkhya school of thought, which construes meaning in terms of feminine and masculine realms. We will begin this discussion with a review of how contemporary feminist theology views sex-linked language, examine the specific instances of Patañjali, and conclude with some reflections on the overall significance of gendered language within the Yoga tradition.

LANGUAGE AND THE FEMININE

Much of contemporary feminist theological writing within the Christian tradition over the past thirty years has focussed on shifting the use of God language from the masculine pronoun *he* to more inclusive terminology, in an attempt to convey a gender-neutral expression of divinity. Writing from the perspective of Christian feminist theology, Rosemary Radford Ruether notes,

> Whereas ancient myth had seen the Gods and Goddesses as within the matrix of one physical-spiritual reality, male monotheism begins to split reality into a dualism of transcendent Spirit (mind, ego) and inferior or dependent nature. . . . Thus the hierarchy of the God-male-female does not merely make women secondary to God, it also gives her negative identity in relation to the divine. Whereas the male is seen essentially as the image of the male transcendent ego or God, woman is seen as the image of the lower, material nature . . . the male identity points 'above' and the female 'below'.[1]

Ruether goes on to note that this subservient status of the female percolates throughout societal attitudes toward women, always relegating women to second-class status. Elizabeth Johnson articulates the problem as one of emphasis: "In spite of the multitude of designations for divine mystery in the Bible and later, lesser-known sources, prevailing Christian language names God solely with male designations, causing the rest to be forgotten or marginalized. The speech about God in female metaphors or in images from the natural world lies fallow, and can even appear deviant."[2] Johnson goes on to quote Mary Daly's apothegm: "If God is male, then the male is God," emphasizing the diminishing effect on the feminine when male imagery shapes cultural values.

Ruether argues for a vision of what she terms the "God/ess" that combines both energies in one transcendent deity. This combined representation of transcendence hence allows for an integrated and equal spirituality and attendant cultural view. She states, "Redeemed humanity as male and female represents the reuniting of the self, in both its spiritual masculinity and its spiritual femininity, against the splitting into sexual maleness and sexual femaleness."[3] However, until recently the Christian tradition has not offered a language that values feminine expressions of divinity. Johnson laments the effect on women's self-image: "Speech about God in the exclusive and literal terms of the patriarch is a tool of subtle conditioning that operates to debilitate women's sense of dignity, power, and self-esteem."[4]

A first step in undoing this bias toward the male gender in regard to divinity requires a restructuring of language usage. Feminist scholars have examined the development of such conventions as "masculine preferred" in the English language and have pointed out that as rules governing English grammar developed in the eighteenth century, a bias toward the male became codified.[5] Nonetheless, it has also been noted that English has the capacity to adapt itself to new cultural standards. Mary Collins notes, "Women's claim to the recognition and inclusion of their full human personhood in all social and cultural institutions, including language, is one such distinctive late twentieth century social reality."[6] As a consequence, several books of prayer in various denominations and in many instances translations of the Bible itself have been recrafted using inclusive language, such as the New Revised Standard Version and the New Jerusalem Bible.

In contrast to the Jewish, Christian, and Islamic traditions, the feminine aspect of divinity has enjoyed great prominence in Indic religions. Both in metaphor and in a proliferation of named goddesses, the feminine has exerted a strong influence on the myth and culture of India. In many Hindu traditions, divinity comes in male-female pairs such as Indra and Indrāṇī, Śiva and Pārvatī /Devī/Śakti, Kṛṣṇa and Rādhā. Additionally, Hinduism includes several unpaired goddesses, including Vāk, Sarasvatī, and Pṛthivī from the Vedic tradition; Dūrgā and Kālī from the *Purāṇas*; and various local and even contemporary manifestations of female divinity such as Santoshi Ma. Buddhism also includes a goddess tradition, particularly in the forms of Tārā and Prajñā, as does the Jaina tradition, which holds special reverence for a goddess known as Padmavatī.

The balancing of gender has long played an important role in Indic religiosity, with goddesses maintaining a vital role in religious expression throughout India's history. Not only is the female principle widely invoked in an abstract, philosophical sense, but there have been numerous female teachers. Tracy Pintchman explains the goddess in Indian tradition in terms of three phases. The first phase[7] includes representations of the feminine in the Vedic tradition, such as the earth (Pṛthivī), the goddess of speech (Vāk) and the goddess of knowledge (Sarasvatī). The Vedas extol the goddess, as associated with these various great powers. In the second phase,[8] the feminine becomes an abstract principle in philosophical discourse. The Vedāntins refer to her as "Māyā"; the followers of Sāṃkhya and Yoga refer to her as "Prakṛti"; the followers of Tantra call her "Śakti." In the third narrative phase,[9] the goddess becomes a great heroine heralded in the many great stories of the Purāṇas. Building on the literature of the Vedas and the Darśanas, these Purāṇas create new theologies with goddesses as central figures. These goddesses include Rādhā (the consort of Kṛṣṇa), Durgā, Lakṣmī, Sāvitrī, Kālī, and many others, associated with both the Vaiṣṇava and Śaiva schools.[10] In contemporary traditions, devout Hindus throughout India venerate various forms of the goddess, from the Himalayas,[11] to northwest India,[12] to eastern India,[13] and throughout the subcontinent. Consistently throughout these traditions, the goddess principle figures prominently in household religiosity and in the more rarefied area of theological discourse, particularly when she is referred to as the "energizing power of the universe" (Śakti).

In this chapter, we will examine feminine religiosity as marked by the use of the feminine gender in technical terms describing yogic practices in the second and third of Pintchman's phases, the philosophical and the narrative. To begin the first part of this investigation, I will discuss the feminine principle in philosophical discourse. Specifically, I will examine briefly below the ontological status of the feminine as seen through the usage of the term *prakṛti*. We will then focus on the use of feminine terminology in Patañjali.

Hence, in a sense we will investigate an important but hitherto unheralded aspect of Yoga that involves the feminine. Patañjali incorporates a string of yogic practices associated with the Buddhist tradition into the *Yoga Sūtra*.

These traditions clearly predate Patañjali and allow him to meld some aspects of Buddhist spiritual practice (*sādhana*) with the prevailing themes of Sāṃkhya tradition. Though Patañjali, standing in the ideological and chronological middle of the Vedic and Purāṇic eras, might not at first glance seem dedicated to a feminine-oriented project, certain aspects of his text clearly honor the strength of feminine power (*śakti*).

The Sāṃkhya and Yoga traditions provide a vocabulary that defies the sort of neuterization proposed by the contemporary endeavors of Christian feminist theology. Though the ultimate reality is referred to in the neuter gender as "Brahman," hundreds if not thousands of others names for the divine appear in either the masculine or feminine gender. Acknowledging and building upon this complex gendered analysis, and drawing upon themes appearing from the Vedas, Sāṃkhya philosophy postulates a twofold analysis of reality divided into masculine and feminine components. However, unlike the Christian subordination of the feminine under the masculine, Sāṃkhya advances a reciprocal relationship between the male and the female, similar to, but certainly not identical with the androgynous theological vision posed by Ruether. The feminine principle or *prakṛti* carries both the potential for creativity and creates the world as a fully manifest reality. Sāṃkhya regards the masculine principle or *puruṣa* as the pure witnessing, spectator consciousness that observes the unfolding dance of *prakṛti*. Through the complicated act of mistaken identity, egoistic aspects of *prakṛti* claim the power of consciousness for herself, leading to repeated delusion and suffering. Release can be gained when this confusion ceases, when the grasping self (*ahaṃkāra*) stimulated by a sullied emotionality (*buddhi*) exhausts its misguided purposes. Finally, in a state of surrender, *prakṛti* retreats, allowing the quiet emergence of *puruṣa*'s solitary witnessing.

The language here clearly makes distinctions of gender. The manifest world of change, movement, and dance, regulated and determined by the three *guṇa*s, carries the marker of the feminine gender. The realm of pure consciousness, of merely looking on, of taking no position and initiating no activity carries the marker of the masculine gender. However, despite the possibility within this system to declare the masculine witnessing capability to be supreme, the Sāṃkhya system does not denigrate the role and importance of the feminine. Without the realm of manifestation, no experience is possible for the *puruṣa*. Without experience, there can be no liberation. *Prakṛti* serves two important functions: experience and liberation. Without *prakṛti* there can be no meaning; as Prajāpati lamented in the *Chāndogya Upaniṣad*, the third level of consciousness (deep sleep with no dreams) renders one stupid, without a context through which meaning and enjoyment may be pursued.[14]

This interest in feminine powers of manifestation and creativity also extends to Sāṃkhya's related system of thought, Yoga. As Ian Whicher has noted:

> Yoga allows for a dynamic interplay and creative tension between identification and association with the empirical world (*prakṛti*) and a trans-empirical or transworldly identity (*puruṣa*) . . . Yoga can thus be recognized as a highly developed and integrated state of mystical illumination that extends and enhances our self-identity . . . [T]he yogin can dwell in a state of balance and fulfillment serving others while feeling/being truly at home in the world. . . . Freedom denotes a transformation of our entire way of being or mode of action as embodied within the lived world itself.[15]

Freedom within this lived world returns one to the process of interacting through the manifest realm, marked with the feminine gender.

The Yoga system of Patañjali outlines and develops a series of more than fifty techniques to bring about a move from an ego-centered consciousness dominated by the grasping play of *prakṛti* to a purified consciousness that transcends affliction and grasping. The bulk of these practices put forth by Patañjali can be found in the first *pāda*. More than twenty distinct disciplines are listed, including practice coupled with released from desire; dispassion; the progressive application of thought, reflection, bliss, and solitariness (*asmitā*); the Buddhist disciplines of faith, energy, mindfulness, concentration, and wisdom; dedication to *īśvara*, the chosen ideal; the practice of mantra recitation; one-pointedness; the Buddhist practice of friendliness, compassion, happiness, and equanimity; breath control; centering the mind; sorrowless illumination; nonattachment; insights gained from sleep; meditation "as desired"; and the fourfold application of meditative states that erases negative past tendencies and leads to the state of seedless *samādhi*. This section of Patañjali's masterwork lists a range of yogic disciplines designed to eradicate the negative influences of karma, moving the practitioner from the feminine-identified realm of change into the masculine-identified realm of changelessness. Interestingly, it is only through the feminine, material aspect of one's being that one can move toward higher awareness. Sāṃkhya philosophy emphasizes the contingency and reciprocity of the feminine and the masculine.

In the second *pāda*, Patañjali outlines a threefold and an eightfold system for advancing in the Yoga path. In the third *pāda* he explains how the cultivation of yogic powers can lead to the distinctive awareness (*viveka khyāti*) that liberates. In the fourth *pāda* he asserts a philosophical position reflective of Jaina and Sāṃkhya ideas on the individuality of the soul and emphasizes the purification of karma as key to the attainment of Yoga. He concludes the text with a remarkable appeal to the power of higher awareness, *citi-śakti*,[16] ending the text with and literally giving the final word to what can be construed as feminine power.

Although Patañjali seems to value the male-designated realm of consciousness (*puruṣa*) over the changing female-designated world of activity (*prakṛti*), a subtle inversion of language takes place that confounds the privileging of the male pole in this dualistic system. First, let us keep in mind that without the feminine principle, there can be no meaning, no purpose. Second, recall that the highest state as described in the *Chāndogya Upaniṣad*[17] mandates a return through which the senses are reemployed but from the perspective of a newly informed, newly shaped, newly purified emotional and cognitive filter. Just as the Buddha returned to teach after forty-nine days of reflection on his *nirvāṇa* experience, so also the enlightened yogi or yoginī may return to energize and give service through the realm of the very manifestation that caused so much difficulty and suffering. So, in a sense, the move is not strictly away from the realm of *prakṛti*, but the move implicitly includes a recognition of the reciprocity of *puruṣa* and *prakṛti* and may involve a "saving" or reclaiming or a skillful redemption of the manifest realm, through which it is put into the service of clarity rather than stimulated by negative past impulses.

Patañjali's *Yoga Sūtra* has been analyzed by traditional commentators as well as modern and contemporary scholars. The writings of Vyāsa, Vācaspati Miśra, Vijñāna Bhīkṣu, Bhoja Rāja, Śankara (most likely not the famous philosopher of the same name), and so forth provide word analyses and illuminate the text's connections with approaches to liberation in Sāṃkhya and Vedānta. The modern interpretations of Dasgupta, Jacobi, Keith, Poussin, Hauer, Frauwallner, Feuerstein, Larson, and others posit various influences and identify key themes knitted together by Patañjali. Focusing on the first *pāda*, I would like to suggest a new interpretation of Patañjali's use of language, using a method that combines the techniques of feminist and biblical text redaction criticism, with particular attention placed on Patañjali's privileging of gender terminology. Though this analysis is tentative, I would posit that this approach might yield fruitful results in understanding the ongoing vitality of yogic thought and practice.

First, I would like to remind the reader of the oral nature of the *Yoga Sūtra*. As noted in the prior chapter, the text was most likely composed as an oral and aural exercise. To this day, the *sūtras* are memorized and recited, as seen in the contemporary teachings of Desikachar in Madras and Gurāṇi Añjali in Amityville, New York. Students of Yoga memorize and recite the *sūtras* as part of their move into the practice of Yoga.

Second, I would like to suggest that we not dismiss the power of gendered language. Though native speakers of English are taught that the feminine and masculine genders do not convey a sense of maleness or femaleness as we learn French, Spanish, or German, even in English we cannot deny that we refer to ships and automobiles in the feminine gender and that we associate certain objects and generalized notions with particular genders. In the Indian context, the Tantric schools developed sequences of *vidyās* or multiword invocations to accompany the practice of mantras. These *vidyās*, referred to in the feminine gender, were associated with magical powers. As John Cort has noted, by the sixth century, "from words of the feminine gender they eventually became goddesses."[18] As noted in the first chapter, Haribhadra renamed each of Patañjali's eight major Yogas with goddess monikers: Mitrā, Tarā, Balā, Dīprā, Sthirā, Kāntā, Prabhā, and Parā.[19] Similarly, in the Buddhist tradition, wisdom or *prajñā*, a feminine term, becomes personified in the Buddhist deity Prajñāparamitā. Because of the highly gendered nature of the Sāṃkhya philosophy that underlies the Yoga system and because of the persistent presence of goddesses or the *Devī* in Hinduism, it is advantageous for the reader to be vigilant about an author's choice in selecting words of the feminine gender when staking out religious or philosophical positions.

THE USE OF THE FEMININE GENDER IN THE SAMĀDHI *PĀDA* OF PATAÑJALI'S *YOGA SŪTRA*

In the orthopractic and philosophical language of the first *pāda* or section of the *Yoga Sūtra*, Patañjali builds a rhythm, a cadence in his text that spirals the reader/reciter toward the spiritual climax of *nirbīja samādhi*. I would like to map the gendered language of the first *pāda* and suggest that Patañjali plays with gender rhythms in this section of the text just as Īśvaraka creates a gendered dance leading to the climax of the *Sāṃkhya Kārikā*.

To begin this analysis, I want to highlight terms from the first *pāda* in the feminine gender that describe accomplishments within the Yoga system. The first term that I want to mention is *puruṣa-khyāti*[20] a compound phrase that also appears in the second, third, and fourth *pādas*.[21] This term describes the very experience of liberation, the discernment of or the discernment by the *puruṣa*. *Khyāti* is a feminine word from the root *khyā*, to name or make known. The same root is found in the term Sāṃkhya. Hence, the very process that culminates in and can be identified with the experience of liberation is the feminine perception of the masculine, a theme in keeping with Sāṃkhya's metaphysics: it is only when *prakṛti* sees herself that she then moves into a state of self-transcendence; without the vision (described in feminine terminology) there can be no release.[22]

The second group of terms I want to discuss includes a cluster of words generally associated with the Buddhist tradition. Noting the prevalence of these words in descriptions of Buddhist meditation, many scholars surmise that these practices were borrowed into Patañjali's Yoga system from well-known popular Buddhist systems. The first is in the five-fold list of meditative practices well known from the Pali canon: faith, mindfulness, wisdom, strength, and concentration (*śraddhā, smṛti, prajñā, vīrya, samādhi*).[23] The first three terms are feminine; the last two are masculine. Of particular interest is the term *prajñā*, wisdom, which moves from being a feminine word in Buddhist traditions into a fully developed goddess symbol, as found in the Mahāyāna texts on the Perfection of Wisdom, the *Prajñāparamitā Sūtras*, as mentioned above. This term later appears in the *Yoga Sūtra* describing a special type of liberative knowledge, as will be discussed below.

An even stronger case for the purposeful use of feminine language derived from Buddhist sources can be found in the list of the four Brahmavihara: *maitrī, karuṇā, muditā*, and *upekṣā*.[24] These appear in the context of advice for appropriate social behavior: to be friendly toward the fortunate, compassionate toward the unfortunate, happy for the virtuous, and dispassionate toward the evil ones.[25] Each of these terms appears in the feminine gender. Richard Gombrich goes so far as to declare that these terms not only describe appropriate prescribed behavior but in fact describe the very state of *nirvāṇa* itself. Gombrich states that when these four are performed, one achieves a state of releasing the mind (*ceto-vimutti*), which he asserts "is simply a term of Enlightenment, the attainment of nirvana."[26] In this state, the monk "pervades every direction with thoughts of kindness, compassion, sympathetic joy and equanimity [*mettā, karuṇā, muditā, upekkhā*]."[27] Gombrich is careful to assert that this accomplishment refers to an activity or process and not to a thing. In this sense, the Buddhist monk becomes an arhant, a liberated or enlightened person. Being established in these four "immeasurables" becomes the Buddhist equivalent to the *jīvan-mukta* of later Vedantic traditions. Gombrich summarizes the significance of this attainment in terms of two "salient characteristics of the Buddha's theory of *kamma* (*karma*)." First, process substitutes for objects: instead of identifying with universal consciousness "one is to think in a particular way; salvation is a matter of *how* one lives, not of *what* one is. Secondly, the process is ethicized: to be totally benevolent is to be liberated."[28] Kindness, a distinctly feminine virtue as indicated by the gender of the terms used, becomes a way to salvation. In the later Mahāyāna tradition, these same benevolent qualities come to be identified with the Buddhist goddess Tārā, a manifestation of the compassion of Avalokitesvara.[29]

The last set of terms I wish to identify from the first *pāda* appear in the culminating section, which, in my assessment, begins with verse I:41. This verse, as has been discussed in the prior chapter, provides the foundational definition for understanding *samādhi*: "The accomplished mind of diminished fluctuations, like a precious (or clear) jewel assuming the color of any near object, has unity (*samāpatti*) among grasper, grasping, and grasped." The term *samāpatti* is used to describe that dissolution of one's identity as separate from the felt world; in David Abram's terms, "The recuperation of the incarnate, sensorial dimension of experience brings with it a recuperation of the living landscape in which we are corporeally embedded. As we return to our senses, we gradually discover our sensory perceptions to be simply our part of a vast, interpenetrating network."[30] '*Samāpatti*,' synonymous with '*samādhi*,' indicates a state of concrescence or merging that stands at the core of Yoga philosophy. It also introduces Patañjali's descriptions of the fourfold phases of this state of absorption.

The fourfold process of *samādhi* is described in terms of four words in the feminine gender, *savitarkā*, *nirvitarkā*, *savicārā*, and *nirvicārā*, which I have translated as "with gross object, free of gross object, with subtle object, free of subtle object"[31] respectively. These states indicate increasingly higher degrees of subtilization within *prakṛti*. The realm of feminine materiality here becomes suffused with *sattva*, bringing *prakṛti* closer to her mission of providing an experience of/for *puruṣa* through the process of discernment (*khyāti*). These stages[32] as indicated with Gombrich's interpretation of the Brahma Vihāra mentioned above, describe both a process and a fulfillment Each of these attainments qualifies for description by the later commentators as a *samādhi*.

Each of these four feminine words, *savitarkā*, *nirvitarkā*, *savicārā*, and *nirvicārā*, may be seen as modalities through which the realm of *prakṛti* is suffused with clarity. To see these states as purified perceptions of the feminine principle accords well with the idea of celebrating *prakṛti* as the tool or key to liberation, an idea upheld by the usage of the term *prajñā* [33] in the forty-eighth *sūtra*: "There the wisdom (*prajñā*) bears righteousness (*ṛtaṃ-bharā*)." Both these critical terms, *prajñā* and *bharā*, appear in the feminine gender. In a sense, the echo and reecho of these feminized descriptions of the final state of Yoga seem to presage the assertion of the feminine in later Tantric traditions. In a sense, the feminine sets one free by departing but is also the occasion for one's ongoing freedom, as it is only in relationship with the feminine realm of activity that the liberated person can feel his or her freedom.

In the first *pāda*, we have seen the prominence of the feminine terms *khyāti, prajñā, śrāddhā, smṛti, maitrī, karuṇā, muditā, upekṣā, samāpatti, savitarkā, nirvitarkā, savicārā,* and *nirvicārā* as central to the accomplishment of Yoga. I have also mentioned that the term *khyāti* appears in all four *pādas*, underscoring its importance as a unifying term for the *Yoga Sūtra*.

The repeated use of the feminine gender to describe yogic practice and accomplishment in the first *pāda* is significant. It affirms the centrality of the manifest world, generally denoted in feminine imagery, as integral to the spiritual path.

CONCLUSION

Patañjali's *Yoga Sūtra*, though not often recognized for its Tantric content, acknowledged the powerful reciprocity between male and female. It also heralded the attainment of highest consciousness with the feminized term *citi-śakti*, denoting the union of consciousness and power and hence upholding the role of the feminine in the process of liberation. Even in the description of yogic practices, the language of the *Yoga Sūtra* includes an attention to gender, particularly in the first *pāda*. This may be seen as reflective of a tendency in Indic religious traditions to bifurcate reality into masculine and feminine components. Most specifically, the Sāṃkhya system characterizes the realm of manifestation and creativity and activity as the property of the feminine, referred to as '*prakṛti*,' and characterizes the state of liberated pure witnessing as masculine or *puruṣa*. It is important to recognize that in this system both are required for liberation; *prakṛti* provides the experience that leads to her self-dissolution. Through her embarrassed departure, *puruṣa*, though remaining forever inactive, can stand in liberated isolation from the distracting and confusing identity issues repeatedly presented by the self-claiming dance of *prakṛti*.

One might expect that such a tradition would degrade the importance of the female gender and advocate a social release from all that is symbolized by female creativity and attachment, hence the tradition of male renouncers or *sadhus*. However, to the contrary, Patañjali, reflective of a parallel movement in Buddhist tradition, employs feminine-gendered terminology to describe the most rarefied yogic practices (*Brahma-vihāra; sa/nir vitarkā; sa/nir vicārā;* and *prajñā*) in his first *pāda*. It also heralded the attainment of highest consciousness within the feminine term *citi-śakti*.

In terms of the contemporary feminist theology summarized at the inception of this chapter, one can interpret the tradition of Yoga and the feminine from a variety of perspectives. A defender of Hindu theology might claim that womanhood in Hinduism is a nonissue precisely because the philosophy upholds the feminine power in the form of *śakti* and that women have access to a wide array of goddesses to fulfill their religious needs. Critics of Hinduism, including adherents to the faith, might protest that the male patriarchy eclipsed the social implications of feminine power by subordinating all women to men. Citing the statement in the *Laws of Manu*, "In childhood a female must be subject to her father, in youth to her husband, when her lord is dead to her son; a woman must never be independent,"[34] it might be argued that this attitude toward women led to the neglect of their education and encouraged such extreme practices as the immolation of widows. Feminists from both Christianity and Hinduism have argued that textual statements made in religious texts have determined cultural values, often to the detriment of women's well-being. However, just as Sally McFague has found and reintroduced feminine images of God from biblical sources, a yogic feminist tradition can cite references and allusions from yogic texts that uphold the integrity and centrality of feminine power.

17 Contemporary Expressions of Yoga

We have surveyed some of the key aspects of the Yoga system, including its approach to and interpretation of spiritual liberation, the role of ethics in the development of a Yoga practice, the symbolic and practical significance of animals in the tradition, the *Yoga Sūtra* and its relationship to Sāṃkhya, and the role of the feminine in Yoga. In this final chapter, Yoga will be examined as a modern, global movement that seeks to find expression and relevance in contemporary culture.

YOGA IN THE MODERN AGE

Yoga, throughout history, has exhibited both flexibility and adaptability. At the start of the book we surveyed some of the "places" where Yoga has found a home, including Buddhism, Jainism, Sikhism, and Vedānta and the broad tradition of Hinduism. In recent times, Yoga has been adapted to meet the special needs of modern and postmodern individuals. The start of the popular appeal of Yoga can be traced to the Victorian era, when Yoga was embraced by free-thinking Britons, including leaders of the Theosophical movement, who arranged the publication of early translations of the *Yoga Sūtra* and other texts.

As Yoga became known in the Western world through the writings of Emerson, Thoreau, and eventually Swami Vivekananda and Paramahamsa Yogananda, some early pioneers ventured forth to encounter and learn the tradition from adepts in India. In addition to the teachings brought back from India and written about by Americans and Europeans, the lecture tour, aptly depicted by the author Henry James in his novel *The Bostonians*, proved to be an effective means for the dissemination of information about Yoga. Starting over one hundred years ago, Swami Vivekananda traveled from coast to coast filling lectures halls. Swami Paramahamsa Yogananda, after addressing an assembly of religious leaders in Boston in 1920, traveled through the country giving lectures during the Coolidge administration (1923–1929), making headlines in various newspapers. He also taught Yoga to the American industrialist George Eastman, founder of Kodak, among many others.

In 1955 the first studio dedicated to Haṭha Yoga was opened in San Francisco by Walt and Magana Baptiste. In the 1960s, centers for the practice of Haṭha Yoga were established throughout the United States by disciples of Swami Sivananda (who had trained Mircea Eliade in the 1930s), including Swamis Satchidananda and Vishnudevananda. Other networks of Yoga centers were opened by Swami Rama, Yogi Bhajan, and many others. Today, in Los Angeles alone, more than three hundred studios can be found, each of which traces its core practice back to one of several root teachers or guru lineages. Many of these centers are solely interested in the physical culture of Yoga. Others maintain direct and pronounced links with the spiritual aspects of the tradition.

The Yoga tradition became known in detail to the Western world with the publication of Swami Vivekananda's *Raja Yoga* in 1902. James Haughton Woods of Harvard University published a comprehensive translation of the *Yoga Sūtra* in 1914, with the somewhat verbose title of *The Yoga System of Patañjali: Or the Ancient Hindu Doctrine of Concentration of Mind Embracing the Mnemonic Rules, Called Yoga-Sūtras, of Patajali and the Comment, called Yoga-Bhāshya, Attributed to Veda-Vyāsa and the Explanation, called Tattva-Vaiçāradi, of Vāchaspati-Miçra Translated from the Original Sanskrit.* This highly technical and generally competent rendering remains an important resource for the study of Yoga. A more accessible translation with a modern interpretation was published by Ernest E. Wood in 1948, under the title of *Practical Yoga: Ancient and Modern.* Theos Bernard published *Hatha Yoga* in 1943, which includes a comprehensive discussion of *āsana* practice. The next widely disseminated books on Yoga appear in the 1960s, *The Complete Illustrated Book of Yoga* by Swami Vishnudevananda (1960) and *Light on Yoga* by B. K. S. Iyengar (1966). These two books present the teachings of two pioneering teachers of Yoga, Swami Sivananda and Sri Krishnamacharya, respectively.

In several recent books and media presentations, sociologists, anthropologists, and documentary filmmakers have turned their attention to the contemporary phenomenon of Yoga. Some of the books deal exclusively with the Indian origins of modern Yoga, while others, including the documentary *Yoga Unveiled*, chronicle the spread of Yoga to the West.

N. E. Sjoman's *Yoga Tradition of the Mysore Palace* documents one of the most widely known traditions of physical Yoga, established by Krishnamacharya (1888–1989) in South India starting in the 1920s. Krishnamacharya had traveled to Tibet and throughout India, studying with a variety of teachers from Vaishnava, Saiva, and Buddhist traditions. While on retreat in caves and other remote locations, he perfected a sequence of Yoga postures or *āsanas* that he then taught at the Mysore Palace, where he received patronage from the Maharaja, Krishnarajendra Woodyar IV. Mysore, one of the many kingdoms that did not come under direct British administration, has long prided itself as a repository for India's rich cultural heritage, and with earnings from rich agricultural and manufacturing endeavors, the Maharaja maintained a magnificent research library and university. Within this environment, Krishnamacharya taught several Indians, who continue to teach in this tradition, and one notable Western woman, Indra Devi (1899–2002), who was born in Latvia.

Sjoman points out that life in the Mysore Palace was not isolated and that the texts on Yoga found in the library there indicate influence from British gymnastics. Sjoman comments, "In the case of the yoga asana tradition we can see that it is a dynamic tradition that has drawn on many sources—traditional yoga texts, indigenous exercises, western gymnastics, therapeutics, and even perhaps the military training exercises of a foreign dominating power."[1] Krishnmacharya's most prominent disciples include B. K. S. Iyengar in Pune, his son and grandson, T. K. V. Desikachar and Kaustub Desikachar in Chennai, Pattabhi Jois in Mysore, Srivatsa Ramaswami, and others. Several prominent American teachers of Yoga trace their lineage back to Krishnamacharya and regularly travel to India to train with one or another of his successors.

Joseph Alter has probed early twentieth-century figures who contributed to the modernization of Yoga in *Yoga in Modern India: The Body between Science and Philosophy.* The first figure, Swami Kuvalayananda (1883–1966), attempted to show how science affirms the beneficial effects of Yoga practice. He established Kaivalyadhama Yoga Ashram in Lonavala (between Pune and Bombay) in 1924, where he conducted laboratory experiments to establish the efficacy of Yoga. Several American scientists conducted research into Yoga at his center, including K. T. Behanan of Yale University. Prime Minister Jawaharlal Nehru and his daughter, Indira Gandhi, visited the Ashram in 1958. The Ashram's early studies attempted to measure air volume and oxygen content in relation to breathing exercises. Studies in the 1970s and 1980s focused on asthma, obesity, cancer, diabetes, sinusitis, and emotional disorders. Alter notes, "Yoga was not simply modernized by Kuvalayananda; Yoga was analyzed in such a way that it has come to harmonize with the modernity manifest in science to create an alternative. And to a large extent it is this harmonic hybridity that has enabled Yoga to colonize the West."[2]

Other medical linkages with Yoga can be found in the work of K. N. Udapa, who wrote *Stress and Its Management by Yoga* (1980). This book blends technical terms from traditional Indian physiology and contemporary biochemistry. Some of the experiments conducted to establish the efficacy of Yoga by Dr. Udapa seem almost bizarre, such as holding mice in test tubes in unnatural inverted postures to demonstrate the health effects of the shoulder stand and handstand. Though these experiments were part of an overall project to measure "acetylcholine, cholinesterase, diamineoxidase, and catecholamine levels" of one's biochemistry,"[3] Alter suggests, rather provocatively, that such research constitutes a "complex kind of mythmaking." Noting similarities between the perfectionism of Yoga and the techniques of the modern scientific method, Alter writes that "modern Science is a kind of pseudo-Yoga insofar as it seeks endless progress and perfect knowledge."[4]

BEYOND NATIONALIST YOGA

Yoga has played a role in the development and maintenance of India's national identity. The "neo-Hinduism" developed by Swami Vivekananda, Sri Aurobindo, and others uses the language and terminology of Yoga extensively. However, due to the globalization of Yoga, it can no longer be "owned" by a single culture or national identity. The Rashtriya Swayamsevak Sangh (RSS), established by Dr. Keshav Baliram Hedgewar in the 1920s, hoped to promote a "muscular Hinduism" and adapted several Yoga postures as part of a fitness regimen for its members. Dr. Kumar Pal was affiliated with the Bharatiya Yoga Sansthan (BYS), which later gave birth to the Vishwa Hindu Parishad (VHP) and helped to develop the nationalist rhetoric that undergirds the Bharatiya Janata Parishad (BJP) political party that held power in India during the late 1990s and early 2000s. However, Dr. Pal, like many others, eschewed any links between Yoga and politics or even religion, claiming that "the basic philosophy of the RSS was incompatible with Yoga, since Yoga is universal and not limited to Hinduism."[5] Joseph Alter notes that "Yoga's definition of universal truth as simply beyond belief, and the embodiment of what is beyond belief . . . does not make sense as a nationalist project."[6] Demonstrating that Yoga cannot be "owned," he writes that "As a cultural system Yoga does not present a threat to the integrity of any other cultural system."[7]

The global spread of Yoga was facilitated in large part by the Divine Life Society. This organization was established by the now-legendary Sivananda (1887–1963), who moved to the Himalayas from his native Tamil Nadu, after practicing western-style allopathic medicine successfully for ten years in Malaysia as Dr. Kuppuswami Iyer. Inspired by the writings of Swami Vivekananda, he eventually settled in northern India, taking the vows of renunciation and his new name. Because Swami Sivananda knew little Hindi, his primary language of communication in his adopted home of Rishikesh was English. He eventually published several dozen books on Yoga in English, starting in 1929. Students flocked to receive his teachings from all parts of India and the rest of the world, including the father of the modern academic discipline of the history of religions, Mircea Eliade, who spent six months studying with him on the banks of the Ganges. Eliade's doctoral dissertation, which launched an illustrious career, was eventually published under the title *Yoga: Immortality and Freedom* and remains a classic in the field.

Many of the forerunners of the worldwide Yoga movement trained at Sivananda's Divine Light Society, including Swami Chidananda (b. 1916, trained Lilias Folan, who popularized Yoga on American public television in the 1970s), Swami Vishnudevananda (1927–1993, established centers worldwide and helped promote dialogue between Western and Eastern Europe before the collapse of the Soviet Union), Swami Satchidananda (1914–2002, founder of Integral Yoga and teacher of Dean Ornish, prominent health advocate), Swami Chinmayananda (1916–1993, cofounder of the Vishva Hindu Parishad, a forerunner of the global "Hindutva" movement), Swami Satyananda (b. 1924, founder of the Bihar School of Yoga), and many others.[8] From this remote location in the upper Ganges Valley, Sivananda launched a template for the practice of Yoga that has spread worldwide. Yoga in its globalized form has developed "shared communities of practice" and has come to rely on computer-enhanced communication. Sociologist Sarah Strauss has commented on Yoga as a way of "bringing a measure of calm to our harried lives."[9]

YOGA AS PUBLIC ESOTERICISM

Esotericism, according to Elizabeth De Michelis, includes the promotion of correspondences with the natural world, the development of imagination, and self-transformation through practice. In India, the Neo-Hindu and Neo-Vedanta movements articulated these core ideas and experiences in a manner that could be communicated beyond the standard guru-disciple relationship to a broader public. Rammohan Roy, Rabindranath Tagore, and Keshubchandra Sen all played an important role in the ninteenth century at communicating the core religious experiences outside the normal confines of religious institutions. Inspired by the ecstatic mystic Sri Ramakrishna, Swami Vivekananda in the late nineteenth and early twentieth centuries became the harbinger of a new, globalized way of being spiritual that entailed practices of Yoga, not adherence to religious orthodoxy or orthopraxy. Vivekananda sought to establish Yoga as a science and achieved widespread acceptance of its principles and practices.

De Michelis highlights Vivekananda's *Raja Yoga* as providing the frame upon which Modern Yoga became woven. By emphasizing an integrated body-cosmos continuum mediated through the breath or life force (*prāṇa*), Vivekananda sought to establish the healing powers and transcendent possibilities of Yoga practice. Modern Yoga, according to De Michelis, developed into two primary forms: Modern Postural Yoga (MPY) and Modern Meditational Yoga (MMY). In the former category, she lists Iyengar Yoga, and in the latter, Transcendental Meditation (TM) and modern Buddhist meditation groups. She identifies three primary phases in the development of this movement: popularization (1950s to mid-1970s), consolidation (mid-1970s to late 1980s), and acculturation (late 1980s to date). In this latest phase, self-regulating guilds such as Yoga Alliance arose that standardized the practice of Yoga, and certain styles of Yoga, most notably the form originated by B. K. S. Iyengar, rose to prominence. Citing the history and development of Iyengar through his three well known books (*Light on Yoga*, 1966; *Light on Pranayama*, 1981; *Light on the Yoga Sutras of Patanjali*, 1993), she tracks the emergence of Yoga as an accepted, global, cultural form. She characterizes MPY as a "healing ritual of secular religion." Following Turner, she suggests that a Yoga *āsana* class allows one to separate from the humdrum of daily life, transition into a state of serenity, and then incorporate the benefits of this relaxing experience into one's lifestyle. To account for the success of Yoga, De Michelis writes that it offers "some solace, physical, psychological or spiritual, in a world where solace and reassurance are sometimes elusive."[10]

In addition to these sociological and anthropological studies of Yoga, empirical science has been used to validate or at least understand the physical changes that take place through the regular practice of Yoga. Building on some of the earlier and ongoing studies in India, the Menninger Foundation conducted detailed studies of Swami Rama in the 1970s and the Harvard Medical School performed research into the Tibetan Yoga tradition of heat generation (*tummo*). One study by K. S. Gopal "compared a group who had practiced hatha-yoga for six months with a group who had no yoga experience but engaged regularly in other forms of light exercise, and found the basal breath rate of the former group to be 10 breaths per minute as opposed to 23 per minute in the latter."[11] The International Association of Yoga Therapists continues to report on similar research in its publications.

In this media age, it is important to note that not all studies of the Yoga tradition have been confined to the printed page. The DVD *Yoga Unveiled: The Evolution and Essence of a Spiritual Tradition* narrates the history of Yoga and includes interviews with scholars such as Georg Feuerstein. It includes footage of senior teachers such as B. K. S. Iyengar, Patabhi Jois, and Indra

Devi, as well as contemporary teachers Rodney Yee and Patricia Walden. In the second part, it updates the quest begun by Swami Kuvalyananda by citing studies and interviewing physicians and scholars who have continued to affirm the salubrious benefits of Yoga and meditation. These include Dean Ornish, Mehmet Oz, and Jon Kabat-Zinn. Ideally suited for classroom use, this digital recording allows one to witness Krishnamacarya's now-famous sequence of Yoga postures and hear scientific testimony about the health benefits of a Yoga practice.[12]

YOGA, HEALTH, AND ENVIRONMENT

The health and relaxation benefits of Yoga are well known. De Michelis has written that "practitioners remove themselves from the hustle and bustle of everyday life to attend the yoga class in a designated 'neutral' (and ideally somewhat secluded) place . . . [T]hey leave their social personae, responsibilities, commitments, plans and worries behind for the time being."[13] She goes on to write that the practitioner "embodies, and is trained to perceive, the identity of microcosm and macrocosm,"[14] referring to the Vedic worldview that sees correlations between the nose and the earth; the mouth, water, and saliva; the breath and the wind, and so forth.

The concept of 'cosmic correlations,' which perhaps found earliest expression in India, also was developed in early Greek thought.[15] By the tenth century, the Islamic movement Ikhwan al Safa also explored this philosophy, as found in their encyclopedia *The Epistles of the Brethren of Purity*[16] which lists, in the style of the *Puruṣa Sūkta*, more than twenty microcosm-macrocosm correspondences, such as a correlation between human hair and the plants that grow on the "face" of the earth. Many of these appear in the *Pool of Nectar* or *Amṛtakuṇḍa*, an Arabic translation of a Hindu text on Haṭha Yoga (also translated into Persian and Turkish) that appeared perhaps as early as the thirteenth century.[17] Just as this text was found and "Islamicized," the practice of modern postural yoga is being adapted to fit the prevailing secular worldview. According to De Michelis, "The lack of pressure to commit to any one teaching or practice, the cultivation of 'Self' and of privatized forms of religiosity make modern postural yoga highly suitable to the demands of contemporary developed societies."[18] Yoga, in other words, because it attempts to get beyond belief through the body, presents a nonthreatening, health-enhancing practice that transcends cultural constraints. Alter suggests that Yoga provides a way to claim one's place in the world without asserting that this way must suffice for all others. For Alter, Yoga solves the problem of cultural relativism by pointing beyond culture and body through the engagement and training of the body into states of cosmic connectivity. Today, as many as 15 million Americans, not in any way affiliated with the Hindu faith, regularly attend a Yoga class, probably for reasons not dissimilar to those given by Alter (health) and De Michelis (anonymity; no commitment to religion).

The microphase/macrophase philosophy that undergirds the Yoga tradition has come under threat in the age of industrialization and pollution. We live in environments that are suffused with chemical agents that did not exist when Patañjali wrote the *Yoga Sūtra*. From the foam in our furniture to household cleaning products, we are surrounded with and ingesting through our breath and our food chemical agents that do not exist in nature. According to a European study in 2001, "the average human body is accumulating more than 300 artificial chemicals, many of which could be damaging."[19] Breast cancer rates have increased significantly. In Hamburg, Germany, the "incidence has doubled over the past forty years."[20] The United Kingdom has the highest rate of breast cancer in the world, and it is the "most common cause of death in women between the ages of 35 and 54 years."[21] Among men, sperm counts have decreased, and there is an "increased incidence of testicular cancer."[22] According to a study by Dr. Cecil Jacobsen of the Reproductive Genetics Center in Vienna, Virginia, one-half of one percent of men were functionally sterile in 1938, while today that number has risen fifteen-fold to between 8 and 10 percent.[23]

How do these sobering statistics relate to the practice of Yoga? How might Yoga practice be applied to help reduce the risk to human health posed by artificial chemical agents? I would like to suggest Yoga, with its philosophy of the small reflecting the large and the large being located through the small, can help us understand the intimate relationship between the body and the world. The Upaniṣads talk of the food-made body and proclaim that "life is the essence of food."[24] The discussion of food implicitly warns people to be careful to avoid adulterated foods, a warning that holds true several centuries later. By examining the finest points of the food that we eat, the water that we drink, and the air that we breathe, one is able to avoid potential unseen health problems. No sane person would willingly ingest poison, but in our altered environment, it requires a skilled, scientific eye in order to avoid poison. For instance, studies have shown that the near-ubiquitous plastic water bottle, the emblem of health awareness, in fact may contain polycarbate plastics such as Lexan that can cause the array of health problems mentioned above.[25] The Environmental Protection Agency has been urged by scientists, who have examined more than one hundred studies, to reevaluate bisphenol A or BPA, which has been "detected in nearly all humans tested in the U.S."[26] When plastic containers are heated or stressed, the chemical, which has been known to skew developing animal fetuses and cause hyperactivity in lab animals, leaches into the food or liquid.

Within what De Michelis refers to as "modern postural Yoga," a movement has begun to bring greater awareness of environmental hazards to practitioners of Yoga. One obvious example is the Yoga mat, an accessory of Yoga practice that has gained immense popularity within the past ten years. The standard Yoga mat is made from polyvinyl chloride, a known carcinogen. Laura Cornell, founder of the Green Yoga Association, further discovered that "plasticizers are added to make the PVC soft and sticky" and that the "most common additives include lead, cadmium, and a class of chemicals called phthalates."[27] After a great deal of searching, Cornell found and has arranged for the U.S. distribution of a compostable mat made of rubber and jute with no additives to avoid off-gassing from the artificial product.

Making changes with such immediate and simple objects as food and a Yoga mat constitutes the beginnings of cultivating a greater sensitivity to the relationship between our bodies and the things we consume. In classical Indian thought, much care and attention are given to the itemization and categorization of physical and metaphysical realities. In the Sāṃkhya system, the rudiments of which are found in Vedic literature more than three thousand years ago, reality unfolds when consciousness connects with the world of emotion, ego, thought, sensation, and the elements. In order to understand the relationship between self and world, Sāṃkhya advocates progressive concentration on the elements of earth, water, fire, air, and space. By observing these foundations of experience, one gains an intimacy with the processes that allow their construal through the senses (including the mind) and their grasping through the body. Yoga teaches a practice through which one concentrates on smelling earth with the nose; tasting water with the mouth; seeing radiance and color with the eyes and the work accomplished through the action of the hands; feeling the caress of the air upon skin and boldly walking in the breeze with the legs; hearing sounds within space and filling space with the voice. Recognition of and reflection on the elements, the senses, and the action organs allow one to feel a deep connection between self and world.

The *Yogavāṣiṣṭha*, an eleventh century Sanskrit text that combines aspects of Buddhist thought with Vedānta, includes beautiful poetic descriptions of how a Yogi, trapped within a rock, learns from the goddess Kāli how to dance through the universe by enlivening each of the senses in turn. Beginning within the rock that entombs him, he explores flowing streams, feels the radiance of the sun, celebrates the wind as it "teaches the creeping vines to dance"[28] and enters the vastness of space. The relationship here is more than metaphorical, more than imitative or representational. The rock and the earth constitute a totality, a present reality, an immediacy that invites an experience of feeling connected, fulfilled, complete.

Yoga, in addition to advocating the physical culture for which it is so well known in America and Europe, contains ethical precepts and practices that advocate a simple approach to life. The entry point of classical Yoga can be found in the discipline of nonviolence. Nonviolence or *ahiṃsā* forms the foundation for developing an inclusive ecological ethics. By attempting to do no harm to any life form, one must take into account the interconnections of all life forms. If harm is done to the air, earth, or water, effects will be found in those beings that dwell therein. The diminishment or sacrifice of one species will affect other species as well, making life more difficult. The protection of one life form may very likely allow others to flourish as well. A conscious practice of nonviolence or *ahiṃsā* will provide an ongoing point of conscience when making decisions that have environmental impacts, including the choice of one's food, the choice of one's car, and even the choice of one's Yoga mat.

The other major ethical practice of Yoga that holds environmental potential would be nonpossession or *aparigraha*. By restricting one's ownership of things, one is able to release attachment from external objects. The market-driven economy relies on constant growth in the consumer sector. Advertising, seductive shops, and the bombardment of media from the internet to television and magazines draw a person out from his or her core into a world of false and ephemeral images. Mahatma Gandhi, though he certainly supported and promoted the development of industrial technology, advocated a locally based village economy. Each village would produce its own food, grow its own cotton, spin its own thread, and weave its own clothes. Although an utterly local economy is not very practical in today's urbanized, globalized business environment, buying strategically and sparingly can help contribute to one's own health and the health of others.

In an effort to simplify and "green" their operations, many Yoga studios are taking manageable steps to reduce their energy reliance and minimize the potential for indoor pollution. The Green Yoga Association has developed an audit whereby flyers would be printed on tree-free paper, students would be encouraged to walk or bicycle to class, nontoxic cleaning supplies would be used, and building materials would be "sustainable, non-toxic and fair-trade."[29] This transformation of the Yoga community into careful and prudent consumers could serve as positive examples for the private homes and business practices of Yoga students.

Laura Cornell has developed a theory of Green Yoga that suggests the adoption of an eightfold eco-Yoga practice. She writes,

> Knowledge (Jñāna Yoga) and a reverential mindset (Bhakti Yoga) form the foundational entry point for Green Yoga. The practitioner then establishes and maintains a relationship with nature (Āraṇyaka Yoga), heals the physical and energy bodies (Haṭha Yoga), and purifies the mind (Raja Yoga). Action to heal the world (Karma Yoga) becomes natural and joyful, prompting one to enter into community (Saṅgha Yoga). Realization of one's non-separation from nature (Tantra Yoga) grows out of the sum of all the other practices.[30]

The Green Yoga Association advocates practicing Yoga outdoors in order to connect with nature, to be mindful of one's purchases and ecological imprint, and be wary of studios that do not respect the environment.

Health begins with oneself. By making lifestyle choices, one can lessen the risk of ill health to oneself and one's family. Yoga, as practiced in the modern world, offers guidelines and pathways that can help reduce our tendencies to overconsume. It helps to energize our physicality and challenge our decision-making processes. As Joseph Alter has noted, "By no stretch of the imagination can Yoga be considered dangerous. If practice does not in fact bring about enlightenment or relief from stress and ill health, it most certainly does not threaten the well-being of those who practice it."[31] Without requiring a fixed belief system, Yoga offers a pragmatic course to change one's behavior and cultivate inner health. In turn, this heightened awareness can lead one to adopt an environmentally responsible and mindful lifestyle.

Yoga provides a way for the modern person, unwilling to commit to a fixed ideology, yet in need of solace and meaning in a turbulent world, to engage body and mind in a practice that brings relief from the onslaught of everyday busy-ness and stress. Yoga has a long history on the world stage, and interest in Yoga shows no sign of abatement. Yoga offers a felt, visceral experience, simultaneously physical and emotional. Yoga emphasizes movement and breath more than words and urges its practitioners to adopt a comprehensive ethical lifestyle. Yoga has been applied in different ways by different communities, whether Vedantin, Buddhist, Sikh, Muslim, secularist, Jewish, or Christian. In the challenging world of postnationalism and postmodernism, Yoga may provide some practices needed to move one from disequilibrium to personal, social, and ecological balance.

Notes

1. THE YOGA TRADITION

1. *Time* magazine, in its April 26, 2004, issue selected B. K. S. Iyengar as one of the top one hundred People in the "Heroes and Icons" category.

2. Jonathan Mark Kenoyer, *Ancient Cities of the Indus Valley Civilization* (Oxford: Oxford University Press, 1998).

3. A comprehensive history of Yoga can be found in Eliade, *Yoga Immortality and Freedom*, Georg Feuerstein, *The Yoga Tradition: Its History, Literature, Philosophy and Practice*, and *Yoga: India's Philosophy of Meditation* by Gerald J. Larason and Ramshankar Bhattacharya.

4. SU 3:9–10. See also Robert Ernest Hume, *The Thirteen Principal Upaniṣads* (London: Oxford University Press, 1931), pp. 400–01.

5. Antonio T. deNicolás, *Avatāra: The Humanization of Philosophy through the* Bhagavad Gītā (New York: Nicolas Hays, 1976), p. 269.

6. *Sāṃkhya Kārikā* 19 (hereafter noted as *SK*).

7. *Yoga Sūtra* II:17 (hereafter noted as *YS*).

8. *YS* I:2.

9. *YS* I:6.

10. *YS* II:16.

11. *YS* I:12–14, I:20.

12. *YS* I:24.

13. *YS* I:33.

14. *YS* I:34.

15. *Chāndogya Upaniṣad*, V:1:12, (hereafter noted as *CU*); see also Hume, p. 228.

16. *YS* I:34, II:49–53.

17. *YS* I:35–39.

18. *YS* II:5.

19. *YS* II:6–9.

20. Georg Feuerstein, *The Essence of Yoga* (New York: Grove, 1974), pp. 71–72.

21. *SK* 67.

22. *YS* I:41

23. *YS* II:44.

24. *YS* I:24.

25. *Ṛg Veda* I:164.46.

26. *Ṛg Veda* X:2.

27. *Complete Works*, II:334.

28. Lionel Trilling, *The Experience of Literature* (New York: Holt, Rinehart and Winston, 1967), p. 1130.

29. W. Somerset Maugham, *The Razor's Edge* (New York: Doubleday, 1944), pp. 268–69.

30. Ibid., 277.

31. Brockington, John, "Yoga in the Mahābhārata," in *Yoga: The Indian Tradition*, eds. Ian Whicher and D. Carpenter (Routledge-Curzon, 2003), pp. 13–24.

32. *Yogavāsiṣṭha* III:5–7. For a summary of the historical developments of the *Yogavāsiṣṭha*, see Mainkar, *The Vāsiṣṭha Ramayānā: A Study*, Chapple, *Introduction to Concise Yogavāsiṣṭha*, and Walter Slaje's extensive studies.

33. Christopher Key Chapple, *Reconciling Yogas: Haribhadra's Collection of Views on Yoga* (New York: State University of New York Press, 2003).

34. Winston L. King, *Theravada Meditation: The Buddhist Transformation of* Yoga (University Park: Pennsylvania State University Press, 1980), pp. 42–43.

35. Har Dayal, *The Bodhisattva Doctrine in Buddhist Sanskrit Literature* (London: Kegan Paul, 1932).

36. Trilochan Singh, "Sikhism and Yoga: A Comparative Study in the Light of Guru Nanak's Encounter with the Yogis," in *Perspectives on Guru Nanak: Seminar Papers*, ed. Harbans Singh (Patiala: Guru Gobind Singh Department of Religious Studies, 1975), p. 296.

37. David Gordon White, *The Alchemical Body: Siddha Traditions in Medieval India* (Chicago: University of Chicago Press, 1996), pp. 242–46.

38. Trilochan Singh, "Sikhism and Yoga: A Comparative Study in the Light of Guru Nanak's Encounter with the Yogis," in *Perspectives on Guru Nanak: Seminar Papers*, ed. Harbans Singh (Patiala: Guru Gobind Singh Department of Religious Studies, 1975), p. 298.

39. Alan Tobey, "The Summer Solstice of the Healthy-Happy-Holy Organization," in *New Religious Consciousness*, ed. Charles Y. Glock and Robert N. Bellah (Berekely: University of California Press, 1976), pp. 5–30, 18–19.

40. Mojtab'i, Fathullah, "Muntakhab'i Jug-busasht or Selections from the *Yogavāsiṣṭha* Attributed to Mir Abu I-qasim Findirski." Doctoral dissertation, Haravard University 1977.

41. Carl W. Ernst, "Sufism and Yoga according to Muhammad Ghawth" in *Sufi*, 29 (Spring 1996), 9–13.

42. See Thomas J. McEvilley, *The Shape of Ancient Thought* (New York: Allworth Press, 2002), pp. 1–22, 237, 299.

43. See "Declaration on the Relationship of the Church to Non-Christian Religions: Nostra Aetate," in *The Documents of Vatican II: With Notes and Comments by Catholic, Protestant, and Orthodox Authorities*, ed. W. M. Abbott and J. Gallagher (New York: New Century, 1966), pp. 660–71.

44. The Sanskrit word for meditation (*dhyāna*) became transliterated as *Ch'an* in China. and *Zen* in Japan

45. C. L. Tripathi, "The Influence of Indian Philosophy on Neoplatonism," in *Neoplatonism and Indian Thought*, ed. R. Baine Harris (Norfolk, Virginia: International Society for Neoplatonic Studies, 1982), pp. 273–92.

2. SĀṂKHYA-PHILOSOPHY AND YOGA PRACTICE

An earlier version of this chapter was published as "*Citta-vṛtti* and Reality in the *Yoga Sūtra*" in *Sāṃkhya-Yoga: Proceedings of the IASWR Conference*, 1981 (Stony Brook: The Institute for Advanced Studies of World Religions, 1981), pp. 103–19. Some of the ideas in this chapter have been more fully explained by Ian Whicher in *The Integrity of the Yoga Darshana* (Albany: State University of New York Press, 1999).

1. *SK* 64.

2. Georg Feuerstein, *The Philosophy of Classical Yoga* (New York: St. Martin's Press, 1980), p. 58.

3. *YS* I:5–11.

4. Cf. Buddhist *saṃvṛtti-satya.*

5. *YS* II:5.

6. *YS* I:13.

7. *YS* II:1.

8. *YS* I:20.

9. *YS* I:33.

10. *YS* I:36.

11. *YS* III:1.

12. *YS* III:2.

13. *YS* III:3; James Haughton Woods, *The Yoga-System of Patañjali* (Cambridge, MA: Harvard University Press, 1914), p. 42.

14. *Yogasārasangraha of Vijñānabhiksu*, trans. Ganga Nath Jha, ed. Avanindra Kumar, revised ed. (Delhi: Parimal, 1995), p. 3.

15. *YS* I:43.

16. *YS* I:41.

17. *Yogasārasangraha,* op.cit., p.12.

18. Ibid., p. 33.

19. E.g., Patañjali states that many people see it (*prakṛiti*), and therefore it does not proceed from the mind alone (*YS* IV:15, 16). The *Sāṃkhya Kārikā* asserts that "effects relate directly to their cause" (*SK* 9).

20. Max Müller, *The Six Systems of Indian Philosophy* (London: Longmans, Green, 1899), p. 310.

21. Georg Feuerstein, *The* Yoga-Sūtra *of Patañjali: A New Translation and Commentary* (Kent, UK: Dawson, 1979), p. 76.

22. Feuerstein, *Philosophy*, p. 24.

23. *SK* 67.

24. *YS* II:9.

25. *BG* XIII:29, and Antonio T. deNicolás, *Avatāra: The Humanization of Philosophy through the Bhagavad Gītā* (New York: Hays, 1976), p. 140.

26. Cf. *SK* 66.

27. See deNicolas, *Avatāra*, p. 5.

28. Thomas J. J. Altizer, *Total Presence: The Language of Jesus and the Language of Today* (New York: The Seabury Press, 1980), p. 36.

29. Alex Comfort, *I and That: Notes on the Biology of Religion* (New York: Crown, 1979), p. 12.

30. *SK* 19.

3. PRECEPTS AND VOWS

An earlier version of this chapter was published in *Archiv für Religionsgeshichte* 9 (2007), 9–21.

1. William James, *The Varieties of Religious Experience* (London: Collier, 1961), p. 160.

2. Ibid., p. 165.

3. Ibid., p. 221.

4. William Bucke, *Cosmic Consciousness: A Study in the Evolution of the Human Mind* (Philadelphia, 1901), pp. 182–86, as quoted in James, *Varieties*, pp. 82–83.

5. Bucke, *Cosmic Consciousness*, p. 2, as quoted in James, *Varieties*, p. 313.

6. James, *Varieties*, p. 314.

7. Swami Vivekananda, *Raja Yoga* (London, 1896), as quoted in James, *Varieties*, p. 315.

8. *Yoga Sūtra* II:41.

9. *YS* I:33.

10. *YS* II:30–39.

11. *YS* IV:7.

12. *YS* II:12.

13. *YS* II:3.

14. *YS* II:5.

15. *YS* II:16.

16. *YS* I:50.

17. *YS* II:34.

18. Swami Jyotir Mayananda, *Yoga of Sex-Sublimation, Truth and Non-Violence* (Miami: International Yoga Society, no date), pp. 22–23. Other books on ethical practices of Yoga include John McAfee, *The Secret of the Yamas: A Spiritual Guide to*

Yoga (Woodland Park: Woodland, 2001) and Georg Feuerstein, *Yoga Morality: Ancient Teachings at a Time of Global Crisis* (Prescott: Hohm Press, 2007).

19. Ibid., p. 30

20. Ibid., p. 49.

21. Ibid., p. 99.

22. Ibid., p. 77.

23. Ibid., p. 105.

24. For a description of this training, see "Rāja Yoga and the Guru: Gurāṇi Añjali" in *Gurus in America*, edited by Thomas A. Forsthoefel and Cynthia Ann Humes (Albany: State University of New York Press, 2005), pp. 15–35.

25. Christopher Key Chapple, *Nonviolence to Animals, Earth, and Self in Asian Traditions* (Albany: State University of New York Press, 1993), p. 71.

26. Padmanabh S. Jaini, *The Jaina Path of Purification* (Berkeley: University of California Press, 1979), p. 144.

27. Ibid., p. 149.

28. James Laidlaw, *Riches and Renunciation: Religion, Economy, and Society among the Jains* (Oxford: Clarendon, 1995), p. 157.

29. Herman Jacobi, *Jaina Sutras Translated from Prakriti* (New York: Dover, 1968), p. 202. First edition published by Clarendon, Oxford, 1884.

30. Ibid., p. 204.

31. Ibid., p. 205–06.

32. Ibid., p. 207.

33. Ibid., p. 208.

34. Ibid.

35. Ibid., pp. 80–81.

36. Arun Gandhi, at the American Academy of Religion Annual Meeting 2002, Toronto. Vasudha Narayanan, University of Florida, Presiding, Theme: Have We Distorted the Essence of Religion?

4. IMITATION OF ANIMALS IN YOGA

1. See *A Communion of Subjects: Animals in Religion, Science, and Ethics*, ed. Paul Waldau and Kimberley Patton (New York: Columbia University Press, 2006).

2. Significant writers and researchers in this field include Marc Bekoff, Donald Griffin, and Frans de Waal.

3. See Christopher Key Chapple, *Nonviolence to Animals, Earth, and Self in Asian Traditions* (Albany: State University of New York Press, 1993).

4. See Derek Lodrick, *Animal Shelters in India* (Berkeley: University of California Press, 1981).

5. See Steven J. Rosen, *Holy Cow: The Hare Krishna Contribution to Vegetarianism & Animal Rights* (New York: Lantern Books, 2004).

6. Jonathan Kenoyer, *Ancient Cities of the Indus Valley Civilization* (Karachi: Oxford, 1998) pp. 84–88.

7. Ibid., p. 218.

8. Ibid. pp. 112–13.

9. Mircea Eliade, *Shamanism: Archaic Techniques of Ecstasy* (Princeton: Princeton University Press, 1963) p. 460.

10. P. O. Bodding, "Studies in Santal Medicine," in *Memoirs of the Asiatic Society of Bengal* 10:1 (1925): 45.

11. For an extended discussion of the Jātaka tales, see Chapple, 1997, and of animals in the broader Buddhist tradition, see Chapple, 1994 and Waldau and Patton, 2006.

12. *Ācārāṅga Sūtra* II:15:21.

13. *Kalpa Sūtra*, Jacobi, p. 261.

14. *YS* III:24.

15. *YS* II:46.

16. Svatmarama, *The Hatha Yoga Pradipika* (New Delhi: Munshiram Manoharlal) p. 20.

17. Ibid., p. 24.

18. Ibid., p. 25.

19. Ibid., p. 32.

20. Ibid., pp. 52–54.

21. Personal communication, February 1999.

22. Thomas Berry, *The Great Work: Our Way into the Future* (New York: Bell Tower, 1999) pp. 81–82.

23. *Yoga Sūtra* I:33–34.

24. *Yoga Sūtra* I:30–31.

25. *Yoga Sūtra* I:52.

5. PATAÑJALI ON MEDITATION

This originally appeared as "Practice and Dispassion: Patañjali's Meditation," in *Darshan*, 78/79 (1993): 78–83.

1. *Yoga Sūtra* I:2.

2. *Yoga Sūtra* I:5–11.

3. *Yoga Sūtra* II:2–10.

4. *Yoga Sūtra* II:12–15 and IV:7–11.

5. For Patañjali's theory of mind, see *Yoga Sūtra* I:2–11 and IV:3–5, 15–25. For relationship to afflicted action, see II:3–15.

6. For a discussion of the process of achieving liberation or *kaivalyam*, see *Yoga Sūtra* I:47–51, II:16–28, III:47–55; IV:26–34.

7. *Yoga Sūtra* I:12–22.

8. *Yoga Sūtra* II:30–31, 33–39.

9. *Yoga Sūtra* I:33.

10. *Yoga Sūtra* I:23–32; II:1, 32, 44–45.

11. *Yoga Sūtra* I:23–28.

12. *Yoga Sūtra* II:29, 46–48; III:21.

13. *Yoga Sūtra* I:34, II:29, 49–53.

14. *Yoga Sūtra* III:29–34.

15. *Yoga Sūtra* I:35–39.

16. *Yoga Sūtra* I:17, 35, 42–46; II:53–55; III:12, 43–48.

17. *Yoga Sūtra* III:2.

18. *Yoga Sūtra* IV:6.

19. *Yoga Sūtra* II:11.

20. *Yoga Sūtra* I:41.

21. *Yoga Sūtra* III:16–34.

22. *Yoga Sūtra* III:37.

23. *Yoga Sūtra* I:48–49.

24. *Yoga Sūtra* II:17–26.

25. *Yoga Sūtra* III:48–55.

26. *Yoga Sūtra* IV:29–34.

27. *Yoga Sūtra* I:41.

28. *Yoga Sūtra* I:50.

29. *Yoga Sūtra* II:3–15.

6. LUMINOSITY AND YOGA

An earlier version of this chapter appeared in *Yoga: The Indian Tradition*, ed. Ian Whicher and David Carpenter (London: Routledge Curzon, 2003), pp. 83–96.

1. *YS* I:2.

2. *svarūpa*, I:3.

3. *YS* I:1.

4. *YS* I:2, 3.

5. *YS* I:4–11.

6. *YS* I:16.

7. *YS* I:33.

8. Richard Gombrich, *How Buddhism Began: The Conditioned Genesis of the Early Teachings* (New Delhi: Manoharlal, 1997).

9. Christopher Chapple, "Reading Patañjali without Vyāsa: A Critique of Four *Yoga Sūtra* Passages" in *Journal of the American Academy of Religion* 42:1 (1994): 85–106, and chapter 15 in this book.

10. *YS* I:41.

11. *YS* I:47–48.

12. See Antonio T. deNicolas, *Meditations through the Ṛg Veda* (New York: Nicolas-Hayes, 1976) chapter 5.

13. *YS* I.20–22

14. See Gerald J. Larson, *Classical Sāṃkhya* (Delhi: Motilal Banarsidass, 1979) 199–200.

15. *YS* III:54, IV:29.

16. *YS* II:40–41.

17. *YS* II:51.

18. *YS* II:53.

19. *YS* III:5.

20. *YS* III:26.

21. *YS* III:35.

22. *YS* III:40.

23. *YS* III:42.

24. *YS* III:43.

25. *YS* I:19.

26. YS I:19.

27. *YS* III:43.

28. *YS* II:52.

29. *YS* III:44.

30. *YS* III:46.

31. *YS* III:47.

32. *YS* III:48.

33. *YS* III:49.

34. *YS* III:50.

35. *YS* III:51.

36. *YS* III:52.

37. *YS* III:53.

38. *YS* III:54.

39. *YS* III:55.

40. See Vācaspatimiśra's gloss on *YS* III:35: "It is the sattva of the thinking-substance which reflects the Self united with this presented-idea, and which depends upon the Intelligence (*caitanya*) which has been mirrored (*chāyāpanna*) in it [as the intelligence] of the Self. Thus it exists for the sake of the Self." James Haughton Woods, *The Yoga System of Patañjali* (Cambridge: Harvard University Press, 1914), p.264.

41. *YS* IV:5.

42. *YS* III:55.

43. *YS* IV:6.

44. *YS* IV:7.

45. *YS* IV:18.

46. *YS* IV:17.

47. *YS* IV:18.

48. *YS* IV:19.

49. *YS* IV:25.

50. *YS* IV:30.

51. *YS* IV: 29.

52. *YS* IV:30.

53. *YS* IV:31.

54. *YS* IV:32.

55. *YS* IV:33.

56. *YS* IV:34.

57. *YS* II:52.

58. *YS* IV:31.

59. George James, "Ethical and Religious Dimensions of Chipko Resistance" in *Hinduism and Ecology: The Intersection of Earth, Sky, and Water*, ed. Christopher Key Chapple and Mary Evelyn Tucker (Cambridge: Harvard Divinity School, 2000), p. 526.

60. See Ortega y Gasset, *Man in Crisis* (New York: Norton, 1958).

7. LIVING LIBERATION IN SĀṂKHYA AND YOGA

An earlier version of this chapter appeared in *Living Liberation in Hindu Thought*, ed. Andrew O. Fort and Patricia Y. Mumme (Albany: State University of New York Press, 1996), pp. 115–34.

1. Gerald Larson dates Īśvarakṛṣṇa at CE 350–450 and Patañjali at CE 400–500. See *The Encyclopedia of Indian Philosophies,* volume 4: *Sāṃkhya, Dualist Tradition in Indian Philosophy* (Delhi: Motilal Barnarsidass, 1987), p. 15.

2. See *Sāṃkhya Kārikā*, verse 67. For a full translation of the text see Gerald J. Larson, *Classical Sāṃkhya: An Interpretation of Its History and Meaning* (Delhi: Motilal Banarsidass, 1979). Hereafter, the text will be abbreviated as *SK*. For the most part, my own translations of the text are used.

3. See *YS* IV:29.

4. See *YS* IV:19.

5. See the description of the state of *prakṛti-laya* in *YS* I:19.

6. According to sixth-century commentator Gauḍapāda, this pain is internal (both psychological and physical), external (caused by living beings other than oneself), and from "above" (in modern parlance, acts of God). See his commentary on the second *kārikā* in *Sāṃkhya Kārikā of Īśvarakṛṣṇa with the Commentary of Gauḍapāda,* trans. T. G. Mainkar (Poona: Oriental Book Agency, 1972). Hereafter abbreviated as *SKGB*.

7. *SK* 57.

8. *SK* 21.

9. *SK* 58.

10. *SK* 64–68.

11. *SK* 61.

12. *SKGB* 58.

13. *SK* 66.

14. *SK* 64.

15. *SK* 68.

16. *SK* 9.

17. *SKGB* 66.

18. See Gerald James Larson and Ram Shankar Bhattacharya, ed., *Samkhya: A Dualist Tradition in Indian Philosophy, Encyclopedia of Indian Philosophies,* volume 4 (Delhi: Motilal Banarsidass, 1987), pp. 29ff.

19. Ibid., p. 353.

20. Ibid., p. 411.

21. Ibid., p. 482.

22. Ibid., p. 574.

23. *SK* 19.

24. T. S. Rukmani, "Samprajñāta in the Patañjali Yoga System—Difference in Interpretation between Vācaspati Miśra and Vijñānabhikṣu," appendix 3 in *Yogavārttika of Vijñānabhikṣu* (New Delhi: Munshiram Manoharlal, 1989), p. 159.

25. *YS* II:11.

26. *Bhagavad Gītā* VI:17. See also B. Srinivasa Murthy, tr., *The Bhagavad Gita* (Long Beach, CA: Long Beach, 1991). Hereafter referred to as *BG*.

27. *YS* II:15.

28. *YS* II:16.

29. *YS* II:18.

30. *YS* II:28.

31. *YS* I:50.

32. *YS* II:29–III:8.

33. *YS* II:51.

34. *YS* III:13.

35. *YS* III:9.

36. *YS* III:11.

37. *YS* IV:2, 14.

38. *YS* IV:32, 33.

39. *YS* I:50–51.

40. See Vyāsa's *Bhāṣya* on II:2, 4, see also James Haughton Woods, *The Yoga System of Patanjali* (Delhi: Motilal Banarsidass, 1977 [first published in 1914]). pp. 105–08

41. Swami Hariharananda Aranya, *Yoga Philosophy of Patañjali* (Albany: State University of New York Press, 1983 [first published in 1963]), p. 119.

42. *YS* IV:30.

43. *YS* IV:34.

44. *Kleśa-karma-nivṛttau jīvanneva vidvan vimukto bhavati* (*YS Vyāsa-bhāṣya* IV:30).

45. *BG* V:28.

46. *BG* V:8.

47. *YS* I:24.

48. *YS* I:26.

49. *YS* I:27.

50. *YS* II:45.

51. *YS* IV:25.

52. *YS* I:2.

53. *Adhyātma prasāda, YS* I:47.

54. *YS* I:51.

55. *YS* II:21, 22.

56. *YS* II:20.

57. *YS* III:35, 49, 55.

58. *YS* IV:29.

59. *YS* IV:30.

60. *YS* IV:34.

61. *YS* IV:34.

62. "*Dharmamegha samādhiḥ . . . asyāmavasthāyāṃ jīvanmukta ityucyate,*" as found in Vijñānabhikṣu, *Yoga-Sāra-Sangraha* (Madras: Theosophical, 1933), p. 17.

63. For other references to the relationship between Yoga and Buddhism, see Emile Senart, "Bouddhisme et Yoga" in *La Revue de l'histoire des religions,* vol. 42 (1900), pp. 345–64; Louis de la Vallee Poussin, "Le Bouddhisme et le Yoga de Patañjali," in *Melanges Chinois et Bouddhiques,* vol. 5 (1936/37), 232–52.

64. Har Dayal, *The Bodhisattva Doctrine in Buddhist Sanskrit Literature* (New York: Samuel Weiser, 1932), p. 291.

65. *YS* IV:30.

66. *Dharmādinam akaraṇāpraptau, SK* 67.

67. Īśvarakṛṣṇa states that "by virtue (*dharma*) [one obtains] ascent to higher planes" (*SK* 44), interpreted by Vācaspati Miśra to be heaven. This attainment is clearly at variance with the goal of liberation, which is achieved only through knowledge (*jñāna*).

68. See *Self Knowledge* (*Ātmabodha*), tr. Swami Nikhilananda (New York: Ramakrishna-Vivekananda Center, 1970), pp. 117–72.

69. The very first verse of the *Ācārāṅga Sūtra* indicates Jainism's commitment to *ahiṃsā*; the second section of the text is devoted to a detailed description of the practices of *satya, asteya,* and *aparigraha,* all of which find direct parallels in *YS* 2:30–39. The earliest sections of the *Ācārāṅga Sūtra* date from the third or fourth century BCE, several centuries before the *Yoga Sūtra.* See Christopher Key Chapple, *Nonviolence to Animals, Earth and Self in Asian Traditions* (Albany: State University of New York Press, 1993), pp. 10, 17–18, 71.

70. It is interesting to note that the Jainas use the term *karma-prakṛti.* One possible way to interpret the Sāṃkhya tradition in light of Jainism would be to see Sāṃkhya's *prakṛti* not as a universal or cosmological principle but as a discrete karmic pattern. Perhaps it could be conjectured that the insight mode of Sāṃkhya allows one to quell a particular karmic configuration, but that this insight or knowledge must be used repeatedly according to new karmic circumstances that arise.

71. Helmuth von Glasenapp, *The Doctrine of Karman in Jain Philosophy* (Bombay: Bai Vijibai Panalal Charity Fund, 1942), pp. 5–19. See also Muni Shivkumar, *Doctrine of Liberation in Indian Philosophy* (New Delhi: Munshiram Manoharlal, 1984), pp. 66–72.

72. See Padmanabh S. Jaini, *The Jaina Path of Purification* (Berkeley: University of California Press, 1979), pp. 141–56.

73. Reprinted from Christopher Key Chapple, *Reconciling Yogas: Haribhadra's Collection of Views on Yoga* (Albany: State University of New York Press, 2003), p. 36.

74. Jaini, op. cit., p. 142.

75. Nathmal Tatia, trans., *That Which Is: The Tattvārtha Sūtra of Umāsvāti* (San Francisco: HarperCollins, 1994), p. 284.

76. Padmanabh S. Jaini, *Gender and Salvation: Jaina Debates on the Spiritual Liberation of Women* (Berkeley: University of California Press, 1991), p. 95.

77. Also referred to in the *Yoga Sūtras* as clinging to life or *abhiniveśa* (II:9).

78. Jaini, *Gender and Salvation*, p. 98.

79. *YSVB* 4.30.

80. *SK* 19.

8. APPROACHING THE *YOGA SŪTRA*

1. *YS* I:35–39.

2. *YS* II:1–27.

3. *YS* II:28–III:3.

4. See Christopher Chapple, "*Citta-vṛtti* and Reality in the *Yoga Sūtra*," in *Sāṃkhya-Yoga: Proceedings of the IASWR Conference, 1981* (Stony Brook, NY: Institute for Advanced Studies of World Religions, 1983), pp. 103–110, which has been revised as chapter 2 in this book.

5. Georg Feuerstein, *The* Yoga Sūtra *of Patañjali: A New Translation and Commentary* (Folkestone: Dawson, 1979), p. 3.

6. T. S. Rukmani, *Yogavārttika of Vijñānabhikṣu, Samādhipāda* (Delhi: Munshiram Manoharlal, 1981), p. 3.

7. For a summary of the views of these and others, see Mircea Eliade, *Yoga: Immortality and Freedom* (Princeton: Princeton University Press, 1969), pp. 370–72.

8. Ibid., p. 9.

9. Gerald James Larson, "Introduction," *Yoga: India's Philosophy of Meditation, Encyclopedia of Indian Philosophies*, vol. 8 (Delhi: Motilal Banarsidass, 2007), pp. 33, 42.

10. Mircea Eliade, *Yoga: Immortality and Freedom* (Princeton: Princeton University Press, 1969), p. 162. See also Emile Senart, "Bouddhisme et Yoga," *La Revue de l'histoire des religions* 42 (1900): 345–64.

11. Louis de la Vallee Poussin, "Le Bouddhisme et le Yoga de Patañjali" *Melanges chinois et bouddhiques* 5 (1936–37): 232–42.

12. A. B. Keith, *Indian Historical Quarterly* 3 (1932): 434, as quoted in la Vallee Poussin.

13. Georg Feuerstein, *The* Yoga Sūtra *of Patañjali: An Exercise in the Methodology of Textual Analysis* (New Delhi: Heinemann, 1979), pp. 87–88.

14. Paul Deussen, *Allgemeine Geschichte der Philosophie* vol. 1, pt. 3 (Leipzig, 1920), as summarized in Feuerstein, ibid., p. 37.

15. J. W. Hauer, *Der Yoga* (Stuttgart: Kohlhammer, 1958), as summarized in Feuerstein, ibid., p. 42.

16. Erich Frauwallner, *History of Indian Philosophy*, vol. I, tr. V. M. Bedekar (Delhi: Motilal Banarsidass, 1973), pp. 344–45.

17. S. N. Dasgupta, *Yoga Philosophy in Relation to Other Systems of Indian Thought* (University of Calcutta, 1951), p. 51.

18. *Ṛg Veda,* X:22:13.

19. *Chāndogya Upaniṣad* III:17:4.

20. Ibid., VIII:15:1.

21. In the *sūtras* of Baudhāyana, five disciplines are mentioned as "rules for an ascetic: abstention from injuring living beings, truthfulness, abstention from appropriating the property of another, continence, and liberality" (II:10:18:1). At a later date, the Laws of Manu prescribe "*ahiṃsā, satya, asteya, śauca,* and control of the senses to be performed by all castes. The *Anuśāsanaparvan*, chapters 113 to 116, of the *Mahābhārata*, greatly extols *ahiṃsā.*

22. Jan Gonda, *The Ritual Sūtra* (Wiesbaden: Harrassowitz, 1977), p. 476. (*A History of Indian Literature*, vol. 1, fasc. 2).

23. Judith A. Berling, *The Syncretic Religion of Lin Chao-en* (New York: Columbia University Press, 1980), p. 9.

24. Frauwallner, p. 335.

25. Max Mueller, *The Six Systems of Indian Philosophy* (London: Longmans, Green, 1928), p. 40.

26. *Mahābhārata* XVIII:113:8.

15. READING PATAÑJALI WITHOUT VYĀSA

This chapter was originally published in the *Journal of the American Academy of Religion* 62, no. 1 (1994): 85–105. This research was funded by a grant from the National Endowment for the Humanities.

1. *YS* I:19–22.

2. *YS* I:41.

3. *YS* II:17–27.

4. *YS* III:53.

5. Of particular note are the essays "Formula and Meter" by Gregory Nagy and "Is 'Oral' or 'Aural' Composition the Cause of Homer's Formulaic Style?" in Benjamin A. Stolz and Richard S. Shannon, III, eds. *Oral Literature and the Formula* (Ann Arbor: Center for the Coordination of Ancient and Modern Studies, 1976). References to the oral tradition in India are included in Jack Goody, *The Interface between the Written and the Oral* (Cambridge: Cambridge University Press, 1987) and Jan Vansina,

Oral Tradition: A Study in Historical Methodology (Chicago: Aldine, 1961). Michael N. Nagler is particularly sensitive to Indian literary tradition in his *Spontaneity and Tradition: A Study of the Oral Art of Homer* (Berkeley: University of California Press, 1974), noting that "there was a highly developed theory of meaning, language, and language acquisition built around . . . the term *sphota* . . . , 'to burst,' its application to language being the intuitive perception of meaning which in our language also 'bursts' upon the mind in some unknown way either spontaneously or when triggered by a linguistic symbol: word, phrase, or sentence."

6. Harold Coward, Sacred *Word and Sacred Text: Scripture in World Religions* (Maryknoll, New York: Orbis Books, 1988), p. 116.

7. See especially chapter six, "Scripture as Spoken Word: The Indian Paradigm" in William A. Graham, *Beyond the Written Word: Oral Aspects of Scripture in the History of Religion* (Cambridge: Cambrige University Press, 1987).

8. Kofi Awoonar, *Breast of the Earth: A Survey of the History, Culture, and Literature of Africa South of the Sahara* (Garden City: Anchor Press/Doubleday, 1975), p. 80.

9. My own experience with the *Yoga Sūtras* has included memorization and group recitation in Sanskrit of the second *pāda* at Yoga Anand Ashram in Amityville, New York.

10. *YS* I:23–24; II:1; II:32, 45.

11. Bruce M. Metzger, *The Text of the New Testament: Its Transmission, Corruption, and Restoration* (New York: Oxford University Press, 1968).

12. *YS* I:41, IV:34.

13. For a narrative description of these, see Edward Conze, *Buddhist Thought in India* (Ann Arbor: University of Michigan Press, 1967). See also the *Visuddhimagga* (XXI:128).

14. *YS* I:41.

15. *YS* I:23–40.

16. *YS* I:40.

17. *YS* I:41.

18. *YS* I:2.

19. *YS* I:3.

20. *YS* I:12–16.

21. *Laṅkāvatāra Sūtra,* II:VIII [Suzuki]. See also II:XXXV, 78.

22. *Laṅkāvatāra Sūtra* II:X, 44.

23. *Laṅkāvatāra Sūtra* II:XLVII, 115.

24. *Laṅkāvatāra Sūtra* II:LIV, 128.

25. *Laṅkāvatāra Sūtra* III:LXXIII, 177.

26. Malcolm D. Eckel, "The *Madhyāntavibhāgabhāṣya*: A Commentary on the Distinction between the Middle and the Extremes," unpublished trans. 1983.

27. This translation and those that follow are taken from Sarvepalli Radhakrishnan and Charles A. Moore, *A Source Book in Indian Philosophy,* which is based on translations by S. S. Suryanarayana Sastri and Ganganatha Jha.

28. *YS* II:23–24.

29. *YS* II:25.

30. *YS* II:26.

31. *SK* XLIV, LXIII, LXIV.

32. *SK* XL–LV.

33. *YS* I:44, 45; II:10, 50; III:25; IV:13.

34. *SK* LXIV–LXV, my translation.

35. See p. 172.

36. Katherine Harper, *The Iconography of the Saptamatrikas: Seven Hindu Goddesses of Spiritual Transformation* (Lewiston: Mellen, 1989).

37. *Laṅkāvatāra Sūtra* IV:LXXX, 213

38. *Laṅkāvatāra Sūtra* IV:LXXX, 215

39. Haribhadra (eighth century CE) lists Patañjali's system and then aligns it with his own eightfold scheme (*mitrā, tārā, balā, dīprā, sthirā, kāntā, prabhā, parā*) as well as with two other eightfold systems that are otherwise unknown: Bandhu Bhagavaddatta (*adveṣa, jijñāsa, śuśrūṣā, śravaṇa, sukṣmabodha, mīmāṃsā, pratipatti, sātmī-kṛta-pravṛtti*) and Bhandanta Bhāskara (*akheda, anudvega, akṣepa, annuttānavatī, abhrānti, ananyamud, arug, saṅga vivarjitā*). For a full discussion, see Chapple, *Reconciling Yogas* (Albany: State University of New York Press, 2003).

40. *YS* IV:23.

41. *YS* IV:25–26.

42. *YS* IV:29.

43. See *Sāṃkhya Kārikā* X.

44. *YS* III:48.

45. *YS* III:49.

46. *YS* III:50.

47. *YS* III:51.

48. *YS* III:52.

49. *YS* III:53.

50. *YS* III:54.

51. *YS* III:55.

16. THE USE OF THE FEMININE GENDER IN PATAÑJALI'S DESCRIPTION OF YOGIC PRACTICES

1. Rosemary Ruether, *Sexism and God-talk: Toward a Feminist Theology* (Boston: Beacon, 1983) p. 54.

2. Elizabeth A. Johnson, *She Who Is: The Mystery of God in Feminist Theological Discourse* (New York: Crossroad, 1993) p. 33.

3. Ruether, pp. 100–01.

4. Johnson, p. 38.

5. Mary Collins, *Worship: Renewal to Practice* (Washington: Pastoral Press, 1987) p. 201.

6. Ibid., p. 202.

7. Ca. 1500 BCE to 200 BCE.

8. Ca. 200 BCE to 600 CE.

9. Ca. 600 to present.

10. Tracy Pintchman, *The Rise of the Goddess in the Hindu Tradition* (Albany: State University of New York Press, 1994).

11. William Sax, *Mountain Goddess: Gender and Politics in Himalayan Pilgrimage* (New York: Oxford University Press, 1991).

12. Kathleen M. Erndl, *Victory to the Mother: The Hindu Goddess of Northwest India in Myth, Ritual, and Symbol* (New York: Oxford University Press, 1993).

13. James J. Preston, *Cult of the Goddess: Social and Religious Change in a Hindu Temple* (Prospect Heights, IL: Waveland, 1980).

14. See Chapple, *Karma and Creativity*, pp. 19–21.

15. Whicher, *The Integrity of the Yoga Darsana: A Reconsideration of Classical Yoga*, p. 306.

16. *YS* IV:34.

17. *CU* VIII:12.

18. John Cort, "Medieval Jaina Goddess Traditions" in *Numen* 34, no. 2 (1987): 239.

19. See Chapple, "Haribhadra and Patañjali," *Reconciling Yogas*, for a full discussion of the parallels, pp. 15–38.

20. *YS* I:16.

21. *YS* II:26, 28; III:49; IV:29.

22. *Sāṃkhya Kārikā*, 66; see Larson 1979, p. 27.

23. *YS* I:20.

24. *YS* I:33.

25. For a listing where these terms appear in Buddhist texts, see Dayal, 225–29. In particular, see Buddhaghosa's *Visuddhimagga*, IX.

26. Richard F. Gombrich, *How Buddhism Began: The Conditioned Genesis of the Early Teachings* (Delhi: Munshiram Manhoharlal, 1997), p. 60.

27. Ibid., p. 60.

28. Ibid., p. 62.

29. Martin Willson, *In Praise of Tara: Songs to the Saviouress* (Boston: Wisdom, 1996), pp. 35, 41.

30. David Abram, *The Spell of the Sensuous: Perception and Language in a More-Than-Human World* (New York: Pantheon, 1996), p. 65.

31. *YS* I:42–44.

32. *Bhūmi*, also a feminine term used in I:14 and I:30.

33. Again, a carry-over term from Buddhism.

34. V:148, George Bühler, tr., *Laws of Manu* (Oxford, 1884, reprinted Delhi: Motilal Banarsidass, 1964).

17. CONTEMPORARY EXPRESSIONS OF YOGA

1. N. E. Sjoman, *The Yoga Tradition of the Mysore Palace*, 2nd ed. (New Delhi: Abhinav Publications, 1999), p. 60.

2. Joseph S. Alter, *Yoga in Modern India: The Body between Science and Philosophy* (Princeton: Princeton University Press, 2004), p. 106.

3. Ibid., p. 67.

4. Ibid., p. 69.

5. Ibid., p. 167.

6. Ibid., p. 171.

7. Ibid., pp. 211–12.

8. Sarah Strauss, *Positioning Yoga: Balancing Acts across Cultures* (Oxford and New York: Berg, 2005). For a complete bibliography of Sivananda's writings, see Tilak Pyle and Calvin Mercer, *A Bibliographic Study of Swami Sivananda* (Lewiston: Edwin Mellen, 2007).

9. Ibid., p. 143.

10. Elizabeth De Michelis, *A History of Modern Yoga: Patanjali and Western Esotericism* (London and New York: Continuum, 2004), p. 260.

11. Mikel Burley, *Hatha Yoga: Its Context, Theory, and Practice* (New Delhi: Motilal Banarsidass, 2000), p. 228.

12. Gita and Mukesh Desai, *Yoga Unveiled: The Evolution and Essence of a Spiritual Tradition*, two DVD set. 3 hours, 15 minutes. 2005. www.yogaunveiled.com.

13. De Michelis, *A History of Modern Yoga*, p. 252.

14. Ibid., p. 256.

15. See George Boas, "Macrocosm and Microcosm," in *Dictionary of the History of Ideas*, ed. Philip P. Wiener (New York), vol. 3, pp. 126–31.

16. Carl W. Ernst, "The Islamicization of Yoga in the *Amṛtakuṇḍa* Translations," *Journal of the Royal Asiatic Society*, third series, vol. 13, pt. 2 (July 2003): 213.

17. Ibid., p. 204.

18. De Michelis, *A History of Modern Yoga*, p. 260.

19. "Health Threats of Untested Chemicals," BBC News, February 13, 2001.

20. Dieter Flesch-Janys, "Explaining Breast Cancer and Chemical Links: Health Hazards for Women Workers," in *Silent Invaders: Pesticides, Livelihooods and Women's Health*, ed. Miriam Jacobs and Barbara Dinham (London: Zed Books, 2003), p. 148.

21. Jill Day, "The Campaign against Lindane: The Lessons of Women's Action," in *Silent Invaders*, p. 273.

22. Miriam Jacobs, "Unsafe Sex: How Endocrine Disruptors Work," in *Silent Invaders*, p. 178.

23. Wayne Sinclair and Richard W. Pressinger, "Environmental Causes of Infertility," www.chem-tox.com. Consulted May 12, 2005.

24. *Maitri Upanisad*, VI:13. See *Taittiriya Upanisad* III:1–10 and *Maitri Upanisad*, VI:10–13, as translated in Robert Ernest Hume, *The Thirteen Principal Upanishads*, 2nd ed. pp. 292–93, 430–33.

25. Patricia Hunt, Case Western University in *Current Biology* (2003) summarized in www.greenfeet.net. Consulted May 12, 2005.

26. Marla Cone, "Study Cites Risk of Compound in Plastic Bottles," *Los Angeles Times*, April 13, 2005, p. A10. See also, by the same author, "Estrogen Imitator in Womb May Lead to Cancer in Men," *Los Angeles Times*, May 3, 2005, and by Steve Lopez, a journalist who underwent testing for his chemical content, "Chemical Stew: What's a Body to Do?" *Los Angles Times*, May, 2005. California Assemblywoman Wilma Chan has introduced legislation that would ban the sale of toys and feeding products that include BPA and other estrogen-mimicking compounds.

27. Laura Cornell, "Rethinking Yoga Mats: The Search for a Green Solution," *Green Yoga Times* vol. 1, no. 1 (2004–2005): p. 8.

28. Swami Venkatesananda, tr., *Vasiṣṭha's Yoga* (Albany: State University of New York Press, 1993), p. 582.

29. Felicia M. Tomasko, "The Greening of Yoga," *L.A. Yoga* 4, no. 3 (2005): p. 35.

30. Laura Cornell, "Green Yoga: A Collaborative Inquiry among a Group of Yoga Teachers," Doctoral dissertation, California Institute of Integral Studies (Ann Arbor: Proquest, 2006) pp. 310–11.

31. Alter, *Yoga in Modern India*, p. 211.

References

Abram, David. *The Spell of the Sensuous: Perception and Language in a More-Than-Human World*. New York: Pantheon Books, 1996.

Agrawala, P. K. *Goddesses in Ancient India*. New Delhi: Abhinav Publications, 1984.

Alter, Joseph S. *Yoga in Modern India: The Body between Science and Philosophy*. Princeton: Princeton University Press, 2004.

Aranya, Swami Hariharananda. *Yoga Philosophy of Patanjali: Containing His Yoga Aphorisms with Vyasa's Commentary in Sanskrit and a Translation with Annotations Including Many Suggestions for the Practice of Yoga*. Translated by P. N. Mukherji, Albany: State University of New York Press, 1983. First published in English by Calcutta University Press in 1963.

Arya, Usharbudh. *Yoga Sūtras of Patañjali with the Exposition of Vyāsa. Vol. 1, Samādhi-pāda*. Honesdale, PA: Himalayan International Institute of Yoga Science and Philosophy, 1986.

Awoonar, Kofi. *Breast of the Earth: A Survey of the History, Culture, and Literature of Africa South of the Sahara*. Garden City: Anchor Press/Doubleday, 1975.

Baba, Bengali. *Yoga Sutra of Patanjali with the Commentary* of *Vyāsa*. Translated from Sanskrit into English with Copious Notes. Delhi: Motilal Banarsidass, 1976.

Ballantyne, J. R., and Govind Sastry Deva, trs. *Yogasutras of Patanjali (sic) with Bhojavritti called Rajamartanda*. Akay Book Corporation, 1980. First published in the *Pandit*, 1852.

Bharati, Veda. *Yoga Sūtras of Patañjali with the Exposition of Vyāsa. Vol. 2. Sādhana-pāda*. Delhi: Motilal Banarsidass, 2007.

Bodding, P. O. "Studies in Santal Medicine and Connected Folklore." *Memoirs of the Asiatic Society of Bengal*. Vol. X, no. 1. Calcutta: The Asiatic Society of Bengal, 1925.

Buddhaghosa. *The Path of Purification (Visuddhimagga)*. Translated from the Pali by Bhikkhu Nanamoli. Fifth Edition. Kandy: Buddhist Publication Society, 1991.

Burley, Mikel. *Hatha Yoga: Its Context, Theory and Practice*. New Delhi: Banarsidass, 2000.

Callahan, Daren. *Yoga: An Annotated Bibliography of Works in English, 1981–2005*. Jefferson, NC: McFarland, 2007.

Chapple, Christopher. *Karma and Creativity*. Albany: State University of New York Press, 1986.

———. "Theology and the World Religions." In the *College Student's Introduction to Theology*, edited by Thomas P. Rausch. Collegeville, Minnesota: Liturgical, 1993. Pp. 189–205.

———. "Monist and Pluralist Discourse in Indian Traditions." In *East-West Encounters in Philosophy and Religion*, edited by Ninian Smart and Srinivas Murthy. Long Beach: Long Beach, 1996. Pp. 120–129.

Chapple, Christopher Key, and Yogi Anand Viraj (Eugene P. Kelly, Jr.). *The Yoga Sūtras of Patañjali: An Analysis of the Sanskrit with Accompanying English Translation*. Delhi: Sri Satguru, 1990.

Chapple, Christopher Key. *Nonviolence to Animals, Earth, and Self in Asian Traditions*. Albany: State University of New York Press, 1993.

———. "Reading Patañjali without Vyāsa: A Critique of Four *Yoga Sūtra* Passages." *Journal of the American Academy of Religion* 42 no. 1 (1994): 85–106.

———. "Animals and Environment in the Buddhist Birth Stories." In *Buddhism and Ecology: The Interconnection of Dharma and Deeds*, edited by Mary Evelyn Tucker and Duncan Ryuken Williams. Cambridge: Harvard University Center for the Study of World Religions, 1997.

———. "Haribhadra's Analysis of Patañjala and Kula Yoga in the *Yogadṛṣṭisamuccaya*." In *Open Boundaries: Jain Communities and Cultures in Indian History*, edited by John E. Cort. Albany: State University of New York Press, 1998.

———. *Sāṃkhya-Yoga: Proceedings of the IASWR Conference, 1981*. Stony Brook, NY: The Institute for Advanced Studies of World Religions, 1983.

———. *Reconciling Yogas: Haribhadra's Collection of Views on Yoga*. Translation of Haribhadra's *Yogadṛṣṭisamuccaya* by Christopher Key Chapple and John Thomas Casey. Albany: State University of New York Press, 2003.

Chapple, Christopher Key, and Mary Evelyn Tucker, ed. *Hinduism and Ecology: The Intersection of Earth, Sky, and Water*. Cambridge, Massachusetts: distributed by Harvard University Press for the Center for the Study of World Religions, Harvard Divinity School, 2000.

Collins, Mary. *Worship: Renewal to Practice*. Washington, DC: Pastoral, 1987.

Cornell, Laura, "Green Yoga: A Collaborative Inquiry among a Group of Kripalu Yoga Teachers." California Institute of Integral Studies, 2006. Ann Arbor: Proquest, 2006.

Conze, Edward. *Buddhist Thought in India: Three Phases of Buddhist Philosophy*. Ann Arbor: University of Michigan Press, 1967.

Cort, John. "Medieval Jaina Goddess Traditions." *Numen* 34, no. 2, (1987): 235–255.

Coward, Harold G. *Sacred Word and Sacred Text: Scripture in World Religions*. Maryknoll: Orbis Books, 1988.

Dasgupta, S. N. *Yoga Philosophy in Relation to Other Systems of Indian Thought*. Calcutta: University of Calcutta, 1951.

———. *Yoga as Philosophy and Religion*. London: Kegan Paul, 1924.

Dayal, Har. *The Bodhisattva Doctrine in Buddhist Sanskrit Literature.* London:Kegan Paul, 1932.

Dehejia, Vidya. *Yoginī Cult and Temples: A Tantric Tradition.* New Delhi: National Museum, 1986.

De Michelis, Elizabeth. *A History of Modern Yoga: Patanjali and Western Esotericism.* London and New York: Continuum, 2004.

DeNicolás, Antonio T. *Avatāra: The Humanization of Philosophy through the* Bhagavad Gītā*: A Philosophical Journey through Greek Philosophy, Contemporary Philosophy, and the* Bhagavad Gītā *on Ortega y Gasset's Intercultural Theme: Man and Circumstance.* New York: Nicolas-Hays, 1976.

———. *Meditations through the Ṛg Veda.* New York: Nicolas-Hays, 1976.

Desai, Gita and Mukesh. *Yoga Unveiled: The Evolution and Essence of a Spiritual Tradition.* 2 DVD set. 3 hours, 15 minutes. www.yogaunveiled.com. 2004.

Desikachar, T. K. V. *The Heart of Yoga: Developing a Personal Practice.* Rochester, VT: Inner Traditions, 1995.

Deussen, Paul. *Allgemaine Geschichte der Philosphie* 1, no. 3. Leipzig: Brockhaus, 1920.

Dvivedi, M. N. *The Yoga Sutras of Patanjali.* Revised edition. Dehli: Satguru, 1980. First published in Madras, 1890.

Eckel, Malcolm D. "The *Madhyāntavibhāgabhāṣya:* A Commentary on the Distinction between the Middle and the Extremes." Unpublished translation quoted with permission, 1983.

Eliade, Mircea. *Shamanism: Archaic Techniques of Ecstasy.* Translated by Willard R. Trask. Princeton: Princeton University Press, 1963.

———. "Spirit, Light, and Seed." *History of Religions* 11, no. 1: 1–30.

———. *Yoga: Immortality and Freedom.* Translated by Williad R. Trask. Princeton: Princeton University Press, 1958.

Erndl, Kathleen M. *Victory to the Mother: The Hindu Goddess of Northwest India in Myth, Ritual, and Symbol.* New York: Oxford University Press, 1993.

Ernst, Carl W. "Sufism and Yoga according to Muhammad Ghawth." *Sufi: Journal of Sufism* 29 (Spring 1996).

Feuerstein, George. *Yoga Sūtra: An Exercise in the Methodology of Textual Analysis.* New Delhi: Heinemann, 1979.

———. *The Essence of Yoga.* New York: Grove, 1974.

———. *The Philosophy of Classical Yoga.* New York: St. Martin's, 1980.

———. *Yoga Morality: Ancient Teachings at a Time of Global Crisis.* Prescott, AZ: Hohm, 2007.

———. *The Yoga Sūtra of Patañjali: A New Translation and Commentary.* Folkeston, England: Dawson, 1979.

———. *The Yoga Tradition: Its History, Literature, Philosophy, and Practice.* Prescott, AZ: Hohm, 1998.

Forsthoefel, Thomas A. and Cynthia Ann Humes, eds. *Gurus in America.* Albany: State University of New York Press, 2005.

Frawallner, Erich. *History of Indian Philosophy*. Delhi: Motilal Banarsidass, 1973.

Fuller, C. J. *The Camphor Flame: Popular Hinduism and Society in India*. Princeton: Princeton University Press, 1992.

Gheranda. *The Gheranda Samhita*. Translated by Rai Bahadur Srisa Chandra Vasu. Delhi: Satguru, 1979. First published 1914–15.

Ghosh, Shyam. *The Original Yoga as Expounded in Siva-Samhita, Gheranda-samhita and Patanjali Yoga-sutra*. New Delhi: Munshiram Manoharlal, 1980.

Gombrich, Richard F. *Theravada Buddhism: A Social History from Ancient Benares to Modern Colombo*. London: Routledge and Kegan Paul, 1988.

———. *How Buddhism Began: The Conditioned Genesis of the Early Teachings*. New Delhi: Munshiram Manoharlal, 1997.

Goody, Jack. *The Interface Between the Written and the Oral*. Cambridge University Press, 1987.

Gonda, Jan. *The Ritual Sutra*. A History of Indian Literature, Vol. 1. Wiesbaden: Harrassowitz, 1977.

Graham, William A. *Beyond the Written Word: Oral Aspects of Scripture in the History of Religion*. Cambridge: Cambridge University Press, 1987.

Granoff, Phyllis. "Jain Lives of Haribhadra: An Inquiry into the Sources and Logic of the Legends." *Journal of Indian Philosophy* 17, no. 2 (1989): 105–128.

HansrajYadav, Yogacharya. *Yoga Course for All*. Bombay: Bhavan, 1977.

Haribhadra. *Yogadṛṣṭisamuccaya*. Jaina Grantha Prākāśa Sabhā 25, 1940.

Harper, Katherine A. *The Iconography of the Saptamatrikas: Seven Hindu Goddesses of Spiritual Transformation*. Lewiston: Mellen, 1989.

Harris, R. Baine. *Neoplatonism and Indian Thought*. Norfolk, VA: International Society for Neoplatonic Studies, 1982.

Hauer, J. W. *Der Yoga*. Stuttgart: Kohlhammer, 1958.

Houseman, A. E. "The Application of Thought to Textual Criticism." *Proceedings of the Classical Association, August 1921*. London, 1922.

Hume, Robert Ernest. *The Thirteen Principal Upaniṣads*. London: Oxford University Press, 1931.

Jacobi, Hermann. *Jaina Sutras Translated from the Sanskrit*. Part I. *The Acaranga Sutra* and *The Kalpa Sutra*. Oxford: Clarendon, 1884.

Jaini, Padmanabh S. *The Jaina Path of Purification*. Berkeley: University of California Press, 1979.

———. *Gender and Salvation: Jaina Debates on the Spiritual Liberation of Women*. Berkeley: University of California Press, 1991.

James, William. *The Varieties of Religious Experience*. New York: Modern Library, 1929.

Jha, Gangānātha. *An English Translation with Sanskrit Text of the Yogasārasaṅgraha of Vijñāna Bhikshu*. Bombay: Tatva-vivechaka, 1894. Madras: Theosophical, 1933. Revised edition, Avanindra Kumar. Delhi: Parimal, 1995.

———. *Sāṃkhya Kārikā*. 2nd ed. Poona: Oriental Book Agency, 1934.

Jhavery, Mohanlal Bhagavantas. *Comparative and Critical Study of Mantraśāstra*. Ahmedabad: Nawals, 1944.

Johnson, Elizabeth A. *She Who Is: The Mystery of God in Feminist Theological Discourse*. New York: Crossroad, 1993.

Jyotir Maya Nanda, Swami. *Raja Yoga Sutras*. Miami, FL: Yoga Research Foundation, 1978.

Kenoyer, Jonathan Mark. *Ancient Cities of the Indus Valley Civilization*. Karachi: Oxford University Press, 1998.

Kinsley, David. *Tantric Visions of the Divine Feminine: The Ten Mahāvidyās*. Berkeley: University of California Press, 1997.

King, Winston L. *Theravada Meditation: The Buddhist Transformation of Yoga*. University Park: Pennsylvania State University Press, 1980.

Larson, Gerald J. *Classical Sāṃkhya: An Interpretation of Its History and Meaning*. Delhi: Motilal Banarsidass, 1979.

Larson, Gerald J. and Ram Shankar Bhattacharya. *Sāṃkhya: A Dualist Tradition in Indian Philosophy*. Encyclopedia of Indian Philosophies, vol. IV. Delhi: Motilal Banarsidass, 1987.

———. *Yoga: India's Philosophy of Meditation*. Encyclopedia of Indian Philosophies, vol. XII. Delhi: Motilal Banarsidass, 2007.

Lodrick, Derek. *Animal Shelters in India*. Berkeley: University of California Press, 1981.

Mainkar, T. G. *Sāṃkhyakārikā of Īśvarakṛṣṇa with the Commentary of Gauḍapāda*. Poona: Oriental Book Agency, 1972.

———. *The Vāsiṣṭha Rāmāyana: A Study*. New Delhi: Meharchand Lachhmandas, 1977.

McAfee, John. *The Secret of the Yamas: A Spiritual Guide to Yoga*. Woodland Park, CA: Woodland, 2001.

McEvilley, Thomas. *The Shape of Ancient Thought: Comparative Studies in Greek and Indian Philosophies*. New York: Allworth, 2002.

Mayananda, Swami Jyotir. *Yoga of Sex-Sublimation, Truth and Nonviolence*. Miami: International Yoga Society, no date.

Metzger, Bruce M. *The Text of the New Testament: Its Transmission, Corruption, and Restoration*. New York: Oxford University Press, 1968.

Miller, Barbara Stoler. *Yoga: Discipline of Freedom*. Berkeley: University of California Press, 1996.

Müller, Max. *The Six Systems of Indian Philosophy*. London: Longmans, Green, 1899.

Muzumdar, S. *Yogic Exercises for the Fit and the Ailing*. Bombay: Orient Longmans, 1949.

Murthy, B. Srinivasa, trans. *Bhagavad Gita*. Long Beach: Long Beach, 1991.

Nagler, Michael. *Spontaneity and Tradition: A Study of the Oral Art of Homer*. Berkeley: University of California Press, 1974.

Nagy, Gregory. "Formula of Meter." In *Oral Literature and the Formula*. Edited by Benjamin A. Stolz and Richard S. Shannon III. Ann Arbor: Center for the Coordination of Ancient and Modern Studies, 1976.

Nikhilananda, Swami. *Self Knowledge (Ātma bodha)*. New York: Ramakrishna-Vivekananda Center, 1970.

Onishi, Yoshinori. *Feminine Multiplicity: A Study of Groups of Multiple Goddesses in India*. Delhi: Satguru, 1997.

Ortega y Gasset, Jose. *Meditations on Quixote*. Chicago: University of Illinois Press, 2000.

Pintchman, Tracy. *The Rise of the Goddess in the Hindu Tradition*. Albany: State University of New York Press, 1994.

Prasada, Rama. *Patanjali's* Yoga Sutras *with the Commentary of Vyasa and the Gloss of Vachaspati Misra*. New Delhi: Oriental Books and Reprint Corporation. First Published in 1912 by Panini Office, Allahabad.

Preston, James J. *Cult of the Goddess: Social and Religious Change in a Hindu Temple*. Prospect Heights, IL: Waveland Press, 1980.

Pyle, Tilak and Calvin Mercer. *A Bibliographic Study of Swami Sivananda*. Lewiston, NY: Edwin Mellen Press, 2007.

Radhakrishnan, Sarvepalli, and Charles A. Moore. *A Source Book in Indian Philosophy*. Princeton: Princeton University Press, 1957.

Ramaswami, Srivatsa, and David Hurvitz. *Yoga beneath the Surface: An American Student and His Indian Teacher Discuss Yoga Philosophy and Practice*. New York: Marlowe, 2006.

Rosen, Steven J. *Holy Cow: The Hare Krishna Contribution to Vegetarianism and Animal Rights*. New York: Lantern Books, 2004.

Ruether, Rosemary Radford. *Sexism and God-talk: Toward a Feminist Theology*. Boston: Beacon, 1983.

Rukmani, T.S. *Yogavārttika of Vijñāna-bhikṣu: Text with English Translation and Critical Notes along with the Text and English Translation of the Patañjala Yogasūtras and Vyāsabhāṣya. Volume I: Samādhipāda*. New Delhi: Munshiram Manoharlal, 1981.

———. *Yogavārttika of Vijñānabhikṣu*, vol. 4. Delhi: Munshiram Monoharal, 1987.

Russo, Joseph A. "Is 'Oral' or 'Aural' Composition the Cause of Homer's Formulaic Style?" In *Oral Literature and the Formula*, edited by Benjamin A. Stolz and Richard S. Shannon III. Ann Arbor: Center for the Coordination of Ancient and Modern Studies, 1976.

Saraswati, Swami Muktibodhananda, trans. *Hatha Yoga Pradipika: Light on Hatha Yoga*. Munger, India: Bihar School of Yoga, 1985.

Saraswati, Swami Satyananda. *Asana Pranayama Mudra Bandha*. Munger, India; Bihar Yoga Bharati, 1966.

Sarbacker, Stuart Ray. *Samādhi: The Numinous and Cessative in Indo-Tibetan Yoga*. Albany: State University of New York Press, 2005.

Sastri, S. S. *Sāṃkhya Kārikā*. Madras: University of Madras, 1935.

Sastry, R. Ananthakrishna, trans. *Lalitā-Sahasranāma with Bhāskararāya's Commentary*. Madras: Adyar Library and Research Centre, 1899.

Schimmel, Annemarie. *Mystical Dimensions of Islam*. Chapel Hill: University ofNorth Carolina Press, 1975.

Shivkumar, Muni. *Doctrine of Liberation in Indian Philosophy*. New Delhi: Munshiram Manoharlal, 1984.

Singh, Trilochan. "Sikhism and Yoga: A Comparative Study in the Light of Guru Nanak's Encounter with the Yogis." In *Perspectives on Guru Nanak: Seminar Papers*, edited by Harbans Singh. Patiala: Guru Gobind Singh Department of Religious Studies, Punjabi University, 1977. Pp. 296–309.

Sjoman, N. E. *The Yoga Tradition of the Mysore Palace*. Second edition. New Delhi: Abhinav, 1999. First edition, 1996. 124 pp., with 20 additional color plates.

Strauss, Sarah. *Positioning Yoga: Balancing Acts across Cultures*. Oxford and New York: Berg, 2005.

Suzuki, D. T. *Laṅkāvatāra Sūtra*. London: Routledge, 1932.

Svatmarama. *The Hatha Yoga Pradipika*. Translated by Pancham Sinh. New Delhi: Munshiram Manoharlal, 1997.

Taimni, I. K. *The Science of Yoga: The Yogasutras of Patanjali in Sanskrit with Transliteration in Roman, Translation in English and Commentary*. Wheaton, Illinois: Theosophical, 1961.

Tatia, Nathmal. *That Which Is: The Tattvārtha Sūtra of Umāsvāti*. San Francisico: HaperCollins, 1994.

Tobey, Alan. "The Summer Solstice of the Healthy-Happy-Holy Organization." In *New Religious Consciousness*. Edited by Charles Y. Glock and Robert N. Bellah; with contributions by Randall H. Alfred, foreword by P. J. Philip. Berkeley: University of California Press, 1976. Pp. 5–30.

Vansina, Jan. *Oral Traditions: A Study in Historical Methodology*. Chicago: Aldine, 1961.

Venkatesananda, Swami. *The Concise Yoga Vasistha*. Albany: State University of New York Press, 1984.

Vishnudevananda, Swami. *The Complete Illustrated Book of Yoga*. New York: Bell, 1960.

Vithaldas, Yogi. *The Yoga System of Health and Relief from Tension*. New York: Bell, 1957.

Vivekananda, Swami. *The Complete Works of Swami Vivekananda*. Calcutta: Advaita Ashram, 1989.

———. *Raja Yoga*. Revised edition. New York: Ramakrisha-Vivekananda Center, 1975.

von Glasenapp, Helmuth. *The Doctrine of Karman in Jain Philosophy*. Bombay: Bai Vijiba: Panalal, 1942.

Waldau, Paul and Kimberly Patton, eds. *A Communion of Subjects: Animals in Religion, Science, and Ethics*. New York: Columbia University Press, 2006.

Whicher, Ian. *The Integrity of the Yoga Darśana: A Reconsideration of Classical Yoga*. Albany: State University of New York Press, 1999.

Whicher, Ian and David Carpenter, eds. *Yoga: The Indian Tradition*. London: Routledge Curzon, 2007.

White, David Gordon. *The Alchemical Body: Siddha Traditions in Medieval India*. Chicago: University of Chicago Press, 1996.

Willson, Martin. *In Praise of Tara: Songs to the Savioures*s. Boston: Wisdom, 1996.

Woodroffe, Sir John. *The Garland of Letters: Studies in the Mantra-Śāstra*. Pondicherry: Ganesh, 1979.

Woods, James Haughton. *The Yoga System of Patanjali or the Ancient Hindu Doctrine of Concentration of Mind Embracing the Mnemonic Rules, Called the Yoga-Sutras, of Patanjali and the Comment, Called Yoga-bhashya, Attributed to Veda-Vyasa and the Explanation, Called Tattva-vaicaradi, of Vachaspatimisra*. Delhi: Banarsidass, 1977. First published Cambridge: Harvard University Press, 1914.

Yardi, M. R. *The Yoga of Patanjali with an Introduction, Sanskrit Text of the Yogasutras, English Translation and Notes*. Poona: Bhandarkar Oriental Research Institute, 1979.

Zaehner, R. C. *Hindu and Muslim Mysticism*. Oxford, England: One World, 1994. New York: Schocken Books, 1969.

Index of Sanskrit Terms

akaraṇa III:51
akalpita III:43
akusīda IV:29
akṛṣṇa IV:7
akrama III:54
akliṣṭa I:5
aṅga I:31; II:28, 29, 40
ajñāta IV:17
ajñāna II:34
añjanatā I:41
aṇiman III:45
aṇu I:40
atad I:8
atiprasaṅga IV:21
atīta III:16; IV:12
atyanta III:35
atha I:1
adṛṣṭa II:12
adhigama I:29
adhimātra II:34
adhimātratva I:22
adhiṣṭātṛtva III:49
adhyātman I.47
adhyāsa III.17
adhvan IV:12
ananta I:34; II:47
anabhighāta II:45, 48
anavacchinna II:31
anavaccheda I:26; III:53
anavadhāraṇa IV:20
anavasthitatva I:30
anaṣṭa II:22
anāgata II:16; III:16; IV:12
anātman II:5
anāditva IV:10
anāśaya IV:6
anitya II:5
aniṣṭa III:51
anukāra II:54
anugama I:17
anuttama II:42
anupaśya II:20
anupātin I:9; III:14
anubhūta I:11
anumāna I:7, 49
anumodita II:34
anuśayin II:7, 8
anśāsana I:1
anuṣṭhāna II:28
aneka IV:5
anta I:40
antara IV:2, 21, 27
antar-aṅga III:7
antarāya I:29, 30
antar-dhāna III:21
anya I:18, 49, 50; II:22
anyatā III:49 ,53
anyatva III:15
anvaya III:9, 44, 47
aparānta III:22; IV:33
aparāmṛṣṭa I:24
aparigraha II:30, 39
apariṇāmitva IV:18
apavarga II:18
api II:9, 20, 22, 26, 29, 51; III:8, 50; IV:9, 24, 29
apuṇya I:33; II:14
apekṣitva IV:17
apeta IV:31
apratisaṁkrama IV:22

apramāṇaka IV:16
aprayojaka IV:3
abhāva I:10, 29; II.25; IV:11
abhijāta I:41
abhiniveśa II:3, 9
abhibhava III:9
abhimata I:39
abhivyakti IV:8
abhyantara II:50, 51
abhyāsa I:12, 13, 18, 32
ariṣṭa III:22
artha I:28, 32, 42, 43; II:2, 18, 21, 22; III:3, 17, 35; IV:23, 24, 32, 34
arthatā III:11
arthatva I:49; III:35
arthavattva III:44, 47
alabdha I:30
aliṅga I:45; II:19
alpa IV:31
avasthā III:13
avasthāna I:3
avidyā II:3, 4, 5, 24
aviplava II:26
avirati I:30
aviśeṣa II:19; III:35
aviṣayībhūtatva III:20
avyapadeśya III:14
aśukla IV:7
aśuci II:5
aśuddhi II:43
aṣṭa II:29
asaṁkīrṇa III:35
asaṁkhyeya IV:24
asaṅga III:39
asaṁpramoṣa I:11
asaṁprayoga II:54
asamyoga III:21
asaṁsarga II:40
asti IV:12
asteya II:30, 37
asmitā I:17; II:3, 6; IV:4
asya I:40
ahimsā II:30, 35
ā II:28
ākāra IV:22
ākāśa II:41, 42
ākṣepin II:51
āgama I:7
ātmaka II:18
ātmatā II:6
ātman II:5, 21, 41; IV:13, 25
ādarśa III:36
ādi III:23, 24, 39, 45
ānantarya IV:9
ānantya IV:31
ānanda I:17
ānuśravika I:15
āpatti IV:22
āpūra IV:2
ābhāsa IV:19
āyus II:13
ālambana I:10, 38; IV:11
ālasya I:30
āloka III:5, 25
āvaraṇa II:52; III:43; IV:31
āveśa III:38
āśaya I:24; II:12
āśis IV:10
āśraya IV:11
āśrayatva II:36
āsana II:29, 46
āsanna I:21
āsevita I:14
āsvāda III:36
itara I:20; III:17; IV:7
itaratra I:4
iti II:34; III:54, 55; IV:34
idam [see asya, eṣām]
indriya II:18, 41, 43, 54, 55; III:13, 47
iva I:41, 43; II:6, 54; III:3
iṣṭa II:44
īśvara I:23, 24; II:1, 32, 45
ukta IV:28
utkrānti IV:39
uttara II:4
utpanna I:35
udaya II:11
udāna III:39
udāra II:4
udita II:12, 14
upanimantraṇa III:51
uparakta IV:23
uparāga IV:17
upalabdhi III:23
upasarga III:37
upasthāna II:37
upāya II:26
upekṣā I:33
ubhaya IV:20
ṛtaṁbhara I:48
eka I:32; II:6; IV:5, 9, 16, 20
eka-tānatā III:2
ekatra III:4
ekatva IV:14

ekāgratā III:11, 12
ekāgrya II:41
etayā I:44
etena III:13
eva I:44, 46; II:15, 21; III:3; IV:8
eṣām IV:11,28
oṣadhi IV:1
kaṇṭaka III:39
kaṇṭhā III:30
kathaṁtā II:39
karaṇa III:18
karuṇā I:33
karman I:24; II:12; III:22; IV:7, 30
kalpita III:43
kāya II:43; III:21, 29, 42, 45, 46
kāraṇa III:38
kārita II:34
kāritva IV.24
kāla I:14, 26; II:31,50; IV:9
kim IV:16
kūpa III:30
kūrma III:31
kṛta II:22; IV:32
kaivalya II:25; III:50, 55; IV:26, 34
krama III:15, 52; IV:32, 33
kriyā II:1, 36; II:18
krodha II:34
kliṣṭa I.5
kleśa I:24; II:2, 3, 12, 13; IV:28, 30
kṣaṇa III:9, 52; IV:33
kṣaya II:28, 43; III:11, 43, 50
kṣīṇa I:41
kṣīyate II:52
kṣudh III:30
kṣetra II:4
kṣetrika IV:3
khyāti I:16; II:26, 28; III:49; IV:29
gati II:49; III:28
gamana III:42
guṇa I:16; II:15, 19; IV:13, 32, 34
guru I:26
grahaṇa I:41; III:47
grahītṛ I:41
grāhya I:41; III:21
ca I:29, 44, 45; II:2, 15, 41, 53; III:20, 22, 38, 39, 42, 45, 48, 49, 54; IV:10, 16, 20, 21
cakra III:29
cakṣus III:21
caturtha II:51
candra III:27
citi IV:22, 34
citta I:2, 30, 33, 37; II: 54; III:1, 9, 11, 12, 19, 34, 38; IV:4, 5, 15, 16, 17, 18, 21, 23, 26
citra IV:24
cetanā I:29
chidra IV:27
ja I:50; III:52, 54; IV:1, 6
janman II:12, 39; IV:1
japa I:28
jaya II:41; III:5, 39, 40, 44, 47, 48
jala III:39
javitva III:48
jāti II:13, 31; III: 18, 53; IV:2, 9
jāyante III:36
jugupsā II:40
jña I:25
jñāta IV:17, 18
jñātṛtva III:49
jñāna I:8, 9, 38, 42; II:28; III:16, 17, 18, 19, 22, 25, 26, 27, 28, 35, 52, 54; IV:31
jñeya IV:31
jyotiṣmant I:36
jyotis III:32
jvalana III:40
tatas I:22, 29; II:48, 52, 55; III:12, 36, 45, 48, 53; IV:3, 43
tattva I:32; IV:14
tatra I:13, 25, 42, 48; III:2; IV:6
tathā II:9
tad I:12, 16, 28, 32, 41, 50; II:11, 13, 21, 22, 25, 35; III:3, 5, 8, 17, 20, 21, 22, 28, 45, 50, 52; IV:8, 11, 16, 17, 18, 19, 22, 24, 27
tadā I:3; IV:16, 26, 31
tanu II:4
tantra IV:16
tapas II:1, 32, 43; IV:1
tayoh IV:5
tasmin II:49
tasya I:27, 51; II:24, 27; III:6, 10, 20
tā I:46
tāpa II:15
tāraka III:54
tārā III:27
tāsām IV:10
tīvra I:21
tu I:14; IV:3
tulya III:12, 53
tūla III:42
te I:30; II:10,14; III:37; IV:13
tyāga II:35
traya III:4, 7, 16

trividha IV:7
darśana I:30; II:6, 41; III:32
darśin IV:25
divya III:41
dīpta II:28
dīrgha I:14; II:50
duḥkha I:31, 33; II:5, 8, 15, 16, 34
dṛḍha I:14
dṛś II:6
dṛśi II:20, 25
dṛśya II:17, 18, 21; IV:21, 23
dṛśyatva IV:19
dṛṣṭa I:15; II:12
devatā II:44
deśa II:31, 50; III:1, 53; IV:9
doṣa III:50
daurmanasya I:31
draṣṭṛ I:3; II:17, 20; IV:23
dvandva II:48
dveṣa II:3, 8
dharma III:13, 14, 45; IV:12,29
dharmin III:14
dhāraṇā II:29, 53; III:1
dhyāna I:39; II:11, 29; III:2; IV:6
dhruva III:28
na III:20; IV:16
naṣṭa II:22
nāḍī III:31
nābhi III:29
nitya II:5
nityatva IV:10
nidrā I:6, 10, 38
nibandhanin I:35
nimitta IV:3
nimna IV:26
niyama II:29, 32
niratiśaya I:25
nirupakrama III:22
nirodha I:2, 12, 51; III:9
nirgrāhya IV:33
nirbīja I:51; III:8
nirbhāsa I:43; III:3
nirmāṇa IV:4
nirvicārā I:44, 47
nirvitarkā I:43
nivṛtti III:30; IV:30
nairantarya I:14
nyāsa III:25
paṅka III:39
pañca II:3
pañcataya I:5
panthan IV:15
para I:16; II:40; III:19, 35; IV:24
parama I:40; II:55
paramāṇu I:40
pariṇāma II:15; III:9, 11, 12, 13, 15, 16; IV:2, 14, 32, 33
paritāpa II:14
paridṛṣṭa II:50
pariśuddhi I:43
paryavasāna I:45
parvan II:19
pipāsā III:30
puṇya I:33; II:14
punar III:12, 51
puruṣa I:16, 24; III:35, 49, 55; IV:18, 34
pūrva I:18, 26; III:7, 18
pūrvaka I:20; II:34
prakāśa II:18, 52; III:21, 43
prakṛti IV: 2, 3
prakṛti-laya I:19
pracāra III:38
pracchardana I:34
prajñā I:20, 48, 49; II:27; III:5
praṇava I:27
praṇidhāna I:23; II:1, 32, 45
prati II:22
pratipakṣa II:33, 34
pratipatti III:53
pratiprasava II:10; IV:34
pratibandhin I:50
pratiyogin IV:33
pratiṣedha I:32
pratiṣṭha I:8
pratiṣṭhāya II:35, 36, 37, 38
pratyak-cetanā I:29
pratyakṣa I:7
pratyaya I:10, 18, 19; II:20; III:2, 12, 17, 19, 35; IV:27
pratyāhāra II:29, 54
pradhāna III:48
prabhu IV:18
pramāṇa I:6, 7
pramāda I:30
prayatna II:47
prayojaka IV:5
pravibhāga III:17
pravṛtti I:35; III:25; IV:5
praśānta III:10
praśvāsa I:31; II:49
prasaṁkhyāna IV:29
prasaṅga III:51
prasāda I:47
prasādana I:33

prasupta II:4
prāgbhāra IV:26
prāṇa I:34
prāṇāyāma II:29, 49
prātibha III:33, 36
prādurbhāva II:9, 45
prānta II:27
phala II:14, 34, 36; IV:11
bandha III:1, 38
bala III:23, 24, 46
bahis III:43
bahir-aṅga III:8
bādhana II:33
bāhya II:50,51
bīja I:25; III:50
buddhi IV:21, 22
brahmacarya II:30, 38
bhava I:19
bhāva III:48, 49, IV:25
bhāvana I:28; II:2, 33, 34
bhāvanā IV:25
bhāvanātas I:33
bhuvana III:26
bhūta II:18; III:13, 17, 44
bhūtatva III:20
bhūmi I:14; II:27; III:6
bhūmikatva I:30
bheda IV:3, 5, 12, 15
bhoga II:13, 18; III:35
bhauma II:31
bhrānti I:30
maṇi I:41
madhya I:22; II:34
manas I:35; II:53; III:48
mantra IV:1
mala IV:31
mahant II:31; III:43
mātra I:43; II:20; III:3, 49; IV:4
mithyā I:8
muditā II:33
mūrdhan III:32
mūla II:12, 13
mṛdu I:22; II:34
megha IV:29
maitrī I:33; III:23
moha II:34
yatna I:13
yathā I:39
yama II:29, 30
yoga I:1, 2; II:1, 28
yogin IV:7
yogyatā II:53
yogyatva II:41
ratna II:37
rasa II:9
rāga I:37; II:3, 7
rūta III:17
rūpa I:8, 17; II:23, 54; III:3, 21, 46; IV:34
rūpatva IV:9
lakṣaṇa III:13, 53
laghu III:42
laya I:19
lābha II:38, 42
lāvaṇya III:46
liṅga-mātra II:19
lobha II:34
vajra III:46
varaṇa IV:3
vaśīkāra I:15, 40
vaśyatā II:55
vastu I.9; IV.14, 15, 16, 17
vā I:23, 34, 35, 36, 37, 38, 39; III:22, 33; IV:34
vācaka I:27
vārtā III:36
vāsanā IV:8, 24
vāhitā III:10
vāhin II:9
vikaraṇa III:48
vikalpa I:6, 9, 42
vikṣepa I:30, 31
vicāra I:17
vicchinna II:4
viccheda II:49
vitarka I:17; II:33, 34
vitṛṣṇa I:15
viduṣa II:9
videha I:19; III:43
vidvāṃs II:9
vidhāraṇa I:34
viniyoga III:6
vinivṛtti IV:25
viparyaya I:6, 8
vipāka I:24; II:13; IV:8
viprakṛṣṭa III:25
vibhakta IV:15
virāma I:18
virodha II:15
viveka II:26, 28; III:52, 54; IV:26, 29
vivekin II:15
viśeṣa I:22, 24, 49; II:19; IV:25
viśoka I:36
viṣaya I:11, 15, 33, 37, 44, 49; II:51, 54; III:54

viṣayatva I:45
viṣayavant I:35
vīta I:37
vīrya I:20; II:38
vṛtti I:2, 4, 5, 10, 41; II:11, 15, 50; III:43; IV:18
vedanā III:36
vedanīya II:12
vaitṛṣṇya I:16
vaira II:35
vairāgya I:12,15; III:50
vaiśāradya I:47
vyakta IV:13
vyavahita III:25; IV:9
vyākhyāta I:44; III:13
vyādhi I:30
vyutthāna III:9, 37
vyūha III:27, 29
vrata II:31
śakti II:6, 23; III:21; IV:34
śabda I:9, 42; III:17
śarīra III:38
śānta III:12, 14
śīla II:18
śuci II:5
śuddha II:20
śuddhi II:41; III:55
śūnya I:9, 43; III:3; IV:34
śeṣa I:18
śaithilya II:47; III:38
śauca iII:32,40
śraddhā I:20
śrāvaṇa III:36
śruta I:49
śrotra III:41
śvāsa I:31; II:49
sa I:14
saṁyama III:4, 16, 17, 21, 22, 26, 35, 41, 42, 44, 47, 52
saṁyoga II:17, 23, 25
saṁvid III:34
saṁvega I:21
saṁvedana III:38; IV:22
saṁśaya I:30
saṁskāra I:18, 50; II:15; III:9, 10, 18; IV:9, 27
saṁhatya IV:24
saṁhananatva III:46
saṁkara III:17; IV:21
saṁkīrna I:42
saṁkhyā II:50
saṅga III:51
saṁgṛhītatva IV:11
saṁjñā I:15
sati II:13, 49
satkāra I:14
sattva I:41; III:35, 49, 55
satya II:30, 36
sadā IV:18
santoṣa II:32, 42
saṁnidhi II:35
saptadhā II:27
sabīja I:46
samaya II:31; IV:20
samādhi I:20, 46, 51; II:2, 29, 45; III:3, 11, 37; IV:1, 29
samāna III:40
samāpatti I:41, 42; II:47; III:42
samāpti IV:32
saṁpad III:45, 46
saṁprajñāta I:17
saṁprayoga II:44
saṁbandha II:41, 42
saṁbodha II:39
sarva I:25, 51; II:15, 31, 37; III:11, 17, 33, 49, 54; IV:23, 31
sarvarthā III:54; IV:29
savicārā I:44
savitarkā I:42
sahabhuva I:31
sākṣa III:18
sādhāraṇatva II:22
sāmya II:55; IV:15
sārūpya I:4
sālambana III:20
siddha III:32
siddhi II:43, 45; III:37; IV:1
sukha I:33; II:5, 7, 42, 46
sūkṣma I:44, 45; II:10, 50; III:25, 44; IV:13
sūrya III:26
sopakrama III:22
saumanasya II:41
stambha II:50; III:21
styāna I:30
stha I:41
sthānin III:51
sthiti I:13, 35; II:18
sthira II:46
sthūla III:44
sthairya II:39; III:31
smaya III:51
smṛti I:6, 11, 20, 43; IV:9, 21
syāt IV:16
sva II:9, 23, 40; III:35; IV:19, 22, 50

svapna I:38
svabuddhi IV:22
svarasa: II:9
svarūpa I:3, 43; II:23, 54; III:3, 44, 47; IV:34
svarūpatas IV:12
svāṅga II:40
svādhyāya II: 1, 32, 44
svābhāsa IV:19
svāmin II:23
svārtha III:35
hāna II:25, 26; IV:28
hiṁsā II:34
hṛdaya III:34
hetu II:17, 23, 24; III:15; IV:11
hetutva II:34
heya II:10, 11, 16, 17
hlāda II:14

Index

abhiniveśa, 6, 63, 90, 121, 163, 164, 166, 272n.77, 288
Absolute, the x, 8, 21, 26, 40–41. *See paramārtha.*
abhyāsa, 21, 24–25, 29, 72, 103, 116 (I.12), 117 (I.18, I.32), 146–7, 149, 154
Abram, David, 245, 276n.30, 279
Ācārāṅga Sūtra, 34, 45, 51, 111, 266n. 271n.69, 282
Advaita Vedanta, 8
adharma, 20
adhyātma, 25, 160, 271n.
Agni 112
ahaṃkāra, 4, 19, 21–23, 26–27, 84, 140, 169, 229–30, 240
ahiṃsā, 2, 11, 31, 34, 37–38, 44, 46, 49, 62, 96, 98, 100, 104, 110–13, 124–5 (II.30, II.35), 173, 175, 258, 271n.69, 273n.21
akliṣṭa, 7, 144, 233
al-Biruni, 13
Alter, Joseph, 251–2, 255–6, 259, 277n.2, 278n.31, 279
Altizer, Thomas J.J., 27, 264n.28
Amṛtakuṇḍa, 31–32, 255, 277n.16
anitya, 24, 34, 164, 287
Añjali, Gurāṇi, x, 37, 57, 242, 265n.24
aparigraha, 31, 34, 37–41, 47, 62, 96, 98, 124 (II.30), 126 (II.39), 173, 176, 258, 271n.68, 287
Aranya, Swami Hariharananda, 91, 140, 270n.41, 279,
Āraṇyaka Yoga, 259
Arhat, 73, 98
Aristotle, 49
Arjuna, 26, 95, 112, 195,
āsana, x, 11, 22, 24, 49, 52–56, 58, 64, 90, 104, 106, 126 (II.46), 172–173, 178, 227, 250–251, 254, 284, 288
asmitā (egotism), 6, 23, 63, 90, 121 (II.3, II.6), 133 (III.47), 135 (IV.4), 148, 163–165, 198, 204, 241, 288,
aṣṭāṅgayoga, 104, 110–11, 221
asteya, 31, 34, 37–38, 62, 96, 98, 124 II.30), 125 (II.37), 173, 176, 271n.69, 273n.21, 288
aśuci 24, 34, 121 (II.5), 164
Ātmabodha, 95, 271n.68
ātman, 3, 5, 9, 27, 29, 164, 177, 207, 225, 227 *See puruṣa.*
Aurobindo, 15, 252
Avalokitesvara, 245
avidyā, 6, 24, 34, 63, 90, 109, 121 (II.3, II.5), 124 (II.24), 163–164, 171. *See* ignorance.
Awoonar, Kofi, 219–220, 274n.8, 279

Bahuguna, Sunderlal, 81
Baptiste, Walt and Magana, 250
Behanan, K.T., 251
Bernard, Theos, 250
Berry, Thomas, xiii, 57, 266n.22
Bhagavad Gītā, xv, 2–3, 8–11, 26, 88, 90, 92, 95, 107, 112, 195, 198, 261n.5, 264n.25, 270n.26, 275n.39, 281, 283
Bhai, Gurdas, 13
Bhai, Rajchandra, 46
Bhajan, Yogi, 13, 250
bhakti, ix, 1–2, 7, 259
Bhakti Yoga 2, 259

bhāva, 20–21, 24, 35–36, 65, 85–87, 91, 95, 98–99, 117 (I.19), 118 (I.28), 119 (I.33), 121 (II.2), 125 (II.33–34), 133 (III.48–49), 137 (IV.25), 145, 149, 152, 154–155, 163, 171, 174–175, 185, 199, 211–212, 225, 230–234, 270n.44, 282, 291,
Bhojarāja, 26
Bihar School of Yoga, 253
Bodhidharma, 15, *See* Zen
bodhisattva, 7, 12, 93–94, 224–225, 227, 232, 262n.35, 271n. 64, 281.
bondage, 83–86, 89, 91, 96, 100, 105, 125 (II.33), 132 (III.38), 174, 194–195, 230–231
Brahma, 8, 10, 12
Brahman, 88, 240
Brahma Vihāra, 12, 63, 72–74, 109, 190, 223, 244–246
brahmacarya, 31, 34, 38, 46, 62, 96, 98, 124 (II.30), 126 (II.38), 173, 176, 291,
Brahmanical, ix, 33, 108, 109, 111,
Brahmin, 9, 11
Brahmo Samaj 16
Bucke, William, 32–33, 264n.4–5
Buddha, 2, 7, 12, 14, 20, 49, 51, 73, 81, 110, 242, 244
buddhi, 19–22, 24, 28, 65, 78, 87, 137 (IV.21), 140, 169, 210, 229, 230, 235, 240, 291
Buddhism, ix, x, 2, 7–12, 24, 28, 33, 43, 49, 51, 62–63, 72–73, 80, 94, 108–111, 221–227, 235, 239–246, 249, 251, 254, 257, 259, 262n.34–35, 263n.4, 266n.11, 267n.8, 271n.63–64, 274n.13, 276n.25–26, 276n.33, 279–283; Mahāyāna, 93, 94, 109; Yogācāra, 107, 224, 226; Mādhyamika, 10, 28; Theravada, 12, 262n.34, 282–283; Vajrayāna, 12; Abhidharma, 108
buddhīndriyas, 22,
breath, x, 3–5, 11–14, 24, 40–41, 50, 58–59, 64, 67, 75–77, 90, 99, 104, 106, 119 (I.34), 124 (II.29), 127 (II.49, II.51), 132 (III. 39), 154–155, 160, 164, 173, 179–180, 190, 195, 198, 223, 241, 251, 254–256, 259

cakra, 12–13, 66, 76, 131 (III.29), 192, 289,
Chidananda, Swami, 253
Chinmayananda, Swami, 253
Chipko movement, 81–82
Christian, ix, 1–2, 14, 16, 81, 84, 237–238, 240, 247, 259, 263n.43.
citi śakti, 26, 62, 66, 80, 92, 105, 109, 138 (IV.34), 214 (IV.34), 215, 242, 246
citta, 22, 25, 29, 105–107, 110, 115 (I.2), 118 (I.30), 119 (I.33, I.37), 127 (II.54), 128 (III.1, III.9), 129 (III.11–12), 130 (III.19), 132 (III.34, III.38), 135 (IV.4–5), 136 (IV.15–18), 137 (IV.19, IV.21, IV.23, IV.26), 140, 143, 153–156, 180–181, 183, 185–186, 188–189, 193–196, 204, 207–212, 231, 272n.4, 289; *prasāda,* 58, 72, 90, 119 (I.33), 154; *pariṇāma,* 91, 107
citta-vṛtti, 22–27, 29, 79, 104, 137 (IV.21), 209, 263, 272n.4, 289; *nirodha*, 4, 22, 25, 71, 73, 103, 115 (I.2), 143
Collins, Mary, 238, 275n.5, 280
Comfort, Alex, 28, 264n.29
consciousness, x, 2–4, 6–8, 10–11, 19, 22–24, 27–29, 32–33, 35, 38, 40–41, 45, 57, 59, 63, 65, 66, 72–73, 76, 78–81, 84–85, 87, 96, 98, 100, 104–105, 107, 118 (I.29), 137 (IV.22), 138 (IV.34), 140, 148, 152, 155, 186, 195, 210, 215, 225, 227, 240–242, 244, 246, 257, 262n.39, 264n.4–5, 285
Cornell, Laura, xiii, 257–258, 278n.27 and 30, 280. *See* Green Yoga
Cort, John, 276n.18
Coward, Harold, 220, 274n.6, 280

Daly, Mary, 238
Daśabhūmika Sūtra, 93
Dasgupta, Surendranath (S.N.), ix, 108, 110, 242, 273, 280,
De Michelis, Elizabeth, 277n.(10, 13 and 18), 253–257, 281
deity, 5, 7, 31, 51, 63, 92, 126 (II.44), 178, 238, 243 *See iṣṭa devatā*. *See* also *Īśvara*.
Descartes, Rene, 49, 61
Desikachar, T.K.V., xiii, 251, 281
Desikachar, Kaustub, 242, 251
Devi, Indra, 251, 254–255
devotion, 1–2, 6–7, 15, 24, 36, 63, 178, 200, 223 *See bhakti*
dhāraṇā, 11, 24–25, 64, 104, 119 (I.34), 123 (II.22), 124 (II.29), 127 (II.53), 128 (III.1), 137 (IV.20), 155, 170, 172–173, 180, 183, 209, 220, 290
dharma, 10, 20, 80, 81, 83, 86–87, 94, 112, 129 (III.13–14), 133 (III.45). 136

(IV.12), 140, 160, 186–187, 197–198, 207, 213, 271n.67, 280, 290
dharma-megha, 4, 6, 27, 29, 93–94 *dharma-megha samādhi*, 12, 25–26, 66, 80, 93–94, 100, 138 (IV.29), 213, 233, 271n.62
Dharmaśāstra, 14, 33
dhyāna, 11–12, 24–25, 64–65, 104, 109, 111, 119 (I.39), 122 (II.11), 124 (II.29), 128 (III.2), 135 (IV.6), 157, 166, 172–73, 183, 204, 263n.44, 290,
Digambara, 98
Divine Life Society, 252
dualism, 21, 84, 237
duḥkha, 2, 4, 12, 20, 24, 34–35, 61, 66, 85, 90, 106, 109, 118 (I.31), 119 (I.33), 121 (II.5), 122 (II.8), 123 (II.15–16), 125 (II.35), 154–155, 164–165, 167–168, 174–175, 290
dveṣa, 6, 63, 90, 121 (II.3), 122 (II.8), 163, 164–165, 290

Eastman, George, 250
Eliade, Mircea, ix, 50–51, 71, 108–109, 227, 250, 253, 261n.3, 266n.9, 272n.7 and 10, 281
Emerson, Ralph Waldo, 8, 249
equanimity, 5, 11–12, 24, 34, 63, 72, 104, 119 (I.33), 155, 241, 244
Ernst, Carl, 14, 262n.41, 277n.16, 281
existential, 7, 15, 24, 27, 65, 210

Familia, Sal, x. *See* Satyam, Yogi Anand
feminine, viii, x, 19, 141, 237–247, 249, 275, 276n.32, 283–284,
Feuerstein, Georg, ix, xiii, 6, 26, 108, 110, 149, 221, 242, 254, 261n.3 and 20, 263n.2, 264n.21–22, 265n.18, 272n.5, 273n.13–15, 281
five (categories of); *karmas*, 96; types of fluctuations *(vṛttis)*, 22, 115 (I.5), 144
Folan, Lilias, 253
freedom, x, 1, 4, 6–7, 38, 40, 50, 71, 87, 92, 96–96, 133 (III.43), 146, 148, 197, 224, 241, 245, 253, 261n.3, 272n.7 and 10, 281, 283
Freud, 29

Gandhi, Arun, 47, 265n.36
Gandhi, Indira, 251
Gandhi, Mahatma, 36, 46, 258
Gandhi, Rajiv, 47
Ganesh, 51, 286
Gasset, Ortega y, 27, 82, 269n.60 281, 284
Gauḍapāda, 86, 87, 269n.6, 283
Gheraṇḍa Saṃhitā, 56, 282
God, 7–9, 13–14, 28, 36, 46, 50–51, 63, 67, 92, 110, 112, 178 (II.44), 237–238, 247, 269n.6, 275n.1–2, 283–284
Goddess, 7, 11, 14, 67, 237, 238–239, 243, 257, 275n.36, 276n.10–13 and 18, 279, 280–282, 284,
Gombrich, Richard, 73, 244–245, 267n.8, 276n.26, 282
Graham, William A., 220, 274n.7, 282
Green Yoga Association, 257–259, 278n.27 and 30, 280
Guru Granth Sahib, 13 *See* Sikh
Gurmat Yoga, 13 *See* Gurmukh Yoga or Sahaja Yoga
Gurumukh Yoga, 13
Gurdas, Bhai, 13
guṇa, 19, 27, 29, 34, 72, 80–81, 85, 93, 105, 108–109, 117 (I.16), 123 (II.15 and II.19), 135 (IV.8), 136 (IV.13), 138 (IV.32 and IV.34), 140, 148–149, 167–168, 172, 187, 205, 207–208, 214–215, 228–229, 231, 240, 289
guṇasthāna, 87, 96–98, 100
guru, x, 1, 12–13, 67, 84, 92, 118 (I.26), 151, 250, 253, 262n.36 and 38, 265n.24, 281, 285, 289

Hanuman, 51
Harappa, 50
Hare Krishna, 1, 265n.5, 284
Haribhadra, 9, 11, 15, 91, 232, 243, 262n.33, 270n.44, 272n.71 and 73, 275n.39, 276n.19, 279–280, 282
Haṭha Yoga, 12–14, 56, 76, 250, 254–255, 259, 266n.16, 277, 279, 284–285
Hedgewar, Dr. Keshav Baliram, 252
Hellenist, 14
Houseman, A.E., 219, 282

ignorance 20, 24, 34–35, 62–63, 86, 88–89–92, 96–97, 109, 121 (II.3–5), 124 (II.24–25), 125 (II.34), 161, 163–165, 171, 175, 228, 230–232, *See avidyā*
impermanence, 12
Indra, 110, 112, 169, 238
Indus Valley Civilization, 2, 14, 50, 261n.2 and 6, 283

Islam, 9, 13–14, 238, 255, 277n.16, 284
iṣṭa devatā, 7, 63, 126 (II.44), 178
Īśvara, 5–7, 24, 28, 31, 63, 90, 92, 104, 106, 110, 117 (I.23–2), 121 (II.1), 125 (II.32), 126 (II.45), 150–151, 163, 174, 178, 221, 223, 241, 243, 288
Īśvarakṛṣṇa, xv, 19, 72, 83, 85–89, 95, 99, 228,230, 269n.1 and 6, 271n.67, 283
Iyengar, B.K.S., 1, 250–251, 254, 261n.1
Iyer, Dr. Kuppuswami, 252

Jacobsen, Dr. Cecil, 256
Jaini, Dr. Padmanabh S., 45, 98, 265n.26
Jainism, vii, ix, 2, 7–9, 11–12, 14, 31, 33–35, 37, 39, 41, 43–47, 49, 51, 62, 79–80, 83, 87, 95–100, 108–112, 221, 239, 241, 249, 265n.26 and 28–29, 271n.69–70, 272n.71–72, 74, 76, 78, 276n.18, 280, 282, 285
Jambū, 98
James, George, 81, 269n.59
James, Henry, 249
James, William, 31, 33, 44, 249, 264n.1
Jātaka, 49, 266n.11
Jesus, 14, 264n.28
jewel, x, 33, 35, 65, 72–73, 105, 108, 112, 120 (I.41), 125 (II.37), 158, 176, 223–224, 226–227, 245
Jina, 2, 51, 98
jīva, 79, 96
jīvan-mukta, 25, 82–84, 88–89, 91–94, 98–100, 116 (I.8–9), 119 (I.38), 120 (I.42), 124 (II.28), 129 (III.16–17), 130 (III.18–19 and 22), 131 (III.25–29) 244, 271n.62
jñāna, 19–21, 25, 72, 83, 85–89, 93–94, 98, 131 (III.25–29), 132 (III.32), 134 (III.52 and 54), 138 (IV.31), 145, 156–158, 172, 175, 187–189, 193, 201–202, 213–214, 230–234, 267n.67, 289
Jñāna Yoga, 2, 259,
Johnson, Elizabeth, 238
Jois, Pattabhi, 1, 251, 254

Kabat-Zinn, Jon, 255
kaivalyam, 6, 27, 71, 77–78, 81, 86–87, 93, 103, 105, 107–111, 113, 124 (II.25), 134 (III.50 and 55), 137 (IV.26), 138 (IV.34)., 140, 171, 200–202, 204, 212, 214–215, 230, 233–235, 266n.6
Kāli, 239, 257
Kapleau, Philip, x
karma, x, 2, 8, 11, 22, 33–35, 45, 72, 75, 79, 84, 90–92, 94, 96, 99–100, 105, 107, 110, 117 (I.24), 122 (II.12), 130 (III.22), 135 (IV.7–8), 138 (IV.30), 141, 151, 154, 166, 190, 195, 205, 213, 241–242, 244, 259, 270n.44, 271n.70, 272n.71, 276n.14, 280, 285, 289
Karma Yoga, 2, 11, 259,
karmendriya, 22
Kaufman, Denise, xiii, 57
Kenoyer, Jonathan Mark, 50, 261n.2, 265n.6, 283,
kevala, 2, 11, 21, 51, 79, 86, 96–98, 110, 171, 230, 233
kevalin, 98
King, Winston, 12
kleśa, 4, 6, 24, 34, 66, 89–92, 98, 104, 117 (I.24), 121 (II.2–3), 122 (II.12), 138 (IV.28 and 30), 151, 163–164, 166, 212–213, 230, 270n.44, 289
kliṣṭa, 7, 90–91, 94, 100, 115 (I.5), 144, 233, 289
Koran, 14
Kripalu movement, 2, 280
Krishna, 1, 26, 90, 95, 112, 195, 265n.5, 284
Krishnamacharya, Sri, 1, 250–251
kuṇḍalinī, 13

Laghu Yogavāsiṣṭha, 13
Laidlow, James, 45
Larson, Gerald, xiii, 108, 269n.1
Laṅkāvatāra Sūtra, 224, 227, 232, 274n.21–25, 275n.37–38, 285
liberation, vii, 4, 6, 9, 11, 20–21, 26, 46, 51, 72–73, 78, 80, 83–100, 105, 123 (II.18), 169, 172, 201–202, 211, 225, 228, 230, 231, 233–235, 240, 242–243, 245–246, 249, 266n.6, 271n.67, 272n.76, 282, 285

Madhyāntavibhāgabhāṣya, 225, 274n.26, 281
Mahābhārata, 9, 95, 109, 112, 262n.31, 273n.21 and 26,
Maharshi, Ramana, 36
mahat 19, 119 (I.40), 157, 229. *See buddhi*
mahāvākya *See* Upaniṣad, 8
Mahavira, 46, 51, 96, 98, 110
Mahāvrata, 62, 111, 125 (II.31), 173
mantra, 39, 134 (IV.1), 200, 203, 223, 241, 243, 283, 286, 291
Manu, Laws of, 247, 273n.21, 278n.34,

Maugham, W. Somerset, 9, 262n.29,
māyā, 239
Mayananda, Swami Jyotir, 35–36, 264n.18, 283
McFague, Sally, 247
Menninger Foundation, 254
Miśra, Vācaspati, 78, 220, 233, 242, 268n.40, 270n.24, 271n.67,
Modern Meditational Yoga, 254
Modern Postural Yoga, 254–255, 257
Mohenjodaro, 50
Mojtaba'i, Fathullah, 14, 262n.40
monism, 9–10, 21
Muller, Max, 26, 263n.20, 283
Muslim, ix, 13–16, 51, 259, 286

Nanak, Guru, 13, 262n.36 and 38, 285
ṇadīs, 13
Nehru, Jawaharlal, 251
Neo-Vedantic, 1, 8, 14, 253
Nietzsche, 42
nirvāṇa, 2, 26, 242, 244
nirvicārā, 25, 65, 73–74, 77, 90, 120 (I.44 and 47), 159–160, 227, 245–246, 290
nirvitarkā, 25, 65, 73, 90, 120 (I.43), 159, 227, 245–246, 290
niyama, 6, 11, 24, 31, 63, 75. 90, 104, 106, 124 (II.29), 125 (II.32), 172, 174, 290
nondualist, 8
non-violence, 31, 36, 124 (II.30), 125 (II.35), 264n.18. *See ahiṃsā*

Ornish, Dean, 253, 255
Oz, Mehmet, 255

Padmasambhava, 15
Pal, Dr. Kumar, 252
Panipati, Nizam al-Din, 13
paramārtha, x, 227
Parliament of World Religions, 1
Paśupati, 50
Pintchman, Tracy, 239, 276n.10, 284
prakṛti, 3–6, 13, 19–23, 25–27, 29, 66, 72, 77–79, 84–88, 93, 96, 99–100, 104–107, 117 (I.19), 124 (II.23), 134 (IV.2), 135 (IV.3), 140–141, 148–149, 160, 169, 199–201, 203–204, 208–211, 222, 228–231–235, 239–243, 245–246, 263n.19, 265n.29, 269n.5, 271n.70, 290
prajñā, 5, 104, 109, 117 (I.20), 120 (I.48–49), 124 (II.27), 128 (III.5), 149–150, 160–161, 172, 184, 239, 243, 244–246, 290
prāṇāyāma, 11, 24, 58, 64, 75, 81, 104, 124 (II.29), 127 (II.49), 172–173, 179, 254, 284, 291
pratibhā, 78, 131 (III.33), 132 (III.36), 193–194, 225, 291. *See* reflection
pratyāhāra, 11, 24, 59, 64, 90, 124 (II.29), 127 (II.54), 172–173, 180–181, 290
prāṇava, 28, 118 (I.27), 152, 290
puruṣa, 2–4, 10, 13, 19–23, 26–29, 66, 72–81, 84–88, 92–93, 100, 107–109, 117 (I.16 and 24), 123 (II.21), 124 (II.23), 132 (III.35), 133 (III.49), 134 (III.55), 136 (IV.18), 137 (IV.20), 138 (IV.34), 140–141, 148, 151, 161, 170, 172, 184, 193, 199–202, 204, 209, 211, 214–215, 225, 227–231, 233–234, 240–243, 245–246, 255, 290

Quaker, 27, 58

Rāja, Bhojam, 26, 242
Raja Yoga, ix, 250, 254, 259, 264n.7, 265n.24, 283, 285
rajas, 19, 34, 72, 74, 105, 148, 169
Rama, Swami, 250, 254
Rāma, 10, 262n.32, 283
Rāmakṛṣṇa, 1, 14, 81, 253, 271n.68, 284–285
Rāmānanda, 233
Rashtriya Swamyamsevak Sangh, 252
reincarnation, 49
renunciation, ix, 26, 51, 82, 96, 173, 222, 252, 265n.28
restraint, 5–7, 22, 24–26, 31, 34, 35–36, 44, 46, 61, 71–72, 91–92, 98, 103–105, 107–108, 115 (I.2), 116 (I.12), 124 (II.30), 126 (II.38), 128 (III.9), 143, 146, 172–173, 176, 184–185, 229
Roman Catholic Church, 14–15
Roy, Ram Mohan, 16
Ruether, Rosemary Radford, 237–238, 240, 275n.1 and 3, 284
Rukmani, T.S., 89, 108, 153–154, 224, 270n.24, 272n.6, 284
Ṛg Veda, 7–8, 110, 112, 262n.25–26, 267n.12, 273n.18, 281
ṛta, 66, 74, 120 (I.48), 160–161, 245, 288

sabīja, 65, 120 (I.46), 160, 292
Saddarśanasamuccaya, 11, *See* Haribhadra

sādhaka, 43
Sahaja Yoga, 13
samādhi, viii, 3, 5, 8, 11–12, 24–27, 33–34, 44–45, 59, 64–66, 73, 77–77, 80–81, 89–94, 99–100, 103–107, 109, 111–112, 115, 117 (I.20), 120 (I.46), 121 (I.51 and II.2), 124 (II.29), 126 (II.45), 128 (III.3), 129 (III.11), 132 (III.37), 134 (IV.1), 138 (IV.29), 141, 145, 149–150, 160–163, 173, 178, 183–186, 194, 203, 213, 222–224, 226, 232, 233, 241, 243, 245, 271n.62, 272n.6, 279, 284, 292
Sāṃkhya, 7, 10–11, 13, 19, 20–21, 23–25, 28, 33, 74–75, 83–100, 105–109, 127 (II.50), 148, 179, 193–194, 210–211, 219, 228–235, 237, 239–243, 246, 249, 257, 268n.14, 269n.1, 270n.18, 271n.70, 272n.4, 280, 283, 292
Sāṃkhya Kārikā, xv, 6, 19, 26, 73–74, 79, 83–84, 87–89, 91, 95, 98–99, 106, 140, 201, 209, 221, 228, 230–231, 234, 243, 261n.6, 263n.19, 269n.2 and 6, 275n.43, 276n.22, 282, 284
saṃsāra, 4, 29, 34
saṃskāra, 22–25, 27, 34–35, 66, 74, 77–79, 86–92, 94–95, 99, 103, 117 (I.18), 121 (I.50), 123 (II.15), 128 (III.9), 129 (III.10), 130 (III.18), 135 (IV.9), 136 (IV.11), 138 (IV.27), 149, 161, 167–168, 185, 188, 203, 205–207, 210, 212, 222, 228, 230, 292
saṃyak dṛṣṭi, 44–45,
saṃyama, 65–66, 76, 78, 128 (III.4), 129 (III.16–17), 130 (III.21–24), 131 (III.26), 132 (III.35 and 41, 133 (III.42, 44, and 47), 134 (III.52), 140, 184, 187–191, 193, 196–199, 201, 234–235, 292
Saṅgha Yoga, 259
Santal tribe, 50, 266n.10, 279
Santoṣa, 31, 63, 125 (II.32), 126 (II.42), 174, 177, 292
Sartre, Jean Paul, 63
sat, 42, 147, 177
Satchidananda, Swami
sattva, 19, 34, 72, 74–80, 92–93, 96, 98, 105, 107, 109, 126 (II.41), 132 (III.35), 133 (III.49), 134 (III.55), 140–141, 148, 169, 177, 193, 199, 201–202, 204, 232, 234, 235, 245, 268n.40, 292
satya, 31, 34, 37–38, 41–42, 58–59, 62, 124 (II.30), 125 (II.36), 173, 175, 263n.4, 271n.69, 273n.21, 292; *graha,* 46,
Satyam, Yogi Anand, x, xiii
Satyananda, Swami, 253, 284
savicārā, 25, 65, 73, 90, 120 (I.44), 159, 227, 245–246, 292
savitarkā, 25, 65, 73, 90, 120 (I.42), 158–159, 227, 245–246, 292
Śaiva, 14, 239, 251
Śankara, 8, 242
śauca, 31, 63, 75, 125 (II.32), 126 (II.40), 174, 176, 273n.21, 292
Sen, Keshubchandra, 253
sex, 7, 33–36, 38, 44, 46, 63, 96, 98, 124 (II.30), 126 (II.38), 173, 176, 237–238, 264n.18, 275n.1, 277n.22, 283–284
Śiva, 50, 238, 282
śraddhā, 5, 103, 109, 117 (I.20), 149, 244, 246, 292
Second Vatical Council, 14,
seen, 3–4, 7, 26, 27, 29, 66, 74–76, 79, 86, 90, 93, 106, 109, 115 (I.3), 121 (II.6), 123 (II.17, 21 and 22), 124 (II.25), 137 (IV.19 and 23), 143, 165, 168, 170, 209, 211, 226–230, 233 *See prakṛti*
seer, 3–4, 7, 19, 23, 26, 27, 28, 29, 66, 74–76, 79–80, 82, 84–86, 90, 93, 98, 106, 109, 121 (II.6), 123 (II.17, 18 and 20), 137 (IV.23), 143–144, 165, 168, 170, 211, 224–230, 233 *See puruṣa*
Self-Realization Fellowship, 1
Shaman, 25, 50–51, 56–57, 227, 266n.9, 281
siddha, 44, 76, 79, 131 (III.32), 132 (III.37), 134 (IV.1), 192, 194, 203, 262n.37, 285, 292
siddhi, 29, 66, 126 (II.43 and 45), 178, 201, 292
Sikh, ix, 2, 9, 13–14, 16, 249, 259, 262n.36 and 38, 285
Singh, Trilochan, 13, 262n.36 and 38, 285
Sjoman, N.E., 250–251, 277n.1, 285
Strauss, Sarah, 253, 277n.8, 285
Śrāmanical, ix, 49
śraddhā, 5, 103, 109, 117 (I.20), 149, 244, 246, 292
śūnya, 10, 12, 25, 27, 128 (III.3), 138 (IV.34), 145, 159, 183, 214–215, 292
svarūpa, 12, 25, 27, 120 (I.43), 127 (II.54), 128 (III.3), 133 (III.44 and 47), 136

(IV.12), 138 (IV.34), 171, 183, 197–198, 207, 214–15, 267n.2, 293
Svatmarama, 56, 266n.16, 285
Śvetāmbara, 98
Sufi, 2, 14, 16, 262n.41, 281
sukha, 20, 34, 119 (I.33), 121 (II.5), 122 (II.7), 126 (II.42 and 46), 154–155, 164–165, 177–178, 292
svādhyāya, 24, 31, 63, 126 (II.44), 163, 174, 178, 293

Tagore, Rabindranath, 253
tamas, 19, 34, 72, 74–75, 80, 105, 148, 169
tanmātra, 19, 189–190, 194
Tantra, 12, 136 (IV.16), 195, 208, 239, 259, 289
Tantra Yoga, 259
tapas, 24, 31, 37, 63, 126 (II.43), 178, 289
Tarkabhūṣana, Pramathanātha, 88
Tarkatīrtha, Rāmeśacandra, 88
tathāgatagarbha, 110
tattva, 19, 21–22, 85–85, 106, 118 (I.32), 136 (IV.14), 154, 198, 207, 210, 223, 231, 250, 272n.75, 285, 286, 289
tauḥīd, 2
Tibetan, x, 15, 251, 254, 284,
tolerance, 14–15, 104
transcendent, 1, 8, 10, 28, 88, 237–238, 254
Transcendental Meditation (TM), 254
Tyrrell, George, 27

Udapa, K.N., 251–252
Upaniṣad, 1–3, 5, 8–9, 27, 34, 75, 77, 109–111, 210, 219, 240, 242, 256, 261n.4 and 15, 273n.19, 277n.24, 282
unity, 8, 27, 33, 41, 73–74, 84, 108, 112, 120 (I.41–42), 127 (II.47), 128 (III.4), 133 (III.42), 158–159, 178, 184, 196, 223–224, 226–227, 245

Vaiṣṇava, 14, 49, 239
Varuna, 112
Vāsiṣṭha, 10, 262n.32, 278, 283, 285 *See Yogavāsiṣṭha*
vāsanā, 22, 74, 87, 120 (I.45), 135 (IV.8), 137 (IV.24), 205, 211, 230, 291
Vasubandhu, 225
Vedānta, ix, x, 8–11, 14, 21, 83, 88, 95, 242, 249, 253, 257
Vedas, 2, 7–8, 11, 88, 110, 112, 219, 239–240
vegetarianism, 13, 44, 49, 265n.5, 284
Vijñānabhikṣu, 25, 28, 78, 88–89, 93–94, 139, 220, 233, 242, 263n.14, 270n.24, 271n.62 and 67, 272n.6, 282, 284
Vijñāptimātra, 10
Viraj, Yogi Anand, x, 280
Vishnudevananda, Swami, 250, 253, 285
Vishwa Hindu Parishad, 252–253
viveka khyāti, 25–27, 83, 90, 93–94, 100, 103, 124 (II.26 and 28), 138 (IV.29), 171–172, 213, 230, 231, 233, 241, , 291
Vivekananda, Swami, ix, 1, 8, 14–16, 33, 249–250, 252–254, 264n.7, 271n.68, 284–285
viyoga, 26
Vyāsa, viii, xv, 28, 79–80, 91–94, 99, 107, 111, 139–140, 149, 154, 156, 158, 160, 172, 201, 219–235, 242, 250, 267n.9, 270n.40 and 44, 273, 279–280, 284, 286,

wheel, 6, 21, 26, 58, 83, 86, 88, 91, 94–95, 99, 192. *See cakra*
Whicher, Ian, ix, xiii, 241, 262n.31, 263n., 267n., 276n.15, 285
Whitman, Walt, 31–32
witness, x, 2–4, 10, 19, 22–23, 26, 28–29, 62, 66, 72, 78, 85, 87, 89, 93, 100, 107, 140, 148, 210, 229, 240, 246, 255
Woods, James Haughton, 250, 263, 268n.40, 270n.40, 286

yajña, 74
yama, 6, 11, 24, 31, 62–63, 75, 90, 104, 106, 110–111, 124 (II.29 and 30), 172–173, 184, 264n.18, 283, 291
Yogadṛṣṭisamuccaya, 9, 11, 232, 280, 282. *See* Haribhadra
Yogavāsiṣṭha, 9–10, 13, 15, 88, 257, 262n.32 and 40

Zaehner, R.C., 14, 286
Zen, x, 15, 263n.44
Zoroastrian, 14